Acknowledgments

The writing of this book is the result of a continuous effort of many years, involving study, research, and survey of a large body of materials on the subject. No work is perfectly complete, and what I have put together is only the beginning of the long and arduous task of setting the foundation for the history and development of Arab art. I am sure that young and open-minded art historians will further this discourse with innovative and constructive work.

The publishing of this book involved many individuals who assisted in the process. My thanks go to the Linus Creative Publishing team and Senior Editor Jay Herath who encouraged me to write this book for years; and Mr. Dilup Gamege for his relentless work on the layout design. I also would like to thank my friend and colleague Dr. Cynthia Finlayson from Brigham Young University for her support while working together on archaeological projects in Syria and Jordan.

My gratitude goes to my institution: Henry Ford College; namely, The Office of the President; Vice President for Academic Affairs, Dr. Michael Nealon; and Vice President of Strategy and Information, Ms. Becky Chadwick, for providing me the needed Sabbatical and support to complete the project. My thanks are due to the wonderful team at Nantes Institute for Advanced Studies in Nantes, France for granting me a fellowship in 2011 that helped greatly in the details pertaining to research in preparation for this book. Similarly, I am grateful for the Fulbright Association for offering me a senior research grant in 2007 in Italy to study and research Arab art in Sicily.

My utmost thanks go to my editorial director at Linus, Dr. Steven Darian, who has been a tremendous help in the editing process. His insights and suggestions guided crucial moments of this book in the right direction. I am indebted for his patience, constructive suggestions and sharp acumen. Special thanks are due to Wihad Al-Tawil for her painstaking help in text proofreading, polishing, and formatting; to my wife Eman Ali for her support; to Bashshar Al-Tawil for his assistance; to Ahmed Al-Tawil for helping in the design of the book cover.

The book contains images of works of art, architectural structures, and related objects that were kindly provided with permission for publishing from many museums, institutions, archaeological sources and libraries. Record of the credits for these sources are listed in the credit appendix, but I would like to especially thank the following professionals for their valuable help in Sicily: Vittoria Allibate, Pietro Militello, Francisco Tomasello, Andrea Lo Bue, Fabiola Ardizzone, Rino Francaviglia, Maria Mastelloni, Elisabetta Pagello and Hasan Salamah.

I also thank the many individuals who extended assistance in the Office of the Superintendent, Palermo, Sicily; the authorities at the Cappella Palatina, the Martorana, Palermo Cathedral, Palermo University, Palermo Archaeological Museum, Catania University, Catania Archaeological Museum, Catania Cathedral Library, The Vatican Museum; The Library of Congress, Washington DC; Freer Sackler Gallery of Art, Smithsonian Institution, Washington DC; The MET Museum, NY;

the Trustees of the British Museum; Società Geografica Italiana; The Louvre Museum; Harvard Art Museums; The Iraqi Museum; The National Museum, Damascus; The Department of Archaeology, King Saud University, KSA; Wereldmuseum Rotterdam; Biblioteca Medicea Laurenzina; Museum of Fine Arts, Boston; Museum of Islamic Arts, Cairo, Egypt; Museum Für Islamische Kunst, Staatliche Museen, Berlin; Dr. James B. Kiracofe for his kind permission to publish some of his own photographs; Yale University; Francesco Guazzelli; Cushing/Whitney Medical Library; Qatar National Library; US National Library of Medicine; National Museum of San Mattero, Pisa, Italy.

    My appreciation is also due to the many colleagues and friends who helped in providing related sources, references and materials.

Dedication

To my parents

who taught me that seeking

knowledge is virtue.

To **Ahmed, Wihad**,

and

Bashshar

as they steadfastly

create their paths in life.

INTRODUCTION

History of Arab Art is a brief study of the visual arts and architecture of the Arab people, based on archaeological material and historic accounts dating back as far as 2000 BCE. Although Arab cultural characteristics existed in the Arabian Peninsula and the nearby regions in Iraq, Syria, and North Africa, they have not been adequately studied and identified. Tracking, recording, and studying such characteristics helps to develop a better understanding about the identity of Arab art. Thus, this book is an effort to identify and describe those traditions, explore their chronologies, and explain the relevance to the regions where Arab culture is found.

Language is a major feature of Arab culture as the shared communication system along with social, geographic and ritualistic characteristics. The Arabic language, in its various early Aramaic dialects, is key in tracing the formation of the Arab visual tradition. Linguistically, the various groups of the Arab population shared different dialects of the familiar Aramaic tongue in both the southern and northern regions of the Arabian Peninsula. Ultimately, that linguistic bond evolved into the unifying Arabic language, and continued to be an essential element of Arab visual art. With regard to the study of later periods, particularly from the 7th century CE on, historians commonly include Arab art within the field of "Islamic Art." Similarly, present scholarly literature on the subject tends to subsume Arab art under the reigning culture or cultures of the time; hence they identify it as a reflection of the hegemonic culture.

Arab Art and Islamic Art

Since the establishment of the field of art history and the methodological foundations of the field in the 19th and 20th centuries, the term "Arab art" was more or less equated with Islamic art. The term "Islamic art" itself was coined by Western scholars following the common European perspective, for lack of a more defining term, to describe the "art of the Muslim people." According to this conventional interpretation, religious identity was imposed as the principle characteristics of "Islamic art." In that context, "Arab art" was and to a certain degree still is, included marginally within the fluid concept of "Islamic art."

Historically, Arab art encompasses more cultural elements than those related to the Islamic faith. It comprises cultural materials and artworks produced by Arabs and their ancestors who were of Jewish, Christian, Islamic or non-monotheistic background. Evidence of such cultural material has been dated to precede the advent of monotheism. Such plurality is found in the visual vocabularies and cultural materials of the body of artistic production in central Arabia and Yemen; the Canaanite-Phoenicians in the Mediterranean region; the Nabataeans in the Syrian region; Hatra and Hirah in Iraq. This culturally coherent heritage continued and persisted among independent and semi-independent Arab kingdoms under the control of foreign civilizations such as the Hellenistic, the Parthian-Sassanian, and the Byzantine.

The Beginning

Lack of research and the persistence of the given traditional view of the origin and development of Arab culture have contributed to the continued perplexity on the chronology of Arab culture. Starting in ancient times (around 2000-1500 BCE) and into the period of late antiquity (around 200-800 CE), we encounter Arab culture and artistic practices in literary, visual, and architectural forms presented in different regions. Scholars and art historians have generally overlooked such materials and habitually misinterpreted them by affiliating such materials with the realm of the dominant culture. Such examples can be found throughout the Arab regions across time. For example, Phoenician art is presented within Greek art; Nabataean art from Petra and Palmyra is categorized as "Hellenistic" or "Roman" in style and iconography, the art of Hatra and Hirah in Iraq is identified with the usual Parthian-Sassanian attribution, and the art of the Arab Ghassanids in Syria is presumed Byzantine.

Semite, Semitic and Semitism

The tradition inherited from the 18th century defines the Arab people as part of the "Semite" group. Most studies on this subject rely on, or indirectly use religious views as the basis for interpreting the related cultural materials. The use of the term "Semite" in identifying the culture and ethnicity of the population of the Arabs in Mesopotamia, Syria, Egypt and East Africa is an example of that approach. The term "Semite", originated in the literature of the Old Testament, was adopted and maintained by Western Judeo-Christian scholars in the middle ages, and was further bolstered in the 18th century. The perspective has been accepted by Muslim historians and writers by association, since much of the theological exegeses and narratives of the Islamic teaching concur with Biblical content. The use of the terms Semite, Semitic, and Semitism alludes to certain racial and ethnic identities, and convey veiled nepotism. These applications do not conform with the current academic line of scientific objective research. When used in this book, the term Semite and its derivatives refer to the cultural and linguistic structure among the Aramaic-dialect speaking populations, especially the Arabs, and it does not carry specific religious implication or allusions.

The Problem of Chronology

The earliest indications of Arab culture can be associated with the rise and expansion of the Phoenicians, also known as the Can`anites (Canaanites) in the Mediterranean region sometime around 1500 BCE, but perhaps earlier. Their power centered around the eastern coastal cities of the Mediterranean in the greater Syrian region; Palestine; in the Sinai of Egypt; North Africa at Carthage; Sicily; Malta; Sardinia; and eastern Spain. Their expansion was primarily through commercial activity, with recorded contact in trade and cultural exchange with the ancient Egyptians, the Assyrians and early Greek cities. The Phoenicians rivaled the Greeks and later posed continuous military challenges to the Romans (3rd – 2nd centuries BCE). In the adjacent region closer to Mesopotamia, archaeological records show Phoenician trade activity with the Mesopotamians (1500- 600 BCE).

Cultural Contact and Exchange

In Mesopotamia, Assyrian records of the 8th century BCE show interaction and exchange with the Arabs during the Assyrian and New Babylonian reigns. Arab culture was strongly present during Hellenistic and Roman times as evidenced in Petra, Palmyra, Dura-Europos and other locations in Syria (3rd–5th centuries CE). That presence continued during the Late Roman-Byzantine and Parthian-Sassanian rivalry for domination (4th–7th centuries CE). With the rise of Arab power under Islam in the 7th century CE, "Arab culture" was instrumental in shaping what was to become "Islamic art." It contributed to the formation of Islamic art in the early centuries of Muslim rule in the Arabian region and the expanded Muslim world during the Umayyad, Abbasid, Fatimids, and succeeding dynasties. In the 8th–9th centuries and after, Arab culture and art reached the Iberian Peninsula (Al-Andalus) in Spain, and across the Mediterranean region, Sicily, south Italy and Malta. It left its marks on contemporary European art and architecture continuously through the 17th century and beyond. During the early centuries of Islamic reign, the identity of such "Arab" artistic trends has been typically associated with, and/or overshadowed by the prevalence of "Islamic" art. Very little work has seriously been done to define the characteristics and continuity of Arab art in the regions of the Muslim world.

Western Historians and the Traditional View of the Arabs

Western scholarship inherited a tendency of culture that manifested itself steadily through classical Western sources, which usually characterized the Arab people as wandering Bedouins and nomads, void of civility, and lacking cultural norms. These perceptions were reinforced by 18th century Orientalism and persisted throughout the 19th and 20th centuries, with additional popular views stemming from biased religious interpretations. Meanwhile, a process of cultural discrimination was and continues to be applied by the mainstream scholarship, further undermining Arab culture from the main course of historic development, including the visual materials. That approach was developed in Europe during the late 18th–early 20th centuries amid a colonial campaign in the Arab region and was manifested by long-standing societal and military conflict with the Muslim culture that existed beginning in the medieval era. A distorted and discriminatory view towards the Arabs has become an ingrained bias still at work and reverberates in much of current scholarship.

Arab Origin, Migration, and the Silk Road

As we've seen, scholars identify Arab culture with the "Semitic" roots found in the region of the Arabian Peninsula and its adjacent lands as early as 2000 BCE. Semitic Arab culture developed in the central part of the Peninsula and the southern region (Yemen), which at the time was an active area for the Silk Road's trade. Consecutive waves of migration from those areas prompted by commercial, economic and political activities, resulted in new settlements, and the flourishing of new Arab mini-states and urban centers. Waves of migration headed to the north and northwest adjacent to Mesopotamia and Egypt (Minaean, Sabaean, Himyarite, and Qutabanian). Similar migration reached the southeastern region of Africa via Yemen across the Red Sea. A major thrust of this migration followed the trade routes along the eastern shores of the Mediterranean Sea, to the east and northeast, close to the Persian region (Canaanites-Phoenicians, Nabataeans) (Map 1). The influx of migration transmitted Arab artistic and cultural traditions to neighboring societies and are sometimes easily traceable, but often were assimilated by those contemporary cultures.

INTRODUCTION

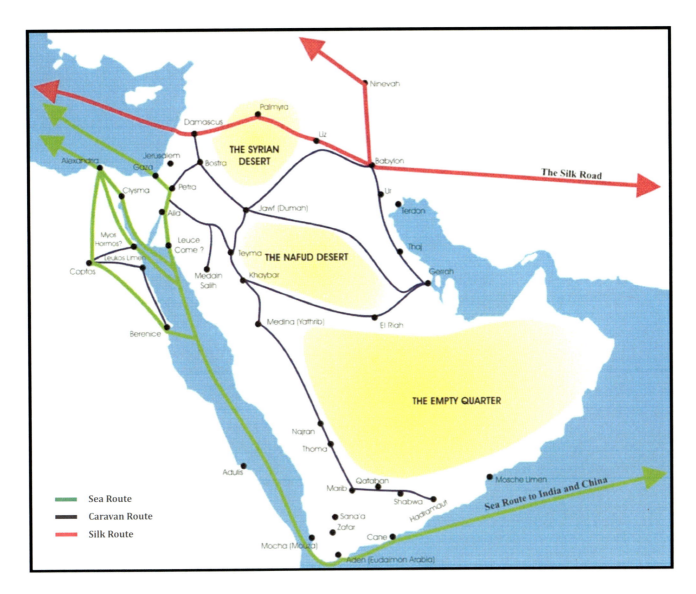

Map 1: The Arabian Peninsula and the trade routes around 1000 BCE.

The contents of the book are presented chronologically:

Part One traces the early period from around 2000 BCE to 650 CE, starting with early archaeological and historical references to Arab culture in the Arabian regions adjacent to Mesopotamia, Egypt, and the Greco-Roman world. The Assyrian records and visual narratives of the 8th century BCE provide us with a fair picture of Arab interaction with powerful neighboring states; especially the Canaanite-Phoenicians with Greeks, Egyptians and Assyrians. The mainland of Arabia was strategically positioned to facilitate trade between the Far East and Southeast Asia and the Mediterranean world. As a result, many Arab semi-states developed along important trade routes next to the territories controlled by different dynastic powers in Mesopotamia and Egypt (943-726 BCE).

This part covers selected monuments, buildings, sculptural works and paintings in the region, against the backdrop of the Greco-Roman control in the west and northwest of the Arabian Peninsula and Persian-Sassanian dominance in the north and northeast. Manifestations of Arab artistic characteristics can be traced through Canaanite-Phoenician cultural materials in the Mediterranean region; especially in cities on the eastern shores, through their contact and exchange with the Mesopotamians, Egyptians, Greeks and Romans. The Canaanite-Phoenicians were a forerunner of Arab culture that interacted with contemporary civilizations, especially the Greeks, who were influenced by Phoenician language, among other things.

The region of central and south Arabia, including Yemen territories, preserved important cultural materials that we have discussed through selected visual and architectural examples from the Minaean, Sabaean, Himyarite, Qutabanian and Hadhramawt kingdoms (800 BCE- 630 CE). Similarly, in the northwest area of the Nabataeans, architecture and sculpture are discussed through selected monuments from Petra and Palmyra in greater Syria, Hatra in northern Iraq, Dura-Europos in Syria and Kindah in central Arabia. In different parts of the Arabian Peninsula, scattered populations of Arabs co-existed with ruling foreign powers, as allies, agents, and adversaries; often as independent or semi-states. Cultural manifestations of their existence indicate various levels of assimilation, integration and impact within the prevailing dominant powers.

Part Two traces the appearance of Arab art in the late pre-Islamic period (200 CE-622 CE) and as a major component of the newly emerging Islamic art from the 7th century through the medieval period. A focus on the late Pre-Islamic period reveals developed visual art traditions in the Hijaz and Najd, along with the Yemen region. Variations of that visual culture in northwest Arabia–Al-`Ula, Mada`in Salih–complete the wider cultural picture. The Ghassanids in northwest Arabia and Syria, the Lakhmids-Mundhirids in Hirah, Iraq, and the Copts in Egypt–exhibited the political affiliation with dominant powers: the Byzantines and the Sassanians. Their cultural tradition, both the literary and the visual, are covered as an important conduit in transmitting the artistic traditions of the Byzantines and Sassanians.

Part Three explores and investigates the Arab literary sources for the cultural activities among the Arabs in the late pre-Islamic and early Islamic period, as attested by poetry, prose, and historical accounts. This includes artistic terms in connection with painting, decoration, sculpture, and the marketing of artworks. It covers the development of Arab art during the early Islamic period in the central and eastern Islamic lands of the newly expanded Muslim state, which includes the Hijaz region (Mecca and Medina), Syria, Iraq, and Egypt. Characteristics of traditional Arab visual culture contributed to and transformed the foundation of early Islamic art during the period of the reign of the Prophet Mohammed, the four succeeding Caliphs (Al-Rashidun), and the Umayyad dynasty to the end of the Abbasid period (622-1258).

Part Four discusses Arab art in the Iberian Peninsula of southern Spain and Portugal. It also covers Arab art in Sicily after the Arab conquest in the 8th and 9th centuries. It includes discussion and analysis of the major survived architectural monuments with associated works of art in sculpture and calligraphic decoration. Covered in this part is the cultural exchange between the Arab-Muslims and Christian Europe to understand the contact, impact, influence and inspiration resulting from such interactions. This part also explains the process of transmitting Arab science, knowledge, and the translated Greco-Roman intellectual heritage to Europe during the 10th-15th centuries. The coverage also includes descriptions of the influence of Arab art forms on European architectural structures and artworks in painting since the 11th century, through the Renaissance and beyond. This part also briefly covers the impact of European Modern art and culture on Arab art during the modern era.

The contents of this book are the product of decades of studying, investigating and analyzing the vast body of literary, cultural, and archaeological materials on the subject. It is a humble effort to establish a reasonable foundation for the study of Arab visual art. I hope that this work will assist students and scholars in their inquiry for better understanding of the formation and development of Arab art and architecture, and Arab culture in general.

Hashim Al-Tawil

Michigan, 2018

Table of Content

Acknowledgements III

Dedication V

Introductions VI

    Arab Art and Islamic Art VI

    The Beginning VII

    Semite, Semitic and Semitism VII

    The Problem of Chronology VII

    Cultural Contact and Exchange VIII

    Western Historians and the Traditional View of the Arabs VIII

    Arab Origins, Migration, and the Silk Road VIII

PART ONE

CHAPTER 1: THE EARLY PERIOD (2000 BCE-650 CE) 1

THE ARAB CULTURAL BACKGROUND 1

Development of the Arabic Language 2

ARABS IN THE REALMS OF MESOPOTAMIA AND EGYPT 2

The Canaanite-Phoenicians 2

Arab Interaction in Mesopotamia 5

ARABS ENCOUNTERS WITH HELLENISTIC AND PERSIAN POWER 9

CHAPTER 2: THE KINGDOMS OF ANCIENT SOUTH ARABIA 11

THE MINAEAN KINGDOM (800 BCE–300 BCE) 13

THE SABAEAN KINGDOM (700 BCE–575 CE) 14

THE HIMYARITE KINGDOM (700 BCE–520 CE)	22
THE QATABANIANS AND HADHRAMAWT (400 BCE–630 CE)	25

CHAPTER 3: ARAB KINGDOMS IN THE NORTH OF THE PENINSULA (400 BCE-600 CE) — 27

NABATAE: PETRA AND PALMYRA (400 BCE-300 CE)	28
PETRA	30
Rock-Cut Architectural Structures of Petra	30
Al-Khaznah – (the Treasury)	32
Al-Dayr (the Monastery)	33
The Tomb of Uneishu	34
The Art of Sculpture at Petra	34
Sculptural Representations of Deities in Petra	34
PALMYRA	41
Architecture of Palmyra	43
Temple of Allat	43
Temple of Ba`l	46
The Tower Tombs of Palmyra	48
Funerary Portraiture	50
HATRA IN NORTHERN MESOPOTAMIA (300 BCE- 200 CE)	54

CHAPTER 4: DURA EUROPOS AND KINDAH — 67

THE CITY OF DURA EUROPOS, SYRIA, (114 CE-257 CE)	67
THE TEMPLES OF DURA EUROPOS	69
Temple of Ba`l at Dura	69
Dura-Europos House-Synagogue	69
Dura-Europos House-Church	71
THE KINGDOM OF KINDAH (200 BCE-600 CE)	75

Qarya Al-Faw 77

PART TWO

CHAPTER 5: VISUAL ART AND ARCHITECTURE IN THE ARABIAN PENINSULA DURING THE LATE PRE-ISLAMIC PERIOD (200 CE-622 CE) 87

CULTURAL AND POLITIC BACKGROUND 87
MECCA AND YETHRIB (MADINAH) REGION 89
SCULPTURAL MONUMENTS OF DEITIES IN PRE-ISLAMIC 90
MADA`IN SALIH (AL-HIJR)- NORTHWEST ARABIA 95
Pre-Islamic Ka`bas and Sanctuaries in Arabia 97
Al-`Ula and Petra 98
Tayma` 98
Temple Wadi Al-Sirhan 98
Ha`il 98
Yemen 98
Hatra 99
Ka`bat Ghatfan 99
Al-Qulays 99
Najran 100
Riyam (Ri`am) 101
GHASSANIDS IN SYRIA 102
LAKHMIDS (MUNDHIRIDS) IN HIRAH, IRAQ 109
COPTS IN EGYPT 115

PART THREE

CHAPTER 6: ARAB ART DURING THE EARLY ISLAMIC PERIOD 119

LITERARY SOURCES TO CULTURAL ACTIVITIES 119
Artistic Terms 120

The Visual Arts	120
The Art of Painting and Decoration	120
The Art of Sculpture	122
`Amru ibn Luhayy, the Patron of Monumental Statues in Mecca	125
EARLY ISLAMIC ART IN THE ARABIAN PENINSULA	126
THE REGION OF MECCA	126
The Ka`ba of Mecca	126
The Kiswah of the Ka`ba and its Decoration	127
The Black Stone of the Ka`ba of Mecca	128
The Sculptural Representations of the Idols in Mecca	129
The Mural Paintings Inside the Ka`ba	133
The Expansion of the Ka`ba During the Umayyad Time	137
THE REGION OF MEDINAH (YETHRIB)	137
The Prophet Mohammed's House-Mosque, Medinah	138
The Minaret of the Prophet's Mosque	139
The Minbar of the Prophet's Mosque	140
The Mihrab of the Prophet's Mosque	140

CHAPTER 7: ARAB ART DURING THE EARLY ISLAMIC PERIOD IN IRAQ, SYRIA, AND PALESTINE — 145

EARLY MOSQUES IN IRAQ	145
The Old Mosque of Basrah	145
The Great Mosque of Kufah and Dar Al-Imarah (governor's house)	146
The Great Mosque of Wasit and Dar Al-Imarah (governor's house)	147
EARLY ARCHITECTURE IN JERUSALEM	149
The Aqsa Mosque	149
The Palatial Complex (Umayyad Royal Residence)	146
The Dome of the Rock	150
EARLY MOSQUES IN DAMASCUS	154

The Great Mosque of Damascus	154
The Mosaic Work at the Great Mosque of Damascus	155
UMAYYAD SECULAR ARCHITECTURE	156
Qusayr `Amra	158
Mshatta Complex	162
Khirbat Al-Mafjar, Jericho, Palestine	164

CHAPTER 8: ARAB ART DURING THE ISLAMIC PERIOD: (800- 1300) — 169

BAGHDAD, THE ABBASID CAPITAL	170
Al-Mustansiriyyah School, Madrasah, Baghdad	173
MANUSCRIPT ILLUMINATION	176
"Kitab Al-Diryaq", Book of Antidotes of Pseudo-Galen	176
The Illustrations of "Maqamat Al-Hariri"	179
THE BAGHDAD SCHOOL OF MANUSCRIPT ILLUSTRATION	181
THE ART OF THE FATIMIDS IN EGYPT	184

PART FOUR

CHAPTER 9: ARAB ART IN EUROPE DURING THE ISLAMIC PERIOD (800- 1500) IBERIA (AL-ANDALUS) — 189

The Great Mosque of Cordoba "Mezquita de Cordoba"	190
Bab Al-Mardum Mosque "The Ermita del Cristo de la Luz"	196
The Great Mosque of Seville, Cathedral of Santa Maria de la Sede and Geralda	199
Alcazar Complex, Seville	201
Madinat Al-Zahra`	203
Al-Hamra` Complex, Alhambra	204
Calligraphic Decoration at the Alhambra	208
The Paintings of the Alhambra, Sala de Los Reyes	212

PORTUGAL	213
The Church-Mosque (Nossa Senhora da Anunciação)	214

CHAPTER 10: ARAB ART IN EUROPE DURING THE ISLAMIC PERIOD (800- 1500) — 217

SICILY (SIQILYAH)	217
Arab architecture in Sicily	218
The Great Mosque of Palermo––The Palermo Cathedral	218
The Martorana, (Concattedrale Santa Maria dell'Ammiraglio)	220
La Zisa Castle/Palace, Palermo	225
La Cuba, Castello della Cuba	229
The Painted Ceiling of the Royal Chapel-the Cappella Palatina, palermo, sicily	232
The Royal Palace of King Roger II and Qasr Al-Amir	236
The Arabic Text on the Ceiling of the cappella palatina	237
The Tradition of the Arab Diwan	238
The Muqarnas Ceiling and the Chapel	239

CHAPTER 11: ARAB CULTURAL IMPACT AND EXCHANGE — 245

Cultural Exchange Through Trade and Commerce	245
Arab-Islamic Art Abroad	246
War and Diplomatic Relationship	246
The Abbasid Caliph Harun Al-Rashid Gifts to Charlemagne	247
Arab Decorative Visual Vocabularies in European Art	247
KNOWLEDGE EXCHANGE AND DISSEMINATION	249
THE TOLEDO SCHOOL OF TRANSLATORS	254
PSEUDO-KUFIC DECORATION	255
Pseudo-Arabic in Byzantium	255
Pseudo-Arabic in Southern Italy	259
Arabs in Southern Italy	260

Pseudo-Arabic as a "Humanistic Mark"	263
Pseudo-Arabic as a Signifier of "High Status"	267
THE DECLINE OF ARAB ART (1700-1900)	269
MODERN ARAB ART	272
Images & Maps Credits	277
Glossary	298
Index	308

THE EARLY PERIOD (2000 BCE-650 CE)

THE ARAB CULTURAL BACKGROUND

Tracing Arab culture to the earliest period is a challenging task, due to insufficient research in the field. The scarce studies done so far provide a hazy picture of the subject, often derived from religious-Biblical interpretations. Nevertheless, the limited archaeological and ethnographic research offer more legible details and reasonable understanding about the subject. These sources agree on the presence of Arab culture as a reflection of the Arabs, found throughout the region centered noticeably around ports and major trading cities along the ancient Silk Road.

In the Mediterranean, the Canaanite-Phoenicians appeared as a strong force dominating trade activity in major cities and islands in the region. The Phoenicians, who can be understood as the eastern branch of the ancient Arab population, engaged in economic, military, and cultural interactions with contemporary cultures such as the early Greeks, Egyptians and later Mesopotamian dynasties. Such interactions are important in constructing the roots of Arab culture. Our knowledge of the Phoenician origin is greatly confused by myths, religious misinterpretation and incorrectly transmitted information by their contemporaries; especially the Greeks.

The term Phoenician comes from the ancient Greeks, who named them "Phoiníkē" and "Punic" meaning purple people, in reference to the unique purple dye that they produced and used in dyeing their cloths. The term Canaanite comes from traditional monotheistic concept of the location and people of the "Northwest Semitic" region – Syria, Palestine, and the Sinai. Recent research on the origin of these people indicate that they were part of the early "Semitic" migration from the Arabian Peninsula to the Fertile Crescent.

Dating back to the early first millennium BCE, two large indigenous ethnic groups emerged in the Arabian Peninsula; one in the South and one in the North. The northern group exhibited mobile lifestyles, sometimes with more advanced characteristics of subtle settlements and expansion similar to the Phoenicians, while the southern group was settled, with a recognizable agricultural and urban sophistication. Continuous migration, trade activity, and intermixing between the south and the north maintained cultural indigenousness in rituals, language, and lifestyle. These two groups originated from indigenous historical traditions that would gradually form the foundation of Arab ethnicity and culture.

Development of the Arabic Language

The Classical Arabic language is traditionally connected to the "Semitic" family of dialects and scripts: Akkadian, Babylonian, Assyrian, Canaanite-Phoenician and Aramaic. Its roots can be traced to around 2000 BCE in the Arabian Peninsula where two indigenous ancient dialects developed; one in the north, known as the North Arabic script *Al-Musnad Al-Shamali,* and one in the southern part of the peninsula; the South Arabic script *Al- Musnad Al-Janubi.* The North Arabic script spread through northern Arabia, from which the Lihyanite, Safaitic and Aramaic dialects developed. Aramaic became the prevalent language in North Arabia around 500 BCE and soon was the official Nabataean script. It was from the Nabataean Aramaic that Arabic writing developed. Meanwhile the use of South Arabic forms of writing also expanded and developed among the Sabaean, Qatabanian, Hadhrami, and Himyarite scripts. Gradually, by 500 CE, Arabic became the language of the whole region, with slight variations in the dialects amongst different localities.

The splendor of South Arabian civilization in the Yemen region has already been attested to by a wealth of archaeological and epigraphic discoveries. Evidence of well-established mini-states governed by structured monarchic systems have been confirmed in different parts of the region as early as 1000 BCE through the first century of the current era. Studies show that South Arabia witnessed an advanced social life with vigorous agricultural and commercial activity. Poetry and oral tradition played a significant role among these groups, and pre-Islamic poetry collections reveal rich descriptive accounts of daily life. The body of oral and recorded literature set the standard for visual narratives produced by Arabs in the pre-Islamic period. Among other things, pre-Islamic poetry provides records of trade, wars, tribal conflicts, accords, and alliances. Furthermore, these texts uncover spiritual and ritualistic practices, revealing indigenous pre-Islamic mythology, deities, and rituals associated with worship, setting the foundation for our understanding of pre-Islamic Arab culture and beliefs.

ARABS IN THE REALMS OF MESOPOTAMIA AND EGYPT

Archaeological records attest the presence of Arabs during the late Mesopotamian, ancient Egyptian, and early Greek eras. Broadly speaking, the Arabs migrated from the Arabian Peninsula to the Fertile Crescent. Mainly settling in the valley of Euphrates and Tigris rivers in ancient Iraq (Greek: Mesopotamia), they coexisted with the Akkadians, Babylonians and Assyrians. Culturally, the Arabs shared similar characteristics with these groups, including language, religion, rituals, social values, history, environment and geography. Trade was a key element in the Arab movement and expansion northward and westward.

The Canaanite-Phoenicians

A pioneer group in trade were the Canaanite-Phoenicians, who extended their commerce and advanced their maritime activity, ultimately establishing many centers along the eastern shores of the Mediterranean Sea. Archaeological evidence indicates that they formed and controlled settlements in key centers such as Sardinia, Corsica, Sicily and around the Aegean Sea. Their lucrative trade, quality of wood (cedar and fir) and agricultural products, and craftsmanship in shipbuilding was sought after by the Assyrians and Egyptians, who imported such commodities from Phoenician cities via ships and caravans. The Canaanite-Phoenicians controlled North African shores, established a strong center at Carthage, and reached southern Spain with major settlements. They had similar activities with the Egyptians and the early Greeks (Map 2). Archaeological records reveal architectural remains, burials, and sculptural monuments in a number of sites that were

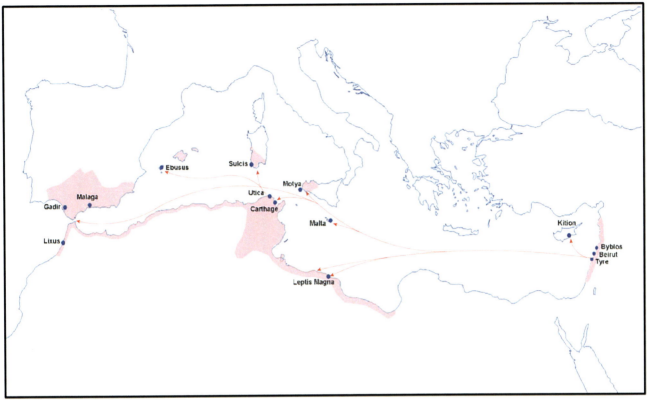

Map 2: Phoenician Expansion in the Mediterranean Region around 800 BCE.

under Phoenician control.

Records reveal Phoenician artifacts, pottery and metal works exported to Mesopotamian, Egyptian and Greek cities. The Phoenician language, which is a dialect of the traditional "Semitic" family of tongues, was a vehicle of communication in that region. Ongoing studies have shown that the Phoenician dialect, an early version of Aramaic, stimulated the development of contemporary dialects such as the Greek early alphabets. Phoenician Aramaic was also infused with Egyptian Hieroglyphics, resulting in a hybrid dialect. The Phoenicians played a significant cultural role in transmitting the heritage of Mesopotamia and Egypt to Europe through the Mediterranean Sea, including mythology, literature, language and visual arts.

Phoenician artistic trends reflect cultural interaction with Mesopotamia, Egypt and Greece, but their artistic production has typically been attributed to those more defined cultures rather than analyzing the motives and sources. Canaanite-Phoenician artists and craftsmen were highly proficient and admired by their clients. By incorporating neighboring traditions, they were able to produce diverse amalgamate styles that catered to a variety of societies.

Fig. 1.1: Sarcophagus of Ahiram, King of Byblos, 1000 BCE, carved limestone, Beirut National Museum, Lebanon.

The sarcophagus of Ahiram, King of Byblos, is an excellent multisource stylistic example of Phoenician art. Dated to around 1000 BCE, it is carved out of limestone, with four royal lions at the base corners. Ceremonial regal scenes present figures depicted with typical Egyptian and Mesopotamian visual characteristics. The narratives also include burial rituals, mourning women, a sacrificial scene, and a portrait of King Ahiram. A remarkable feature of the sarcophagus is the inclusion of a Phoenician-early Aramaic commemorative inscription. (Fig. 1.1). The relief carving is clearly inspired by Babylonian-Assyrian and Egyptian styles, fusing elements together to produce a unique Phoenician visual vocabulary.

Another example is the silver-gilt bowl, which has been dated to the middle of the 8th century BCE. (Fig. 1.2).

The center shows a winged figure-deity of Assyrian type with a sword, overcoming a rampant lion. Surrounding the central scene are two friezes; the inner is occupied with a variety of animals while the outer depicts men battling animals. Egyptian-style subjects, including a Sphinx wearing the Egyptian double crown are present. Ongoing archaeological investigation has uncovered artifacts from Canaanite-Phoenician territories in southern Spain, Sicily and along North African shores. The Canaanite-Phoenicians were instrumental in the transmission of early Arab culture across the Mediterranean regions where they conducted their trade and interacted with contemporary civilizations.

Fig. 1.2: Silver-gilt bowl, Mid 8th century BCE, H. 1 1/4 in. (3.1 cm) diameter 6 5/8 in. (16.8 cm), MET Museum, NY.

Arab Interaction in Mesopotamia

In the North and northwestern areas of the Arabian Peninsula, Arab populations engaged in, managed, and controlled trade activities along the caravan roads that passed through the Syrian territories. Assyrian records documented Arabs living close to the southern border of the Assyrian empire. According to those records of the 8th and 7th centuries BCE, the Arabs extended their control over the Yamamah region in central Arabia. King Assurbanipal campaigned south of Tayma`, an oasis and important trade center on the caravan route in the northwest of the Arabian Peninsula. Assyrian and Babylonian kings reinforced the walls of the city and erected a complex of royal buildings. Later on, the Babylonian King Nebonidus established a seat of power at Tayma`, from around 553–543 BCE. An important find at Tayma` is the so-called "Tayma` Stele" (Fig. 1.3).

This 6th century BCE sandstone stele is inscribed in Aramaic, with a text relating the introduction of the worship of a new Babylonian divinity, Salm of Hagam into the city of Tayma`. Details of the Assyrian inscriptions describe "Arab" tribes, with a notable state of organization, that were at times led by queens. The names of two 8th-century BCE queens, Shamsi and Zabiba, are recorded. It is possible that Assyrian authorities employed the Arab tribes to guard borders, escort their armies in desert regions, and manage commercial activity; especially the lucrative incense trade from Yemen.

The earliest mention of the word "Arab" in Assyrian chronicles is found in the records of King Shalmaneser III, who recorded the history of a battle in around 853 BCE. At the end of the list of his adversaries, Shalmaneser III mentioned Gindibu the Arabian (Arabic: Jundub) and his 1000 camels. Later in the records of the Assyrian kings from Tiglath Pileser III through Ashurbanipal (745-627 BCE), we encounter the mention of a kingdom named Aribi, and "Arabs" appear in the context of both targeted subjects and allies. The Assyrian King Sargon II (reigned 722-705 BCE) claimed to have resettled some Arab nomadic groups in Samaria, Palestine. Later, the Arabs were subdued by the last king of the Neo-Babylonian empire Nabonidus (reigned 556-539 BCE), who made the oasis of Tayma` in the northwest corner of the Arabian Peninsula his capital from 550-540 BCE. These records also list fourteen Arab kings and queens who ruled northern Arabia between 870- 410 BCE.

Through that time, the Arabs established noticeable power to the south of the Mesopotamian Empire. They exerted political pressure when weakness was detected in the centralized government. According to the accounts, they raided the outskirts of cities and villages, instigated rebellions, and disrupted transportation and trade routes. These records also tell of Assyrian kings launching military campaigns against them without decisive victory. They indicate that besides warfare, these Mesopotamian kings had trade relations with Arab cities such as Dedan and Qedar.

Seventh century BCE Assyrian relief panels display narratives of the Assyrian army engaging in warfare with Arabs.

FIG. 1.3: Tayma` Stele, sandstone, 111cm H, 43 cm W and 12 cm D, 6th century BCE, found in Tayma`, Louvre Museum, Paris, France.

THE EARLY PERIOD (2000 BCE-650 CE)

Fig. 1.4: Stone panel from the North Palace of Ashurbanipal (Room L, nos. 9-13), Nineveh, northern Iraq, Neo-Assyrian, around 645 BCE, limestone, Length: 134.62 cm, Width: 226.06 cm, The British Museum.

Fig. 1.5: Fragment of Assyrian relief panel, North Palace of Ashurbanipal, 680-636 BCE, limestone, Height 39 cm, The Vatican Museum.

Fig. 1.6: Assyrians engaged in warfare with Arabs, limestone relief panel, 650 BCE, The British Museum.

A relief carving (Fig. 1.4) of an Assyrian panel from the North Palace of Ashurbanipal in Nineveh depicts such a campaign, with Assyrian soldiers on horseback and foot troops pursuing Arabs on camels. A fragment of a similar relief (Figures 1.5, 1.6), originally part of a more extensive sculptural program, celebrates the victories of King Assurbanipal over Arabs of the Syrian-Arabian desert. In the scene, a dromedary and a burning tent are visible.

Details of these scenes reveal an advanced degree of military organization, weaponry, and a practical use of camels for war mobility, suggesting well-established military engagement on the part of the Arab troops. Late Babylonian records indicate that the same area was occupied during the reign of King Nabonidus (553-543 BCE), and his son Belshazzar continued that policy.

ARABS ENCOUNTERS WITH HELLENISTIC AND PERSIAN POWERS

As we've seen above, the eastern Mediterranean coast in the Syrian region witnessed the rise of Canaanite-Phoenician city-states such as Tyre, Sidon, Byblos, and Baalbek.

As early as 1500 BCE, the Phoenicians established a strong presence of independent city-states in the region and engaged in seafaring trade with Egypt, Mesopotamia, and later, the Greek city-states. Assyrian accounts of the 7th century BCE also recorded Phoenician connection with the Assyrians as professional ship builders and possible suppliers of ships built for the Assyrians military. In 539 BCE Cyrus of Persia conquered "Phoenicia" and the Achaemenids subjugated northwestern Arabia during the late 6th century BCE. Persian control reached south Arabia as well, in the 5th century BCE.

In 332 BCE Alexander of Macedonia conquered the Phoenician city-states and the area continued to be a battleground for domination after his death. A succession of Macedonian rulers followed but finally fell to the Ptolemies of Egypt in 197 BCE. In 65 BCE Pompey annexed the territory as part of the Roman province of Syria. The Romans continued their control of the greater Syrian region, and cities such as Petra and Palmyra would be client states under the Romans. Egypt was also under Roman control through the end of the Roman power in mid 4th century CE. The Byzantine Empire inherited the former Roman colonies, and hence parts of North Africa, Syria and Egypt became Byzantine territories.

In the eastern region of the Arabian Peninsula, the Persians held political dominance and the Sassanians succeeded in penetrating the Arabian Peninsula. There, they established a stronghold in southern Iraq through the client Arab mini-state Hirah. Around 570 CE the Sassanians succeeded in establishing an alliance with a semi-independent Yemeni state against the Byzantine client state of Aksumites across the Red Sea in Abyssinia, who had invaded Yemen. Around the end of the 6th century CE, southern Arabia became a Persian dominion managed by a Yemenite vassal. The Sassanid control of Arab lands in both Iraq and Yemen ended soon after the rise of the unified Arab tribes under Islam in 622.

The cultural picture of the land of the Arabs during the middle of the 7th century CE was that of scattered mini-states, independent, semi-independent, or clients to ruling powers. In this light, we can understand the rise and expansion of "Islam" as a campaign to reclaim colonized Arab territories and populations from dominant powers of the time, namely the Sassanian and Byzantine Empires and their allies. It is important to look at these scattered communities, their cultural activities, art, and architecture as a reflection of this cultural interaction.

Selected Bibliography

Barnett, Richard D, *Sculptures from the North Palace of Ashurbanipal at Nineveh (668-627 B.C)*, London: British Museum, 1976.

Gabrieli, Francesco, *The Arabs: A Compact History*, New York: Hawthorn Books, Inc., 1963.

Gadd, Cyril John, *The Stones of Assyria: the surviving remains of Assyrian sculpture, their recovery, and their original positions,* London: Chatto and Windus, 1936.

Hitti, Philip, *History of the Arabs*, 10th edition, London: Palgrave Macmillan, 2002.

Hourani, Albert, *A History of the Arab People*, Cambridge: Harvard University Press, 2010.

Hoyland, Robert G, *Arabia and the Arabs: from the Bronze Age to the coming of Islam*, London & New York: Routledge, 2001.

Moscati, Sabatino, *Ancient Semitic Civilizations*, London: Penguin, 1960.

Paterson, A, *Assyrian Sculptures* (12 parts), H. Haarlem & London: Kleinmann, 1901.

Rossi Pierre, *La Cite d Isis Histoire Vraie des Arabes*, Nouvelles Editions, Paris: Latines, 1976.

CHAPTER 2

THE KINGDOMS OF ANCIENT SOUTH ARABIA

Yemen, the southern region of the Arabian Peninsula, was strategically important for the two-way trade activities and transportation between China, Southeast Asia and the Mediterranean. A major producer of frankincense, myrrh and other desirable spices, Yemen's location and connection to Africa and the Red Sea made it equally critical for military and political control. In such an active and lucrative region with trade revenue, political and economic competition drove the population. Ultimately, this resulted in the development and creation of many semi-independent kingdoms that collaborated, competed and struggled for control. The thriving activity in South Arabia also exhibited a cultural interaction between the indigenous Arabs and foreign merchants operating across Yemen. Such multicultural interaction manifested in the diversity of beliefs, rituals and styles of artistic production.

These mini-states in the Yemen region monitored and supervised the sea route of the Silk Road and the overland caravan route through the Arabian Peninsula. They were active along this important trade route that connected China and India in the east with the Mediterranean and the Roman territories in the west (Map 3). These mini-states or kingdoms competed, contested, collaborated and at times consolidated their powers for economic and political interest. Political alliance with dominant powers of the time took place among these kingdoms, and at times resulted in protracted wars.

Because of the flourishing economy, many cities thrived in different parts of South Arabia, with advanced cultures, art forms, and architectural structures. Early on and around 1000 BCE, contact with both Mesopotamia and Egypt is found in Yemen, as evidenced by stylistic evaluation of certain artworks and architectural structures. Similarly, archaeologists have registered Hellenistic, Byzantine and Persian influence on the visual art during the 2nd-5th centuries CE.

Polytheism, and later monotheism, spread among South Arabian inhabitants, with funerary and ritualistic practices similar to other Arab groups in the mainland and in the outskirts of Arab lands in Iraq and Syria (Hirah, Hatra, Petra, Palmyra). In the early 7th century CE monotheism alone prevailed with the predominant religion of Islam. Smaller communities of Jewish and Christian Arab tribes were already residing in major ancient Arab cities. The limited archaeological investigation of inscriptions found in "South" Arabia reveal a unified Arab culture with dialects of "Semitic" origins that contributed considerably to the development of the classical Arabic language.

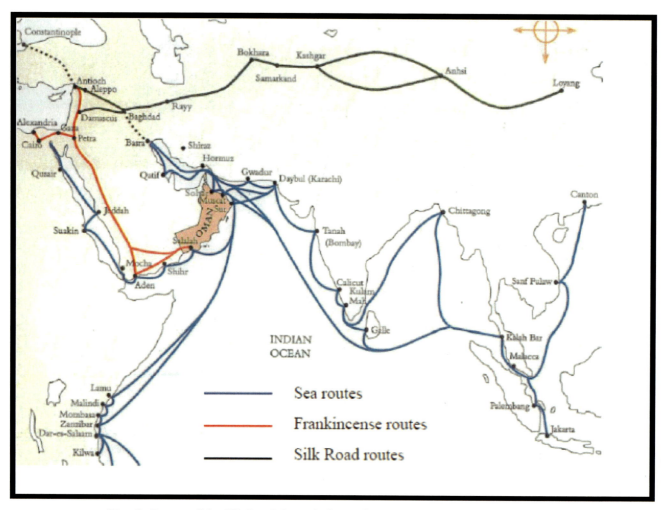

Map 3: Routes of the Silk Road through the Arabian Peninsula (1000 BCE-700 CE).

The chronology of these kingdoms is not clear enough, and more analysis and research are needed to update the approximate dates of the beginning and end of each kingdom. It is clear that some of these kingdoms coexisted in many phases of the South Arabian historical timetable.

Powerful kingdoms also extended their control to the central and northeastern regions of the Peninsula. Results of carbon dating with analysis of written inscriptions reveal that the culture of South Arabia dates back to around 1200 BCE and merged in the new sociopolitical setting of the early 7th century CE. Considerable South Arabian cultural characteristics would be instrumental in the formation of early Islamic art and architecture.

Three powerful kingdoms have been identified. Chronologically: the Minaean Kingdom centered in Ma`in (800 BCE- 300 BCE), followed and overlapping with the kingdom of the Sabaens (700 BCE–525 CE), which was centered in Ma'rib and was contemporary with the later Roman era; and finally, the the Himyarite (700 BCE–520 CE), who experienced the ongoing confrontation between the Romans and the Persians (4th-6th centuries CE.). Two notable kingdoms followed and should be mentioned, the Qatabanians and the Hadhramawt (400 BCE–630 CE). These kingdoms were instrumental in the trading activities, both domestic and foreign; including: China, Southeast Asia and the Mediterranean region in the west.

THE KINGDOMS OF ANCIENT SOUTH ARABIA

Archaeological excavation, although limited in different parts of South Arabia (Yemen region), produced many artifacts, such as votive offerings, funerary plaques, and inscriptions in temples and other locations. The rituals and religious beliefs associated with the deities worshipped in that region indicate that a production of naturalistic, abstract and symbolic imagery on objects was common in South Arabia. These objects (busts, heads, portraits, incense burners, plaques, models of altars, etc.) are mostly sculptural, typically depicting an image of the donor or dedication of text and symbolic relief images carved in naturalistic style on stone. The majority of these offerings were directed toward gaining favor from the deity, and some were meant to probably show the wealth of a donor as well. Sometimes, these votive offerings are identified with inscriptions. Other times, the carvings commemorate the deceased with a combination of text and images. Many of the objects portray the deceased in a particular pose, along with other figures in the presence of important persons or deities.

THE MINAEAN KINGDOM
(800 BCE–300 BCE)

An ancient southern Arabian kingdom occupied the northern part of Yemen, with its earlier capital in Yathil-Baraqish and later at Ma`in, according to early records of the 6th and 5th centuries BCE. The Minaeans, named for the city of Ma`in, flourished in the incense trade. They controlled commercial routes through Arabia from the 4th through the 2nd century BCE. Their territories extended to the north in Dedan, also known as Al-`Ula. In the 1st century

Fig. 2.1: The ruins of the ancient city of Baraqish, Yemen.

BCE, the Minaean kingdom came under the rule of the Qatabanian Kingdom and was soon incorporated into the kingdom of Saba`.

The ruins of the city of Baraqish (Fig. 2.1) reveal many inscriptions on the walls of buildings (Fig. 2.2). A large Minaean votive alabaster stele carved in relief sculpture (Fig. 2.3) and dated to 6th-4th centuries BCE displays a 10-line Minaean inscription in the center that reads:

"Amm-dhara, son of Ya'wsi its family 'Ahir, family Sahr, Administrator [gods] and Wadd' Athtar-de-Qabdu and Nakrah, and the gods of Ma'in, and [the kings] Il-yafa 'and Waqah he, the priest Sahr, he has devoted to this' Athtar de Qabdu and made a monument Sahar. Ma'in by the gods and kings and Il'yafa Waqah it."

The borders of the stele are decorated with symbols of deities while sacrificial animals surround the text on three sides. Sculpture in the round along with reliefs of full human figures, busts, and portraits were made to honor deities, commemorate nobilities and record information for individuals.

THE SABAEAN KINGDOM (700 BCE–575 CE)

The Sabaean Kingdom rose to power around the time of the construction of the Ma`rib Dam. The city of Ma`rib was the center of power and administration where the Sabaeans controlled the trade route and oversaw the protection and transport of the frankincense and myrrh.

The fortified city of Ma`rib in north-central Yemen and its associated dam was the principal center of the state of Saba' (950–115 BCE). The kingdom of Saba` reached its peak around the 7th century BCE. Ma`rib was located on one of the primary caravan routes of the Silk Road

Fig. 2.2: Wall with Minaean inscriptions, Baraqish, Al Jawf province, Yemen, 5th-1st centuries BCE.

Fig. 2.3: Votive alabaster stele carved in relief sculpture with Minaean inscription, 6th-4th centuries BCE.

linking the Mediterranean world with the Arabian Peninsula. The city prospered; especially because of its trade monopoly of frankincense and myrrh from Yemen and the southern coastal region of Hadhramawt (Fig. 2.4).

The Sabaean kings established the city of Ma`rib as their capital and constructed the Ma`rib dam as part of a wider irrigation system that continued to support flourishing agricultural prosperity. Magnificent stonework of high quality was employed, with sluices and anchor towers rising to a height of 18 meters (59 feet). The dam was 750 meters (2460.63 feet) across and held back water to a depth of 15 meters (49 feet) and was used to irrigate a vast area. The rerouting of the trade path away from Ma`rib in the 6th century BCE marked the gradual deterioration of the city. This development, coupled with the negligence of the dam, inevitably led to its total decline.

Fig. 2.4: The remains of ancient Ma`rib, Yemen.

Fig. 2.5: Barran Temple, Ma`rib, Yemen.

THE KINGDOMS OF ANCIENT SOUTH ARABIA

Fig. 2.6: Calcite incense burner showing a camel rider, Sabaean, 3rd century BCE.

Fig. 2.7: Painted limestone incense burner, 5th-4th centuries BCE, Height: 9.50 cm. Width: 9.50 cm. Thickness: 9.50 cm., Yemen.

Fig. 2.8: Calcite statue of standing female figure, 3rd-2nd centuries BCE, Height: 74.5 cm, Width: 33 cm (at shoulder), Thickness: 24 cm, Sabaean from Ma`rib or Qataban, Yemen.

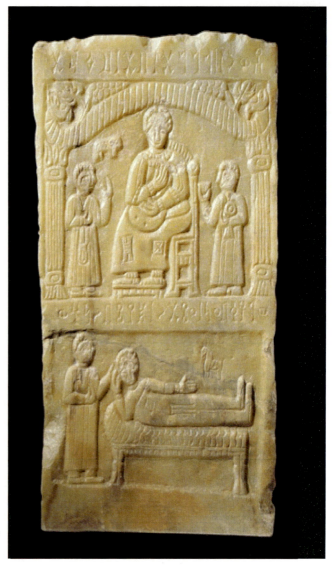

Fig. 2.9: Dedication calcite Stele: Ghalilat, daughter of Mafaddat, 1st c. BCE-1st c. CE. Width: 27.50 cm., Yemen.

Many temples were erected in and nearby the city of Ma`rib, whose remains are still standing today. One important example is the temple of Barran, with four imposing monolith pillars, a courtyard, porticos, and altars (Figure 2.5). The temple is associated with the moon deity Almuqqah. The architectural plan is a typical Arab square layout with a surrounding wall, open courtyard, and a ritualistic well in the center, next to a platform with six towering pillars, 12-meters high. Religious beliefs, deities and rituals were shared among these different kingdoms and the use of visual images and symbols of deities were common in temples and the funerary field. Such images are found on ritualistic objects and burial plaques. Incense burners are found in many temples as seen in Figure 2.6. This incense burner displays a camel rider and an inscription in the Sabaean alphabet. It refers to 'Adhlal, son of Wahab'il', who had presumably dedicated the burner in a temple as an act of piety.

A more abstract example can be seen in Figure 2.7, a painted limestone incense burner that comes from the 5th-4th century BCE. This cubic form was common for incense burners and was often inscribed with the names of specific aromatics from the range of woods, barks, roots and resins used in South Arabia, but can also carry names of donors or deities. This example is inscribed with the names "rand, darw, kamkam and qust."

Other votive offerings are presented with full human figures, such as (Fig. 2.8). It is a smaller than life-size statue of a standing woman and may originally have held an offering.

A funerary stele (Fig. 2.9) is a gravestone or possibly a dedication slab deposited inside a temple as a votive offering to the deity Attar. The Sabaean inscription states "The image of Ghalilat–daughter of Mafaddat. May Attar destroy him who breaks it." This is an interesting work of art that not only commemorates the deceased but also provides a glimpse into the details of everyday life. The composition has two registers. The upper register displays the full figure of Ghalilat. The depiction of this female personality reflects wealth and important social status. She is seated on an intricate high chair with her feet resting on a footstool, flanked by two smaller female attendants. She is playing a musical instrument, probably the `Ud, and one attendant holds another musical instrument, a drum. The three figures are positioned underneath an arch with dragon's heads at both ends, possibly representing the protection of deities like Attar (Athtar), who was one of the main deities in Yemen, associated with irrigation. Stylized depictions of acanthus leaves top the two columns and fill the triangular spaces on

Fig. 2.10: Aylward Stela- Funerary Qatabanian calcite Stele, Wadi Bayhan (Qataban), Hayd ibn Aqil (Timna)Yemen, 1st c. BCE-1st c. CE. Height: 29 cm, Width: 27 cm, Thickness: 6.3 cm, Yemen.

both sides. The lower register shows a female figure reclining on a decorated couch, with an attendant next to her. Details fill the scene, such as symbols on the dress and miniature depictions of animals in the background.

Such funerary presentations may have been standard in use and reused for multiple deceased individuals. Furthermore, the practice of "erasing" an old name and inscribing a new one may have taken place. The presentation in Figure 2.10 shows such a variation, with a funerary slab depicting a related composition of a seated woman playing music accompanied by two attendants. The upper register contains an "erased" inscription, possibly the name of the deceased. This slab reveals striking similarities with the stele seen in Figure 2.9, and may provide strong evidence of an established typecast tradition of a ready-made funerary format that functioned within the burial tradition.

`Awwam, also Awam Temple is another important site near Ma`rib, also known as "Mahram Balqis," which was dedicated to the Sabaean moon god, Almaqah-Allumqah (Figures 2.11, 2.12). This temple has been traditionally associated with the fabled Queen of Sheba-Balqis based on common folklore and religious interpretation. Excavations at the temple have yielded many inscriptions and show that Al-Maqah was represented by the crescent and the bull and invoked with other female deities such as "Athtar" and Dhat-Himyam.

South Arabian visual narratives are plentiful and found abundantly in temples, tombs, and residential quarters. They display an established tradition of visual narratives presented in a naturalistic and descriptive style.

Fig. 2.11: `Awam Temple "Mahram Balqis", Sabaean, near Ma`rib, Yemen.

THE KINGDOMS OF ANCIENT SOUTH ARABIA   21

Fig. 2.12: Mahram Balqis, interior, Yemen.

Fig. 2.13: Sabaean hunting scene, Alabaster carving, 500 BCE, Height. 88 Cm, Width 32.5 Cm, Thickness 6 Cm., Yemen.

A Sabaean alabaster stele (Fig. 2.13), carved in low relief, depicts a hunting narrative divided into four registers on a rectangular slab dated to around 500 BCE. In the lower register, a male figure riding a horse is depicted along with an attendant–perhaps his servant. The main figure tackles and overpowers a bull in the second scene with two attendants. He appears again in the third register, this time riding a camel with his hunting prize along with an attendant. On the upper register, our figure is presented walking stridently with an attendant. On top of the upper register is a Sabaean identifying inscription with the wording "ṣwr w-nṣb Sʿdʾwm ḏ-Mḏmrm," which roughly translates to "Image and dedicatory monument to Saʿd ʿAwm of Medmarm."

THE HIMYARITE KINGDOM (700 BCE–525 CE)

The Himyarites established their power in the city of Zafar near present-day Sanʿaʾ. By 300 CE the Himyarite kingdom extended its power over the Sabaeans, the Qutabanians, and Hadhramawt. Their kings continued the tradition of supervising the transport of spices and precious commodities throughout Yemen

Fig. 2.14: Funerary Commemorative slab of ʿAban of the tribe of Mahdhar, calcite-alabaster stele, Height: 30 cm, Width: 19.01 cm, Thickness: 7 cm (at nose) 1st c. BCE – 2nd c. CE., Yemen.

Fig. 2.15: Life size stone relief of alleged Himyarite king, 450-525 CE., 1.70 meters height. Dhafar (Zafar), Yemen.

while exporting ivory from Africa, to be sold in the Roman territories. Judaism and Christianity spread among Himyarite territories, and in 520 CE the Christians of Najran–supported by Abyssinia, a client of the Byzantine Empire– defeated the Himyarites.

A gravestone slab relief sculpture on calcite-alabaster stone shows a bust of a young standing female (`Aban) on a rectangular plaque. She is holding her right hand up in a ceremonial or ritualistic pose, with a bundle of wheat in her left hand, perhaps a symbol of fertility. Such a pose must have been characteristic of certain social or ritualistic gestures. The inscription records her name as `Aban of the tribe of Mahdhar (Fig. 2.14). The work is commemorative and shows the wealth of the woman and the abundance she enjoyed in life. She wears bracelets and a short-sleeved dress. Two holes in the earlobes suggest hanging earrings. Such funerary plaques may have been part of a tomb or placed in a niche. The stylistic representation of the figure is reminiscent of the style found in funerary monuments in Palmyra.

Depictions of human figures were common in the various burial and funerary rituals throughout Yemen. Carved images of the deceased along with inscriptions of names

Fig. 2.16: Funerary dedication of a man head, calcite-alabaster Stele, 1st c. BCE–2nd c. CE., Timna`, Yemen.

and other contextual information are found on many stone plaques. Archaeologists have unearthed numerous slabs from various sites in the region. They commonly depict a simple portrait— a stylized human head with or without identifying text.

An important full-sized frontal relief portrait of a high-ranking person believed to be a Himyarite king (Fig. 2.15) has recently been unearthed. This relief sculpture comes from the ruins of a stone building in Dhafar (Zafar), which was the capital of the last powerful kingdom, the Himyarite, in southwest Yemen, that ended with the Sassanid conquest in 575 CE. Zafar was one of the most important and celebrated towns in Southern Arabia and witnessed Exumite and Sassanid occupation. The naturalistic relief sculpture depicts a crowned and bearded man, dressed in an official tunic, and adorned with jewelry and weapons. In his left hand, the man holds a bundle of twigs or branches, probably a symbol of peace, while he holds a court staff in his right hand. Evidence of stylistic affinity with the Ethiopian, Coptic, and Sassanian visual traditions is noticeable, but more evident are the persisting indigenous Arab visual conventions found in Yemen and to the north in the paintings of Qaryat al-Faw (see chapter 4). Such characteristics would reemerge later with the Umayyad style in Syria in the 8th century. Archaeologists have attributed elements such as the crown, staff, and the rounded face with curly hair to Ethiopian or Coptic roots and can be connected to the Abyssinian incursion in Yemen during the 6th century.

THE QATABANIANS AND HADHRAMAWT
(400 BCE–630 CE)

The Qatabanians and the Hadhramawti kingdoms came on the scene along with the Sabaeans and Himyarites and lasted to the end of the 2nd century CE. The kingdom of Qataban thrived in the Bayhan valley, with its capital Tamna` in the Aden region, and Hadhramawt, with its capital Shabwa located in present-day Hadhramawt continued the control of the caravan route, trade activity and related business in their territories. The Qatabanians were probably supervised by the other stronger kingdoms of the Sabaeans and the Minaeans. They shared prevailing religious beliefs and rituals and worshiped common deities in temples that exhibited the unique architectural characteristics of South Arabia. Figurative representations were used in the same manner: for dedication, honoring and commemoration.

Funerary dedication plaques are found in plenty throughout Yemen. Visual representations on these plaques vary from inscriptions to stylized human depictions expressed by a portrait or bust of the deceased. An example here is a Qatabanian head of a man, carved in relief sculpture (Fig. 2.16).

Shabwa was the capital of Hadhramawt in the southern end of the Arabian Peninsula, near the Ma`rib area. Its ruins are still visible, with remains of architectural structures. Many funerary plaques are also found. Studies of many pieces show a mixture of stylistic influence from Mesopotamia and Egypt, along with indigenous South Arabian characteristics. Archaeologists also detected certain connections between South Arabian art and early Islamic (Umayyad) art of the 8th century CE in the Syrian region.

Selected Bibliography

Avanzini, A., "The Hegemony of Qataban", *Caravan Kingdoms: Yemen and the Frankincense Trade*, ed. Ann C. Gunter, Washington DC: Arthur M. Sackler Gallery, Smithsonian Institution, 2005, 20-25.

Daum W. ed., *Yemen: 3000 years of art and civilization in Arabia Felix*, London: Penguin, 1988.

De Maigret A., *Arabia Felix: An Exploration of the Archaeological History of Yemen*, Stacey International, 2009.

De Maigret A., "The excavations of the Temple of Nakrah at Baraqish (Yemen)". Proceedings of the Seminar for *Arabian Studies* 21, 1991, 159–171.

Doe B., *Southern Arabia*, London & New York: Thames and Hudson, 1971.

Fedele Francesco G., "The wall and talus at Baraqish, ancient Yathill (al-Jawf, Yemen): a Minaean Stratigraphy", Proceedings of the Seminar for *Arabian Studies* 41, 2011, 101–120.

Hoyland, Robert G, *Arabia and the Arabs: from the Bronze Age to the coming of Islam*, London & New York: Routledge, 2001.

Philby, St. J. H., *The Queen of Sheba*, London: Quartet, 1981.

Seipel W. and others, *Jemen: Kunst und Archäologie I*, Vienna, 1999.

Simpson St J. ed., *Queen of Sheba: Treasures from Ancient Yemen*, London: The British Museum Press, 2002.

CHAPTER 3

ARAB KINGDOMS IN THE NORTH OF THE PENINSULA (400 BCE-600 CE)

The northern Arabian Peninsula thrived through trade between Yemen and the Mediterranean through Syria and Iraq. Records show that the Arabs played a key role in the management of movement and commerce in the north and northwest. Their control of the routes extended through Syria, the coastal city of Gaza in Palestine, and through Sinai in Egypt. The contemporary powers–Greeks, Romans, and Persians–struggled to secure control of the Arab region. Between the 5th century BCE and the 7th century CE, Arab populations in this vast area were under the control of powerful empires. Against the backdrop of the Greco-Roman political domination in Syria-Iraq, and with a turbulent Persia on the border, independent Arab mini-states emerged along major trade roads and militarily strategic locations.

Noticeable among these mini-state kingdoms are **Hatra** (300 BCE-200 CE) in northern Iraq; **Iturea** near Biqa` in present day Lebanon (2nd century BCE); **Edessa** (Arabic: Raha) in Syria (1st-7th century CE); **Misan** in southern Iraq (150 BCE-222 CE); **Emessa** (Arabic: Hims) in Syria (4th century BCE-7th century CE); and **Petra, Palmyra, Bosra,** and **Al-Hijr** (400 BCE-300 CE) in greater Syria. Other semi-independent kingdoms located in North Arabia were the **Adomites, Dedanites** and **Lihyanites.**

Alexander the Macedonian expanded the dominion of Greek imperial power by annexing lands in Anatolia, Egypt, Babylon, and Persia. After his death in 323 BCE, his generals, specifically Antigonnus, Ptolemy, and Seleucus, divided the colonized territories among themselves. Ptolemy took Palestine and Egypt, Antigonnus took Macedonia and Asia Minor, while Seluces I Nicator took Syria, Iraq and Persia. Hence, most of the Arab population came under foreign occupation. This pattern continued during the Roman, Persian, and later Byzantine and Sassanian rule. The Arab populations in Iraq, Syria, Palestine and Egypt were subject to those dominant powers, in turn impacting the culture at the hands of foreign control and influence. Nevertheless, the fundamental substance of Arab culture persisted and survived through centuries of various occupations. Arab culture, language, religious beliefs and visual art went through assimilation, adaptation, and incorporation during these periods, though the roots of their traditions were preserved. The following is a brief survey of the visual art, architecture and artistic trends among selected kingdoms.

In the North Arabian Peninsula, the Nabataeans emerged through two important Arab kingdoms in **Petra** and **Palmyra.** Aramaic was the language of both states, from which the Arabic language evolved later. Other smaller but important nearby states were **Lihyan,** with its center at **Dedan (Al-`Ula)** connected to both the Minaeans in the south and the Nabataeans in the north. These urban centers yielded numerous architectural and sculptural monuments that displayed both South and North Arabic dialects in their inscriptions beginning in the 1st century CE. The visual tradition of the Lihyanite reveals a blending of typical Arab stylizations with Hellenistic influence, similar to that found in Petra and Palmyra.

Between the 3rd and 6th centuries CE two Arab buffer states emerged. The **Ghassanids** in Syria as an agent state to the Romans (and later the Byzantines), and the **Lakhmids** (Mundhitids)– centered in Hirah, Iraq along the Euphrates, who served as client states to the Parthian-Sassanians. Although both mini-states were Arab Christians, they followed their respective patron empires and exhibited a mutual antagonistic rivalry, with occasional coalitions formed as necessitated by the wider political situation. Arabic historical records describe aspects of magnificent buildings and luxurious lifestyles that existed within the two states, especially at Hirah, particularly in accounts of churches and the Mundhirid palaces. Both states survived into the 7th century until they lost power to the emerging Arab state under the banner of the new faith of Islam.

NABATAE: PETRA AND PALMYRA (400 BCE-300 CE)

The Nabataeans arose through two important Arab kingdoms in **Petra** and **Palmyra** (400 BCE-300CE). Both states were connected by active trade routes and were instrumental in commercial activities between the east (China, Central Asia, India, and Southeast Asia) and the Mediterranean. The Nabataeans were Arab "Semites" who shared cultural bonds with their neighboring Arab communities in other parts of the region such as Hatra, Dura Europos, Bosra and Hirah. Aramaic and its various dialects were primarily used in both states, along with other languages for commercial transactions. Evidence of the use of Greek and Pahlavi (Persian), the languages of the dominant occupying powers of the Hellenistic, Roman and Parthian authorities, has been attested to by the wealth of archaeological materials found in cities such as Hatra, Hirah, Bosra, Palmyra and Dura Europos.

As Nabataean states struggled between the Parthians in the east and the Romans in the west, their political endurance showed various phases of compliance, containment and defiance. At times, they appeared independent or expansive while at others functioned as clients of dominating powers. In Mesopotamia, Hatra and Hirah were secured by the Parthians, while in Syria, Petra and Palmyra were controlled first by the Greeks and later by the Romans and Byzantines.

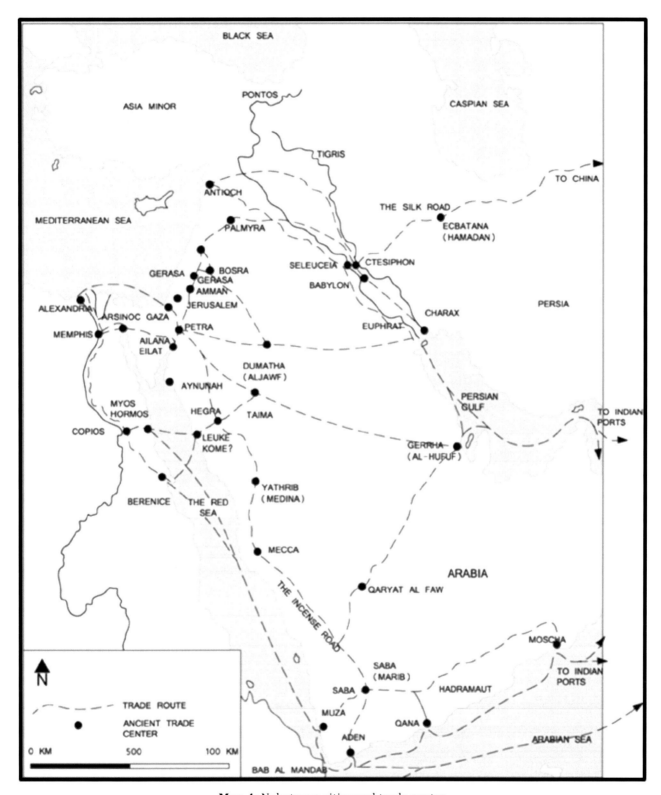

Map 4: Nabataean cities and trade routes.

At the height of their power and before they were conquered and annexed to the Roman Empire, the Nabataeans controlled a vast area of the region from Egypt, Syria, Palestine and Jordan into the northern Arabian Peninsula (Map 4). They produced innovative networks of water conservation cisterns, hydraulic engineering, funerary structures, and transportation systems.

PETRA

The Nabataeans controlled trade traffic in the northwest Arabian Peninsula with connections to Syria, Palestine, Egypt and Iraq. Migrating from the mainland, most probably South Arabia around 400 BCE, they were an essential population on the Peninsula. A progressed society, they established vibrant cities filled with urban lifestyle, excelled as merchants and traders, and administered a vast independent region with Petra as the primary metropolitan center. Petra was strategically located at the crossroads of the lucrative trade caravan route that connected South Arabia with the Mediterranean world.

The Greeks realized the significance of Petra and targeted the territory unsuccessfully in 312 BCE. At its height, between the 1st century BCE and the 1st century CE, Petra extended its territory to include greater Syria, northern Arabia, the Sinai and Palestine. Profitable trade revenue made it a rich cosmopolitan center, enabling the creation of highly efficient water conservation systems such as dams, canals, and reservoirs in an otherwise arid environment.

Eventually the Romans incorporated Petra into the Roman province of Arabia under Trajan in 106 CE and moved its center to the city of Bosra (Bostra). The great wealth of Petra facilitated the construction of outstanding rock-cut architectural structures, tombs, and temples throughout the city. Under Roman control, much of Petra's architecture, sculpture and religious rituals were influenced by Hellenistic and Roman styles. However, Arab cultural characteristics shared in the stylistic transformation, while Aramaic continued to be the predominant language of communication for centuries. Limited archaeological investigations have revealed some significant information about the Nabataeans and their culture. In their early centuries, they formed a monarchic system of kingship and called it "Kings of the Nabtu," along with a pantheon of deities such as Dhushara, (also Dhul-shara) Allat, and Al-`Uzza. After Roman colonization, Hellenistic elements impacted the religious beliefs and the visual arts of the Nabataeans.

ROCK-CUT ARCHITECTURAL STRUCTURES OF PETRA

The outstanding carved structures and enormous rock-cut facades of Petra are still an enigma to archaeologists. Rock-cut facades are found throughout Petra and functioned as tombs, funerary/ceremonial facilities, residential spaces and communal meeting rooms. While some facades are unfinished, most contain moderate decoration; many are superbly carved and decorated on a royal scale. Very limited archaeological research has been conducted in Petra; what we know at present is minimal compared to what is presumably waiting to be uncovered.

The architectural style of the rock-cut facades displays a combination of elements and decorative motifs. Researchers have detected stylistic elements from Mesopotamia and Egypt in earlier structures, and Hellenistic and Roman influence in facade details of the later period. The general interior plans of the spaces are square or semi-rectangular; a common Arab architectural blueprint found throughout Arabia: as in Yemen, Hatra, Hirah and Syria. Tomb facades have been recognized, with the presence of arches, gables, obelisks, steps and tombs with elaborate temple-like decorations. Carvings on facades range from complete to unfinished in various stages. Larger tombs have multiple doors leading to different burial chambers while single tombs have one doorway leading to the burial space. Harsh climate conditions and excessive vandalism have destroyed almost all interior painting in the structures. There are over 3000 rock-cut structures, residential and burial, that have been dated from the 3rd century BCE to the 2nd century

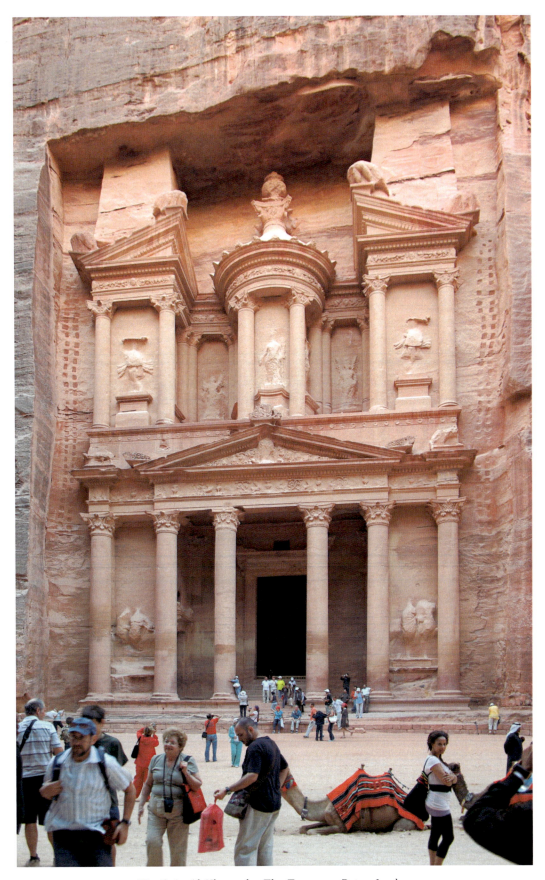

Fig. 3.1: Al-Khaznah - The Treasury, Petra, Jordan.

CE. Although the Hellenistic style is dominant in these structures, indigenous Arab architectural elements are easily traceable and recognizable.

Al-Khaznah – The Treasury

Al-Khaznah is an outstanding monument that resembles a temple, mausoleum or royal structure carved in the rose-colored rocks of Petra, with Hellenistic architectural characteristics present (Fig. 3.1). The facade dates to the 1st century CE, during the period of the Nabataean King Aretas IV (Al-Harith Al-Rabi`), who likely was the patron of the structure. Hence, the structure may well have functioned as the mausoleum of the Arab King. The name Khaznah–or Treasury–was probably applied by a later local population based on a legend that the facade's upper level urn contained a treasure. Another legend claimed that an "evil pharaoh's treasure" was hidden in the urn. These legends made the structure a prime target for treasure hunters and adventurers to cause extensive damage while in search of loot and fortune. Furthermore, the high relief figurative sculptures have either eroded over time or were intentionally defaced by repeated iconoclastic-driven assaults.

The figurative sculptural representations on the facade contains attributes of Roman mythological entities, which prompted archaeologists and art historians to conclude heavy Roman influence in style and iconography. Sculptures of male and female figures are in fact representations of Arabian mythological entities and deities, depicted in an amalgamate style that would have served Arab populations and Roman authorities alike. This hybrid-style approach was common among Arab borderline communities under foreign rule, as was the case with the Canaanite-Phoenicians.

Fig. 3.2 Al-Dayr, The Monastery, Petra, Jordan.

No inscriptions have been found in the structure to identify it, but the location and elaborate carvings of rosettes and eagles point to a royal attribution. The Khaznah's two-storied facade measures 82 ft. (24.9 meters) wide and 127 ft. (38.7 meters) high. The entrance leads to a corridor with three burial rooms. The properties of this structure have inspired researchers to consider it as Petra's first monumental colonnaded mausoleum. The Corinthian style capitals draw striking similarity with Roman architecture of the 1st century CE. The grandeur of this structure is a remarkable testament to the patron of the mausoleum, who would have been deified in this temple-like setting.

Al-Dayr - The Monastery

Al-Dayr is another monumental rock-cut structure that, according to recent research, was neither a monastery nor a tomb but a chamber with a podium setting in the back, possibly for official royal or ritual activities (Fig. 3.2). The interior walls may have originally been painted with visual narratives but did not survive, as is the case with almost all of Petra's structures. It dates to the 1st century BCE, with possible patronage of King Obodas I (Arabic: `Ubaydah). The facade features Hellenistic components and measures 50 meters wide and 45 meters high. It is an unfinished structure, though its magnitude and opulence prompted Byzantine authorities to use it as a Christian church and/or monastery in the 5th century CE. The plaza courtyard

Fig. 3.3: The tomb of Uneishu, Petra, Jordan.

in front of the structure was rock-cut and leveled, probably to accommodate large congregations at public events or religious ceremonies.

The Tomb of Uneishu

The tomb of Uneishu is an elegant tower tomb with a facade that is adorned with a double cornice, crowned with a single monumental crow-step (Fig. 3.3). The facade also features crenellations typical of Arab-Nabataean design deriving from Mesopotamian sources. According to an inscription found near the structure, the tomb belongs to the individual Uneishu who may have been the minister of Queen Shaqillath II. Based on that assumption, the tomb has been dated to the 1st century CE.

THE ART OF SCULPTURE AT PETRA

The Nabataeans incorporated the art of sculpture in their buildings, residential quarters, temples and tombs. Facades of different structures were adorned with relief carvings and figural compositions. They produced portraits of individuals for tombs and mausoleums, along with monumental figural images of deities for temples and larger public enclosures. These figural representations demonstrate a blending of local artistic trends with neighboring styles including Mesopotamian, Egyptian and Parthian. Earlier examples display Hellenistic characteristics, and in the 2nd century CE, Roman characteristics dominated much of the architecture and sculpture throughout Petra as a result of Roman conquest.

SCULPTURAL REPRESENTATIONS OF DEITIES IN PETRA

Monumental figural images are found at major temples and decorate the facades of tombs, such as Al-Khaznah and Khirbat Al-Tannur. As mentioned above, the appearance of these carved figures indicates a fusion of Nabataean and Hellenistic elements. Khirbat Al-Tannur (Ruins of Al-Tannur), named after its location at the top of Mount Tannur (about 70 km north of Petra), is a sanctuary built on the summit of Jebel Tannur, which is about 300 meters high.

Construction of the temple may have started between the 3rd and 2nd centuries BCE and continued in three phases until the 1st century CE. The sanctuary was highly decorated and exhibited sculptures and reliefs of many local Arab deities such as Haddad, Atargatis, and personifications of the goddesses of fish, grain and the sun (Greek Helios). Numerous figural representations have been excavated in the altar area (Fig. 3.4) and on friezes inside the temple. These relief sculptures carry the Nabataean style blended with Hellenistic aspects (Figures. 3.5, 3.6, 3.7, 3.8, 3.9).

The altar of the temple contains figural representations of local Arab-Nabataean deities including Qaws, Haddad, Allat and possibly Dhu Al-Shara (Dusares). Some of these depictions echo the visual attributes from the Hellenistic pantheon such as Nike, Tyche, and Helios. Research regarding these images is ongoing with details yet to be analyzed. Archaeologists and art historians have not fully identified the images; which accounts for the broadly applied designations such as the goddess of "Grains," "Prosperity" and "Fertility."

The Nabataean tradition of erecting monumental images of deities in major temples was shared by other Arab populations for centuries. It is known that pre-Islamic Arabs used large-scale images of deities in Mecca, Yethrib, Najran, Hirah, Hatra and in Syria. Small sculptures of deities were used in residences and as personal guardians for travelers. The Nabataeans experienced consistent contact with other cultures through daily exchanges with traders, travelers, and merchants from as far as China and India, along with those from the nearby Mediterranean world. Presumably, such

Fig. 3.4: Axonometric drawing of the altar, Khirbat Al-Tannur, 1st Century CE., north of Petra, Jordan.

Fig. 3.5: Sandstone relief sculpture of Nabataean deity Qaws (Qos, Koz), h. 115 cm., 2nd Century BCE-1st Century CE, Khirbat Al-Tannur, Petra, Jordan.

Fig. 3.6: Limestone relief sculpture of the bust of the "Grain Goddess," h. 27 cm, 2nd Century BCE-1st Century CE, Khirbat Al-Tannur, Petra, Jordan.

a multicultural and cosmopolitan scene would have impacted the population; through cultural exchange, adaptation, and the catering of local residents to outside traders and travelers.

On this note, the impact of a foreign dominating power would also result in adaptation to the cultural preferences of the occupier. This is most clearly exhibited by Arabs populating the frontiers between the Persians and the Roman-Byzantines. As a result, hybrid varieties of the visual attributes of deities were created, as we have seen in Nabataean art and architecture.

The depiction of deities found at Khirbat Al-Tannur is a good example of stylistic amalgamation using Hellenistic, Mesopotamian, Egyptian, and Arab sources. However, the unique details found in such figures: long dresses, regal jewelry, specific weaponry, distinct stylized eyes, beards, curly hair, and headdresses all indicate a persistent indigenous visual tradition.

Fig. 3.7: Limestone relief sculpture of the winged Goddess (Greek Nike) carrying the Goddess (Greek Tyche)-Arab Allat surrounded by a presentation of the Zodiac, 2nd Century BCE-1st Century CE., Khirbat Al-Tannur, Petra, Jordan.

Fig. 3.8: Limestone relief sculpture of the Sun deity (Greek Helios), h. 55 cm, 2nd Century BCE-1st Century CE., Khirbat Al-Tannur, Petra, Jordan.

Fig. 3.9: Limestone sculptural presentation of eagle wrestling with a serpent, h.46.1 cm, 2nd Century BCE-1st Century CE., Khirbat Al-Tannur, Petra, Jordan.

PALMYRA

To the north of Petra, the Nabataeans developed another trading center at Palmyra (Arabic: Tadmur), which may refer to the Arabic origin `Ardh al-Tamr, or "land of dates." Palmyra, an oasis immersed with date palm trees, rose after the decline of Petra and reached its greatest power in the 3rd century CE. Like Petra, Palmyra was struggling between two imperial powers: the Romans and the Parthians. In the 3rd century CE, the Palmyrans were able to defeat Parthian forces and in turn consolidated the independent Arab state. The celebrated Queen Zenobia expanded Palmyra's borders while resisting growing Roman authority in the region. In 273 the Romans marched into Palmyra, conquered and incorporated it into the Roman Province of Syria.

The city grew wealthy from trade and caravan routes; one originating in the Far East, passing through India to the gulf between Mesopotamia and Persia; the other stretched across the Eurasian continent to China. Enjoying economic stability, Palmyrans were able to administer extravagant urban projects and

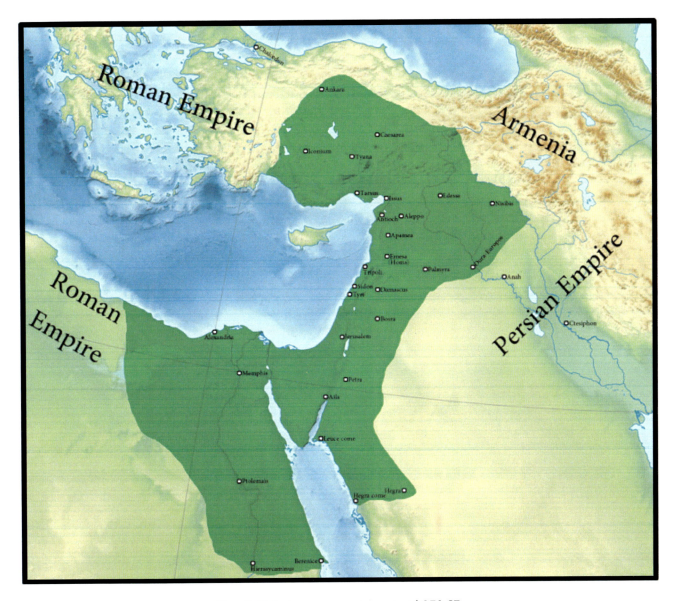

Map 5: Nabataean expansion around 270 CE.

constructed temples, public buildings and spectacular tower tombs. Similar to Petra, the political-cultural conditions of Palmyra facilitated a diverse visual language, particularly in the incorporation of Parthian and Roman elements in art and architecture. The inhabitants of Palmyra spoke a dialect of Aramaic, but also utilized the Greek language for commercial transactions. In religious practices, Palmyrans worshipped deities of Mesopotamian and Greco-Roman origin, overlapping them with local Arab deities such as Shamash, Rahim, Allat and Ba`l. Palmyra reached its greatest power in the second half of the 3rd century CE, annexing Roman provinces in the east including Egypt, Sinai, Phoenicia, Palestine, and Syria, along with parts of Arabia, Mesopotamia and Anatolia (Map 5).

As described above, Palmyran visual arts and architecture essentially continued the formulas we've encountered with the Nabataeans. Located between two superpowers, continuous war impacted the existence of Palmyra on many fronts. As circumstances necessitated, the Palmyrans adopted shrewd political maneuvers of obedience, coalition, or defiance. Palmyran art and architecture adopted Hellenistic and Persian elements, and furthermore, Palmyrans exhibited Hellenistic and Persian mythological themes in their rituals. Although the official language was Aramaic, they also employed languages and dialects from neighboring states.

Since Roman occupation of Palmyra was prominent and lengthy, a clear impact can be observed in official architecture and monumental works of art. Roman mythology was incorporated into Arab traditions as evidenced by the deities worshiped throughout Palmyran territories. Palmyran architects, artists and artisans may have had training in Roman territories, and it is also likely that Roman artists and architects worked alongside Palmyrans. This cultural exchange was essential in the dynamic region; a

Fig. 3.10: Remains of the Temple of Allat, Palmyra, Syria.

multicultural, multilingual society produced a diverse population. Variations of this distinct metropolis were found in frontier cities such as Dura-Europos and Bosra in Syria and Hatra in Iraq.

ARCHITECTURE OF PALMYRA

Temple of Allat

Erected in two phases, the first construction took place in the 1st century CE using the basic Arab rectangular format. In the second phase, the Temple of Allat was enlarged during the 2nd century CE when Palmyra was under Roman control; hence the architectural details reveal strong Roman elements, though still adhering to the typical Arabian enclosure design (Fig. 3.10). The temple incorporates the Roman characteristics of a Corinthian portico with columns and pediments along with common Arab features.

A monumental sculpture "the lion of Allat" (Fig. 3.11) was associated with this temple and may have occupied a prominent location near the entrance. The giant sculpture depicts a fierce lion protecting a crouching antelope, which represents Allat; embodying the idea of divine protection within the sanctuary boundaries. This is reinforced by an Aramaic inscription on the lion's left paw which reads "May Allat bless whoever does not spill blood on this sanctuary."

Fig. 3.11: "The lion of Allat" after conservation, Limestone ashlars, h. 3.5 m., 1st century CE., Palmyra, Syria.

Fig. 3.12: Relief sculpture of the deity Allat, Palmyra, Syria.

The deity Allat was worshiped by Arab communities in the Arabian Peninsula, Hatra, Petra, and Palmyra. Her worship continued into the early years of Islam around 630 CE. In Palmyra, Allat's identity was integrated with that of the Roman deity Athena and possibly with another local Arab female deity Atargatis. Visual representations of Allat have been found across the Arabian Peninsula. Allat provided protection to her worshippers; a concept that existed among the Arabs in sanctuary cities of major deities all over the region. The tradition sustained through the pre-Islamic era and the Islamic period with the exclusive concept of monotheistic divine power.

As a primary deity, Allat was vastly popular. Many monumental artworks containing her image were erected in sanctuaries and public places, while small statuettes of her image were placed inside homes or carried along by travelers. Many images of Allat have been found in Palmyra in the form of relief sculpture. These sculptural works depict her either alone, with lions or with other deities and figures. Figure 3.12 is a limestone relief portraying Allat holding a date palm branch and seated on a throne next to a lion. The slab, which contains an Aramaic inscription, was found inside the temple of Ba`l.

Archaeological excavations at the temple of Allat brought to light many important artifacts, including honorific sculptures. Some 70 funerary plaques have been found, 60 of them containing relief portraits of male and female individuals (Fig. 3.13).

Fig. 3.13: Limestone funerary portraits of female figures, Temple of Allat, Palmyra, Syria, 2nd century CE. Palmyra Archaeological Museum, Syria.

Temple of Ba`l

The Temple of Ba`l is dated to the beginning of the 1st or early 2nd century CE. It was constructed for the worship of the Mesopotamian deity Ba`l, built on a high ground, possibly with an older structure (Fig. 3.14). It was converted to a church during the Byzantine period, and in the 12th-20th centuries was used as a mosque. In the summer of 2015, the temple was destroyed by the so-called the Islamic State of Iraq and Syria (ISIS). The architectural structure and layout revealed local, Mesopotamian, and Greco-Roman elements. Inner colonnades, a high wall, and a walkway all led to a courtyard. The Corinthian columns and rectangular enclosure attested to the diverse cultural sources of the structure.

Palmyrans worshiped many deities, including Ba`l, Ba`l Shamin, and Allat. A relief sculpture from Palmyra (Fig. 3.15) dated to the 1st century CE shows three such Arab-Nabataean deities. Ba`l Shamin flanked by Aghlibel––the personification of the Moon––and Malakbel; personification of the Sun. Once again, Parthian, Roman and local styles are synthesized in this fine composition.

Fig. 3.14: Temple of Ba`l from the south, Palmyra, Syria.

Fig. 3.15: Ba`l Shamin flanked by Aghlibel and Malakbel, Palmyra, 1st century CE. Louvre Museum, Paris, France.

Fig. 3.16: Tower tomb "Illahbel," 103 CE, Palmyra, Syria (destroyed 2015).

The Tower Tombs of Palmyra

Palmyrans created highly unique standing tower mausoleums that were used as family tombs. Many tower tombs have been identified outside the city of Palmyra. The tower of Ilahbel, known locally in Arabic as "Qubbat Al-`Arus," meaning "the shrine of the bride" (Fig. 3.16), is four stories high and dates to 103 CE (destroyed by ISIS in 2015). It had a square plan and was constructed with large sandstone blocks.

A single door led to the interior, which was enclosed by four walls with cubiculum where the bodies of the deceased were placed. Each compartment was sealed with a slab containing a carved and painted image of the deceased (Fig. 3.17). The images were identified with Aramaic inscriptions, while the painted coffered ceiling contained portraits of important family members.

Fig. 3.17: Interior of Tower tomb from Palmyra, Syria. Istanbul Archaeological Museum, Turkey.

FUNERARY PORTRAITURE

Palmyran artists excelled in the realm of portrait relief carving. Funerary portraiture was utilized in order to represent the importance of an individual's life on earth through visual details but also wording of text. The production of funerary portraits was firmly established in Palmyra, with consistent demand for their use. The portraits displayed important iconographic details regarding the social status of the individual through dress, jewelry, hairstyle and other features that referred to the profession of the deceased. Colors were added to finished reliefs. Archaeological accounts evidence the looting of desirable carved portraits since the late 19th century, in part due to their ease of transport. They average in size to about 23 in. x 20 in. (58 cm x 50 cm) and about 9 in. (23 cm) in thickness. The images are carved on limestone slabs; realistic renderings accompany identifying inscriptions in Aramaic.

An example is a relief bust of a Palmyran woman dressed in an elegant costume and flanked by her two children (Fig. 3.18). An Aramaic inscription on the panel lists her name as "Ba'altega, daughter of Hairan. Alas," and her two children as "Si'mon" and "Hairan."

Ba`altega is touching the edge of her veil with her raised right hand, a very common gesture found in the funerary portraits of Palmyra. With her left hand, she holds a ceremonial or dignifying object with tassels. She wears fancy jewelry, gold bands in the hair, triple-pendant earrings, four different types of necklaces, bracelets on both wrists, and a ring on the finger of her left hand. Her two children flank her shoulders, perhaps emphasizing their strong family ties.

Another Palmyran funerary limestone relief dated to 50-150 CE displays the bust of what has been labeled as a priest (Fig. 3.19) wearing a flat-top cylindrical headdress. He holds a bowl and a vase, probably used in rituals. In the space to the left is a small figure (with broken head), wearing woman's attire, holding in her left hand a duck; in her right is a bundle of grapes. The Aramaic inscription reads: "Moqimu, son of Gediah, son of Ate'aqab the servant."

A superbly carved funerary limestone relief, dated to 150-200 CE, depicts a dignified middle-aged Palmyran woman wearing a fancy dress and holding her veil. She wears a triple necklace with a chain adorning her chest. The Aramaic inscription identifies her as "Aqmat daughter of Hagagu, descendant of Zebida descendant of Ma'an. Alas" (Fig. 3.20).

Fig. 3.18: Funerary relief of a woman and two children, Palmyra, 150 CE., carved limestone, 71.5 cm h x 56.5 cm w x 27 cm d (28 1/8 x 22 1/4 x 10 5/8 in.). Harvard Art Museums/Arthur M. Sackler Museum.

Fig. 3.19: Funerary bust of a priest, limestone, 25" x 21", 50-150 CE, Palmyra. The British Museum.

Fig. 3.20: Bust of woman, relief, limestone, Palmyra. 20" x 16.5", (51 x 42 cm). The British Museum.

HATRA IN NORTHERN MESOPOTAMIA (300 BCE- 200 CE)

Hatra is located in the Jazeerah (Jazirah) region of northern Iraq, in the valley between the Tigris and Euphrates Rivers, southwest of Mosul. Hatra (Arabic: Al-Hadhar) flourished as a small kingdom (Map 6). It was a trading stop guarding the two main caravan routes that connected Mesopotamia with Syria and Anatolia. The city controlled the trade route between east and west beginning in the 3rd century BCE; extending its power to a wide territory beyond its walls and onto the frontiers of the Parthian Empire. Hatra thrived as a semiautonomous state on the caravan road linking with Palmyra in Syria, Petra in Jordan, and Baalbek in Lebanon.

Hatra was a desired target for its strategic trade location and wealth by the two rival empires, the Parthians-Sassanians on one side, and the Romans on the other. The kingdom enjoyed a strong military capacity and was able to resist repeated Roman and Parthian attacks in the 2nd century CE. Eventually, the Parthians successfully occupied Hatra around 240 CE. While Petra and Palmyra were frontier states under Roman control, Hatra became a frontier kingdom affiliated with the Parthians. Foreign Roman and Persian control influenced Hatran art and architecture as well as aspects of religious practices.

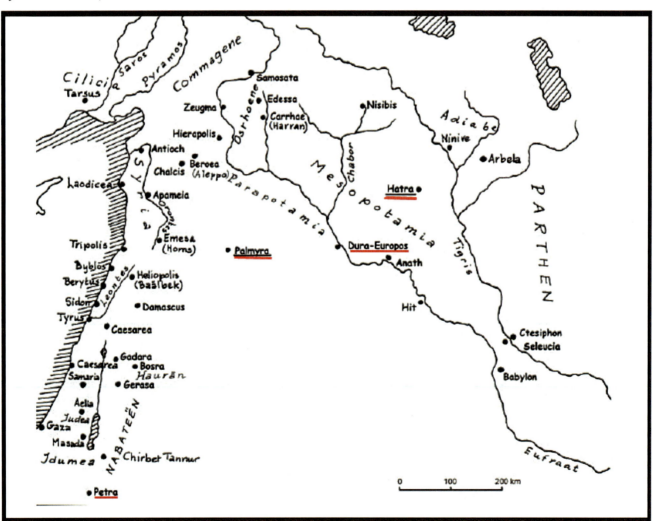

Map 6: Major trade cities on the Silk Road in the Jazeerah region including Hatra.

Fig. 3.21: Aerial view of Hatra, Iraq.

With its sub-circular plan (Figures 3.21 & 3.22), Hatra was fortified with defensive double walls and 160 hollow square towers surrounded by a trench. The outer wall, constructed of dried clay brick extended to a circumference of nearly 5 miles (8 kilometers), while the taller inner wall was constructed using local sandstone and extended nearly 4.7 miles (6 kilometers) with 4 gates. Temples, palaces, castles, and public buildings occupied the center of the city.

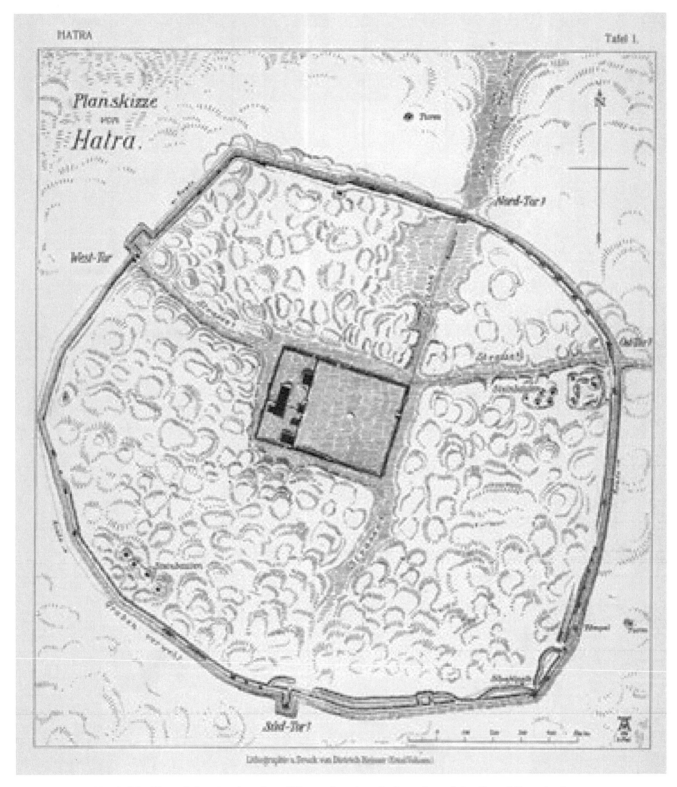

Fig. 3.22: Plan of the circular city of Hatra showing the location of the Grand Temple, Iraq.

ARAB KINGDOMS IN THE NORTH OF THE PENINSULA (400 BCE-600 CE) 57

Fig. 3.23: General view of Hatra with Temple of Shamash in the back, Iraq.

Fig. 3.24: Bronze coin from Hatra shows radiate head of the Sun God "Shamash" with Aramaic text, and an eagle on the other side, 2nd century CE.

Hatra was another prosperous multicultural urban city that contained important religious centers. The limited archaeological excavations in Hatra reveal architectural monuments, large sculptural figures in the round, as well as carved relief panels, facades and other decorated surfaces. There were also a number of ceramic objects, paintings, coins and some 500 Aramaic inscriptions found. In the center of the city stood a massive temple complex known as the Grand Temple Enclosure dedicated to the primary deity of Hatra Shamash, also pronounced Shamsh––the Sun God. The worship of Shamash in Hatra clearly indicates a continued tradition that began during the Sumerian/Akkadian era. The sacred precinct points to the importance of Hatra as a religious center. Within the Grand Temple precinct were at least fourteen smaller temples honoring a host of deities. Chief among the temples was that of the main deity in Hatra: "Shamash" the Sun God, who was worshiped throughout Hatra (Fig. 3.23).

The plan and architecture of the Grand Temple exhibited distinct Arab Hatran features, primarily the rectangular open space. Such a concept continued on in early Islamic architecture; especially mosques. Inscriptions found in the Grand Temple indicate that King Sanatruq and his son 'Abdsamia were responsible for planning and building the temple. Both kings had their images carved in high relief in two niches within the complex (Fig. 3.29).

Fig. 3.25: Facade of the Temple of Allat, Hatra, Iraq.

Fig. 3.26: Female head adorned the facade of the Temple of Shamash in Hatra, Iraq.

Fig. 3.27: Details of figural representations on the facade of the Temple of Shamash, Hatra, Iraq.

Hatra was ruled by a notable Arab dynasty and Aramaic was the official language of the kingdom. Similar to major trade cities in the region, Hatra exhibited a diversity of religious and cultural traditions, and a pantheon of deities were venerated in its temples. Religious traditions in Hatra were nourished by diverse sources: ancient Mesopotamian, Greek, Roman, and Persian-Parthian, and were redefined by Arab-Nabataeans. Along with the Mesopotamian (Sumerian-Akkadian) Sun God Shamash at Hatra, we find the deity Nergal, an epithet of the Greek Heracles; Hermes; and the local Atargatis. Besides Shamash, however, the most prominent was the female Arab deity Allat. Worshiped at an imposing temple, dedications were made to her within the Grand Temple complex. Allat, the goddess and protector of the city of Hatra, was venerated throughout the Arabian Peninsula until the early 7th century CE.

At Allat's temple within the Grand Temple Enclosure, a cubic "Ka'ba" has been excavated, dating to around 200 CE, surrounded by a circumambulatory enclosure. Excavations also uncovered a giant edifice built of ashlar masonry located within Temple. The structure was a sanctuary dedicated to the worship of Allat as identified by epigraphic evidence and sculptural representations (Figures 3.25 and 3.26). Some of the images of Allat at Hatra indicate assimilation with the Greek deities Nemesis and Athena. Furthermore, the worship of Shamash has been confirmed by inscriptions found on many Hatran coins (Fig. 3.24). Sculptural representations of deities and kings adorned temple facades, outer walls, and interior surfaces alike (Figures 3.25, 3.26, 3.27, 3.29, 3.30).

Fig. 3.28: Relief sculpture of male head with Aramaic inscription, The Grand Temple, facade of Iwan, Hatra, Iraq.

Fig. 3.29: King Sanatruq and his son `Abadsamia on the facade of the Temple of Allat, Hatra, Iraq.

Hatran sculptures included portraits of kings, queens, royal figures, deities and a variety of scenes with animals and symbolic representations. Sculptures of kings holding miniature images of a deity were common in Hatra, perhaps to indicate the king's authority and power. These images were carved in relief sculpture or in the round, executed in naturalistic styles with degrees of realism and often accompanied by Aramaic inscriptions. Closer examinations of sculptural images reveal similarities with the artistic traditions found in Petra, Palmyra and Dura-Europos.

A relief sculpture depicting a male portrait head with a mustache and flanked by two snakes was found on the facade of the Grand Temple. Two commemorative Aramaic inscriptions accompanied the image, probably referring to the individuals who contributed to the building of the Temple. The inscription lists names of family members "Zebido and Yehbeshi, sons of engineer Berneni, who received blessing and wisdom from the God" (Fig. 3.28).

Fig. 3.30: Head portrait of Arab king wearing a crown adorned with eagle, limestone, h. 35 cm, 2nd century BCE, Hatra, Iraq.

Representations of female figures were abundant in Hatra, usually depicting deities and royalty. Some were executed in relief carving, while others were sculpted in the round at life-size or larger than life-size. The monumental statue of "Bubint Damyoun" (Fig. 3.31) displays the regal and imposing personality of a sophisticated refined young woman; she is dressed in lavish garments complete with elaborate headdress, earrings and jewelry.

The site of Hatra was severely damaged by destruction and plundering caused by ISIS during their brief occupation of the city (2014-2017).

Fig. 3.31: Monumental statue of royal female "Bubint Damyoun," limestone, h. 210 cm, located within the Grand Temple, Hatra, Iraq.

Selected Bibliography

Al-Tawil, Hashim, *Early Arab Icons: Literary and Archaeological Evidence for the Cult of Religious Images in Pre-Islamic Arabia*, University of Iowa, IA, University Microfilms, Ph.D. Thesis, 1993.

Alcock, Susane, E. (Ed.), *The Early Roman Empire in the East*, Oxford: Oxbow Books, 1997.

Baird, J. A., "The Houses of Dura-Europos: Archaeology, Archive, and Assemblage", in L.Brody and G. Hoffman (eds), *Dura-Europos: Crossroads of Antiquity*, Boston: McMullan Museum, 2011, 235-250.

Ball, Warwick, *Rome in the East: The transformation of an empire*, London: Routledge, 2000.

Barnett, Richard D., Wiseman, Donald J., *Fifty Masterpieces of Ancient Near Eastern Art*, London: British Museum, 1960.

Borgia, E., *Jordan: Past & Present: Petra, Jerash, Amman*, Oxford: Oxford University Press, 2003.

Butcher, Kevin, *Roman Syria and the Near East*, Los Angeles: Getty Publications, 2003.

Dirven L, Hatra: A "Pre-Islamic Mecca" in the Eastern Jazirah, *ARAM*, 18-19 (2006-2007), 363-380.

____, Palmyrenes in Hatra: evidence for cultural relations in the Fertile Crescent, *Studia Palmyrenskie*, 12, 2013, 49-60.

____, (Ed.), *Introduction to Hatra. Politics, Culture and Religion between Parthia and Rome*, Proceedings of the conference held at the University of Amsterdam, 18–20 December 2009, 9-20.

Glueck, N., *Deities and Dolphins: The Story of the Nabataeans*. New York: Farrar Straus and Giroux, 1965.

Kaizer Ted. "Some remarks about the religious life of Hatra", *Topoi*, volume 10/1, 2000, 229-252.

Markoe, Glenn, (Ed.), *Petra Rediscovered: Lost City of the Nabataeans*. New York: Abrams, 2003.

McKenzie, J., "The Development of Nabataean Sculpture at Petra and Khirbet Tannur", *Palestine Exploration Quarterly*, 1988, 81-107.

Safer, Fouad, "Al-Hadhar, Madinat al-Shams", *Hatra, the City of the Sun*, Baghdad: Ministry of Information, Iraq, 1974.

Smith II, Andrew M. *Roman Palmyra: Identity, Community, and State Formation*, Oxford: Oxford University Press, 2013.

Stoneman, Richard, *Palmyra and Its Empire: Zenobia's Revolt Against Rome*, Ann Arbor: University of Michigan Press, 1995.

Tanabe Katsumi, *Sculpture of Palmyra*, Tokyo: Ancient Orient Museum, 1986.

Taylor, Jane. *Petra and the Lost Kingdom of the Nabataeans,* Cambridge, Mass.: Harvard University Press, 2002.

Walker, John, "The Coins of Hatra", The Numismatic Chronicle and Journal of the Royal Numismatic Society, Sixth Series, Vol. 18, 1958, 167-172.

Wood, Robert, *The Ruins of Palmyra, Otherwise Tedmor, in the Desert*, London: Robert Wood Collection, 1753.

CHAPTER 4

DURA-EUROPOS AND KINDAH

THE CITY OF DURA-EUROPOS, SYRIA, (114 CE-257 CE)

A fortified border city that functioned as a garrison and trade center was located on an escarpment on the Euphrates River in Syria (Map 6 in Chapter 3). Dura was naturally fortified on three sides, either by deep ravines or by the Euphrates. On the sloping side, a formidable wall was built, equipped with towers. The city was named **Dura** by the indigenous Semitic inhabitants, a common word in the region that translates to "fortress" or "palace" in the Semitic language; apparently originated by the Assyrians. The Greeks-Seleucids colonized the city and called it Europos.

The strategic location of the city made it a desirable military post for dominating powers. The Assyrians used it for military activity, while the Greeks established a military colony there in the late 3rd century BCE. The Parthians captured Dura around 113 BCE and the Romans seized it in 116 CE. During the latter period, Palmyra was able to control Dura as well. Dura continued to be a hot confrontational site between the Romans and the Persians, who struggled to control the prosperous commercial center on the caravan route. The Romans conquered Dura again in 165 CE, but the rising Sassanian power managed to defeat the Romans and razed the city in 256 CE. Consequently, the city lost significance and gradually was abandoned.

The Greeks, Romans and Parthians impacted the Arab city as a result of prolonged occupation: control of the city experienced changing hands for over 600 years. Dura's inhabitants consisted of an indigenous population connected to Palmyra and Hatra, Greek and Persian colonists, and other visitors and traders. Many languages were spoken as evidenced by over a hundred parchment and papyrus fragments with inscriptions written in Greek, Aramaic (Palmyran and Hatran dialects), Hebrew, Safaitic, and Iranian Pahlavi. Religious structures excavated at Dura reveal a multitude of rituals and practices. Greek, Judaic, Nabataean, Mithraic and Christian artifacts have been found in temples, houses and other archaeological sites. This multicultural, multi-religious society is further evidenced by the plethora of temples, wall decorations and inscriptions that have been found. Prized archaeological finds were transferred to museums in the 20th century, and in 2015, news sources reported that ISIS had damaged or looted much of the remaining structures.

Scholars have typically considered Dura-Europos to be the eastern frontier city of the Roman Empire with Hellenistic culture as a driving feature, although ongoing research and excavations have provided a clearer cultural profile of Dura. It is important to note that Dura, like Palmyra and Hatra, was an Arab city inhabited by an indigenous Arab population. Primarily speaking Aramaic, Durans were also able to communicate in other languages, as required by the trade and travel businesses. Durans had a knowledge and understanding of outside cultures, though frequent foreign occupation did not change the core identity of the Arab people. Rather, outside interaction and influence worked to enhance diversity and daily life; similar to what we have encountered in Petra, Palmyra, Hatra and other cities in the region.

Many places of ritual and worship (temples) with various religio-cultural affiliations have been excavated and identified at Dura. Some appear to have been officially sponsored by the city authorities while others were community-developed using simplified, intentionally discrete appearances. These house-temples were affiliated with Greek, Roman, Persian, and Arab cultural origins and religious practices. This is further confirmed by archaeological finds associated with local deities but also exhibiting Greco-Roman, Parthian, Palmyran, Hatran and Mesopotamian characteristics. Among these examples are the house-temples of Zeus, Adonis, Jupiter, Artemis, Atargatis, Aphlad, and Ba`l. Also identified in Dura is a Jewish house-synagogue, a Mithraeum and a Christian house-church.

Fig. 4.1: Temple of Ba`l, outside the wall. Dura, Syria.

THE TEMPLES OF DURA-EUROPOS

Among the many temples found in and around Dura, at least three have been identified with characteristics of indigenous Nabataean worship. Researchers have labeled them as "Palmyran" or "Pagan," in part to differentiate them from "Hellenistic" or "Monotheistic" temples. One such sanctuary was built outside Dura's walls around the year 33 BCE. Due to its unprotected location, most of the temple's structure deteriorated by 200 CE. Originally a smaller sanctuary, it was enlarged in a later period. A second small temple of "Palmyran" designation was found inside the city and called "Temple of Gades." The third and most important is the "Temple of Ba`l"––god of the sky, also called the "Temple of the Palmyran Gods" based on Aramaic inscription with the words "bayt `ilhy" or "the house of the gods."

Temple of Ba`l at Dura

The Temple of Ba`l at Dura dates to around 250 BCE and is located near the fortified wall in the northern part of the city (Fig. 4.1). Key finds include inscriptions and a fragmentary painting from the temple that contain dedications to the deities "Ba`l" and "Iarhibol," both of whom had temples dedicated to their worship in Palmyra. The inscriptions reveal the names of other indigenous Mesopotamian and Arab deities such as `Ishtar and Manat. The deity "Ba`l" is the epithet of the Babylonian/Mesopotamian Marduk, who headed the Babylonian pantheon.

The plan of the Temple of Ba`l reveals similarities with Mesopotamian temples, primarily in the square foundation and high walls. A wall painting datable to the 1st century CE (Fig. 4.2) depicts the "sacrifice of Conon," a Greek military general, shown with members of his family and temple officials presenting a sacrifice to Ba`l. The painting reflects a mixture of styles: Greek, Arab-Nabataean and Parthian.

Another wall painting dated to the 3rd century CE from the temple depicts the Roman army general Julius Terentius—identified by a Latin inscription—performing a sacrifice (Fig. 4.3). The painting displays Greek, Roman, and Palmyran artistic trends. In the scene, the general performs a sacrifice in front of a military standard, with soldiers looking on behind him. Two labeled female figures seated at the lower left personify the cities of Dura and Palmyra. The three male statues depicted in the upper left may represent Palmyran gods.

Dura-Europos House-Synagogue

During the final siege of the town of Dura by the Sassanians in 256 CE, the Roman defenders strengthened the western wall. The fill that they used to increase the height and thickness of the wall covered a number of buildings, including house-sanctuaries, which resulted in their preservation. One of these preserved building is the Jewish house-synagogue, which contains decorated walls with elaborate visual narratives from the Old Testament. As inscriptions indicate, that Jewish house-synagogue was refurbished and expanded in 244-45 CE by an individual called "Samuel." The walls of the synagogue were illustrated with Biblical events and Old Testament figures.

At least 28 panels portray 58 Biblical scenes such as the Consecration of the Tabernacle, Solomon and Sheba, Abraham's Sacrifice, Infancy of Moses and the Pharaoh, Elijah Restoring the Widow's Son, Samuel Anointing David, and Moses' Exodus from Egypt. There are also individual full figure portraits, possibly of prophets such as Abraham. The panels are organized in three horizontal bands flanked on top and bottom by decorative bands. The whole composition converges at the Torah niche in the west wall (Fig. 4.4). A few Aramaic inscriptions were found on the lower part of the west wall with commemorative statements along with names of individuals, probably

Fig. 4.2: Conon Sacrifice: Details of the wall painting in the temple of Ba`l, 1st century CE., Dura, National Museum, Damascus, Syria.

Fig. 4.3: Julius Terentius Performing a Sacrifice, wall painting, Temple of Ba`l, Dura, Yale University Art Gallery.

community members of Dura. The synagogue was discovered in 1921 and excavated by a Yale University archaeological team from 1928-1937. The paintings along with the synagogue court were cut out and reconstructed at the National Museum in Damascus, Syria where they are now on display.

The unassuming location of the Jewish house-synagogue, in a poor area of the city and next to a Christian house-Church, seems to have been intentionally planned. The inconspicuous building and location may have helped to divert the attention of Roman authorities when Dura was under Roman control. Both buildings were ordinary in appearance, with flat roofs and modest layouts. This can be attributed to the fact that neither Judaism nor Christianity were permitted to be practiced publicly under Roman rule in Dura or any Roman colony.

Although the paintings in the house-synagogue and house-church reveal a blend of styles––Hellenistic, Nabataean and Parthian––the iconographical presentation shows a clear difference with typical Biblical visual narratives elsewhere. The depictions are more naturalistic and focused on storytelling when compared to Western visual conventions of the same theme. The Jews and Christians who painted the walls were local, and their interpretation of Biblical themes reflected their unaffected understanding of the monotheistic narratives.

Dura-Europos House-Church

The nearby Christian house-church was probably constructed around the same time as the synagogue, between 240 and 250 CE. It is smaller in size and the decorative program is modest compared to the paintings in the syna-

Fig.4.4: Interior of the Jewish Synagogue, Dura, Syria with wall paintings of Old Testament narratives, 245-256 CE. Tempera on plaster wall. Reconstructed at the National Museum Damascus, Syria.

gogue. The house-church, probably the oldest known Christian place of worship, was excavated in the early 20th century and the surviving wall paintings were transported to and reconstructed at Yale University Art Gallery. Similar to the synagogue, the house was filled with sand and debris in order to strengthen the wall of the city against the anticipated Sassanian attack. This measure inadvertently preserved the paintings in both structures. The building consists of a residential dwelling attached to a separate space that functioned as a meeting room.

The surviving painting fragments from that room (Fig. 4.5) show similarity in style and presentation with the synagogue paintings. It is possible that some of the artists worked on both buildings. The wall paintings in the church depict Christian themes relating to the New Testament, such as "the original sin," "the rite of baptism," and "salvation." Such themes were suitable for teaching new converts the stories of the Bible. One of the most interesting images is Christ as the "Good Shepherd," which has been considered to be the earliest known depiction of Jesus (Fig. 4.6).

Scholars are still not clear about the identity of the artists who rendered these visual narratives. Were they Romans, Parthians, or local Ar-

Fig. 4.5: The Christian house-church (Baptistery), Dura, Syria, 250 CE. Reconstructed at Yale University Art Gallery.

ab-Durans? Dura, like neighboring trade cities of Palmyra, Hatra and Hirah, was culturally systematized to cater to and host diverse populations and utilized art as an important vehicle in shared communication. Based on conventions, the iconography and stylization of the Biblical visual narratives adheres more closely to local Arab-Nabataean style than what is commonly perpetuated by scholars as being Hellenistic or Parthian. Nonetheless, Greek, Roman, and Persian occupation of Petra, Palmyra, Hatra, Dura and Hirah certainly influenced local Arab artists and artisans in the fields of architecture, sculpture, and painting.

Such influence is clearly evidenced in the artistic production of those cities, but the art also maintained a fundamentally indigenous Arab character, reinforced by the use of Aramaic inscriptions. The visual interpretations of the Biblical narratives in both buildings––the house-synagogue and the house-church––more closely resemble the Biblical theology understood and practiced by the early Jewish and Christian populations of Syria and Palestine than that of the Western Greco-Roman/Byzantine world. For example, the Arabs of greater Syria, Palestine, and Sinai espoused an Orthodox understanding of Judaism and Christianity; ideological idiosyncrasies relevant to this can be traced in the paintings, noticeably distinguishing the visual language in the east from that of the west with regard to Biblical narratives.

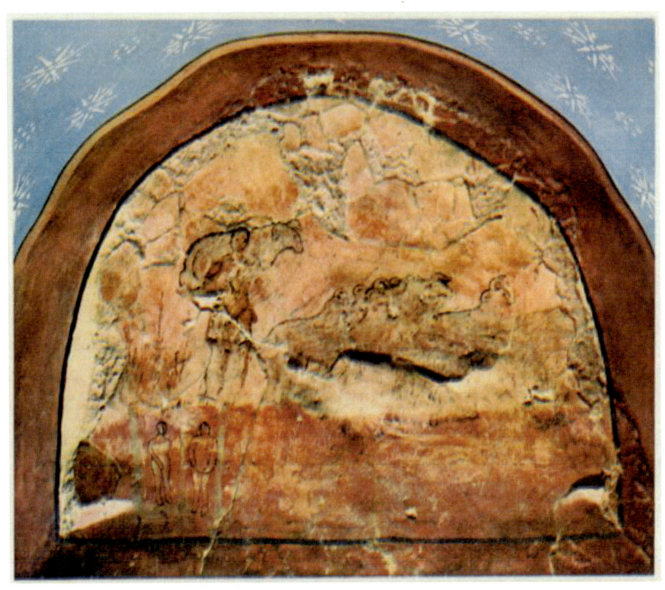

Fig. 4.6: Depiction of Jesus as the Good Shepherd, wall painting, house-church, Dura, Syria. Reconstructed at Yale University Art Gallery.

THE KINGDOM OF KINDAH (200 BCE-600 CE)

An Arab kingdom led by the tribe of Kindah originated in the south of Arabia but was active in the central and northern region where it controlled a great part of the peninsula. Archaeological evidence shows that the Kindites had strong cultural connections with South Arabians in culture, language and rituals. They appeared as early as the 2nd century BCE and were active in central Arabia. Their first capital was "Qaryat That Khal," known today as Qaryat Al-Faw, located south of the present-day city of Riyadh, and was an important urban and administrative center (Map 7). Its location on the main ancient trade route serviced merchants and travelers between Iraq and Syria. The Kindites followed the same pattern

Map 7: The location of Qaryat Al-Faw, the Arabian Peninsula.

as their neighbors; especially the South Arabian kingdoms, in controlling, managing and servicing major caravan routes in their area. Qaryat Al-Faw hosted merchants, commercial activities, and goods from many destinations. Diverse cultures and languages––besides the official indigenous Semitic dialects––were present among the inhabitants and traveling merchants in the city.

The limited excavated area at Qaryat Al-Faw revealed a fortified marketplace, temple, palace, graveyards and a residential quarter. The site is datable to the period of the 2nd century BCE to the 6th century CE. The religious picture was diverse, with rituals involving the adoration and worship of many deities among the Kindites, as attested by archaeological finds. Many inscriptions at Qaryat Al-Faw, mostly in South Arabian Musnad script, corroborate the worship of Arab deities. Most popular among them were the three female deities Allat, Al-`Uzza and Manat, along with the male deities Kahl and Wadd, with sanctuaries common across Arabia including at Qaryat Al-Faw.

Monotheism may have spread among the Kindites, especially Judaism, in the later period.

Fig. 4.7: Aerial view of the remains of Qaryat Al-Faw, Saudi Arabia.

Fig. 4.8 : Aerial view of the remains of Qaryat Al-Faw, Saudi Arabia – details.

Under Sassanian expansion in South Arabia, the Kindites may have supported the Jewish King Dhu Nuwas in his struggle with the Axumite Christian forces, backed by the Byzantine Empire in Yemen in the 6th century CE. In the 7th century CE the Kindites joined other Arab semi-kingdoms in the new unified state under the banner of the monotheistic faith "Islam."

Recent archaeological excavations at Qaryat Al-Faw reveal a well-developed system of urban planning that exhibited traditional Arab architectural layouts in the city (Figures 4.7, 4.8). The archaeological excavations at Qaryat Al-Faw uncovered two major areas of the town. The first was a residential area, consisting of houses, public squares, streets and a marketplace, while the second was a sacred area dedicated to rituals, burial and worship. Three temples and an altar have been discovered, along with tombs and cemeteries.

The foundation of a temple has been identified near the main site of Qaryat Al-Faw (Fig. 4.9). Among the deities worshiped there was Wadd, depicted in an imposing pose and naturalistic style. The oversized image was incised on the slope of a mountainous escarpment in the area (Fig. 4.10). The image represents a male figure, carrying in his left hand a long spear, and in the right a spearhead, while a sword rests in his belt. Underneath this image, the word "WDDM" is incised in bold South Arabian Musnad script. The setting and the relatively large size of the image suggest that communal rituals were likely conducted on behalf of the cult of Wadd at this location.

Fig. 4.9 : Foundation of a temple, Qaryat Al-Faw, Saudi Arabia.

Fig. 4.10 : Carving depicting the deity Kahl (Wadd), Qaryat Al-Faw.

Fig. 4.11: Upper part of a male figure, may represent King Mu`awiyah Bin Rabi`ah, limestone, Qaryat Al-Faw. Department of Archaeology, King Saud University, Riyadh, Saudi Arabia.

Excavations yielded a great number of objects with inscriptions, sculptural pieces, pottery, fragments of wall painting, glass, jewelry, coins and a variety of other artifacts. Archaeologists identified a workshop of artists/artisans, complete with remnants of tools and related materials. The techniques used and visual characteristics of many of the pieces show inspiration from neighboring traditions such as Mesopotamian, Egyptian and Hellenistic. Yet the dominant style tends to follow the indigenous artistic tradition found in southern, central and northern Arabia. A significant piece is a limestone sculpture of the upper part of a male figure with missing head and arms. The sculpture was found near the identified tomb of King Mu`awiya bin Rabi`ah (King of Qahtan and Mudhhij) and may very well be a depiction of that king (Fig. 4.11).

Also found at Qaryat Al-Faw was a clay ritualistic figure, probably of female gender, that may have been used as a votive offering during certain ceremonies at temples. It is hand-modeled, painted and incised with South Arabian Musnad inscription (Fig. 4.12).

Fig. 4.12 : Clay figure painted and incised with South Arabian *Musnad,* Qaryat Al-Faw, Department of Archaeology, King Saud University, Riyadh, Saudi Arabia.

Fig. 4.13: Fragment of a wall painting with a banquet scene, 2nd century CE, black and red paint on white plaster, 58 x 32 cm, from Qaryat Al-Faw, residential district. Department of Archaeology, King Saud University, Riyadh, Saudi Arabia.

The wall painting fragments found in the residential section of Qaryat Al-Faw include a variety of subjects that demonstrate the culture and artistic tradition of the Arabs of Kindah. One of these wall paintings depicts what can be interpreted as a banquet scene, strongly connected with the traditional hospitality of the ancient Arab Diwan (Fig. 4.13). Another wall painting fragment shows the head of a person labeled with the name "ZKY" (Fig. 4.14), who must have been an important social-royal figure. Other paintings contain various subjects such as animals and zodiacal signs.

Excavation at Qaryat Al-Faw also produced an interesting wall painting fragment (Fig. 4.15) which is worth mentioning. The painting depicts a tower-house, probably three or more stories high, with a square plan layout, built with hewn local stone. A human figure occupies a niche in the lower right side, which can be interpreted as the entrance of the tower-house. The function and gender of the figure are not clear. In the upper and middle parts of the house are depictions of people: they glimpse through windows or are possibly seated on balconies. Arab classical sources mention palaces and elaborate fortresses during the pre-Islamic era that existed in numerous regions. The type of building depicted in this painting is typical of the common residential style found in South Arabia and is still being constructed and used presently in Yemen and Hadhramawt. Further study of these paintings and their iconography will enhance our knowledge of the subject.

Obviously, there is a need for thorough comparative analysis of these paintings, sculptural images and architectural remains. The finds at Qaryat Al-Faw reflect the level of cross-cultural interactions that occurred at the site which was an important center on the trade route near the edge of the empty quarter (Al-Rub` Al-Khali) of the peninsula. The examples discussed help build our picture of preserved indigenous Arab artistic traditions, architectural forms, and a continued Arab visual vocabulary. There are probably more sites such as Qaryat Al-Faw on the peninsula waiting to be unearthed.

Fig. 4.14: Fragment of a wall painting with a head of man "ZKY", 2nd century CE, black, yellow and red paint on white plaster, Qaryat Al-Faw, residential district. Department of Archaeology, King Saud University, Riyadh, Saudi Arabia.

Fig. 4.15: Fragment of a wall painting depicts a tower-house with inhabitants (3rd century BCE–3rd century CE), black, red and yellow paint on white plaster, 59 x 64 cm, from Qaryat Al-Faw, Department of Archaeology Museum, King Saud University, Riyadh Saudi Arabia.

Selected Bibliography

Al- Ansari, Abd Al-Rahman, *Qaryat Al-Faw: A Portrait of Pre-Islamic Civilization in Saudi Arabia*, Riyadh, KSA, 1982.

Al-Tawil, Hashim, "Literary References to Early Arab Sculpture and Painting", *"Early Arab Icons: Literary and Archaeological Evidence for the Cult of Religious Images in Pre-Islamic Arabia"* University of Iowa, IA, University Microfilms, Ph.D. Thesis, 1993, 43-100.

Baird, J. A., "The Houses of Dura-Europos: Archaeology, Archive, and Assemblage", in L. Brody and G. Hoffman (eds) *Dura-Europos: Crossroads of Antiquity*, Boston: McMullan Museum, 2011, 235-250.

Baur, P. V. C., and Michael I. Rostovtzeff, eds. *The Excavations at Dura-Europos conducted by Yale University and the French Academy of Inscriptions and Letters: Preliminary Report of Fourth Season of Work, October 1930-March 1931.* New Haven: Yale University Press, 1933.

Borgia, E., *Jordan Past & Present: Petra, Jerash, Amman*, Oxford: Oxford University Press, 2003.

Butcher, Kevin, *Roman Syria and the Near East.* Los Angeles: Getty Publications, 2003.

Dirven L, Hatra: A "Pre-Islamic Mecca" in the Eastern Jazirah, *ARAM*, 18-19 (2006- 2007), pp. 363-380.

Gutmann, J., *The Dura-Europus Synagogue: A Re-Evaluation* (1932-72), Missoula: Scholars Press, 1972.

_____, The Dura Europos Synagogue Paintings and Their Influence on Later Christian and Jewish Art. *Artibus et Historiae*, Vol. 9, No. 17 (1988), 25-29.

Hopkins, C., *The Discovery of Dura-Europos*, New Haven: Yale University Press, 1979.

King, Geoffrey, *The Traditional Architecture of Saudi Arabia*, I. B. Tauris 1998.

Kraeling, C. H., *The Christian Building*, The Excavations at Dura-Europos, Final Report, New Haven: Yale University Press, 1967.

_____, *The Synagogue*, The Excavation at Dura-Europos, Final Report, New Haven: Yale University Press, 1956.

Margaret, O. "Early Christian Synagogues" and "Jewish Art Historians". The Discovery of the Synagogue of Dura-Europos, *Marburger Jahrbuch für Kunstwissenschaft*, 27, 2000, 7-28.

Matheson, S., *Dura-Europos*: The Ancient City and the Yale Collection, New Haven: Yale University Press, 1982.

Perkins, A., *The Art of Dura-Europos*, Oxford: The Clarendon Press, 1973.

Rostovtzeff, M. I., *Dura and the problem of Parthian art*, New Haven: Yale University press, 1935.

_____, *Dura-Europos and its Art*, Oxford: The Clarendon Press 1938.

Saudi Society for Archeological Studies, *Kindah*, Report # 1, King Saud University press, Riyadh, KSA 1989.

CHAPTER 5

VISUAL ART AND ARCHITECTURE IN THE ARABIAN PENINSULA DURING THE LATE PRE-ISLAMIC PERIOD (200 CE-622 CE)

CULTURAL AND POLITICAL BACKGROUND

During the late pre-Islamic period (mid 3rd century to around 622 CE), the Arabian Peninsula witnessed an ongoing power-struggle between the Sassanian (Sassanid) and the late Roman/early Byzantine empires. The first epoch of this struggle started with the rise of the Sassanians to power in 226 when their conflict with the Romans resulted in Sassanian political control over the Arabs of Hirah and the Lakhamids-Mundhirids in southern Iraq, who consequently became their allies. On the other hand, the Romans strengthened their control over the Arab Nabataeans in Syria. This power confrontation continued through the Byzantine era with the Ghassanids Arabs becoming their vassal. Both Arab semi-

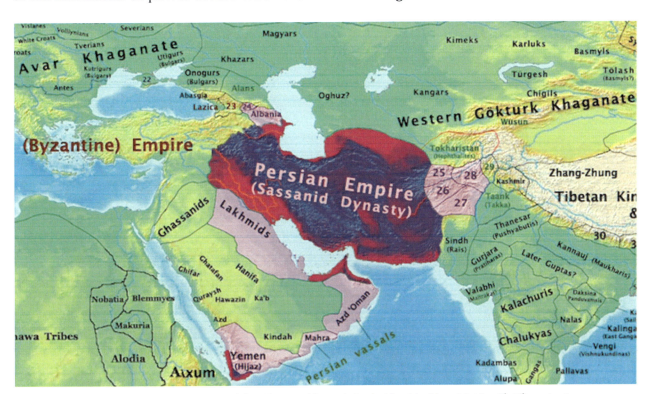

Map 8: Map of the territories of the Ghassanids and the Lakhmids-Munthirids, 6th-7th centuries.

independent kingdoms––the Lakhmids in Hirah and the Ghassanids in Syria–– became buffer states to their sponsors (Map 8).

During this time, Hirah, under the Lakhmids-Mundhirid, flourished and expanded its power over parts of the peninsula, with the support of the Sassanians, who extended their domains along the eastern coast of the Arabian Peninsula. Zoroastrianism, the official religion of the Sassanians was established in and around 'Uman, also Oman and partially along the eastern coast, while Christianity, the official religion of the Byzantines, penetrated Arabia during the 4th century, especially when the late Roman/ Byzantine Empire and Abyssinia officially professed Christianity. By that time, Judaism had already established presence in Arabia. Constantinople politically supported Orthodox Christian Arabs, while the Persians supported Jewish Arabs and also some Christian Arabs, especially the Nestorians, who were not favored by Constantinople.

The second phase of the late pre-Islamic period is marked by the end of the 4th century, witnessed by great Byzantine political expansion into north and northwest Arabia, while the Sassanian hegemony continued along the eastern coast of the peninsula. During this time, the tribe of Kindah, originally from South Arabia, rose to power as a kingdom in Central Arabia and was favored politically by the Byzantine empire.

It is generally believed that during this period, the South Arabian tribe of Khuza'ah occupied Mecca. The most famous member of this tribe was 'Amru ibn Luhayy, to whom the Arab historian Ibn Al-Kalbi (d. 819), and other early Arab historians ascribe the introduction of idolatry into Mecca and the import of monumental statues of polytheistic deities to the region.

Around the beginning of the 6th century the two powerful kingdoms of Kindah, along with their Ghassanid allies and the Lakhmids of Hirah backed by the Sassanians, were driven into military conflict. This period also witnessed famous tribal wars in Arabia. The Basus war occurred around the end of the 5th century, and the war of Dahis and Ghabra' in the 6th century. To a certain degree these wars echoed the then ongoing struggle for domination between the Sassanians and the Byzantines.

At the same time, the two Arab kingdoms, Kindah and especially Hirah, continued to develop and became significant trading and cultural centers. Meanwhile, the city of Mecca continued to grow in importance as a religious and commercial center that linked South Arabia and Syria. When the tribe of Quraysh took power in Mecca around the beginning of the 6th century, the city became an important political, economic and religious center. Thus, the three centers, Mecca, Kindah and Hirah, grew, producing distinctive indigenous cultures. The Classical Arabic language developed, replacing the existing local dialects both in northern and southern Arabia.

The third phase of this period witnessed the ultimate competition between Byzantium and the Sassanians over Arabia, particularly during the reign of their respective emperors, Justinian (527-565) and Khusraw Anushiruwan (531-579). The Abyssinians, with the support of Constantinople, marched to Yemen and overthrew the Himyarite Kingdom in 525. Later, the Abyssinian viceroy in Yemen, Ibraha (Abraham), led an unsuccessful expedition to conquer Mecca. In 575 the last Himyarite King, Sayf Ibn Dhi Yazan, backed by the Sassanian military, succeeded in recapturing Yemen.

The fourth and last phase of the late pre-Islamic period included the continuing war between the Sassanians and the Byzantines over Arabia. The Sassanians expanded their hegemony along the eastern and southern coasts of the peninsula to the gate of the Red Sea. The Byzantines started to lose hold on Arabia. Kindah began to decline and Hirah tried to resist Sassanian control. The final war between the Byzantines and the Sassanians (610-628) coincided with the birth of the Islamic faith and the rise of the Prophet Mohammed in Mecca. Under Islam, for the first time, the Arab tribes of the Arabian Peninsula witnessed total political unification.

The cultural picture was a direct reflection of the political situation in the peninsula. In general, there were three cultures that governed the population in Arabia during the late pre-Islamic period: Byzantine, Sassanian and, most importantly, South Arabian. The latter cultural drive had a strong impact on the peninsula. This South Arabian cultural tradition continued to influence not only the late pre-Islamic period, but early Islamic culture as well.

MECCA AND YETHRIB (MADINAH) REGION

Limited systematic archaeological investigation in the Arabian Peninsula started in the second half of the 20th century. But interest in this field goes back to the 18th century, with Western travelers, adventurers, missionaries and a few serious scholars.

The central and western regions of the peninsula, namely Najd and Hijaz, were major points of attraction to visitors. In 1812-1815 the Swiss expeditor Ludwig Burchart visited Ta'if, Mecca and Medina and produced photographic research of the pilgrimage rite in the region. In 1877 R. Burton toured the northwestern region, where he recorded some ancient sites. In 1875 C. Doughty traveled through the sites of Mada'in Salih and Al-'Ula, recorded inscriptions, and made valuable photographs and drawings of these sites. Huber and Euting made their discoveries in the Yemen and Hijaz in 1878-1883. They produced significant maps of the northern region and unearthed some antiquities and inscriptions from Tayma`.

At the beginning of the 20th century a significant contribution to the archaeological study of the peninsula was made by the French Missionaries F. Savignac and A. Jaussen. They recorded and studied thousands of inscriptions and sculptures mainly from the northern region. Other travelers to the area were B. Moritz in 1906, and A. Musil in 1910 who left a detailed account of his trip.

Between 1909-1915 W. E. Shakespeare, a British officer, made six trips to the north and northeastern regions and parts of the central region. He recorded some epigraphic material from Thaj. H. Philby traveled in central Arabia in 1917 and recorded his account in a series of publications. Again in 1936 he traveled in central and south Arabia. In 1941 P. B. Cornwall followed Shakespeare's footsteps and re-excavated a 6th century headless statue in Qatif, near Dhahran, in the eastern region. This less than life-size statue has been suggested to have portrayed a Sassanian king, but a definite interpretation is yet to be pursued.

In the 1960's a major preliminary survey program in Northwest Arabia was carried out by an expedition team sponsored by the University of London Institute of Archaeology. It was the first official archaeological expedition which laid the foundation of subsequent similar activities. Many sculptures, foundations and remains of temples were recorded, but neither dated nor identified definitely. In 1976, a large-scale comprehensive archaeological survey program was inaugurated by Saudi authorities with the intention of covering the whole of Saudi Arabia. The program started in 1976 and is still ongoing. Reports of the survey have been, and are still, periodically published in the major Saudi archaeological publication Atlal and other publications. Meanwhile an international symposium on the History of Arabia was held in Riyadh in

1977, the result of which has been compiled in three volumes. Apart from this major survey program, an important excavation campaign was carried out in two sites; Qaryat Al-Faw and Al-Rabadhah. Future archaeological activity in major sites in Mecca, Medina, Ta'if, Najran and other locations will add more information to our knowledge of this subject.

It is important to note that classical Arab writers recorded valuable Information about the use of sculptural and other visual representations of worshiped deities with their associated architectural structures in the region of Mecca and nearby towns. The literary accounts of the statues and monuments to the idols (called Awthan, Ansab, and Asnam in Arabic), have come down to us through the writings of Arab historians as early as the 7th century CE. Important historians who contributed to this subject are many, and prominent among them are Al-Azraqi, Al-Baladhuri, Al-Bukhari, Al-Hamdani, Ibn Ishaq, Ibn Al-Athir, Ibn Hisham, Ibn Sa`d, Ibn Al-Kalbi, Al-Mas`udi, and Al-Tabari.

These sources provide considerable information about the nature of architectural and sculptural forms that were readily found or dug out from the scattered archaeological sites throughout the peninsula and its adjacent regions. The southern Arabian region was a major source for such finds, and abundant examples have been unearthed through limited excavation activities. Beside the few monumental sculptures of kings and royal figures, the majority of these finds consist of inscriptional slabs, grave markers and small-scale sculptures or funerary portraits of deceased persons. These small-scale pieces were easily obtained and transferred. Similar finds have been unearthed in central, western and northern Arabia as well.

SCULPTURAL MONUMENTS OF DEITIES IN PRE-ISLAMIC ARABIA

According to early Arabic sources the pre-Islamic population in Arabia worshipped many deities in designated temples and shrines that contained monumental visual representations, mostly in the form of sculpture. Many of these deities are mentioned in the Qur`an and related Hadiths. Besides large figural representations, small-scale statues and statuettes were also used inside houses; furthermore, it was customary for travelers to carry a small statuette of their preferred guardian deity. There are also elaborate reports of the presence of some 360 statues inside the Ka`ba in Mecca, on its roof, around it and nearby its location. Literary sources indicate that these statues were destroyed in the year 630 upon the return of the Prophet Mohammed to Mecca.

Archaeological evidence of these Meccan statues have not been found yet, but there is a considerable body of literature referencing their nature, the materials used to make them, and even their artistic styles. Among these monumental sculptures, we learn that a prominent deity called Hubal was worshiped in Mecca and other regions, and held an extremely important position in the pre-Islamic Arabian pantheon. Inside the Kaa`ba stood a life-size, free-standing stone statue of Hubal. So far, there has been no archaeological trace of the supposed statue of Hubal, but it was likely similar to other monumental statues found across the region. A few of these are worth mentioning.

A colossal statue of male figure was found in Mada`in Salih at Dedan, now called Al-`Ula, in northwest Arabia (Fig 5.1). It is an oversize free-standing statue carved in sandstone and has been dated to the 4th century BCE. The statue has stylistic affinity to Egyptian and Mesopotamian prototypes. It may represent a king, a leader, a royal personality or a personification of a deity.

Fig. 5.1: Statue of a man, broken at knee, 4th–3rd centuries BCE, Red sandstone, 230 x 83 cm, Al-`Ula. Archaeology Museum, King Saud, University, Riyadh, Saudi Arabia.

Three other similar oversized statues have been excavated in the approximate area (Fig. 5.2). They are carved in red sandstone and stand approximately 198 cm (6' 5") tall.

Another colossal statue from the region is now at Istanbul Museum of Archaeology (Fig. 5.3) and displays similar iconographic and stylistic trends. Most of the statues are

Fig. 5.2: Colossal sandstone statues, Al-`Ula, 4th-2nd centuries BCE. Archaeology Museum, King Saud, University, Riyadh, Saudi Arabia

missing heads, likely from intentional damage during later periods. Interestingly, many large male sculptural heads have been found in the area close to Al-`Ula (Mada`in Salih) from approximately the same time period (Fig. 5.4).

Fig. 5.4: Colossal head of male figure, Northwest Arabia, 3rd-1st centuries BCE, Istanbul Archaeology Museum, Turkey.

Fig. 5.3: Colossal statue of male figure, northwest Arabia, 3rd-1st centuries BCE, Istanbul Archaeology Museum.

Further analysis of these example will help develop our understanding of the iconography of pre-Islamic idols: Hubal, Wadd, Dhu Al-Shara, Dhu Al-Khalasa, Yaghuth, Ya`uq, Manaf, `Amm-'Anas, Sa`d, Nasr, Nuhm, `Awdh and other male deities.

Similar details are related to female deities of pre-Islamic Arabia. The most prominent among them was Allat. In literary sources, she is frequently grouped with the goddesses Al-`Uzza and Manat. Many tribes worshipped her and a major shrine was erected at Ta`if and contained a monumental statue of Allat. Her other epithets were Al-Taghiyah, (the tyrant) and Al-Rabbah, the Goddess. Archaeological and literary

Fig. 5.5: Relief sculpture of Allat flanked by two female attendants above a lion, Hatra, 2nd century CE., Limestone, 115 cm. h., 75 cm. w. The Iraqi Museum, Baghdad, Iraq.

sources show that Allat was worshipped across the mainland of Arabia, including Hatra, Hirah, and Palmyra (Figures 3.10, 3.11, 3.12, 3.13), Busra, near the gulf of Aqaba, in the Hawran region and in south Arabia. Many temples have been excavated and identified with her worship in Hatra (Figures 3.25, 3.29), Palmyra (Figures 3.10. 3.11, 3.12), Dura-Europos, Jebel Druze, Kindah and other locations.

From various parts of Syria, sculptural representations of Allat appear as a typical female figure clad in a military outfit. Examples of such depictions can be seen in Palmyra, Dura Europos, and throughout Syria. To the Nabataeans, Allat was a consort of the male deity Dusares. She was a goddess of fertility who corresponded to the Greco-Roman Aphrodite-Venus, the indigenous Arab Atargatis and her cult may have also been incorporated with Athena.

From Hatra, Allat appears as a Goddess of war on a limestone relief in the center flanked by two lesser female deities (untenably labeled as Al-`Uzza and Manat) or attendants above a lion (Fig. 5.5). She wears a helmet and holds a spear and shield. Characteristics of Parthian art are noticeable as well as the Greek attributes of the Goddess Athena. But the overall presentation is typical of Hatran iconography.

The prominence of the worship of Allat is attested by the discovery of many visual images of that deity. From Palmyra, a relief of a seated Allat (Fig. 3.12) appears on an altar from the Ba`alsamin (Ba`l Shamin) sanctuary and is dated to the mid or late 1st century CE. The head and torso are frontal and she is dressed in civilian clothes. The lion seated beside the throne of Allat is believed to be a borrowing from the iconography of the Arab-Syrian goddess Atargatis.

During the 2nd century Allat was also being represented as the armed Athena. However, Palmyran Allat appeared as an Arabian deity and images of Allat/Athena must have enjoyed preference at Palmyra as suggested by the 23 examples that have been discovered so far.

MADA`IN SALIH- HEGRA (AL-HIJR)- NORTHWEST ARABIA

Mada'in Saleh, also called Hegra (Al-Hijr), is an urban settlement dated to 1st century BCE – 1st century CE, and located in the Al-`Ula sector, within the Al-Madinah region of Hijaz in present day Saudi Arabia. The site is located some 12 miles (20 km) north of Al-`Ula. Mada`in Salih may have been the southernmost expansion of the Nabataeans of Petra on the trade route. The site contains over 100 rock-cut monumental tombs with elaborately decorated facades similar in style and techniques to those at Petra. Predecessors of the Nabataeans at the area were the Dedanites and then the Lihyanites. Islamic tradition treats the site as a cursed place, based on the story of the Thamudic people and Prophet Salih in the Qur`an. The Nabataeans called it Hegra (Arabic Al-Hijr, "the stone"). The location of Mada`in Salih was a crossroads where the major north-south incense route intersected a road from the Red Sea to the Arabian Gulf (Map 8).

A large number of inscriptions discovered at the site attest to the spread of the cult of Dhu Al-Shara. A tomb dated to the year 1 BCE containing a dedicatory inscription, mentions Dhu Al-Shara and the deities Manat and Qays. Another inscription on a tomb dated to 1 BCE invokes Dhu Al-Shara and Manat twice, along with Allat, Hubal and Qays. A third tomb dated to the 4th century CE provides an inscription where Dhu Al-Shara is invoked twice. Also, from Al-Hijr a long inscription dates a tomb to the year 26 CE and dedicates it to Dhu Al-Shara. More inscriptions of that nature have been found in neighboring Al-`Ula and other locations. The place was annexed by the Romans, along with the area controlled by the Nabataeans and incorporated it into its Arabian province in 106 CE.

The center of the town Al-Hijr is located some distance from the tombs at a meeting point of many trade routes. The ruins of the houses at Al-Hijr indicate that sun-dried mud brick was the primary building material in that town. Excavation is still in progress, and it may yield more information. Much of our knowledge comes from the well-preserved structures: mausoleums, tombs, and other edifices, and the intricate carving and inscriptions on their facades. The fine carving on these facades are reminiscent of Petran styles and techniques. Most of the facades are topped with a pair of crow steps rising up from a central point. Each tomb has a portal with an entrance that leads to the inside, where a large square space is carved. The walls of the space contained grooves or recesses for depositing the deceased bodies (Figures 5.6, 5.7).

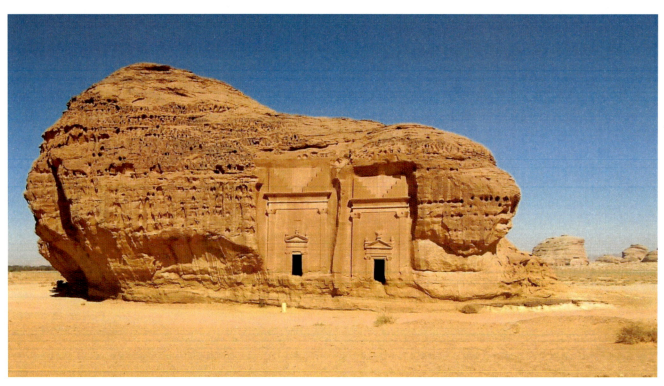

Fig. 5.6: General scene of facades of a tomb in Mada`in Salih, Saudi Arabia.

One imposing section in the complex is called Qasr Al-Bint: The Palace of the Daughter or Maiden (Fig. 5.8). It is the largest tomb facade at the site (16 meters high), with its portal above the ground level. An interesting inscription above the entrance states the name of the sculptor "Hoor ibn Ahi," who carved the tomb facade for "Hani ibn Tafsy, his family and descendants." It also gives the date of 31 CE.

Another 1st century CE monumental tomb at the site known as "Qasr Al-Farid", "the lone" (Fig. 5.9), so-called because it stands alone in an imposing natural rock formation. It has an unfinished facade and the inscription does not provide significant details.

Fig. 5.7: Recesses carved in the walls of Mada`in Salih tombs, Saudi Arabia

PRE-ISLAMIC KA`BAS AND SANCTUARIES IN ARABIA

Arabs of the pre-Islamic times and their associated cults indicate that for every major deity, at least one main sanctuary was dedicated. For example, the Ka`ba at Mecca was an ancient sanctuary dedicated to the worship of the one monotheistic God, Allah since the time of Adam according to Islamic tradition. The tradition relates that later, people associated the worship of pagan deities with Allah. Inside the Ka`ba a large statue of the prominent male deity Hubal and other minor deities were erected. With the advent of Islam, however, this sanctuary was reclaimed for the exclusive use of the original worship of Allah.

The architectural form of the pre-Islamic Ka`ba has survived into the present time without significant alterations to the original design, although the structure has suffered from fire, flooding and demolition. The word "Ka`ba" is derived from the cube-like appearance of the square building. The word has been traditionally associated only with the sanctuary at Mecca. However, the linguistic term also refers to an exalted, esteemed and glorified structure. Arab historical sources show that numerous other pagan sanctuaries were also called "Ka`ba" in pre-Islamic times. There were also sanctuaries associated with minor deities and in some cases more than one sanctuary would be dedicated to the same deity in different towns or regions.

Besides sanctuaries dedicated to pagan Arab deities, the term Ka`ba also appears to have been used to denote other places of worship such as Christian churches and Jewish synagogues, and even some secular buildings. Turning to archae-

Fig. 5.8: Qasr Al-Bint, Mada`in Salih, Saudi Arabia.

ological evidence for early religious architecture in Arabia, it should be noted that most of the sanctuaries mentioned in pre-Islamic literature have not been traced archaeologically, and that very few have been confirmed by systematic excavation or preliminary surveys. Some of the most important sanctuaries and Ka`bas (ka`bat) mentioned in the literary sources of pre-Islamic Arabia are listed below.

**AL-`ULA AND PETRA:** At these sites certain Ka`ba constructions associated with the worship of the deity Thul-Sharah (Dusares) have been discovered.

TAYMA': On the summit of Jebel Ghunaym near Tayma', remains of a temple or open-air sanctuary have been reported. Within this site incised representations of a three faced-head surmounted by bull's horns are noticeable.

TEMPLE WADI AL-SIRHAN: At Wadi Al-Sirhan, near Kaf, Ithra and Qurayyah, the foundation courses of a temple have been reported, measuring about 80 by 20 meters. The floor plan of the structure, which consists of an outer rectangular wall enclosing a rectangular chamber, closely resembles a typical Nabataean sanctuary.

HA'IL: At this important pre-Islamic site, there have been observed the remains of an architectural structure that was possibly a sanctuary.

YEMEN: In Yemen, a major Himyarite palace is known as the "Cubic Palace of Dhu La`wah," so-called because the building contained cubes, shaped like small shields, projecting out of its

Fig. 5.9: Qasr Al-Farid, Mada`in Salih, Saudi Arabia.

walls.

HATRA: At this site in Northern Iraq a Ka`ba has been excavated, dating to around 200 CE, that is surrounded by a circumambulatory enclosure and formed part of the grand temple in that city.

**KA`BAT GHATAFAN:** The sanctuary of the deity Al-`Uzza, located near Mecca, was called Ka`bat Ghatafan. The term refers to the tribe of Banu Ghatafan as custodians and patrons of that sanctuary.

AL-QULLAYS: A cathedral was built in San`a' during the 6th century. Islamic sources argue that the Abyssinian ruler Ibraha built this church as a counter to the Meccan sanctuary. To accomplish this purpose, he decorated the church elaborately, reusing the marbles and stones of Balqis' castle; possibly the `Awwam temple, which had been destroyed at Ma'rib. Arab historians indicate that the Byzantine emperor sent architects and craftsmen to Ibraha in order to embellish the structure with mosaic and marble. Arab lexicographers give the name of this cathedral as Al-Qalis or Al-Qullays, apparently a corruption of the Greek word Ekklesia. Greek inscription from the Syrian region mention the word Ekklesia; with the meaning of "Congregations and New Church." The architectural plan of the church "Al-Qullays" measured 60 cubits (about 30 meters) high, surrounded by a wall located 200 cubits (about 100 meters) from the main sanctuary, according to a 9th century Arab historian.

A recent archaeological study has confirmed the location of this church by the west wall of the citadel in old San`a', not far from the 8th century Great Mosque in that city. Furthermore, this new study suggests that some of the columns at the Great Mosque contain Christian motifs, suggesting that they might have been recycled (spolia) from the original Al-Qullays structure. Scholars have two different opinions on the architectural style of the church (Ka`ba) of Al-Qullays. One claims that it was built in Abyssinian style, while the other asserts that the construction was done in the Byzantine style from Syria.

The interior of the dome of Al-Qullays was decorated with mosaic paintings including narratives of crucifixes covered with gold and silver. A large square stone (5 x 5 meters) was attached to the wall, under which a wooden pulpit with elaborate inlay decoration sat. Al-Qullays survived until the reign of the Abbasid Caliph Al-Mansur (754-775), when his governor in Yemen Al-Abass ibn Al-Rabi` ibn `Ubaydullah Al-Harithi decided to destroy the church. The Arab historian Al-Azraqi claims that a major reason for the long survival of Al-Qullays was the presence of two panels, that the Arabs feared and respected. Al-Abbas destroyed the church and pulled out the two panels of "Ku`ayb and his woman." Consequently, an Iraqi merchant living in San`a' bought the two panels, cut them down and reconstructed the wood for a door that he installed in his house. Recent research suggests that Al-Qullays was a martyrium commemorating the Christian martyrs of Najran and their leader "Al-Harith" or "Al-Harithah." They were persecuted, then suffered mass execution by the Jewish King Dhu Nuwas in 523. Al- Azraqi explained that the two panels represented the images of Arethas (Al- Harith) and Ruhayma, two leading figures among the Christian martyrs of Najran.

NAJRAN

In the region of Najran, remains of architectural structures attest to possible sanctuaries. A place of worship and pilgrimage, apparently affiliated with Christianity, was erected at Najran in the 6th century. It was also called "Bay`at Najran," meaning church, and was still functioning as such during the early decades of the rise of Islam. According to Ibn Al-Kalbi, the tribe of Banu Al-Harith sponsored the temple at Najran. He argues that its function was more social than religious. It might well have been a monastery associated with the cathedral Al-Qullays. This is further confirmed by a verse attributed to Al-A`sha where it is extolled as an asylum for the oppressed. This building was a Christian church run by an organized body of priests from the tribe of Banu Al-Harith. Another account relates that this church was built on a square plan after the model of the Ka`ba at Mecca. Ka`bat Najran was so-called because of the distinct square plan. The interior was adorned with mosaic works.

From historical events, we know that in the year 631 the people of Najran sent delegation to the Prophet Mohammed at Medina to arrange alliances and were granted a peaceful treaty. In the statement of that treaty, the Prophet spared their religious practices, churches, monks, bishops, statues, mosaics, and paintings. This important document informs us that the churches at Najran, including the Ka`ba of Najran, indeed contained sculptures and mosaics. The existence of Ka`bat Najran is attested to by a Hadith attributed to the Prophet Mohammed. He is reported to have said that there are four protected cities: Mecca, Medina, Iylia', "Jerusalem" and Najran. Supportive evidence to this Hadith is the statement by Al-Hamdani––a 10th century Arab historian––where he lists the names of places of worship in the peninsula including Ka`bat Najran. Ka`bat Najran was called the Yemenite Ka`ba as distinctive from the Meccan Ka`ba. From various references, we infer that the city of Najran itself was an important settlement protected by a fortified defensive wall.

As for the nature of the architectural setting of this temple, we have one reference emphasizing that the structure was a dome (Qubba), built on the bank of a river at Najran called Al-Nuhayradan or Al-Bujayrawan. The dome was composed of 300 pieces of leather. The emphasis on the quantity of the leather used for the construction of the dome is a clear reference to the extravagance of the structure. At this point it is important to mention that the sanctuary of the deity Dhu Al-Khalasa at Tabala was also called Al-Ka`bah Al-Yamaniyyah, or the Yemenite Ka`ba, and Al-Ka`bah Al-Shamiyyah or the Syrian Ka`ba. This same sanctuary was also called "Ka`bat Al-Yamamah"; associated with the prevailing cult of Dhu Al-Khalasa in the Yamamah region.

The Qubba mentioned above was a conical tent-like structure, used in pre-Islamic times on important occasions, especially to accommodate arbitration sessions and other social events. As for the shape of this Qubba, scholars argue that it was a geometrical hemisphere, characteristic of imperial Byzantine design, as a distinctive symbol of a "Martyrium," possibly related to the event of the massacre of the Christians of Najran. According to this interpretation, the Ka`ba, or Martyrium was built on an earlier structure (church) from 520 that was later destroyed by the Himyarite king.

The pre-Islamic poet Al-A`sha (d. 629) mentions the Ka`bat Najran in a poem where he refers to its gilded gates. The verses also mention some of the decorations, either on the main entrance or on the interior of the temple. Al-Jahidh (d. 868) includes Ka`bat Najran on a list of impressive monumental buildings credited to the Arabs. Unfortunately, none of the original structure has survived. However, in a recent archaeological survey at Najran, archaeologists have tried to locate the site of this Ka`ba. A semi-circular double row of stones surrounding an offset central pillar was noticed. This may well be the remains of Ka`bat Najran, but confirmation relies on further research.

RIYAM (RI'AM)
A Himyarite sanctuary was constructed at San`a' in Yemen during the 6th century CE. The tribe of Azd patronized Riyam, which was associated with the worship of a South Arabian deity called Ta'lab. The word "riyam" means mercy or pity and appears to have been association with maternal affairs. The word RYM has been found in both North and South Arabian inscriptions. The people of San`a venerated this sanctuary and practiced sacrificial offering as an essential part of the cult. All references point out that a certain man from Yemen called Tubba` Teban destroyed Riyam upon a convincing command from two Rabbis, who subsequently introduced Judaism to that part of Yemen.

According to modern archaeological research supported by epigraphic evidence, the construction of Riyam took place during the reign of the Himyarite kingdom of Sam`ay. The people of that kingdom had their own distinctive cult of a deity named Ta'lab, whose main shrine was at Riyam. However, neither the site of Riyam nor any remain of the structure have been located. Riyam appears to have been an important center of worship; the 10th century historian Al-Hamdani counts it as significant as the Ka`ba at Mecca, Jerusalem, Allat's sanctuary at Ta'if and Ka`bat Najran. He explains that Riyam was a house of worship in the land of Hamdan, where pilgrims flocked to perform their anchoritic-hermitical vows. Around Riyam were pilgrims' campsites. Next to Riyam stood the royal palace of Riyam ibn Nahfan, who sponsored the house. Facing the palace gate was a wall which contained a slab bearing the motifs of the sun and the crescent. Al-Hamdani refers to few pre-Islamic verses that mention Riyam.

Besides these frequently mentioned sites, there are other famous structures: castles, churches, residential spaces and Ka`bat. Names and locations are found in several works, most notably in Arab geographer-historian Al-Hamdani's writing, entitled "Sifat Jazeerat Al-`Arab"–– Geography and Characteristics of the Arabian Peninsula; Yaqut Al-Hamawi, an Arab biographer and geographer (d. 1229) in his encyclopedic work "Mu`jam Al-Buldan," Dictionary of Countries. Examples are Dayr (monastery) of Najran, located in Syrian Najran, better known as Busra (Bostra); Ka`bat Sindad in Hirah; two castles: Al-Khuwarnaq and Al-Sadir in Hirah; the palaces Raydan and Ghamdan in Yemen and other buildings that have not been evidenced by archaeological studies as of yet.

GHASSANIDS IN SYRIA

The Ghassanids were a confederate of Arab tribes that migrated originally from South Arabia as early as the 3rd century CE and more intensely after the deterioration and collapse of the Ma`rib dam in the 6th and 7th centuries CE. The ongoing economic-political conflict between the Arab Jews supported by the Sassanians and the Arab Christians backed by Byzantines in Yemen resumed the upward migration in waves to the Syrian region. Consequently, they settled independently but later submitted to the control of the Romans, followed by the Byzantine powers. Soon the Ghassanids were stimulated by the Greek speaking Christians and the doctrinal institution of the new Eastern Roman Empire--the Byzantine (Map 8). They centered at Busra but controlled a vast region of Syria and Palestine. The Ghassanids followed the eastern Orthodox Jacobite Arab Christianity. In the 7th century, some Ghassanids converted to Islam while other branches of the community remained Christian and joined the Melkite and Syriac churches. Constantinople utilized the Ghassanids and employed them as allies and as a buffer mini-state against the Persian Sassanians and their Arab Christian allies – the Lakhmids (Mundhirids) in Hirah Iraq.

A few interesting milestones are worth mentioning here. The Roman emperor Marcus Julius Philippus, known as Philip the Arab who ruled from 244-249, was of Syrian origin, and was sympathetic to Christianity and early Christians in the region. Born in Shahba in southern Syria, he was likely of Ghassanid descent. The celebrated Byzantine empress Theodora (died 548), wife of the Byzantine Emperor Justinian I, and one of the most influential and powerful Byzantine empresses, was a Syrian. The Byzantine Emperor Nikephoros I (died 811) may have been of Syrian Ghassanid origin. The Ghassanids continued their loyal affiliation with the Byzantines even though the latter disapproved their doctrinal Christianity, which was not in complete agreement with the Byzantine Christian theology. In the 7th century and upon the rise of the new power of the Arab state under the banner of Islam, many factions of the Ghassanids joined with their counterpart Arab tribes. Some converted to Islam while others remained Christians, but ultimately were attracted to their ethnic and cultural identification with the Arabs.

Records indicate that the Ghassanids had a continuous rule of kings in their territory in places such as Raqqa, Rasafa, Golan, Hawran, and around Palmyra from the early 3rd century to the early 8th century. They controlled and secured the trade routes, and consolidated the Byzantine grip on the northern borders of Arabia. The Ghassanids' patronage of the Monophysite Syrian Church, which conflicted with Byzantine Christian Orthodoxy, rendered them unfavorable to the church of Constantinople. The Ghassanids' promotion of a simpler and more rigidly monotheistic form of Christianity in a specifically Arab context paved the way for a closer alliance with the newly emerged power of Islam. The Ghassanids promoted urban development in the Syrian region (Syria, Lebanon, Jordan and Palestine), evidenced by the patronage of several churches, monasteries and palaces. Arab historians describe the Ghassanid courts with luxurious setting and vigorous cultural life. Their kings patronized architecture, the arts, music and especially Arabic poetry. Their legacy can be seen as the backdrop for the cultural and artistic foundation that ensued with the Umayyads in the same region during

Fig. 5.10: Eusebius of Cesarea and Ammonius of Alexandria, Folio 2r, the Rabbula Gospels, Zaghba, Syria, 586, tempera on parchment, 13" x 10.5", Biblioteca Medicea Laurenzina, Florence, Italy.

the 8th century. The Ghassanids' heritage continued to reverberate during the Islamic periods by descendants of the tradition, both Christians and Muslims, well into the succeeding centuries of Islamic rule.

Archaeological and Arab literary sources indicate that Ghassanid structures of palaces, monasteries and churches reveal traces of the traditional south Arabian characteristics overshadowed by Byzantine influence. Remains of churches and other structures in that region are still awaiting full study and analysis. While remains of the Ghassanids' buildings are not clearly defined in the region and almost always identified as Byzantine, Arab literary sources give names of palaces such as Qasr Wardan, Qasr Al-Brays and churches such as Qal`at Sam`an- St. Simon Basilica. We also learn that the Ghassanids were allies to the early Muslim communities, especially the Umayyads against the Byzantines and that early Muslim structures in Raqqa, Rasafa, and the Syrian desert may have had architectural characteristics of Ghassanid origin.

The Ghassanids patronized the spread of monasteries and facilitated their religious activities. In such facilities, Arab monks and priests lived, worked and produced significant religious icons and manuscripts. Such liturgical/artistic production has been typically identified untenably as Byzantine. One important example is the survived 6th century manuscript known as "the Rabbula Gospel." The folios of the manuscript are rather large, (about 13" x 11") and illustrated with narratives painted with tempera on parchment. The text of the manuscript contains Aramaic with later notations in Arabic on some folios (Fig. 5.10).

The gospel was produced and signed by a certain scribe Rabbula at a monastery "Bet Mar Yohannan of Zaghba"— St. John of Zaghba in Syria, present-day Lebanon. It contains more than 24 illustrated pages with paintings and Aramaic text, framed by elaborate floral and architectural motifs. The paintings were modified and painted over later with more illustrations; notes in Arabic and Greek were added later as late as the 15th century. The figurative rendering in the visual narratives show Hellenistic/Byzantine and Persian characteristics but maintain the local identity in both the depiction of the figures and the theological narration according to the Orthodox Arab Christian church. The manuscript is signed by the scribe-illustrator Rabbula, probably a monk affiliated with that monastery. Unfortunately, we do not know more about this 6th century artist, but we can infer that he was aware of and probably enthused and trained by the then established Byzantine artistic trend in visualizing the Biblical narratives.

The name Rabbula, may be derived from the Aramaic to mean "rab alaha" (God "Allah" is the Lord), or "rab `elaya" a cognate of the Arabic expression "rab Al-`ula" (God of Heaven).

The manuscript was completed in 586, and it is probably the earliest illustrated gospel. Along the centuries many artisans/restores added their work to the original paintings, sometime with obvious poor changes or additions as in (Fig. 5.11).

In the crucifixion and resurrection scene (Fig. 5.11), which was repainted later in a more Hellenistic style than the original, Jesus is depicted differently than other portrayals in the manuscript, such as the Canonical Tables scene (Fig. 5.12). The Rabbula depictions generally show Jesus in naturalistic style: black curly hair and fully dressed, rather than partially nude, as is the common rendering of the crucifixion scene in the Byzantine and Catholic tradition. Similar attributes can be seen in the Ascension scene and the rest of the New Testament episodes in this manuscript. The original paintings exhibit an Arab-Christian interpretation of the life of Jesus, rendered with Arab pictorial trends connected to the Ghassanid-Nabataean stylistic traditions. The Rabbula Gospel is a unique 6th century example of Ghassanids-Arab Christian visual Biblical narratives in the Syrian region, which was at the time under Byzantine political control.

The famous 4th century "Namara Inscription" (Figures 5.13, 5.14) has been interpreted as the epitaph of Arab king "Imri`ul-Qays," who

Fig. 5.11: Crucifixion and Resurrection, folio 13r, the Rabbula Gospels, Zaghba, Syria, 586, tempera on parchment, 13" x 10.5", Biblioteca Medicea Laurenzina, Florence, Italy.

Fig. 5.12: Folio 4v, Canon Table with the Prophets Samuel and Joshua and the Annunciation to the Virgin, the Rabbula Gospels, Zaghba, Syria, 586, tempera on parchment, 13" x 10.5", Biblioteca Medicea Laurenzina, Florence, Italy.

Fig. 5.13: Epitaph of "Imri'ul-Qays" inscribed in Nabataean script. H. 45 cm (17 ½ in.), W. 1.73 m (5 ft. 8 in.), D. 15 cm (5 ¾ in.), basalt, dated 328 CE. Found at Namara in the Hawran (Southern Syria), Louvre Museum, Paris, France.

was supported by the Romans. The Nabataen Aramaic text is believed to be an early example of the transition from Aramaic to the Arabic language.

According to Rene Dussaud who, along with Fredric Macler found the epitaph in 1901, the Aramaic text reads:

> "This is the funerary monument of Imri' ul-Qays, son of 'Amr, king of the Arabs, and (?) his title of honour was Master of Asad and Madhij.
> And he subdued the Asadis and they were overwhelmed together with their kings, and he put to flight Madhhij thereafter, and came driving them to the gates of Najran, the city of Shammar, and he subdued Ma'add, and he dealt gently with the nobles of the tribes, and appointed them viceroys, and they became phylarchs for the Romans. And no king has equalled his achievements.
> Thereafter he died in the year 223 on the 7th day of Kaslul. Oh the good fortune of those who were his friends!"

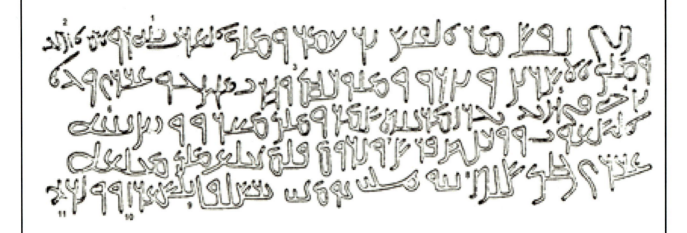

Fig. 5.14: Tracing of the original Nabataean text of "the Namara Inscription" and its Arabic interpretation by Rene Dussaud.

LAKHMIDS-(MUNDHIRIDS) IN HIRAH, IRAQ

The Lakhmids, a confederation of Arab tribes, migrated north from Southern Arabia. They settled at Al-Hirah, on the Euphrates near Kufa, also Kufah in Southern Iraq, which became their capital (4th -7th centuries CE). The Lakhmids developed a powerful kingdom, with an economy rich from their trade activity in Hirah, which was located on the active trade route. Nestorian Christian Arabs from Iraq and Syria joined the Hirans in the 4th and 5th centuries, which further enhanced the cultural development of the Kingdom. Like the Ghassanids who ruled under the Byzantines, the Hirans were an independent semi-state but ended up a vassal to the powerful Sassanian empire.

Arabic historical tradition record aspects of the magnificent buildings and luxurious life among the inhabitants of Hirah especially the later dynasty of the Mundhirids with descriptions of the churches and the Mundhirid luxury palaces. The region of Hirah contains important sites mentioned in literary sources and partially confirmed by archaeological excavations. A major excavation campaign took place in 1931 by Oxford University. Foundation of Churches and residential spaces were unearthed. Plaster works, icons, pottery, stucco and sculptured doors were also found.

More specific sites have been investigated. Archaeological activity continued in the region with subsequent excavations followed by a systematic campaign sponsored by the Directorate General of Iraqi Museums and Antiquities. The archaeological activity (2007-2012) investigated more specific sites uncovering the foundations of buildings assumed to have been Nestorian monasteries and churches. (Figures 5.15, 5.16, 5.17). The results and finds of the relatively recent history of excavation at Hirah appear to be crucial to the question of pre-Islamic art and particularly to the visual sources of early Islamic art. Archaeologists have identified remains of many architectural structures in Hirah. The largest of these structures contains over 30 rooms surrounding two courtyards, a large main space, and various other rooms and spaces within the well-fortified edifice, which may have been originally a monastery. This identification, though not totally conclusive, is supported by the numerous religious objects such as Nestorian carved and painted crosses found within that structure. Hirah is considered an important historical site for the development of the Classical Arabic language.

The stucco work on many of these buildings can be connected to the same traditions, techniques and design elements––vegetal and geometric units–– that were found in Kufah in the early Islamic period (Figures. 5.18, 5.19).

Within this monastery, archaeologists found many crosses: carved in sandstone, molded in plaster and carved in stucco; some painted crosses have also been found. The list of objects found in Hirah includes marble plaques with Arabic writing, pottery, coins and other artifacts (Figures 5.20, 5.21). A marble plaque has two lines incised in early Kufic script and mentions a Christian individual called Abd Al-Maseeh (Fig. 5.20). The 7th century has been tentatively, but reasonably assigned as the general time frame for the monastery and related artifacts.

Arab classical literary sources give vivid records of palaces, monasteries and churches of Arab Christians in Hirah during the pre-Islamic time. Among these important buildings is a pilgrimage shrine called Ka`bat Sindad, also known as Dhu Al-Ka`bat and Dhu Al-Shurufat. This Ka`ba is frequently mentioned in Arab literary sources as an example of the lavish and prosperous secular palace at Hirah, which was patronized by the tribes of Rabi`ah and Eyad at Sindad. It was also called Dhu Al-Ka`bat, or the "Palace with Ka`bas," and "Dhu Al-Shurufat" or the palace with balconies. This Ka`ba was built on the edge of a river or ravine called Al-`Udhayb at Hirah and presented an attractive center for pilgrims who were eager to visit it from many parts of the peninsula.

Al-Isbahani, relying on Ibn Al-Kalbi, mentions that the tribe of Eyad dwelled at Sindad in Hirah and worshipped a deity called "Dhu Al-Ka`batayn." The pre-Islamic poet Al-Aswad ibn Ya`fur documented this Ka`ba in a well-known poem. As for the nature of worship or the deity that was associated with this Ka`ba, we do not have helpful information. At the present time, excavation at Hirah is still being conducted, and it may be a while before we assess any evidence from the site of this Ka`ba. Although both the Lakhmids and the Ghassanids were Arab and Christians, they continually clashed with one another due to their affiliations with the two rival powers, the Byzantines and the Sassanians. Pre-Islamic literary sources mention in detail some important military conflicts between the two camps in prose, poetry and other accounts.

Fig. 5.15: Remains of possible Nestorian monastery, Hirah, Iraq.

Fig. 5.16: Details of stucco beams at the ruins of a Nestorian monastery, Hirah, Iraq.

Fig. 5.17: Stucco work at the ruins of a Nestorian monastery, Hirah, Iraq.

Fig. 5.18: Example of plaster stucco of wall decoration in the monastery, Hirah, Iraq.

Fig. 5.19: Sample of Nestorian crosses found in Hirah, Iraq.

Fig. 5.20: Marble plaque for Abd Al-Maseeh, 6th century, Hirah, Iraq.

COPTS IN EGYPT

During the 4th century BCE, ancient Egypt's power continued to decline and the region was subject to foreign invasions by the Persians, followed by the Greeks in 332 BCE. The Ptolemaic dynasty succeeded Alexander in ruling Egypt, and in 30 BCE it was occupied by the Romans. Around 395 CE the Byzantine Empire conquered Egypt. The Sassanians briefly took over Alexandria in 622, but the Byzantines resumed their control through 645 when the newly risen Arab power expelled the Byzantines from Egypt. The Greco-Roman,

Fig. 5.21: Depiction of Jesus and St. Mina, paint on wood, Deir Baweet, Egypt, late 6th – early 7th centuries, 75 cm x 75 cm x 2 cm, Louvre Museum, Paris, France.

Persian and Byzantine periods in Egypt witnessed prolonged multicultural exposure to the traditional Egyptian culture. Furthermore, Judeo-Christian tradition share Egyptian culture and history according to the Biblical accounts related to Moses and the Exodus.

The Coptic tradition relates that Egyptian Christians (Copts) follow St. Mark, a disciple of Christ, as the introducer of Christianity in Egypt in the second half of the 1st century. Although the Coptic church grew under Byzantine Christianity, it was not favored by the latter for its view of Monophysitism shared by other Orthodox churches of the East such as the Syriac and the Abyssinian.

The Hellenistic-Byzantine domination of Egypt brought in the Greek language alongside the remnant of the old Egyptian Hieroglyphic-Demotic (known as Coptic) throughout that period. The Coptic church was in direct connection with the Church of Jerusalem and the Church of Abyssinia (Ethiopia). Both entities shared similar traditions of indigenous culture. Arabic became the official communication language in the 7th century after the Arabs defeated the Byzantine forces in Egypt, and Egyptian Christians had closer ties to the Arabs and Arab culture. It is within this Coptic community that the characteristics of Arab visual art continued to reverberate in the form of wall painting, metalwork, textiles, ritualistic objects, religious icons and manuscript illustrations

Fig. 5.22: Wall painting of Coptic ascetics, from the monastery of Saint Jeremiahs, Saqqara, Egypt, late 6th -early 7th centuries, the Coptic Museum, Cairo, Egypt.

preserved in monasteries and small churches. Among these icons a painting on wood depicts Jesus and St. Mina (Fig. 5.21) standing in frontal pose with clearly defined facial features. The characterization of the figures follows the common trends found among the Arabs in Yemen and Nabataea.

Another example is a wall painting of Copt ascetics from the monastery of St. Jeremiads at Saqqara (Fig. 5.22).

The wall painting fragment depicts four ascetics of earlier periods such as St. Onophrious, Abbot Makarios along with other ascetics accompanied by a supplicant. Coptic art imbeds diverse sources of Pharaonic, Hellenistic, and Arab traditions. The style of representation in these examples share general characteristics of portrait painting find in many parts of the Arab lands such as in the paintings of Qaryat Al-Faw (Figures 4.13, 4.14, 4.15) or in the royal figures of Himyarite king from South Arabia (Fig. 2.15). The visual narratives of Coptic illuminated manuscripts shows more similarities with that of the Rabbula Gospel from Syria. Notable are the stylistic proximities found in the visual narratives of Egyptian, Ethiopian (Abyssinian) and South Arabian traditions.

It is important to consider the cultural ties between the Christian Arabs in Syria, Palestine, the Sinai, and along the Nile in Egypt during that period through re-evaluation of the artistic production found in the whole region.

Selected Bibliography

Alcock Susane E. Ed., *The Early Roman Empire in the East,* Oxford 1997.

Al- Ansari Abd Al-Rahman, Qaryat Al-Faw: A Portrait of Pre-Islamic Civilization in Saudi Arabia, Riyadh, KSA: Croom Helm Ltd, 1982.

Al-Tawil Hashim, "Literary References to Early Arab Sculpture and Painting", *"Early Arab Icons: Literary and Archaeological Evidence for the Cult of Religious Images in Pre-Islamic Arabia"* University of Iowa, IA, University Microfilms, Ph.D. Thesis,1993, pp. 43-100.

Baird, J. A. 2011, "The Houses of Dura-Europos: Archaeology, Archive, and Assemblage", in L. Brody and G. Hoffman (eds) *Dura-Europos: Crossroads of Antiquity. Boston:* McMullan Museum, 2011, Pp.235-250.

Baur, P.V.C. (Ed.), The Excavations at Dura-Europos conducted by Yale University and the French Academy of Inscriptions and Letters. Final Report IV, Part III, *The Lamps,* New Haven 1929.

Borgia, E., *Jordan Past & Present: Petra, Jerash, Amman,* Oxford University Press, 2003.

Butcher, Kevin, *Roman Syria and the Near East.* Getty Publications, 2003.

Dirven L, Hatra: A "Pre-Islamic Mecca" in the Eastern Jazirah, *ARAM,* 18-19 (2006-2007), pp. 363-380.

Gutmann, J. *The Dura-Europus Synagogue: A Re-Evaluation* (1932-72) (Missoula: Scholars Press, 1972.

____, The Dura Europos Synagogue Paintings and Their Influence on Later Christian and Jewish Art, *Artibus et Historiae,* Vol. 9, No. 17 (1988), pp. 25-29.

Hopkins, C., *The Discovery of Dura-Europos,* New Haven 1979.

King, Geoffrey, *The Traditional Architecture of Saudi Arabia,* I. B. Tauris, 1998.

Kraeling, C.H., The Christian Building, The Excavations at Dura-Europos, Final Report, New Haven: Yale University Press, 1967.

____, C.H., *The Synagogue,* The Excavation at Dura-Europos, Final Report, Yale University Press, New Haven: Yale University Press, 1956.

Margaret, O. "Early Christian Synagogues and Jewish Art Historians. The Discovery of the Synagogue of Dura-Europos. *Marburger Jahrbuch für Kunstwissenschaft,* 27, 2000, Pp. 7-28.

Matheson, S., Dura-Europos: The Ancient City and the Yale Collection, New Haven: Yale University Press, 1982

Perkins, A., *The Art of Dura-Europos.* Oxford, 1973.

Rostovtzeff, M. I., Dura and the problem of Parthian art, New Haven: Yale University Press, 1935.

____, *Dura-Europos and its Art,* Oxford 1938.

Saudi Society for Archeological Studies, *Kindah,* Report # 1, King Saud University Press, Riyadh, KSA 1989.

CHAPTER 6

ARAB ART DURING THE EARLY ISLAMIC PERIOD

The first half of the 7th century witnessed the rise of Islam and the growing power of the Prophet Mohammed in Mecca. The Arabian Peninsula was politically fragmented and much of its regions continued to exist under the control of the Byzantines or the Sassanians. Internally, Arab kingdoms and tribes were in regional conflicts, with recurring wars, fueled by the struggle for the control of commercial activity along trade routes. Three important Arab semi-independent states dominated the scene: The Ghassanids in the north/northwest, poised as agents to the Byzantine Empire; the Lakhmids (Mundhirits), agents to the Sassanians; and the state of Kindah in the central region (Najd), across the south and center of the peninsula, with fluctuating political stands.

LITERARY SOURCES OF CULTURAL ACTIVITIES

The cultural picture of the Arabs in the peninsula and the surrounding regions during this epoch–late pre-Islamic to early Islamic time–is still not fully studied, and more scholarly research is needed. The subject has been muddled with the concept of "ignorance" (Arabic Jahiliyyah); a perception that is historically misinterpreted by both Muslim and Western sources. It simply claims that the Arabs of the pre-Islamic era were mobile Bedouins, lived in tents, raided and pillaged others, were illiterate, void of basic cultural characteristics, and did not produce or appreciate any worthwhile culture. Additionally, the sparse archaeological activity, with its limited unearthed materials in the area during this period, has attributed these materials to other cultural venues. It has been a pattern to attribute such evidence to non-Arab sources. Hence there is a confusing body of new terminologies attached to these cultural materials, such as Semitic, Phoenician, Aramaic, Chaldean, Syriac, Hebrew, and others.

Fortunately, the Arab literal memory saved us tremendous data on the subject, through poetry, rhyme, prose, and narratives. There is a considerable body of literary materials dating as far back as the 4th century CE, that have been orally preserved and transmitted through the centuries. This oral history was eventually codified, compiled and written in books formatted as early as the 8th century CE and later.

This body of pre-Islamic literature and poetry contains valuable information on various aspects of life, such as customs, rituals, economy, politics and even artistic traditions. Pre-Islamic literature reveals that the Arabs were deeply aware of a wide array of visual arts, especially sculpture and painting. In literary references to sculpture, painting, architecture and related minor fields, we find rich material dealing with descriptions of artistic works as well as terms and definitions of various technical processes pertaining to image production. Additionally, a great number of historical accounts confirm the spread of visual images among the Arabs in pre-Islamic times. A tradition of image-making, displaying, and using images was not strange to the inhabitants of the Arabian Peninsula. In fact, a major function of visual images and icons was to propagate monotheistic religious beliefs in Christian churches and Jewish temples at Najran, Hirah, Yethrib - "Madineh," and along the eastern coast of the peninsula, as well as in various polytheistic sanctuaries that were scattered throughout the Arab lands. The following are examples of those literary references to the field of art and architecture.

Artistic Terms

Linguistically, words and phrases denoting artistic activity can be traced back to the very early stage of pre-Islamic period. Such terms have been found in inscriptions in many North Arabian sites as well in South Arabia. The root SWR, meaning "to draw; to imagine" etc. has been found in inscriptions in North Arabia. This root is the origin of the later pre-Islamic, as well as the modern root SWR which means to create, to shape, and the noun MUSAWWIR, which means creator, shaper and fashioner. Both forms were common among late pre-Islamic populations as is evidenced in the Qur'an.

The root RSM has been found in both North and South Arabian inscriptions to mean "to mark" and "to draw." Hence the later Arabic word RASSAM which means "painter-artist." The root NHT, meaning to cut, carve, or hew, has been found on an inscription from Tayma` in North Arabia. In the Qur'an, the word NHT has this same connotation. The Arabic word KHAZZAF, from the root KHZF, means potter. This word has been found in North Arabian and South Arabian inscriptions. HARFF is the North Arabian root for words meaning trade, handicraft and artisanship. Words from this root have been found in two inscriptions from North Arabia. These terms, which were Nabataean and Sabaean in origin, continued to denote the same definitions through the early period of pre-Islam to the late pre-Islamic period. Late pre-Islamic literature attested widely to the use of these and similar words, along with their original definitions.

The Visual Arts

Such artistic terms and their usage in pre-Islamic and early Islamic writings provide a clearer picture of cultural and artistic activity of the time. The Qur`an provides a consistent list of these terms. The denominative verb sawwara: to shape, to portray, to form, and to fashion is used throughout the Qur`an in reference to God, Al-musawwir, the shaper or the fashioner. The noun Sura is also found in the text to mean form or picture. Both words are likely to have come from South Arabia. The word naht in the Qur`an, meaning shaping, forming, and carving sculptures from stone, is applied for both hewing buildings in the mountains and carving statues from stone. The words timthal, wathan, sanam and nusb recur in many verses. Timthal (pl. tamathil) designates sculpted image, painted or carved. Wathan (pl. awthan) denotes an idol. The word sanam (pl. asnam) appears to be synonymous to wathan and also means idol. The word nusb (pl. ansab and nusub) has been interpreted as standing stone, altar, or idol.

The Art of Painting and Decoration

The awareness of pre-Islamic people with painted images has been confirmed through a variety of sources. Close examination of these references proves that painting, calligraphy, book illumination, pottery and other related minor crafts were common professions among pre-Islamic populations. Some of these objects were used to promote worship or ethical beliefs, while others were simply utilized to meet the needs of daily life. Painting was used in the interior decoration of houses, temples, and religious buildings with narratives. The Ka`ba at Mecca contained such religious mural narratives in pre-Islamic times.

Traveling was a popular activity among pre-Islamic people; especially in connection with trading, resulting in exposure to diverse cultures. `Abdah Ibn Al-Tabib of the tribe of `Abd Shams, a pre-Islamic poet, witnessed the coming of Islam, and converted at a later age. In a trip to a peripheral region of the peninsula, probably around Hirah, he describes rugs and carpets with geometric designs and images of animals and birds executed in many colors:

"Then we reclined on carpets over which were spread embroidered rugs most sumptuous, with work of many colors. Thereon were seen the pictures of things: manifold fowls of all kinds, and a lion lurking within the brake. In a house, four-square (Ka`ba), which its builder had plastered and beautified, were lamps with twisted wicks that lit up the night."

The early Islamic poet Al-Hasan Ibn Hani' describes a party where he was served wine from a container that was adorned with a portrait of Khusraw, the "Persian King." On another occasion, he elaborates on the iconography of those wine containers: "We were served wine from a golden container that Persian artists had adorned with various pictures. At the bottom of which was a portrait of Khusraw and on its sides, there were pictures of gazelles chased by horseback riders."

In the early years of the Hijrah, the Jewish population at Yethrib were displeased with the Muslim newcomers and became hostile towards them. A certain Malik Ibn `Ajlan, chief of the Muslim tribe of Banu Salim, inflicted damage and fatality among them. To take vengeance, the Jews painted portraits of Malik at their temples and Churches (Biya`ihim wa Kana`isihim), and condemned him upon their entry and exit, every time they attended the temple.

`Alqamah Al-Fahal, a pre-Islamic poet, describes the appearance of a camp after extensive rain and compares it to the colorful semblance of a woven leather mat that depicts various decorative motifs and writings. Tarafah Ibn Al-`Abd, a 6th century poet, compares the traces of a deserted campsite with the ornaments that a professional Yemenite craftsman would produce on a leather scabbard of a sword: "... thou the traces of the abandoned campsite, adorning the barren land like a finely worked Yemenite scabbard?" He also compares the deserted campsite of his beloved Hind to the Yemenite clothes adorned with motifs that were produced at Rayda and Sahool: "On the slopes are marks as if their traces were Yemenite cloth that Rayda and Sahool made."

The Arab poet Jarir, (650 - 728) describes the difficulty of identifying an abandoned campsite and compares the effort to an expert Rabbi who professionally identifies an illuminated book: "...With much difficulty I then recognized the places of Sarah and Al-Qawwaynin, in the same way a Rabbi would recognize an illuminated manuscript." On another occasion Jarir describes an abandoned camp by comparing it to the faded pages of books that Hermits used: "The ruins of the camp looked like faded writing on pages of books belonging to Hermits, or like a tattoo on a hand mastered by a tattooist woman from the tribe of Al-Harith." Muzahim Al-`Uqaili, an early Islamic poet, uses the same impression in comparing the marks of a deserted camp to the tattoo on the hand.

These alternating definitions of the above-mentioned terms are expressed in the same manner throughout the pre-Islamic literature and among the writings of early Arab historians.

Another word that bears artistic identity is *Zukhruf.* It is applied in the Qur`an to denote anything that is elaborately embellished, especially a building that is ornamented and decorated with paintings and relief sculpture. It is also used to describe well-executed speech or written text and Nusb (pl. Ansab), which means standing stone. Ibn Al-Kalbi states that these Ansab were erected in front of sanctuaries.

The Art of Sculpture

Pre-Islamic literature reveals abundant evidence of the existence of these Ansab. In poetry, the mentioning of a nusb generally gives the impression of a statue or a large-scale monument. Tarafah Ibn Al-`Abd, a 6th century poet, swears with Ansab: "I swear by your grandfather and by the Ansab idols, among whom the blood of the sacrifices is scattered, that I did not satirize you, I swore by the Nusb idol that I would die among crowds, not in ease or prosperity."

The poet Hassan Ibn Thabit (563-674) describes the funeral of Hamza, Mohammed's uncle, where he pictures the tears on the faces of wailing women like Ansab smeared with blood.

Scenes of sanctuaries and statues of idols are often mentioned in poetry. Al-A`sha Maymun compares a prosperous house to a sanctuary enshrining the image of an idol (Wathan) that is always attended by worshippers. He also mentions a church (Haykal) that contains a Crucifix decorated with narratives painted inside. At a late age he converted to Islam, abandoning idol worship. In a poem, he defends the new religion: "And sacrifice not to standing stones (Nusub) (Ansab), and worship not idols (Awthan), but God."

We do not have concrete evidence as to the nature of these Ansab. Nowhere do we find descriptions of the artistic nature of the standing stones. However, from various descriptive verses we can safely discern that they were not mere blocks of natural rocks. In fact, one significant statement by Ibn Al-Kalbi helps in defining the visual appearance of some of these stones. He relates that the Arabs also had relic stones (which they obtained from ancient ruins). They erected them, circumambulated and offered sacrifices to them.

The pre-Islamic and early Islamic population's awareness of the existence of antiquities has been confirmed by literary evidence. Al-Hamdani (died 945) gives the name of an early Islamic governor of Yemen, Sinan, who used to excavate ancient Yemenite tombs and acquire their treasures. He also indicates that many people were used to digging ancient sites at and around Mecca for the same purpose.

Fortunately, even with the limited archaeological activities, we now have considerable information about the nature of these Ansab; that they were readily found or dug out from the scattered archaeological sites throughout the peninsula and adjacent regions. The Southern Arabian region was a major source for such finds, and abundant examples have been unearthed through limited excavation activities. Besides the few monumental statues of kings and royal figures, the majority of these finds consist of inscriptional slabs, grave markers and small-scale statues or portraits of deceased persons. These small-scale pieces were easily obtained and transferred. Similar finds have been unearthed in central, western and northern Arabia as well.

Ancient sites in the Syrian region, including Jordan, the Sinai, and Palestine comprise a direct source of Ansab of the pre-Islamic Arabs. A large number of such pieces have been found in Nabataean and Palmyran sites throughout Syria. In Palestine and Jordan many standing stones have been discovered with various shapes and contents. The bulk of these finds consists of memorial, commemorative and cult stones, votive steles, small anthropoid statuettes, effigies, portraits, sculptured images, heads, fragments, figurines and flat slabs with pictorial and inscriptional representations.

It was natural for the pre-Islamic population to prefer certain relics and use them for certain rituals. These were "Ansab," which bore visual images or depicted actual human figures. This fact is strongly supported by the descriptions of many sculptures which functioned as representations of major deities and were executed in naturalistic styles. Therefore, it is important to reconsider and correct the common misinterpretation that the Arabs of the pre-Islamic times, like the contemporaneous Semitic peoples, dealt exclusively with abstract, non-figurative, aniconic images.

References found in pre-Islamic poetry comparing the physical beauty of a woman's body to that of a statue was widespread and occurred frequently. The celebrated poet Al-A`sha Maymun (d. 629) describes a party where he talks about a group of women resembling beautiful statues: "There were maidens (Hur) like painted images or statues (Duma) and servants, cooks, and generous pots and serving plates and dishes." On another occasion, he describes these women as comparable to the statues of semi-nude females that were clothed with delicate garments: "Like statues (Tamathil) depicted with garments that merely cover their bodies." He pictures his beloved as an icon inside a gilded marble mihrab: "She is like an icon (Dumya) enshrined inside a marble mihrab that is adorned with golden decoration."

Likewise, the poet `Umar Ibn Abi Rabi`ah (643-711) represents an analogous picture: "She is like a statue (Dumya) inside a niche belonging to a devout Hermit." Abu Tammam (d. 842) compares the social status of a public figure to the importance of the location of a mihrab in a house or monastery, especially when it is adorned with a Dumya.

Al-Farazdaq, another Arab poet (641-732) compares beautiful women to statues: "Fair-skinned women; elegant like statues (Duma)... I accompanied white women like statues (Duma) to a deserted place..." He compares the abundant food being cooked in big pots attended by crowds of guests with the scene of a Sanam or an idol attended by worshippers. The second Caliph `Umar is reported to have recited a verse attributed to the pre-Islamic poet `Uday Ibn Zayd: "The most pleasing scene is that of statues (Duma) in niches or of fair women like flowers in a field."

Al-A`sha Nahshal, a poet who lived in the early Islamic period, says that light-skinned women are like statues: "And light-skinned women walk like full moons and statues (Duma); they are elegant, wrapped in fancy draperies."

The poet `Umar Ibn Abi Rabi`ah spent his life in Mecca. His collection contains many poems recording his love adventures with women pilgrims, most of whom were of high class. In many cases he compares them to Dumya and Timthal. The two terms express the meaning of a statue of a female figure executed in purely naturalistic style: "Ladies like statues (Tamathil)..."; "She walked away with her three concubines like the icons (Duma) of Monks..."; "They (the ladies) appeared like the presence of statues (Duma), but even statues (Duma) and painted images (Suwar) were not as beautiful as they were"; "She said to her companions, who looked like statues (Duma)..."; "I saw in her the resemblance of late morning sunshine; she is the most attractive, like an icon (Dumya) of a Hermit..."

In other instances he states: "She passed me with her companions who adhered to her like Christian worshippers around an idol (Wathan)"; "Her companions were like statues (Duma) ... they came to her like statues (Duma)"; "Her companions surrounded her like statues (Duma)..."; "She was among her concubines who looked like icons (Tamathil) coated with gold"; "White-skinned women like statues (Duma) ..."; "Then came three women like statues (Duma) surrounding a beautiful woman who looked like a rising sun"; "Her companions were like Huris or maidens and statues (Duma)"; "She went out with her three companions who looked like statues (Duma); they framed her like an elegant deer"; "She said to her companions who had white faces like those of statues (Duma) ..."; "I went chasing women like statues (Duma), but I could not find any one prettier than you."

Bishr Ibn Abi Khazim (644-719) compares the beauty of his tribeswomen to the elegance and beauty of marble statues: "Verily, our sutlers and hirelings had their will with white-skinned women fair as statues (Duma), with their bosoms perfumed with saffron." Antarah (d. 615) describes his displeased beloved as a statue of an idol (Sanam) frequented by worshippers. On another occasion, he says: "She looks at me as a sword falls on me. As if she were an often-visited idol (Sanam)." Abdullah Ibn Al-`Ajlan, a pre-Islamic poet, expresses his longing for his lover, comparing her to a (Timthal) or a statue, evidently in a church.

In a poem, `Ubaydah Ibn Al-Harith Ibn Al-Muttalib commemorated the battle of Badr (624), where he lost his leg defending the early Muslim community. He imagined his perpetual coming happiness in heaven with the maidens (Huris) whom he compares to statues: "A concubine that was created unique; to her, all women look like her servants. When they visit her the scene resembles a statue of an idol (Sanam) surrounded by virgins." Al-Akhtal (640-710) compares the beauty of a woman to the elegance of a statue or a painting in a monastery: "Beautiful with jewels on her neck, like images (Tamathil) in a monastery." Al-Marrar Ibn Munqidh, an early Islamic poet, continued this tradition where he says in a verse: "Once we see there white-skinned women fair as statues (Duma): no blemish had they suffered from time that brings all things to decay."

Interestingly enough, we find this artistic comparison carrying over and surviving more than a century after the Hijrah. The Umayyad Caliph Al-Walid Ibn Yazid is reported to have used the same expression in his poetry: "White hairs--what of them? Foes--who cares? I have had my day: Ripe girls like statues (Duma), wine, slaves, steeds to hunt the prey." A man of the tribe of `Udhra was asked: "Why are you so weak in the affairs of women that you would die of infatuation with women?" He answered: "By God if you appreciate women's charms you would adore them and take them as Allat and Al-`Uzza."

Bashshar Ibn Burd, an Umayyad poet, compares a beautiful concubine among pretty women to a statue of an idol (Sanam) surrounded by worshippers. Although Bashshar was blind by birth, his knowledge of sculpture and figurative representation is clear in this instance, which also reflects a widespread awareness of an artistic tradition among the majority of people who transmitted this perception to him.

Al-Mas`udi, an Arab historian and biographer (896-956), relates a legendary tale concerning a leader of the tribe of Tayy, Hatem Al-Ta'i (d. 578), whose tomb was adorned with statues. There were eight white statues of concubines flanking both sides of the tomb. The eight women were depicted sitting around the tomb, grieving and their hair dropped loose. The account emphasizes the beauty of these statues, especially the faces. No archaeological research has yet confirmed the existence of such a site in the northern part of the Arabian Peninsula. However, the account, fantastic as it may be, reveals a developed awareness and acquaintance with such sculptural depiction which was a rooted tradition in that society.

Al-Bukhari (810-870) relates that the fourth Caliph `Ali refused to pray at Babylon, probably in reaction to the numerous sculptures that must have been scattered throughout the ruins of that city. Ibn `Abbas, an authoritative transmitter of Hadith, is said to have prayed in churches that did not contain statues (Tamathil).

In this connection, the second Caliph `Umar is reported to have said: "We do not enter your church for the sake of (because of the presence of) the representations that contain pictures. This statement suggests that the early Muslim populations did not mind entering monotheist churches and were not offended by the Biblical visual narratives inside but were not eager to enjoy them either.

Information about the possible origin of many sculptures, including those of major deities, is discussed by Ibn Al-Kalbi and other early Arab historians. He claims that `Amru Ibn Luhayy brought all major statues to Mecca, Yethrib and Ta'if from Ma'ab (Moab) in the Balqa' region of Syria. Only the historian Al-Azraqi (d. 865) relates that the origins of the imported statues was Hit, a city located on the west bank of the middle Euphrates in Iraq. Moab contains many important archaeological sites, of which Dibon is the most important one.

Dibon is a major Moabite city situated 64 Km. south of `Amman. The ruins revealed at least five city walls, a square tower and some Nabataean structures. Excavation has also shown that occupation of this site goes back to about 3000 BCE. Early Arab, Byzantine, Roman and Nabataean remains have also been found. The city particularly flourished during the Nabataean era. On the other hand, tradition of imagery at Hit, (also Heet) had a long connection with the Babylonians through the rise of Hatra and Hirah in Mesopotamia. Balqa' and other Syrian and Mesopotamian sites reveal a rich history of image tradition, and the prototypes of many of the Arabian deities derive from the two regions.

`Amru Ibn Luhayy, the Patron of Monumental Statues in Mecca

`Amru Ibn Luhayy, who lived in the early pre-Islamic period, is believed to be the alleged patron who introduced idolatry into Mecca and the Ka`ba, after a tradition of monotheism dating back to Ibrahim (Abraham). This enigmatic `Amru appears to have been the leader of the Yemenite tribe of Khuza`ah. According to Ibn Al-Kalbi, Ibn Hisham, and later historians, `Amru brought the statues from Ma'ab (Moab) in the Balqa' region of Trans-Jordan. Al-Azraqi relates that he brought them from Hit, in Mesopotamia. Another report of this event maintains that he brought the five statues of Noah's contemporaries, which are mentioned in the Qur'an, from the sea shore of Jeddah and distributed them among the tribes.

As a proper name `MRW was common among many regions of the peninsula in pre-Islamic times. Epigraphic evidence confirms the existence of the name in a Nabataean inscription from Mada'in Salih in North Arabia. The name LHY on the other hand, was even wider known. At least fourteen inscriptions from North Arabia and six from South Arabia carry the word Luhayy as a proper name. However, no inscription has yet been found bearing the full name `Amru Ibn Luhayy. The problem with `Amru is that if he was indeed a historical personality, his name does not occur in any pre-Islamic poetry. The last time we hear about him is in a Hadith according to Al-Bukhari, attributed to the Prophet Mohammed. It states that while the Prophet Mohammed was engaged in deep prayer, he had a vision in which he visited heaven. When he passed by hell, he saw `Umru Ibn Luhayy burning in the fires of perdition.

The oldest literary mention of `Amru is transmitted by Wahb Ibn Munabbih, an Arab historian and traditionalist (655-around 730), in his book Al-Tijan. He relates that `Amru Ibn Qam'ah Ibn Luhayy Al-Kindi Al-Jurhami was the first to introduce polytheism to the then monotheistic population of the peninsula, followers of the religion of Isma`il and Ibrahim. Wahb also brings in a legendary tale where he describes the tomb of `Amru which contains his mutilated corpse, obviously due the severe punishment that he had received for his sins. By the corpse, an inscription in Musnad (Himyarite) reads: "This is the Sheikh `Amru Ibn Luhayy, the first who changed the religion of Isma`il and the first to worship Allat."

Al-Asma`i, an early Arabic lexicographer, scientist, and a leading scholar at Basra school of Arabic Grammar (740-832) mentions `Amru in a rather positive way. In his survey of the history of the pre-Islamic Yemenite Kings, he enumerates famous kings and rulers; listing `Amru as a wise monotheist chief, who advises his sons, in a poem, to do good deeds. Surprisingly, he does not mention the story of the idols. As for archaeological search, no epigraphic evidence attesting to his existence has yet been unearthed. Additionally, it would have been more logical to accept the theory of his introduction of idolatry into Mecca, if the statues had been brought from South Arabia, his homeland, and not from Syria or Mesopotamia.

It is important to realize that some of these statues might have been locally produced, for we know from literary and archaeological sources that there were local artists/artisans producing and selling statues, statuettes and icons publicly. There was a demand for such products for use in homes, temples, shrines and as portable ritualistic objects for travelers.

EARLY ISLAMIC ART IN THE ARABIAN PENINSULA

THE REGION OF MECCA

The presence of the new Muslim community in Mecca led by Mohammed, with his pronounced call for social reform, was not welcomed by the prominent Quraysh leaders of the city, who saw an eminent threat to their economic and political power. Upon the escalating harassment and persecution to the new and growing Muslim community in Mecca, Mohammed sent more than 100 of his followers and family members, as refugees to Abyssinia, the Christian kingdom of Axum, present day Ethiopia, around the year 613 or 615. They returned later to Mecca, but the persecution of the Muslim community continued and Mohammed himself was targeted. Learning about an assassination plot, he migrated to Yethrib, located north of Mecca some 213 km (132 miles) away. Yethrib became known as Medinah "the city", and "the Prophet's city," also Al-Medinah Al-Munawwarah, "the radiant city" in or soon after 622. It became the first political and urban capital of Islam, and the year 622 was designated as the first year of the Higrah/Hijrah, (migration), marking the new Islamic-Arabic calendar.

The Ka`ba of Mecca

The Ka`ba (also Ka`bah, Kaabah, Kaaba) of Mecca, and its precinct, is the oldest surviving and the most sacred sanctuary to all Arabs before and after the rise of Islam. Two pillars of the Islamic faith are firmly connected with the building: Prayer worldwide is directed toward the Ka`ba, and it is the center of the pilgrimage "Hajj"; both the annual and the lesser pilgrimage "`Umrah." To the Muslims, the Ka`ba represent a sacred space that embodies the presence of God (Allah). The pre-Islamic population in the Arabian Peninsula, including polytheists, Ahnaf; unaffiliated monotheists, and monotheists Jews and Christians, recognized the sacredness of the building and revered its sanctity.

According to Islamic tradition the Ka`ba was erected originally by Adam & Eve after their expulsion from paradise, to praise God, and as an expression of their repentance. It was lost after Noah flood, went through many phases of deterioration, repair and rebuilding. The most famous of these events was the rebuilding by the Prophet Abraham, as indicated in the Qur`an, probably sometime around 2000 BCE.

The building is a cube shape constructed from the local rocks near Mecca (Fig. 6.1). Its plan is nearly square, and the four sides measure approximately 13.01 m (43 ft) high, with the sides of 11.03 m (36.2 ft) x 12.86 m (42.2 ft). There is one door to the Ka`ba, that measures 3.10 (10.17 ft) x 1.9 m (6.23 ft) with its base at 2.13 m (7 ft) above the ground level. The Black Stone, which is a corner stone, is located at the eastern corner, about 1.10 m (3.60 ft) above the ground. The interior of the building has bare walls and a ceiling held by three wooden columns (Fig. 6.2).

given as gifts to dignitaries and Muslim leaders. Some of these pieces have become valuable and are found in museums and private collections all over the world.

The Kiswah is decorated with a golden embroidered band of Qur`anic text designed in Thulth calligraphic composition. The text contains verses related to the oneness of Allah and the sacredness of the sanctuary, along with commemorative epigraphs, stating the name

Fig. 6.1: General view of the Ka`ba inside the Sacred Mosque in Mecca, Saudi Arabia (Photo 2017).

The Kiswah of the Ka`ba and its Decoration

The building is traditionally covered by a cloth called the "Kiswah" also "Kiswa" made of fine silk dyed in black color and embroidered with silver and gold threads. The Kiswah is changed annually during the Hajj – Pilgrimage rituals (Fig. 6.3). The Kiswah of the preceding year is usually cut carefully into pieces and

of the Muslim leader, who commissioned or sponsored the Kiswah, and the production date. The commemorative epigraph can also be placed on the part of the Kiswah that covers the door--the curtain. The curtain is heavily decorated with textual ornamentation, mostly with Qur`anic verses and some selected attributes of God's names, such as "praise be to

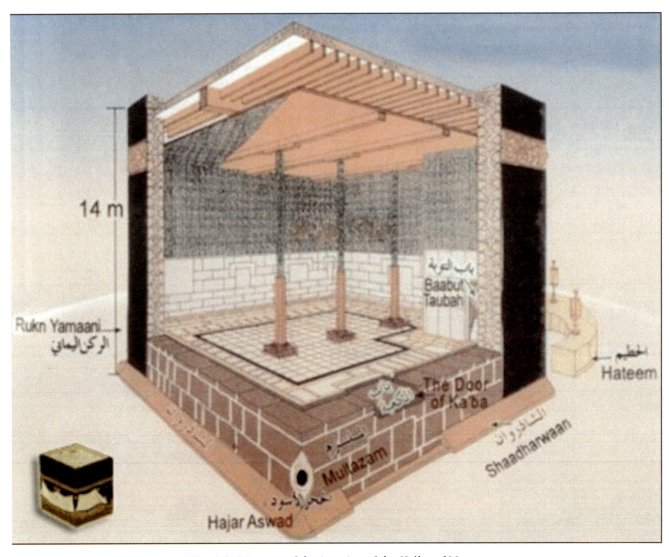

Fig. 6.2: Diagram of the interior of the Ka`ba of Mecca.

Allah, the self-sustaining, the most gracious, the most merciful, ..." (Fig. 6.4).

Arab sources record that the original tradition of covering the Ka`ba is as old as the time of Abraham. References also mention that Yemen supplied the annual Kiswah during the late pre-Islamic period. During the Muslim period, it became the responsibility of the official leader-Khalifah, caliph of the Muslim state, be that the Abbasid, the Fatimid, or the Ottoman. Since the early 20th century, the Kiswah has been manufactured in the city of Mecca and sponsored by the King of Saudi Arabia.

The tradition of covering the Ka`ba dates back to pre-Islamic times; over the long history of that practice, the color of the Kiswah changed. The Ka`ba is located at the center of the most sacred mosque in Islam "Al-Masjid Al-Haram;" also known as "Al-Haram Al-Makki," the sacred Meccan precinct in the city of Mecca.

The Black Stone of the Ka`ba of Mecca

The Black Stone is a corner stone in the building, fragmented, but held together by a ring and silver frame. According to Islamic tradition, it came down from heaven with Adam and Eve, and was originally white. Continuous touching and kissing, according to the tradition, have

Fig. 6.3: Placing a new Kiswah on the Ka`ba, 2015.

turned the color to black because the stone absorbs the sins of pilgrims. It is considered a venerable object, revered by pilgrims of both pre-Islamic and Islamic times. The black stone has survived difficult circumstances, when the Ka`ba was flooded, burned, demolished, rebuilt, and renovated. It is still in the same location-- the eastern corner of the building.

In 605 CE, the Ka`ba suffered damage due to seasonal flood followed by fire. It was rebuilt and Mohammed was involved in the process of replacing the black stone. Historians interpreted the Arab historical resources of that event, and infer that the details of the rebuilding, which was facilitated by an Abyssinian builder, followed the typical architectural method used in Abyssinia. It was during that rebuilding that Mohammed solved a dispute over who would be honored to lift the black stone and place it into its location at the eastern corner, by advising the leaders of Mecca to share the honor collectively. That event was visually depicted later in the work of 14th century Ilkhanid painting (Fig. 6.5). From Jami` Al-Tawarikh "A Compendium of Chronicles" (also known as World History by Rashid Al-Din), written in 1305-04, the artist depicts the Prophet instructing the four leaders to lift the four corners of the carpet while he positions the stone to be carried to its location.

The Sculptural Representations of the Idols in Mecca

Mecca was an important trade and commercial center connected with the trade network in the Arabian Peninsula. Its strategic location near Jeddah, which is a port on the Red Sea, made it an active trade city with bustling traffic of merchants and travelers from the Far East, Yemen, Syria, Persia, Iraq, and East Africa. They were visiting, relocating, and trading goods. Such an active city was host to people of different cultures, languages, rituals, and religious beliefs. It was a cosmopolitan city, with an accommodating outlook similar to all other major cities in the region.

Fig. 6.4: Details of the calligraphic decoration on the door of the Ka`ba.

The multi-religious, multi-cultural picture of pre-Islamic Mecca was necessary for its continually thriving economy. The existence of various rituals, beliefs, and religious places such as temples, shrines and sacred spaces demonstrate such a cultural scene. The Ka`ba itself was a premier center that accommodated various activities, rituals and services in the pre-Islamic era for diverse populations. It hosted polytheistic and monotheistic rituals and services. Arab classical literary sources describe in detail how the Ka`ba was associated with the art of religious sculpture and painting during that era.

There were statues of deities (Asnam, Awthan) installed inside the Ka`ba, on its roof, and around it. These statues represented divinities of different origins: South Arabian, Nabataean, Mesopotamian, Egyptian and probably as far as India and China. Near absent archaeological excavations in Mecca, especially in the immediate area of the Ka`ba, due to religious restriction, has contributed to the lack of helpful information about the subject. A valuable literary source regarding sculptural images at the Ka`ba comes from Ibn Al-Kalbi (737-819), an Arab historian and genealogist. In his most famous book "Kitab Al-Asnam," the

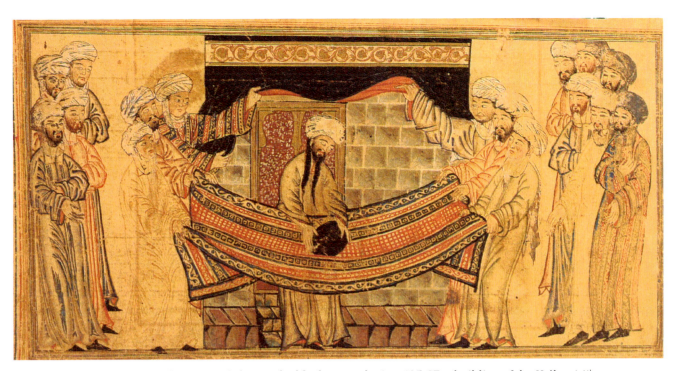

Fig. 6.5: Illustration of the event of placing the black stone during 605 CE rebuilding of the Ka`ba, 14th century illustration in Jami` Al-Tawarikh of Rashid Al-Din, Edinburgh University Library.

Book of Idols," Ibn Al-Kalbi provides a list of idols and deities that were worshipped in pre-Islamic Arabia. Occasionally his text provides details about the iconographical representations of those deities, the size of the statues, materials used in their production and other physical qualities.

Ibn Al-Kalbi also gives the name of a prominent professional sculptor in Mecca, and some details about the marketing of art objects in the peninsula during the immediate pre-Islamic period.

In certain instances, Ibn Al-Kalbi explains the geographical distribution of the cult of a particular deity with an etymological analysis of the deity's name. Although "The Book of Idols" contains some legendary tales associated with the tradition of ancient Biblical Prophets, the historical substance of the content is not devalued, especially when we bear in mind that the legendary tales were meant to substantiate the text of the Qur'an.

Several sources tell us that there were miniature statues in every house at Mecca, Yethrib, Ta'if and neighboring cities. Various copies of miniature statues were regularly displayed and sold at markets. There were also artisans whose professions were painting, decoration, jewelry-making and sculpture. One account mentions a certain Abu Rafi`, a companion of the Prophet Mohammed, and states that before joining Islam he used to work in carving statues of divination arrows at Zamzam by the Ka`ba at Mecca. Another artisan, Abu Tujarah, or Abu Tujrat, was not only a sculptor but also ran the business of selling his own products to the public. At Yethrib "Medinah," another sculptor is identified as Abd Al-Fulan Al-Najjar, apparently an Abyssinian whose profession was carving wooden statuettes of certain deities.

After Mohammed laid siege to Al-Ta'if in 628, the inhabitants of the city expressed their will for peace. They asked the Prophet for permission that their home statues be destroyed by their hands, and not by his followers. But at Najran, in the same year, the people of Najran, who were mostly Christians, yielded to Mohammed on certain terms. He assured the people of Najran that they would not be forced to give up their religion, and that their statues and painted images (icons) would be spared destruction. Statuettes made of ivory bones are reported to have been a favorite toy for children. The Prophet's wife `Aishah (also `Aisha) is reported to have possessed statuettes representing female figures and horses that she used to play with when she was seven years old.

The art of sculpture was popular among pre-Islamic people, not only because it served the rituals, but also because it reflected the aristocratic tastes of the elite in the community. In fact, this attitude continued and was obviously expressed during the Umayyad reign. Al-Tabari (839-923), a historian and Qur`anic exegete, relates that in 746 the Umayyad Caliph Al-Walid appointed Yusuf Ibn `Umar as his governor to Khurasan. Wanting to show his gratitude to Al-Walid, Yusuf sent him a huge convoy of gifts. Beside 1,000 Mamluks armed and mounted on horses and 500 concubines, Yusuf ordered wine jugs of gold and silver to be made.

He also ordered sculptures of gazelles, mountain goats, heads of wild beasts and various other images to be made and included in the convoy. This report legitimizes the existence of different sculptural objects––human, animal and other motifs––throughout Umayyad palaces in Syria and specially at Khirbat Al-Mafjar (see Chapter 7). The inclusion of art work as part of a gift to a Caliph can be interpreted as a gesture reflecting a predominant aristocratic taste.

Inside the peninsula itself, the reproduction of hundreds of statuettes of certain deities must have required artisans, equipment, tools and workshops. Replicas of statues are reported to have been displayed in the public marketplace at Mecca and were sold daily to pilgrims. The claim that every house in the peninsula contained at least one statuette is not unreasonable. In fact, this claim is further supported by the stories of the destruction of these miniature house-statues in various parts of the peninsula.

The sources tell us that the Prophet Mohammed, upon re-entering Mecca, took an immediate measure to terminate paganism. He supervised the destruction of major statues around the Ka`ba, and commanded certain companions to destroy major pagan sanctuaries along with their monumental statues. He then called for people to destroy all icons and images in their homes. In this regard, his wife `Aishah relates that Prophet Mohammed destroyed anything that resembled figurative representation in his house. He also announced the unlawfulness of selling or buying statues. This declaration of the Prophet suggests that the business of producing, selling and buying visual representations, statues, and paintings was common and widespread among the population.

Information on the number, appearance, style, and medium of the statues of the Ka`ba are incomplete and come from many literary sources. These sources state that the deity Hubal held a supreme position among the pre-Islamic population. A cornelian statue of Hubal stood inside the Ka`ba at Mecca and was in the form of a massive male figure. His cult involved divination and the forecasting of future events. According to Al-Azraqi, the cult of Hubal was well organized inside the Ka`ba, and a custodian guarded the statue, received the offerings and sacrifices and conducted future forecasting to pilgrims. Most references attribute the origin of the statue of Hubal to "Ma'ab" in Syria, but Al-Azraqi claims that it was brought from "Hit," also "Heet" in Iraq.

The massive statue of Hubal was a sculpture in the round, in the form of standing man with the right hand broken off, which the Qurayshites restored by replacing it with a golden hand. In 610 when the Meccans rebuilt the Ka`ba, the statue of Hubal was removed, and set beside the Ka`ba. After the rebuilding was completed, the statue was returned to its place. References to the events surrounding the destruction of the statue of Hubal are vague and general. In the year 630 the Prophet Mohammed reentered Mecca and destroyed the supposed 360 (or 36 according to some other sources), standing statues in and around the Ka`ba. It is reported that he did not enter the sanctuary until all images were removed and all paintings were washed off or erased except an icon depicting the Virgin Mary and baby Jesus, which he protected.

The event of removing and destroying those statues has been recorded by major early sources of the 9th and 10th centuries and supplemented by elaborate details from later writers of Islamic history. As for archaeological evidence of those statues, there has not been any official excavation at the site yet.

The iconoclasm of Mecca in 630 continued to reverberate throughout the Muslim world for centuries. There are many illustrations depicting that event, produced during the 16th century and later. The first illustration (Fig. 6.6) comes from a copy of a Safavid manuscript entitled Mir Khawand's Universal History, (Rawdhat Al-Safa), and dates to 1585-1595. The painting shows the Prophet Mohammed carrying Ali on his shoulders to reach the statues of idols. Both figures are depicted with veiled faces engulfed by glowing halos to emphasize their holiness. Ali was Mohammed's cousin, his son-in-law, and the fourth Caliph. He is shown reaching out and taking down the statues from the roof of the Ka`ba.

There are other illustrations of the event, produced between the 16th and 19th centuries in Iran and India. An interesting illustration, (Fig. 6.7), comes from a page of an album labeled as "History of Saints" and now in Rotterdam Museum, the Netherlands. The painting is in opaque colors on gold background. It was produced during the 18th century in Kashmir, and the artist elaborates on the details of the statues. Mohammed and `Ali are shown with their faces veiled but the features are still visible.

A Persian manuscript entitled "Hamla-i haydarî" – The Haydari Campaign, which is a detailed narrative of the life of the Prophet Mohammed, was produced in Kashmir, India in 1808. The manuscript is richly illustrated with descriptive depictions of the life of the Prophet.

A double page illustration, (Fig. 6.8), presents the event of the destruction of the Ka`ba idols' in descriptive details. The general scene depicts the march to the Ka`ba, where the figures of Mohammed and Ali are visualized allegorically as flames. On the right page, Ali is shown riding a white horse, and the Prophet Mohammed rides a camel. They are surrounded and accompanied by their followers. On the left page, the presentation of the actual destruction of the sculptural images is being conducted by Ali, who is depicted as a flame. There are 14 niches on both pages containing images of statues in different positions, and some are being destroyed.

The Mural Paintings Inside the Ka`ba

The accounts of the Prophet Mohammed's reentry into Mecca in the year 630 carry significant information about the wall paintings that were inside the sanctuary. Upon visiting the Ka`ba, he instructed his followers to remove and destroy the idols, statues, and painting that were there. Ibn Ishaq, an 8th century Arab historian, and the author of "The Biography of Mohammed," relates that on the day of the Prophet Mohammed's victory at Mecca, he entered the Ka`ba where he saw paintings of (Biblical) Prophets, angels and other figures on the walls. Among these figures there were depictions of Ibrahim (Abraham) as an old man holding arrows, and his son Isma`il (Ishmael). The Prophet then ordered all paintings to be effaced.

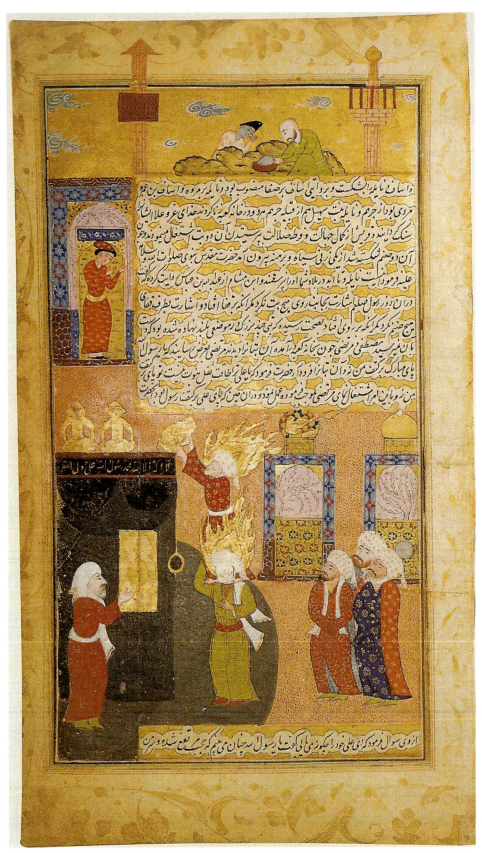

Fig. 6.6: The destruction of the statues of the idols of the Ka`ba, Safavid manuscript entitled Mir Khawand's Universal History, (Rawdhat Al-Safa), 1585-1595.

ARAB ART DURING THE EARLY ISLAMIC PERIOD 135

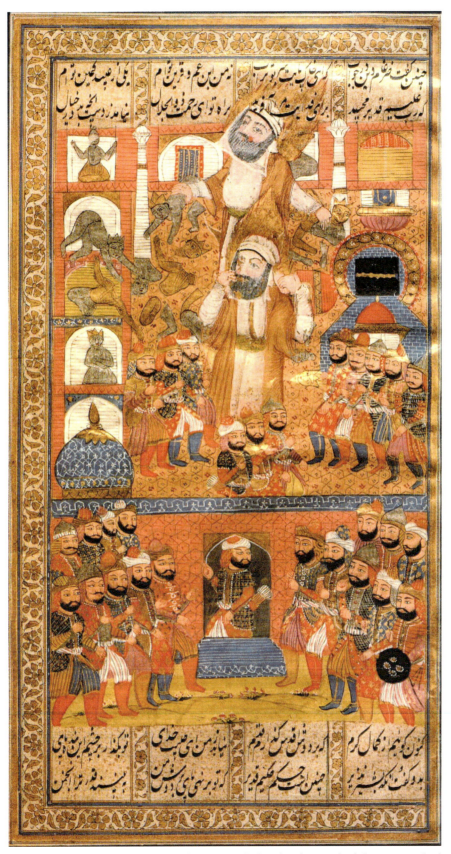

Fig. 6.7: The destruction of the idols of the Ka`ba, page of a book relating the life stories of religious figures, The Museum of Ethnography, Rotterdam (Wereldmuseum Rotterdam) Netherlands.

Fig. 6.8: The Prophet Mohammed approaching the Ka`ba and the destruction of the sculptural representations of the idols, colors and gold on paper, 32 x 20 cm, India 1808, Bibliotheque Nationale de France, Paris.

Al-Azraqi, a native of Mecca, (d. 865), and a major authority on the history of Mecca through his detailed book "Akhbar Mecca," the History of Mecca, is a significant source on this subject. His book contains valuable information about the architectural history of the Ka`ba, as well as the rebuilding and renovations in pre-Islamic and early Islamic periods. Al-Azraqi corroborated the statement of Ibn Ishaq, adding that the narratives included representations of Maryam and her child `Isa (Mary and Jesus). Another version of this event asserts that the Prophet ordered the effacement of all paintings except that of Mary and Jesus. The obliteration of the paintings was done by washing them out with a wet rag, which suggests that the pigment of these paintings was water soluble color on plaster walls. The remaining images are said to have survived until the sanctuary caught fire during the rebellion of the anti-Umayyad governor `Abdullah Ibn Al-Zubayr in 684.

Another interesting reference regarding the iconography of the paintings is reported by Al-Azraqi. A woman from the tribe of Banu Ghassan (Ghassanids) entered the Ka`ba during a pilgrimage. After seeing the painting of Mary, she stated that the features of Mary were very Arabian. The statement implies that the image of Mary was painted by a local artist who reflected the dominant aesthetic tastes of the population.

Al-Mas`udi, an Arab historian and geographer (896–956) elaborates on the subject of these paintings in some detail. He states that besides the paintings of Ibrahim and his son Isma`il riding on horseback, there were other scenes of their descendants, including Qusayy Ibn Kallab, the grandfather of the Qurayshites. About sixty scenes of the type occupied the interior of the Ka`ba according to Al-Mas`udi. Each figure in these scenes was represented along with the deity he embraced. Additionally, each scene showed the quality of the deity involved and the way its cult was practiced.

Al-Mas`udi is the only authority for this statement making it difficult to ascertain the authenticity of its content. However, in this statement he assumes that the paintings existed before the rebuilding of the Ka`ba by the Qurayshites in 608. This assumption is strongly supported by a unique poem attributed to the Yemenite pre-Islamic poet Juma`ah Al-Bariqi. In a verse, he mentions how the tribe of Khuza`ah acquired custody of the Ka`ba at Mecca, which he calls (Dhat Al-Rusum), meaning "the Ka`ba that contains paintings."

We don't know the exact appearance of those mural wall paintings, or the identity of the artists who painted them. But we can surmise that they were executed in a similar style to the painting of Qaryat Al-Faw discussed in Chapter 4, (see Figures 4.13, 4.14, 4.15). Arab historians relate accounts of the existence of artists, artisans and decorators in Mecca and Medinah during the late pre-Islamic and early Islamic time: 400-800 CE. Considering the significance of the city of Mecca during that time, it is reasonable to assume that the profession of art-making was desirable and profitable.

The Expansion of the Ka`ba During the Umayyad Time

The Ka`ba underwent several rebuilding campaigns before and after the time of early Islamic rule. In 683 the building was severely damaged by fire, and the governor of Mecca-- Abdullah Ibn Al-Zubayr, who was defiant to the Umayyads in Syria--rebuilt it and expanded its size with additional space. The rebuilding included thicker stone walls and the addition of mosaics that were taken from a church in San`a, Yemen. We do not know what happened to those mosaic or what they represented. According to the account of Al-Mas`udi, marble columns and marble glazing for the windows came from San`a and were also used in the rebuilding.

In 692 the Umayyad's authority under Abdul Malik sent an army and besieged Mecca, bombarded the Ka`ba, removed the additions, and rebuilt it to the previous form, which supposedly matched the original Abrahamic measurements. The present architectural form of the Ka`ba preserves the original nearly square plan.

THE REGION OF MEDINAH (YETHRIB)

The artistic and architectural scene of Yethrib (later Medinah) is not very clear during the period 400-800 CE. However, scattered references found in early sources help to compose a reasonable picture. One of these sources is Ibn Sa`d (784-845), who was an Arab historian and biographer. His major book "Kitab Al-Tabaqat Al-Kubra," a compendium of major personalities among the early Muslim community, is a valuable source for such cultural information. In the text he explains that the secretary of the Umayyad Caliph, Abd Al-Malik, lived in Medinah at a quarter called "Zuqaq Al-Naqqashin," or the quarter of the artisans: painters, decorators, scribes, and sculptors. This and other sources inform us that the use of brick, stone, and plaster was common in the construction of residential units, palaces, and fortresses in the region including the Tihama (southwest Arabia along the Red Sea). They were equally aware of architectural structures involving colorful interior paintings and exterior sculptural reliefs. Poets used certain terms for such ornamented structures, such as: "Bayt zukhruf," or decorated house.

Al-Azraqi describes in details the Umayyad palaces and relates that Mu`awiyah (d. 680), the founder of the Umayyad dynasty, lived in Mecca before assuming power in Damascus in 661. At Mecca, he built many luxurious houses. One was called "Al-Baydha'"or "the white one" because it was covered completely with plaster. Another house was called "Al-Raqta`" or "the dotted one," because it was built with red bricks and gypsum mortar. A third one was built by his servant Sa`d Al-Qasir, the exterior of which was adorned with "Tamathil," or sculptures carved in either plaster (stucco) or stone. This house must have exhibited artistic motifs and styles analogous to those of the Umayyad palaces in Syria.

The method of building houses of bricks and gypsum seems to have been widespread in Mecca and Medinah, before and during the early years of Islam, and was also known to South Arabian inhabitants in pre-Islamic periods. Luxurious materials were also used in the construction of domestic buildings. Accounts report that the Caliph Abu Bakr constructed a house where teak and cypress woods were used for the doors. Mu`awiyah imported artisans and construction workers from Iraq to Mecca to build his houses. These few selected references shed new light on the cultural and artistic attainments of pre-Islamic and early Islamic society and should help to dispel the traditional perception of pre-Islamic Arabia as devoid of any significant architectural tradition.

The sources also refer to the oasis area of Khayber, located some 170 kilometers (105.6 miles) northeast of Medinah. It is naturally fortified with high rocky formations, that were at times used as forts and castles. Kahyber's thriving agriculture was supported by plenty of natural spring water in an otherwise arid area. It was a target for the New Babylonians, and later was a safe haven to the Jewish population who were displaced by the Romans after the sack of Jerusalem. The Ghassanids controlled Khayber in the 7th century, and it later became an extension of the new Muslim territory. Ruins of forts are still visible; among them is the famous "Khayber Fort" (Fig. 6.9). Future field research would hopefully bring to light more information about the site.

The Prophet Mohammed's House-Mosque, Medinah

Medinah became the city of the new Muslim community after the Hijrah–the migration of the Prophet Mohammed in 622. It was also the seat of the political power and the first capital of Islam. The house of the Prophet was the first structure initiated in Media after the arrival of Mohammed, his family members, and his small community. It was a simple rectangular enclosure of 56 m (61.2 yards) with an open expandable courtyard, and functioned as a dwelling, meeting place, and space for communal prayer "Masjid," more commonly and incorrectly called "Mosque" (Fig. 6.10).

The original hypostyle building, which measured 30 by 35 m (98.4 ft by 114.8 ft), included a wall about 1.8 m (6 ft) high, surrounding the mostly open courtyard enclosure. It had three entrances, rooms for dwelling on one side, open to the courtyard, and a covered area portico, (Arabic Dhullah, also Zulla), to provide shade on the north side during hot days. The construction materials were mud bricks, palm tree trunks, and leaves. After the death of the Prophet, the mosque was enlarged, and in 707, the Umayyad Caliph Al-Walid demolished the old structure, enlarged the size to 84 by 100 m (275.5 ft by 328 ft), and used stone for the foundation, and a teak roof supported by stone columns.

Fig. 6.9: Aerial view of Khayber Fort, Tabuk area, Saudi Arabia.

According to Al-Tabari, an Arab historian, chronicler, and biographer (839-923), the mosque walls were decorated with mosaics similar to those of the Dome of the Rock and the Great Mosque of Damascus, both built during the reign of Al-Walid. Four minarets were added, along with a Mihrab under a small dome at the Qiblah wall. The structure underwent more change, renovation and expansion during the following periods. The pattern of expansion, modification, and enlargement has continued to the present, with near disappearance of the original structure.

The Minaret of the Prophet's Mosque

It is in the house-mosque that the need for an elevated area to call for prayer (Arabic Mi`thanah) and later Manarah (Minaret) evolved, with the purpose of calling together the community for congregational prayer. Bilal, a close companion of the Prophet, with a strong voice, stood at the top of a wall or on the roof of the mosque, and performed the call to prayer. That tradition later evolved into the incorporation of a tower-like structure with an internal or external staircase leading to the top where a person, the Mu`athin, also Mu`aththin, and Muazzin, would stand on a balcony or projected gallery to perform the call to prayer. The Mi`thanah also served as a point of reference for travelers to the mosque. With the addition of light on top of the Mi`thanah, it became Manarah/Minaret, a visual aid for travelers approaching the city. The origin of the Mi`thanah/Minarah echoes the Greek watch tower.

The original mosque of the Prophet in Medinah did not have a minaret, and the prayer was performed by a person – Mu`aththin, who

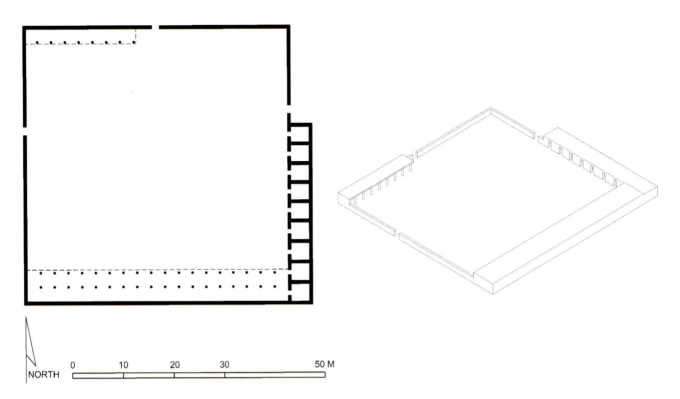

Fig. 6.10: Hypothetical floor plan and perspective drawing of the Prophet Mohammed's house-mosque in Medinah.

would stand on a high spot on the structure to call for the prayer. Hence Bilal, an African companion of the Prophet with a powerful voice was the first Mu`aththin. It was in the year 707 that the Umayyad Caliph Al-Walid renovated, enlarged and added four minarets to the mosque.

The Minbar of the Prophet's Mosque

The high seat, Minbar in Arabic, was a necessary mosque feature developed to address the congregation. It is essentially comparable to the "Ambo" in the early church or the "Lectern" or Pulpit. The need for an elevated platform or pulpit to address the congregation initiated the addition of the feature. Muslim sources record that the first form of Minbar that the Prophet Mohammed used at his mosque was a cut palm tree trunk fixed in the ground that he would lean on while addressing the congregation. Soon after, around 629, a wooden pulpit (Minbar) was made, which was a chair elevated by three steps.

As time passed, this mosque furniture evolved to the traditional elevated seat usually placed to the right of the Mihrab, which is a niche indicating the direction of prayer. In succeeding periods, the Minbar was made of fine wood, bricks or stone, and contained multiple steps.

The Mihrab of the Prophet's Mosque

In the traditional Arab culture, a Mihrab, which is a blind niche, designates the location of the seat of power, and acts as the focal point in an audience's communal space. It is found in community or gathering enclosures where the leader is seated. The architectural concept was adopted in the layout of the mosque with the additional function of the Mihrab as the indicator of the direction of prayer (toward the Ka`ba in Mecca). It is a blind semi-circular niche located on the Qiblah wall of the mosque, usually void of figurative decoration but can contain a Qur`anic calligraphic inscription as well as floral and geometric designs (Fig. 6.11).

ARAB ART DURING THE EARLY ISLAMIC PERIOD

Large mosques may have more than one Mihrab on the Qiblah wall.

The original mosque of the Prophet in Medinah did not have a Mihrab, though prayer was directed towards the east. After more than a year, the prayer was directed to the Ka`ba of Mecca. Sources do not mention the mosque having a special form for the Mihrab during that period; it was probably a flat central area on the Qiblah wall. The first distinguished niche-like Mihrab was added to the Qiblah wall during the Umayyad reign of Al-Walid, as part of a general

Fig. 6.11: Mihrab and Minbar at the mosque of `Amr Ibn Al-`As, (Fustat), Cairo, Egypt.

enlargement of the mosque. In 632, the Prophet Mohammed died and was buried in one of the rooms of his house-mosque at Medinah. Hence the complex included a residential space, a prayer area, a space for general community meetings, and a burial place for the Prophet.

The open courtyard plan of the house-mosque of the Prophet, with its architectural furniture–the Minbar, Mihrab, Minaret–would later become the prototype for the architectural planning of future mosques in Iraq, Syria, Iran, Egypt, Tunisia, and elsewhere in the Islamic territories. The rectangular/square plan of such buildings was derived from the long-standing Arab architectural tradition found in the pre-Islamic era across many regions. The rapid expansion of the Prophet's house-mosque, along with the continued development/additions to the complex throughout time makes it difficult to trace and identify the original structure of the compound.

Selected Bibliography

Al-Hamdani Hasan Ibn Ahmed, *Al-Iklil*, ed. Nabih A. Faris, Princeton: Princeton University Press, 1940.

____, *Kitab Al-Jawharatayn Al-`Atiqatayn Al-Ma'i`atayn min Al-Safra' wa Al-Baydha'*, ed. C. Toll, Uppsala, 1968.

Al-Tabari Mohammed Ibn Jarir, *Tarikh Al-Rusul wa Al-Muluk,* ed. M. Abu Al-Fadhl Ibrahim, Cairo. 1960-69.

Al-Waqidi Mohammed Ibn `Umar, *Kitab Al-Maghazi*, ed. M. Jones, Oxford: Oxford University Press, 1966.

Al-Ya`qubi, Ahmed Ibn Abi Ya`qub, *Kitab Al-Buldan.* ed. M. J. de Goeje, Leiden 1892. trans. G. Wiet as *Les Pays*, Cairo 1937.

Al-Zabidi, M. Murtadha, *Taj Al-`Arus min Jawahir Al-Qamus*, various editions.

Beeston A. F. L., Johnston T. M., Serjeant R. B. and Smith G. R., *Arabic Literature to the End of the Umayyad Period*, Cambridge: Cambridge University Press. 1983.

Bevan A. A., ed., *The Naqa'idh of Jarir and Al-Farazdaq*, Leiden: B. J. Brill, 1905.

Creswell, K. A. C., *Early Muslim Architecture*, Oxford, Clarendon Press, 1940.

Faris Nabih A., ed., *The Book of Idols*, being an English translation of Ibn Al-Kalbi's *Kitab Al-Asnam*, Princeton: Princeton University Press, 1952.

Hamidulla M., *The Battlefield of the Prophet Muhammad*, Hyderabad: Hamid and Company. 1973.

Harding, G. Lankester, *An Index and Concordance of Pre-Islamic Arabian Names and inscriptions*, Toronto: University of Toronto, 1971.

Hillenbrand, Robert. *Islamic Architecture, Form Function and Meaning*, 1972-73. Edinburgh: Edinburgh University Press, 1994.

Ibn Al-Athir, *Al-Kamil fi Al-Tarikh*, Beirut: Dar al-Kitab al-'Ilmiah, 1965.

Ibn Al-Kalbi, Hisham, *Kitab Al-Asnam*, ed. Ahmed Z. Pasha, Cairo 1924, rep. 1965.

Ibn Al-Zubayr, Aḥmead Ibn Al-Rashid. *Kitab Al-Thakha`ir wa Al-Tuhaf, Book of Gifts and Rarities,* Transl. & ed. by Ghada-Al-Hijjawi Al-Qaddumi, Cambridge: Cambridge University Press, 1996.

Ibn Hisham Abd Al-Malik, *Kitab Al-Tijan fi Muluk Himyar `An Wahb Ibn Munabbih*, Hayderabad, 1928.

____, *Kitab Sirat Rasul Allah `An Ibn Ishaq*, ed. F. Wüstenfeld as *Das Leben Muhammed Nach Muhammed Ibn Ishaq*, Gottingen, 1858-60.

Ibn Sa`d, Mohammed, *Kitab Al-Tabaqat Al-Kabir*, eds. E. Sachau and E. Mittwoch as *Biographien Muhammad*, Leiden, 1904-40.

Martin, Frishman and Hasan-Uddin Khan, Ed. *The Mosque: History, Architectural Development and Regional Diversity*, London & New York: Thames and Hudson, 1994.

Michell, George, Ed., *Architecture of the Islamic World: Its History and Social Meaning, with a Complete Survey of Key Monuments*, London: Thames and Hudson, 1984.

Mohammad Gharipour and İrvin Cemil Schick Ed., *Calligraphy and Architecture in the Muslim World.*, Edinburgh University Press, 2014.

Nees Lawrence, *Perspectives on Early Islamic Art in Jerusalem*, Brill Academic Publication, Leiden, 2015.

Potts D. T., "Northeastern Arabia: from the Seleucids to the Earliest Caliphs.", *Expedition*, 26, iii (1984) pp. 21- 30.

Rosenthal F., *A History of Muslim Historiography*, Leiden: E. J. Brill, 1968.

Yaqut Al-Hamawi, *Marasid Al- 'Ittila` 'Ala 'Asma' Al-'Amkinah wa Al-Biqa`*, eds. T. G. J. Juynboll and J. J. Bgaal, Paris, 1850-64.

CHAPTER 7

ARAB ART DURING THE EARLY ISLAMIC PERIOD IN IRAQ, SYRIA, AND PALESTINE

The new Arab state emerged in the 7th century in the Hijaz region, and expanded rapidly during the time of the Prophet Mohammed to include the whole of the Arabian Peninsula. The ensuing years of the four Caliphs–the successors of the Prophet, also known as the Rashidun Caliphs, "the rightly-guided leaders" (632- 661) – witnessed a rapid expansion to the north and northwest of the peninsula. The Arab armies defeated the Sassanian empire, and a vast former Persian territory in central Asia was annexed to the swiftly expanding Arab state. Similarly, the Arab state defeated the Byzantine forces in Syria, Palestine, Egypt, and parts of Anatolia. The heritage of both the Sassanians and the Byzantines was assimilated into many aspects of the new Arab state, now called the Islamic State.

EARLY MOSQUES IN IRAQ

The Old Mosque of Basrah

The city of Basrah is located in southern Iraq, on the Shat Al-`Arab waterway between Kuwait and Iran. It was founded in 635 by the new Arab state and used primarily as a military encampment for the Muslim army. It was there in 635 that the first and oldest mosque outside of Medinah was erected. The mosque was a simple rectangular space, enclosed by a fence of reeds. Following the Medinah model, the mosque was meant to serve multi-functional tasks. Besides daily, seasonal, and annual religious activities, it was used as an office for the community leader, governor, or Caliph.

The Great Mosque of Basrah was used as educational classrooms, a place for community meetings, elections, lodging for travelers, and a variety of other social functions. Furthermore, the space served as a courthouse, and as an office of distribution of public assets and pensions. It was a headquarters for the city government as well as for military leaders, where major issues would be discussed and decided on. The leader of the city lived next door in Dar Al-Emarah (Dar Al-Imarah), with direct access to the main prayer court.

The Basrah mosque suffered fires and flooding and was rebuilt several times. According to Al-Baladhuri, a 9th century Arab historian, the mosque was considerably enlarged during the reign of the Umayyad governor Zeyad ibn Abih in 665. The construction materials included bricks, mortar and stones. A teak roof sat on five rows of stone columns, and the governor's residence was erected adjacent to the mosque. Other accounts suggest that it was in that mosque that the first Maqsurah was constructed. The Maqsurah is a protective enclosure composed of a wooden screen near or around the Mihrab, or in the center of the Qiblah wall, and includes the Minbar. It is likely that the Umayyad authorities in Syria, especially during the reign of Mu`awiyah (661-680), initiated such an addition to the prayer area as a protective measure for the ruler, who was responsible for leading congregational prayer. Eventually the Great Mosque of Basrah developed into a prestigious center of learning, where eminent scholars, historians, scientists, linguists, and philologists lectured regularly. Not much of the original plan and structure has survived due to consecutive alteration and remodeling.

The Great Mosque of Kufah and Dar Al-Emarah (Governor's House)

Medinah was the capital of the Arab-Islamic state beginning in the time of Prophet Mohammed and the Rashidun Caliphs until the time of the fourth Caliph, `Ali ibn Abi Talib, who transferred the capital to Kufah, in Iraq in 657. Kufah is located on the Euphrates River, not far from Hirah–the capital of the Lakhmids. Kufah was originally intended as a military garrison; it was planned with trenches surrounding it in 638, during the time of the second Caliph `Umar.

Fig. 7.1: The Great Mosque of Al-Kufah and the adjacent Dar Al-Emarah, Kufah, Iraq, The National Archives, London, (Photo 1915).

Following the pattern of the Prophet Mohammed, a great mosque, rectangular in plan, was built in Kufah in 639, emulating the same architectural plan of the Medinah mosque (Figures 7.1, 7.2). Its square plan measures about 343 feet on each side – about 104.5 meters. The square mosque is surrounded by a thick wall of about 3 meters high and fortified by semi-round buttresses (Fig. 7.3). The construction materials included marble columns from Iran, and repurposed building materials from ruined palaces in nearby Hirah. Professional Iraqi builders, with knowledge of Hiran and Sassanian building techniques, contributed to the construction process. The residential complex, "Dar Al-Emarah" the home of the governor of Kufah, was constructed on the Qiblah side next to the Mosque. Records indicate that the plan and other details of the palace had similarities with typical Arab palaces in Hirah. The accounts mention that columns from ruined Mundhirids palaces in Hirah were reused in the building. Within Dar Al-Emarah, there was the public treasury, "Bayt Al-Mal." The arrangement of a governor's residence "Dar Al-Emarah" adjacent to a main mosque in the Islamic city became a customary pattern for centuries across Islamic lands. Much of the original structure and materials of the Great Mosque of Kufah complex have changed, again because of renovations and additions that occurred in succeeding periods.

The Great Mosque of Wasit and Dar Al-Emarah (Governor's House)

Similar developments took place in Wasit, located on the Tigris River, midway between Kufah and Basrah. Wasit was established in 702, during the Umayyad period, and a great mosque and Dar- Al-Emarah complex was erected by its governor. The site and remains of the renovated old structure are still visible in Wasit, the present city of Kut in central Iraq.

With the assassination of the fourth Caliph `Ali, in Kufah in 661, the Umayyad governor of Syria seized the opportunity and proclaimed the Khilafah–leadership in Damascus. With that a new phase of a monarchic system was implemented as the Umayyads gradually consolidated their power in Syria, Iraq, Iran, Egypt, North Africa and Southern Spain.

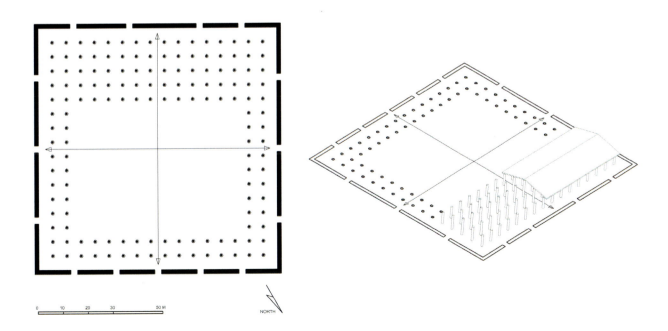

Fig. 7.2: Floor plan of the Great Mosque of Al-Kufah, Iraq.

148 CHAPTER 7

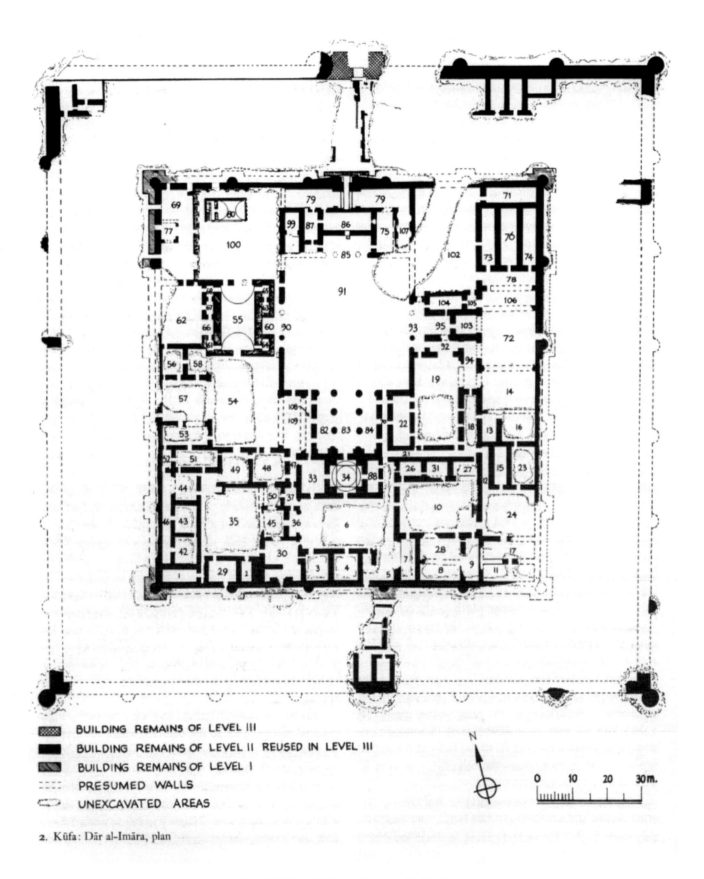

2. Kūfa: Dār al-Imāra, plan

Fig. 7.3: Dar Al-Emarah, plan, Kufah, Iraq.

The Umayyad authorities sponsored official buildings; both religious and secular.

EARLY ARCHITECTURE IN JERUSALEM

The Arab army recovered Jerusalem from the Byzantines in 637 – during the reign of the second Rashidi Caliph `Umar. Following the pattern of planning in a newly acquired city, similar to Basrah and Kufah, a large mosque was planned in Jerusalem. According to Arab historic accounts, a communal prayer area-mosque, probably square, was planned in the area of the sacred precinct, "Mount Moriah." This report is corroborated by the account of the 7th century Frankish Bishop Arculf, who visited Jerusalem around 670. He described a large square place of Muslim prayer – a mosque. He states that the location was on the Temple Mount. Arab sources indicate the location was near the Church of the Holy Sepulcher. We have very little details regarding this early mosque in Jerusalem, but it could very well have been the initial plan for the Aqsa Mosque, which came later.

The Umayyads sponsored a program of architectural structures, both religious and secular, in the greater Syrian region. Jerusalem was a prime city for such a program, due to its religious sacredness shared by the three monotheistic groups: Jews, Christians and Muslims. Three significant structures were erected in the area: the Aqsa Mosque, The Dome of the Rock, and the Palatial Complex (Fig. 7.4).

The Aqsa Mosque

Called "Aqsa," in Arabic meaning the farthest from Mecca and the Ka`ba; the Prophet's mosque in Medinah is called "Adna," meaning the nearest to Mecca. The Aqsa Mosque is located in the Old City of Jerusalem. The rectangular roof measures 80 by 55 meters. It has a silvery lead dome with wooden construction at the center of the Qiblah wall. Historians believe the earliest use of the pointed arch was found in the original structure of the Aqsa Mosque. The Ablaq technique is used in the architecture of the Aqsa Mosque, the Dome of the Rock, and the Great Mosque of Damascus. "Ablaq," which refers to the alternating ashlars of dark and light stone in the facades and walls of the structure, is a Syrian building technique supported by the abundance of local stones of various colors and shades.

Islamic tradition states that the Aqsa Mosque existed during the time of Adam and throughout the times of all of the Biblical prophets. The building has suffered extensive damages since its recorded erection during the reign of the second Caliph `Umar (634-644). It was enlarged and strengthened in 705 during the Umayyad times. Further damage impacted the building; it was rebuilt twice more during the Abbasid period, in 754 and 780.

Records indicate that the building witnessed continued rebuilding, expansion, renovation, and maintenance. The present structure of the Aqsa Mosque (Fig. 7.4) may reflect the last major rebuilding in 1035, during the Fatimid period. When the Crusaders conquered Jerusalem (1099-1187), the Aqsa Mosque was used as a palace, a military facility, and as a headquarters for the Templar Knights. They also transformed the Dome of the Rock to a church. In 1187, the Muslims retook Jerusalem and both mosques were restored to their original functions.

The Palatial Complex (Umayyad Royal Residence)

The Umayyad Royal Residence complex is composed of luxury palaces, pavilions and other residential facilities, located just to the south of the Aqsa Mosque (Fig. 7.4), linked together with a direct access bridge. Archaeological work in the area has confirmed the use of the Umayyad royal family complex as residential in nature; construction began by the builder Al-Walid I (668-715). The main palace measures 84 by 96 meters, with an open

Fig. 7.4: The Sacred Precinct, Jerusalem: Locations of the Aqsa Mosque, the Dome of the Rock, and the Umayyad Royal Residential - Palatial Complex.

central courtyard paved with flagstones. It has a massive foundation that extends 9 meters deep in order to accommodate the original multi-level structure. Amongst the ruins, the presence of a mosque has been suggested by excavators. The familiar arrangement of a leader's palace built next to the main mosque continues the tradition found at Dar Al-Emarah, which was next to and directly accessible by the Great Mosque. As discussed, this trend is also found in Kufah and Basrah. Further research will provide a more comprehensive understanding of the architectural and functional nature of the site.

The Dome of the Rock

The magnificent Dome of the Rock was the first monumental structure built in Jerusalem by the Umayyad Caliph Abd Al-Malik during (687-691). It is a commanding structure built as a mosque, but also served as a political statement of power and might. It was designed and built by local Syrian and Palestinian architects who were knowledgeable of contemporary building trends in the cosmopolitan region. Characteristics of neighboring architecture are found in the details of the mosque, from the form to the decorating techniques.

ARAB ART DURING THE EARLY ISLAMIC PERIOD IN IRAQ, SYRIA, AND PALESTINE

The Dome of the Rock has generated various interpretations among researchers. It has been interpreted as a mosque to commemorate the Qur`anic "Night Journey" called "Al-Isra` wa Al-Mi`raj" of the Prophet Mohammed, a route that went from Mecca to Jerusalem to heaven. Islamic tradition considers the platform of the Aqsa precinct a sacred space for that reason. The mosque is built on the highest point of the stone platform. Some have argued that the monument was intended to divert Muslim pilgrimage from Mecca to Jerusalem, when Mecca was governed by the anti-Umayyad rival, Abdullah ibn Al-Zubayr. Others claim that the Umayyad authority built the superb structure to rival the splendor of the Christian churches in the region, especially the Byzantine Church of the Holy Sepulcher.

Considering the predominantly Christian population of greater Syria at the time (which included Palestine), the Dome of the Rock can be realized as a fulfilment of obligation, a statement of power, and a landmark of the new Muslim authority in the region.

The building has gone through repairs and reconstruction, however the essence of the design and interior decoration has mostly remained unchanged. The octagonal mosque is topped by a wooden dome that sits on marble columns, which form two rows of circular colonnades (Figures 7.5, 7.6).

Fig. 7.5: The Dome of the Rock, general view, Jerusalem, Palestine, completed 691.

The interior is covered with mosaic decoration of non-figurative designs: mainly floral, vegetal, and geometric patterns. The mosaic work reveals Byzantine influence in visual vocabulary as well as method and technique; it is possible that the artisans were skillfully trained in the Byzantine mosaic tradition. There are grilled windows with colored glass positioned near the base of the drum and along the walls, which allows natural light to funnel in, reflecting and shimmering on the mosaic compositions.

Perhaps the most important characteristic of the decoration program in the structure is the inclusion, for the first time, of Arabic calligraphy in the Kufic style. The original mosaic text consists of carefully selected verses from the Qur`an, spread around the interior and possibly on the exterior as well, which were replaced by Ottoman ceramic tiles in the 16th century and later. The selected verses focus on the oneness of Allah (God), and the message and nature of Jesus Christ as a Prophet. The Qur`anic text represents a dialogue addressing the Christian population of Jerusalem directly. In this way, the mosque serves as a forum encouraging theological and cultural discourse.

As mentioned, the Dome of the Rock represents the earliest Arab-Islamic structure to use Arabic text in general and specifically in old Kufic calligraphy. This use introduced a new architectural concept, one in which the building

Fig. 7.6: Sectional axonometric view through the Dome of the Rock, Jerusalem, Palestine.

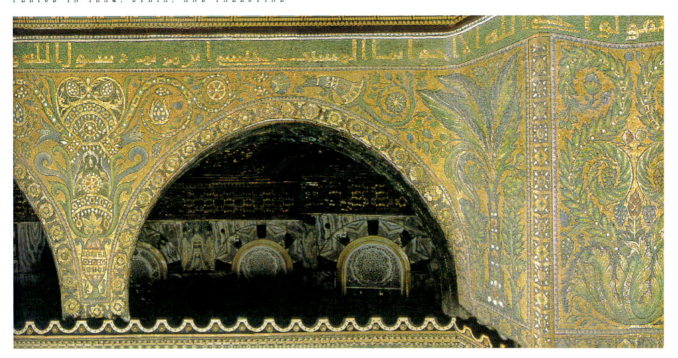

Fig. 7.7: Qur`anic inscription in the inner face of the arcade, the Dome of the Rock, Jerusalem, Palestine.

Fig. 7.8: Mosaic work, interior of the Dome of the Rock, Jerusalem, Palestine.

speaks to, debates, and converses with visitors (Figures 7.7, 7.8).

This new and unparalleled trend in Arab art–within the phase of the Islamic era–would continue to appear through the succeeding centuries across Arab and Islamic lands. Examples include the walls of the Al-Hamra` complex in Granada, Spain; the Muqarnas ceiling of the Cappella Palatina, Palermo, Sicily; the interior of the Taj Mahal Mausoleum at Agra, India and many other structures, both secular and religious. The introduction of the use of decorative writing and the concept of textual interaction in early Arab-Islamic architecture, as early as 691 at the Dome of the Rock, marks the birth of a remarkable Arab visual trend that can be called "Oratorical Architecture."

EARLY MOSQUES IN DAMASCUS

The Great Mosque of Damascus

Also known as the Umayyad Mosque in Damascus (built 705-715), the splendor of the Great Mosque of Damascus represents the primacy of early Arab-Islamic architecture. The mosque is located in the old part of Damascus, built on the layers of former cultural and religious structures. Archaeological research reveals that the site was originally occupied by a temple for the worship of the ancient Arab (Phoenician – Nabataean) deity Haddad in the 8th century BCE. After the Roman conquest in the 1st century BCE, the temple was incorporated as the cult of the Roman god Jupiter. In the 4th century CE, the Byzantines built a Basilica for St. John the Baptist at the same site. The space was utilized by Christians and Muslims for decades

Fig. 7.9: Aerial view of the Great Mosque of Damascus, Syria, (705-715).

Fig. 7.10: Interior view of the Great Mosque of Damascus, Syria.

before it was dedicated as a Muslim mosque by the Caliph Al-Walid in 705.

The open courtyard plan of the mosque follows the ancient Arab tradition as described in Pre-Islamic Arabian architecture, which was then reintroduced with the Prophet's mosque in Madinah. The structure (Fig. 7.9) is rectangular (157 x 100 meters) and consists of two main sections: the open courtyard, which is surrounded by porticos with horseshoe arches, as well as the covered interior space of the prayer area.

The covered interior prayer area is composed of a large rectangle containing three aisles that run parallel to the Qiblah wall (Fig.7.10). There are four Mihrabs on the Qiblah wall. The main Mihrab occupies the center and is highlighted by the dome and the nave. The roof of the prayer area sits on three rows of tall columns, forming double-tiered arches that support the height of the roof. Significant innovative elements introduced for the first time at the mosque included the horseshoe arch, the double-tiered arch, the Maqsurah, and the square minaret. Other important architectural elements found at the mosque are the pointed arch, the Ablaq technique, the colored glass windows, and mosaic painting. Many of these elements were later expressed at the Great Mosque of Cordoba in Spain.

The Mosaic Work at the Great Mosque of Damascus

Mosaics at the Great Mosque of Damascus cover the facade and arcades in the courtyard. Local Syrian workmen, along with imported artisans and materials from Constantinople were utilized in the making of the mosaics. Stylistically and technically speaking, the mosaics bear resemblance to those at the Dome of the Rock. Measuring about 37 meters in length and 5 meters in height, landscape scenes and natural motifs fill the mosaics, with luxury homes, tall trees and flowing rivers lush against golden backgrounds. It is believed that the scenes symbolize the visual concept of paradise as described in the Qur`an. Other researchers have interpreted the scenes as representing the beauty of Syria and its rivers (Fig. 7.11).

UMAYYAD SECULAR ARCHITECTURE

The Arabs during pre-Islam were in direct contact with the two powerful empires at the time: the Byzantines and the Sassanians. Important linking points were via the Ghassanids in Syria and the Lakhmids in Hirah. Through trade and travel, the Arabs were familiar with the cultural commodities and lifestyles among the authorities and citizens of both empires. The Umayyads were not only aware of, but were also keen to match the grandiosity of architectural monuments, splendid palaces, and the aristocratic tastes found in the lands north of Hirah and Syria.

The Umayyads were interested in creating and maintaining their own image of power and wealth, through constructing impressive structures, establishing royal etiquettes, and upholding elegant lifestyles. Such demonstrations of opulence are found in the monumentality of architecture and level of artistry displayed at the Aqsa Mosque, the Dome of the Rock, and the Great Mosque of Damascus. Other expressions of the attitude are

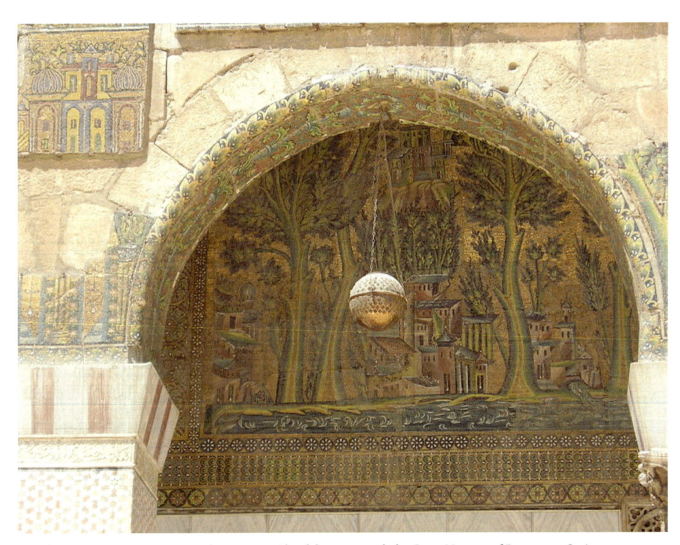

Fig. 7.11: Mosaics at the western side of the courtyard, the Great Mosque of Damascus, Syria.

Fig. 7.12: Aerial view of Qusayr `Amra, 8th century, Jordan.

found in the Umayyad royal palaces, which were scattered across Syria and Palestine.

The Umayyad royal palace complexes vary in size and function. Besides caravan rest and service stations, built for merchants and travelers along trade routes, private royal complexes were also constructed. Some were smaller structures, probably serving as a retreat or rest area for authorities, while others were large with multiple sections and facilities surrounded by heavy walls, gates and defensive systems. Other palatial complexes were built next to farmed and forested fields, providing private hunting areas for the royal family members. These royal palaces are scattered throughout greater Syria (presently in Syria, Lebanon, Jordan, and Palestine).

Some of the well-known palaces are Qasr Burqu`, Qasr Al-Minya, Qasr Harrana "Kharrana," Qasr Al-Hayr Al-Sharqi, Qasr Al-Hayr Al-Gharbi, Qasr Al-Mashta, "Mushatta, also Mshatta" the Palatial complex in Jerusalem mentioned above, and Qusayr `Amra. The latter is particularly notable for the paintings that cover the interior and ceilings of the audience hall, "the Diwan" and the bath.

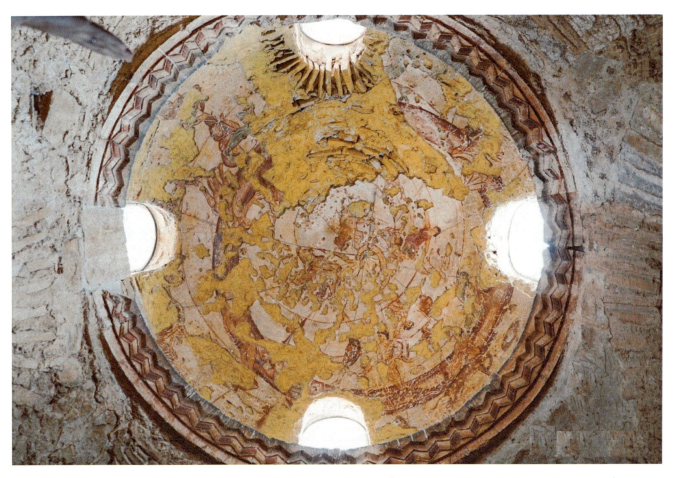

Fig. 7.13: Astronomical chart of the constellations, painting on the ceiling of the bath, Qusayr `Amra, Jordan.

Qusayr `Amra

Qusayr `Amra is a small Umayyad royal retreat, constructed of local limestone, and located some 60 miles east of Amman. The building is part of a hunting lodge, and consists of an audience hall for group activities, and a bath annexed to two service rooms. The rooms were originally paved with marble slabs. The water supply system to the bath was equipped with a furnace (boiler) and was connected to an outside water well that used an animal-powered hydraulic system, water wheel, and cistern. To the northwest of this building, some 300 meters, the remnants of a military garrison with a small castle have been identified by archaeologists. The courtyard of the castle contained a watchtower surrounded by rooms. Evidence of a second hydraulic lifting system has been identified near the castle, which may have been used to irrigate the surrounding fields. The construction of Qusayr `Amra is believed to date to 723-743 (Fig. 7.12).

The interior of Qusayr `Amra comprises a rich program of figurative depictions, executed in painting and applied to the plastered walls. The paintings display a variety of subjects, including scenes of nature, birds, animals; scenes of hunting, wrestling, farming; and scenes of dancers and musicians. There is also a painting on the interior dome ceiling of the bath that depicts the constellations. It is believed to be the oldest visual representation of astronomical subject matter (Fig. 7.13).

The paintings at the Qusayr `Amra retreat-bath compliment the function of the building as a soothing space meant for relaxation. This concept is further emphasized by the inclusion of scenes depicting female figures

ARAB ART DURING THE EARLY ISLAMIC PERIOD IN IRAQ, SYRIA, AND PALESTINE

Fig. 7.14: Painting of a female dancer-server on the spandrel, Qusayr `Amra, Jordan.

Fig. 7.15: Reproduced painting of the "Six Kings," Qusayr `Amra, Jordan.

bathing, dancing, or serving. Their femininity is highlighted: they are partially nude, clothed in mini-skirts and holding plates or dancing. The figures are found on a spandrel near the lower level of the interior (Fig. 7.14).

The decoration program at Qusayr `Amra echoes the power of the Umayyad Empire. The famous scene of the "Six Kings" is the focus of such a theme. It is important to note that most of the paintings in the abandoned structure are

Fig. 7.16: Aerial view of Mshatta complex, Jordan.

severely damaged from centuries of continuous abuse and negligence. The paintings of the Six Kings are badly damaged at the present time, but are undergoing conservation. In 1899, the Czech archaeologist Alois Musil discovered the site and revisited it with a photographer and a professional artist called Mielich. Mielich produced drawings and color sketches of the details of the paintings as well as the structure itself.

Although the reproductions produced by Mielich may seem insignificant, they are considered the best surviving source for study of the original program. In particular, the Six Kings paintings display royal foreign personalities, identified partially by Arabic and Greek text. Further research identifies the figures as Roderick, the ruler of Visigothic Spain, a Sassanian king (Shah), a Byzantine emperor, and the Negus, ruler of Abyssinia. The identities of the other two figures are debatable, but could be Chinese, Anatolian, or Indian leaders (Fig. 7.15). The reasoning behind the inclusion of the Six Kings painting at such a location remains unclear. It is possible that the Caliph who built the structure, most probably Al-Walid II, wanted visual confirmation of his power by symbolically bringing world leaders together in his visiting room, "the Diwan." Another possible interpretation is that Al-Walid II wished to align himself with or show his victory over the imperial powers of the time.

Interestingly, at the top of the alcove facing the entrance, there is yet another painting of an enthroned person, this time with a halo. The identity of the figure is not clear, but could be a depiction of the master of the bathhouse.

Mshatta Complex

"Mshatta" is a vast unfinished square complex, located south of Amman, Jordan. It is believed that the complex was sponsored by Al-Walid II during his short reign (743-744). The complex might have been intended as a temporary government headquarters. The original name of the complex is unknown, and the Arabic name "Mshatta," which simply means winter resort, was given to the complex by local people. It is the largest of all late Umayyad buildings (Fig. 7.16).

The complex has an entrance hall, mosque, audience hall, and residential quarters. The outer wall, which stands about 3 meters high, is built with fine ashlar masonry and regularly spaced with semi-circular buttresses, with a gate flanked by two semi-octagonal towers. The most notable feature of this unfinished complex is the richly carved south facade of the wall, now in The Pergamon Museum in Berlin (Fig. 7.17). It has a continuous band of zigzags, some 47 meters long, with large rosettes occupying the spaces of the zigzag triangles.

The left side of the facade contains carved scenes of a variety of animals and mythological creatures such as birds, lions, griffins and others. The right side of the wall is void of such images and decorated with vegetal and floral motifs. The lack of animals on this side may be

Fig. 7.17: Part of the outer wall of the Mshatta complex at the Pergamon Museum in Berlin, Germany.

Fig. 7.18: Aerial view of Khirbat Al-Mafjar, Jericho, Palestine.

Fig. 7.19: Mosaic work at the bathhouse area, Khirbat Al-Mafjar, mid 8th century, Jericho, Palestine.

Fig. 7.20: Examples of stucco statues from Khirbat Al-Mafjar, Jericho, Palestine.

attributed to its location behind the Qiblah wall of the mosque.

Khirbat Al-Mafjar, Jericho, Palestine

Next, we have a desert fortified royal palace complex, constructed by the Umayyads near Jericho (Arabic: Ariha), in Palestine between 724-743. The authority of the construction was possibly the Caliph Hisham or his successor Al-Walid II. According to historical accounts, the complex was destroyed by a massive earthquake in 747. The rectangular plan of the complex is enclosed within strong walls fortified by circular towers at equal intervals. The complex has the palace proper, which is a two-story structure, with "Diwan" or audience hall, a courtyard, two mosques, a magnificent large bathhouse, a fountain pavilion, a possible khan "caravanserai," and a large forecourt paved with flagstones, probably used for royal sports (Fig. 7.18).

Archaeologists and historians agree that this complex epitomizes the grandeur and sophistication of Arab art in both architectural plan and visual decoration during the late Umayyad period. The complex itself is a masterpiece of architectural ingenuity. Of grand forum, the complex displays superb works of art. The outstanding mosaic works in the palace, audience hall, bathhouse, and other spaces display a variety of geometric, floral and vegetal motifs (Fig. 7.19). Interestingly, many of the mosaic patterns are still used in traditional and contemporary Palestinian textile designs.

Archaeologists recovered many fragments of colored stucco sculptures of partially nude women depicted as dancers and entertainers. Such sculptures were positioned in niches and alcoves in the bathhouse and in the Diwan; Figure 7.20 is an example of such sculptural representation. The figure on the left is believed to be a depiction of the Caliph Hisham, standing on a pedestal, with two lions symbolizing his

Fig. 7.21: Stucco of the dome cap of the Diwan. Khirbat Al-Mafjar, Jericho, Palestine.

royal power and authority. A similar statue of a "Caliph" is found in Qasr Al-Hayr Al-Gharbi. Archaeologists believe that the statue was originally positioned in a prominent upper niche located in the bath porch area of the palace complex. The dignified posture of power, along with the individual details of the figure, share traditional visual characteristics found in the arts of South Arabia (see Fig. 2.15).

The other two sculptures represent dancers and entertainers. These female figures are depicted wearing skirts with elaborately set hair, intricate jewelry, and hold musical instruments and other objects. Their presentation complimented the atmosphere of entertaining guests and visitors within the Diwan; an established tradition that would persist for centuries and continue to appear in Diwans at other locations; the most notable being the painted Muqarnas ceiling of the Cappella Palatina in Sicily (see Chapter 10). The artistic style of the sculptures continues the Arab tradition found in the arts of Petra and Palmyra.

The original ceiling of the dome of the Diwan was decorated with a large six-lobed rosette carved in stucco. There are 6 large acanthus leaves with two smaller rosettes in the center. At the lobes, alternating male and female heads of Arab figures occupy the centers. The male heads are painted with black mustaches, trim beards and curly hair. The heads of the females are adorned with rounded pendant earrings, black painted curly hair and reddish lips. The heads are surrounded by vine leaves, flowers and 18 loops decorated with floral and vegetal motifs (Fig. 7.21). The iconography or identification of the visual composition in the central location is still not clear. Scholars have not reached a satisfying explanation about the splendid display. The treatment of the faces is reminiscent of those found in the paintings of Qaryat Al-Faw and Dura-Europos (see Figures 4.4, 4.13, 4.14).

The architects, builders, painters and sculptors who executed the artworks at Qusayr `Amra, Khirbat Al-Mafjar, and other palaces in the greater Syria and Palestine region during the Umayyad period were local, with adequate knowledge of the architectural and visual traditions found around the Umayyad territories. Much of the cultural heritage of the Persians and Byzantines had already spread among the Arabs in the 6th to 8th centuries, by way of the agent mini-states, the Ghassanids and the Lakhmids. By the turn of the 8th century, the Umayyads were in control of Persia and great swaths of the former Byzantine colonies. Builders, artists, and artisans–Arab, Persian and Byzantine–worked freely throughout the area, and shared their cultural heritage in their productions, which created a new, blended Arab art style that had its roots in the ancient pre-Islamic era.

This is clearly noticeable in the appearance of Sassanian architectural elements in Umayyad buildings, along with Byzantine technical details found in the mosaics and decorations of the structures. These elements, derived from neighboring sources, blended with the Arab cultural and visual traditions already examined in South Arabia: Yemen, Syria-Nabateae, Iraq-Hatra and Hirah, and in the Mediterranean.

The existence of figurative representations in the art of the Arabs during this period was the natural evolution of a long tradition. It came as a surprise to 19th century historians, who were Orientalists, unable to reconcile the trends within their established perceptions of Islamic art as the aniconic and non-figurative antithesis to the Christian West. Hence, their early interpretations categorized such paintings as either Byzantine or Sassanian in origin. Some structures were completely misidentified as Roman, Byzantine or Sassanian.

The presentation of the Aqsa Mosque, the Dome of the Rock, and the Great Mosque of Damascus mark the development of early Muslim art and architecture, which was heavily based in the Arab artistic tradition, but now complimented by the visual vocabulary of neighboring cultural powers. Furthermore, it also marks the continuity of Arab tradition in art and architectural design. The Arab tradition originates in architectural and visual sources found in Yemen, central Arabia, Syria, and Iraq. The 7th and 8th centuries saw the intermingling of visual culture, mainly from Sassanian and Byzantine sources. Building on Arab art in the 8th-10th centuries, a standard was developed and spread throughout the Muslim lands in North Africa, the Mediterranean, Spain, southern Italy and Sicily.

Selected Bibliography

In addition to the list of bibliography in chapter 6

Al-Khamis, Ulrike and Weber Stefan, *Early Capitals of Islamic Culture: The Art and Culture of Umayyad Damascus and Abbasid Baghdad (650-950), Chicago:* University of Chicago Press, 2014.

Ali, Wijdan, *The Arab Contribution to Islamic Art: From the Seventh to the Fifteenth Centuries,* Cairo: American University in Cairo Press, 2000.

Ettinghausen, Richard, Grabar Oleg, Jenkins-Madina Maryilyn. *The Art and Architecture of Islam, 650-1250.* New Haven, Yale University Press. 2001.

Fairchild Ruggles, D., Ed., *Islamic Art and Visual Culture: An Anthology of Sources*, Malden, MA: Wiley-Blackwel, l2011.

Fowden Garth, *Qusayr 'Amra: Art and the Umayyad Elite in Late Antique Syria,* Berkeley, CA: University of California Press, 1969.

Grabar, Oleg. *Ceremonial and Art at the Umayyad Court,* UMI Dissertation Services, 1991.

____, *The Formation of Islamic Art.* Rev. and enlarged ed. New Haven: Yale University Press, 1987.

____, *The Mediation of Ornament.* Princeton: Princeton University Press, 1992.

Grube, Ernst. "A Bibliography of Iconography in Islamic Art," in: *Image and Meaning in Islamic Art, ed. R. Hillen brand.* London: Altajir World of Islam Trust, 2005.

Papadopoulo Alexandre, *Islam and Muslim Art*, translated from the French by Robert Erich Wolf, London: Thames and Hudson, 1980.

8 CHAPTER

ARAB ART DURING THE ISLAMIC PERIOD (800 - 1300)

The Abbasids took control of the political system of the expanding Islamic state in 750, marking the end of Umayyad rule and the start of a new global era. The Muslim empire stretched eastward through Persia and Central Asia to the borders of China and India. Meanwhile, The Abbasids consolidated power in the central region, where Baghdad became the new capital of the empire. Egypt, all of North Africa, and a considerable portion of the Iberian Peninsula—Spain to the borders of France—became Muslim territory. An efficient network of transportation and communication was further developed, and spread without restriction throughout the vast lands. The Abbasid policy of utilizing the cultural heritage of conquered peoples paved the way for a revolution in many fields of learning.

The Abbasids sponsored a massive program of preserving, studying, and developing all known fields of knowledge, centered in many key regions. A network of institutions of higher learning was established, starting with the "Bayt Al-Hikmah" and "Dar Al-Hikmah," literally "House of Wisdom," in Baghdad, and replicated later in Cairo, Jerusalem, Qayrawan, Andalus, and other major cities. These early centers of learning attracted scholars from distant lands and cultures, who brought with them materials from Persia, India, and the Hellenistic world. They included Muslims, Christians, Jews, and others. Besides fluency in Arabic, which was the official language, they employed proficiency in Aramaic, Greek, Pahlavi, Hebrew and other languages. A revolution based in the exaltation of knowledge began, resulting in the preservation, translation, study, annotation and further development of global intellectual heritage, especially the Greco-Roman knowledge base.

The continuing global cultural attainment impacted the development of Arab art as well. New artistic vocabularies of Hellenistic, Turkic, and Persian origin merged with the already established trends in Arab art. This can be recognized in major early architecture and their decorative details, throughout the Muslim empire of the 8th-13th centuries. Examples include Iraq: the circular city of Baghdad; the Abbasid Palace in Baghdad; the fortress of Ukhaydir––south of Baghdad; the Great Mosque of Samarra; and The Caliph's Palace in Samarra, known as Jawsaq Al-Khaqani. In Egypt, examples include the Ibn Tulun Mosque and Al-Azhar Mosque in Cairo. From western North Africa: the Great Mosque of Qayrawan in Tunisia; Al-Qarawiyyin and Al-Kutubiyyin mosques in Morocco. From Andalus: the Great Mosque of Cordoba, Al-Madina Al-Zahira, the Great Mosque of Seville, and the

Al-Hamra` (Alhambra) complex. From Sicily: the Great Mosque of Palermo, the Cappella Palatina Muqarnas ceiling, and the royal palaces. Some of these monuments will be discussed in the following chapters.

BAGHDAD, THE ABBASID CAPITAL

The vastly expanding Abbasid Empire facilitated the movement of people, knowledge, and ideas from as far as Spain to the borders of China and India. The quest for knowledge, officially sponsored by the government and the Caliph's immediate circle in Baghdad, brought in world knowledge sources to the newly established learning institutions. Within a short time of its founding, Baghdad became a center of higher learning, political power, and thriving commerce. The "Bayt Al-Hikmah" House of Wisdom was an educational center fully funded and dedicated to the preservation, translation and development of Greek, Persian, and Indian intellectual culture. The Abbasid authorities diligently succeeded in recruiting scholars from the nearby former Sassanian academy of Jundi-Shapur (Gundi-Shapur) in Iran, and the Hellenistic world, facilitating the introduction of Greek, Persian and Indian sciences into the new empire.

Scholars collaborated on acquiring world knowledge from European, Anatolian, Persian, Byzantine, Indian, and Chinese origin. The translation program targeted original works in philosophy, physics, science, math, alchemy, medicine, chemistry, zoology, geography, astronomy, and literature. Scholars were educated in the languages of the time, along with the official Arabic language. Christian Arab scholars were instrumental in this campaign; besides Arabic, they held knowledge of Aramaic and Greek. Within a few decades, a scientific rebirth was manifest, where science was sought, studied, and implemented in all aspects of life throughout the Muslim lands. The Bayt Al-Hikmah in Baghdad was destroyed by the invading Mongols in 1258.

The plethora of intellectual and cultural exchange was underscored by an emphasis on critical thinking, which produced a wealth of ideas that would ultimately contribute to the shaping of the arts. The Arabs learned Chinese papermaking technology around 751. Soon, the process was improved by substituting the tree bark–mulberry with linen. Paper mills emerged in Baghdad, Basrah, Kufah, and Mosul by the end of the 8th century.

By the beginning of the 9th century, the paper making industry spread to other major Muslim cities such as Damascus, Jerusalem, Cairo, Sicily, and Al-Andalus in Spain. The availability of paper facilitated the growing need for books and records among the relatively literate Islamic world. A new industry of manuscript copying was created, functioning as a large-scale scriptorium. Sources of the period reference "Souq Al-Warraqin," or "the scribes' market." The sources provide the locations of markets, as well as descriptions of the types of works for sale, decorative details, illuminations, materials used, and even names of scribes, who were known to state their names proudly in every copy.

As the book making industry developed rapidly, so did the demand for scribes, illustrators and illuminators. Copies of surviving works show advanced levels of artistic achievement, such as "Maqamat Al-Hariri" (The Assemblies of Al-Hariri), "Kalilah wa Dimnah," "Kitab fi Ma`rifat Al-Hiyal Al-Handasiyyah," (The Book of Knowledge of Ingenious Mechanical Devices), and "Kitab Al-Diryaq," (The Book of Antidotes of Pseudo-Galen), among others. The new capital of the Muslim empire was the round city of Baghdad, "Madinat Al-Salam," which translates to "the city of peace." Built in 762-767, the city plan was a masterpiece of architectural novelty, meant to outshine the glory associated with other cities in the region. Circular in plan, the city was built with four major gates facing the directions of Damascus, Khurasan, Basrah and Kufah. The Great Mosque and the Palace of the

Fig. 8.1: Illustration of Baghdad, the circular city.

Caliph occupied the center area (Fig. 8.1).

Nothing has survived of the original city structure except for some remains of the wall, part of a gate, and scattered remnants of the foundation. Literary sources describe in detail the Great Mosque and the Palace, which had a "Green Dome" capped with a statue of a horseman holding a lance. Al-Jazari, a 13th century Arab mechanical engineer, provides an illustration of an automaton horse rider (Fig. 8.2). The practical function of that statue is unclear, though it is possible that it was used to aid in weather forecast.

Fig. 8.2: Al-Jazari's illustration of the automaton horse rider atop the Green Dome, the Caliph's Palace, Baghdad.

Al-Mustansiriyyah School, Madrasah, Baghdad

Al-Mustansiriyyah Madrasah was built and sponsored by the Abbasid Caliph Al-Mustansir Billah in 1233 along the Tigris River in the heart of Baghdad, to serve students from all four Islamic schools of Jurisprudence. It is a massive rectangular building of 106 x 48 meters with a large open central courtyard 62 x 26 meters. Rooms and Iwans (a vaulted space open from one side) occupy the two levels of the building (Fig. 8.3). The decorations inside consist of carved bricks with calligraphic text, geometric and floral patterns repeated inside the iwans, on the facades and under the arches.

Fig. 8.3: Al-Mustansiriyyah School, Baghdad, 13th century.

Calligraphy is used in a brilliant way to extend the same functionality that we saw inside the Dome of the Rock in Jerusalem. Bands of monumental calligraphy in modified Thulth-Naskh style, adorn the outer walls and the entire facade of the main entrance (Fig. 8.4). The calligraphic text on the entrance and the bands on the upper portion of the exterior create an engaging visual experience. The calligraphic text is a proclamation of achievement and a road map for the building's use, announcing the Caliph's intent and vision. The building speaks, passing the message of the Caliph to visitors. A form of "Oratorical Architecture," the structure emphasizes the monumentality of the Arabic language through the use of calligraphy accentuated by geometric and floral design.

Fig. 8.4: Main entrance, Al-Mustansiriyyah School, Baghdad, 13th century.

The decorative architectural system employed at Al-Mustansiriyyah school was not limited to buildings in Iraq only, but appeared in other locations as well. An example of this is the Ince Minareli Madrasah (1258-1279) in Konya, Turkey (Fig. 8.5). The entrance of this school is carved in stone and contains vertical bands with emphasis on two intertwining banners at the center. Elegant Thulth calligraphy dominates the facade, pronouncing Qur`anic verses from chapters 36 and 110. The entrance becomes the orator; the announcer of the nature, essence, and function of the building.

Fig. 8.5: Facade of the entrance, Ince Minareli Madrasah, Konya, Turkey, 13th century.

MANUSCRIPT ILLUMINATION

The quest for knowledge that swept through the Abbasid Empire produced a vibrant movement of learning everywhere, centralized in major cities. Public and private libraries were constantly acquiring books, driving a demand that prompted the creation of related trades such as paper-making, copying, and illustrating texts. Master artists, calligraphers, and illuminators teamed up with book binders to meet the growing demand for books. Meanwhile, an important development in the field of Arabic calligraphy took place in Baghdad with the innovative works of Ibn Muqlah and Ibn Al-Bawwab, who created new styles of Arabic script. The period of the 10th-13th centuries witnessed an explosion in book production across the eastern, central and western lands of the Islamic empire. The following is an examination of samples from manuscript illuminations produced during the time.

"Kitab Al-Diryaq," Book of Antidotes of Pseudo-Galen

Baghdad, Basrah, Mosul, Kufah and other Abbasid cities housed many active book-making establishments which produced superb illuminated manuscripts. Among them was the unique and sumptuously illuminated 12th century manuscript, "Kitab Al-Diryaq," known as Book of Antidotes of Pseudo-Galen. There are two known copies of this manuscript: one at the Paris Bibliotheque Nationale with the year 1199 as the date of completion, and the other copy, dated to the mid 13th century, is in the Vienna Nationalbibliothek. Each manuscript contains 72 pages with measurements of 37 cm by 29 cm; the medium is color and ink on paper.

The book's subject matter covers an ancient medicinal compound initially used as a cure for the venomous bites of poisonous snakes and other wild animals. The manuscript includes illustrations of the medicinal plants used in formulas produced by important Greek physicians such as Galen and Andromachus. The copy is signed by the scribe (katib), Muhammad ibn Abi Al-Fath. The manuscript functions as a medical reference, but also provides accounts, tales, and anecdotes about the nine great Greek physicians of antiquity, who contributed to the development of the medicines described and are depicted in the manuscript.

The illustrations of the nine Greek physicians depict the figures with typical Arab facial characteristics, postures, and attire (Fig. 8.6). They appear on three separate pages, shown engaged in research, study or conversing with students. They are identified with their names placed in a frame over each individual portrait. The style of the painting is closely connected to that of Yahya ibn Mahmoud Al-Wasiti, the illustrator of Maqamat Al-Hariri.

Noticeable in the illustrations is the use of calligraphy as a visual instrument. Text is written in elegant cursive Naskh style, with full diacritical marks called "tahreek." The headings, titles and names are executed in a most daring modified version of Kufic style with bold colors: black, blue, and red against rich harmonious backgrounds composed of floral and vegetal patterns (Fig. 8.7).

The artist-calligrapher organized the scripts in geometric patterns: horizontal, circular, vertical, and diagonal, using a combination throughout the manuscript. The vertical letters stand like elegant date palm tree or human figures embracing in the dynamic aesthetic forms. Here, the calligraphic compositions compete with the visual narratives, at times overpowering them. The literal narratives in these illustrations – similar to the case of the Dome of the Rock and the Ince Minareli Madrasah – surpass the visual narratives in beauty and presence.

Fig. 8.6: Folio from "Kitab Al-Diryaq" Book of Antidotes of Pseudo-Galen, 12th century, Mosul. Iraq. Bibliothèque Nationale de France.

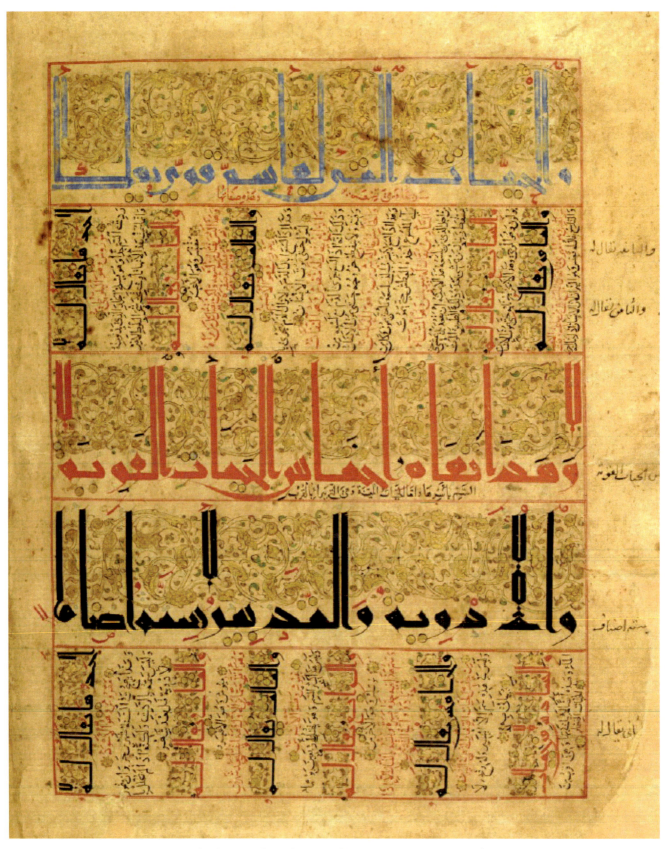

Fig. 8.7: Folio from "Kitab Al-Diryaq" Book of Antidotes of Pseudo-Galen, 12th century, Mosul, Iraq. Bibliothèque Nationale de France.

The Illustrations of "Maqamat Al-Hariri"

Maqamat Al-Hariri is a 13th century illustrated book, written by Al-Hariri (1054-1122) from Basrah, and illustrated by Al-Wasiti from Wasit, Iraq and probably copied in Baghdad. The novelty genre is Arabic rhymed prose composed in poetical form. Multiple copies were produced due to the popularity of the book, and the few surviving copies are now scattered in libraries and museums. The best of these surviving illustrated copies was completed in 1237, and is now in the Bibliotheque Nationale in Paris. It has 99 fully colored illustrations.

The book presents tales and anecdotes narrated by the main figure, along with his companion traveler, with rich descriptions of the daily lives of people in different Arab cities (Figures. 8.8, 8.9).

Fig. 8.8: Folio 19 Recto: Illustration of Maqamah # 7, celebration the end of Ramadan. Bibliothèque Nationale de France.

The artist of this manuscript was Yahya ibn Mahmoud Al-Wasiti, a proficient calligrapher and illustrator. He composed the narratives of this book, some fifty paintings for fifty assemblies called "Maqamat," based on the literary descriptions coupled with his astute observations of people, places and details of daily life.

The writer Al-Hariri, titled each Maqamah with the place of its occurrence, referring to names of cities, villages, or major landmarks. The celebration of the end of fasting (Fig. 7.8) illustrates the seventh Maqamah, entitled "Al-Maqamah Al-Barqa`idiyyah," where the scene is recorded in the small town north of Mosul.

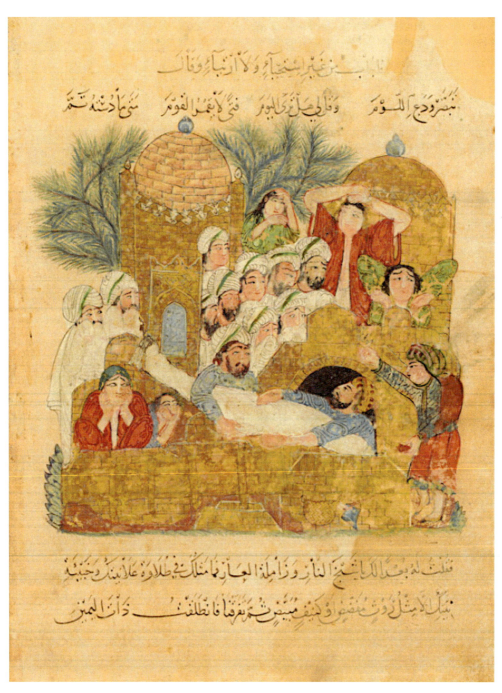

Fig. 8.9: Folio 29 Verso: Illustration of Maqamah # 11, The burial at Sawa Cemetery. Bibliothèque Nationale de France.

The illustration is one of the most famous of Wasiti's collections in Al-Hariri's Assemblies. The superb composition shows men on horseback touring the streets of the city, announcing the beginning of the 4 days Eid Al-Fitr, the end of Ramadan fasting. The men are riding horses, perhaps mules, playing musical instruments of high tones: trumpets and drums. Other young men on horseback are holding flags and banners. The painting reflects an accurate depiction of a familiar scene that continues to take place annually across Muslim lands. Although the event is religious, the style is realistic and straightforward, reflecting secular activity void of allegorical or spiritual implication.

The second example of Al-Wasiti's style is the illustration of the Maqamah no. 11, entitled "Al-Saawiyyah," which is a city located west of Iraq between Ray and Hamedan in Iran (Fig. 8.9). The funerary scene illustrates a cemetery burial, presumably in the city of Saawah. Two men are shown lowering the body of the deceased into the prepared grave. Grieving men watch in sorrow, while mourning women wail. Again, Al-Wasiti's distinct realistic style is present in the composition.

THE BAGHDAD SCHOOL OF MANUSCRIPT ILLUSTRATION

The paintings and illuminated works discussed in this chapter are parts of the body of work produced by the "School of Baghdad," particularly in the art of illustration. Mahmoud ibn Yahya Al-Wasiti's style epitomizes that artistic style. Developed gradually in Baghdad within the field of manuscript illumination, the style and its practice reached a highpoint in the 12th-13th centuries. The manuscript style spread to other major regions such as Iran, Syria, Egypt and Al-Andalus. The Baghdad School style is characterized by an emphasis on figural realism highlighted by the use of expressive emotion. Figures are depicted with distinct identities; remarkable attention is given to individual facial features, clothing, and body movements. The narratives illustrated in the works of the Baghdad School reveal a preoccupation with stylistic realism that was not being practiced contemporaneously in most of Europe.

During the period 800-1300, Baghdad was the world's center of education and culture, where innovations in science and technology were happening regularly. Mechanical engineering was a thriving field; supported by the authorities throughout the Muslim empire. Arab scientists based their research on the already existing Greek knowledge, along with sources from India, China and Persia. There were many Arab and Muslim scientists who excelled in various fields. Famous among them is the brilliant mechanical engineer, Badi` Al-Zaman Isma`il Al-Jazari (1136-1206). He was born in the Al-Jazirah region, which is the upper area between the Tigris and Euphrates Rivers in northern Iraq, and at the time, part of the Artuqid dynasty; a vassal of the Zengid rulers of Mosul.

Like his father and brother before him, he was a skilled engineer, craftsman, and likely a creative artist. He was the chief engineer at the court of three Artuqid rulers. He compiled his brilliant inventions, some 50 of them, in a book called "The Book of Knowledge of Ingenious Mechanical Devices," in Arabic "Kitab fi Ma'rifat Al-Hiyal Al-Handasiyyah," with color illustrations. The book was so popular that many Arabic manuscript copies from his time and later still survive. His inventions include water and candle clocks, as well as mechanical figures (robots) that acted as attendants, serving guests in washing and drinking. He invented music operating machines, water raising machines, hydro-powered figures, hydro-powered gates, and many other automata.

The engineer Al-Jazari is most famous for his monumental device, the elephant clock. Among the visual illustrations of his devices is the "Castle Water Clock" (Fig. 8.10). This 11 ft. tall device has a complicated operation, involving five mechanical musicians (robots), two falcons throwing metal balls, a zodiac dial, and the lunar and solar orbits. The "Castle Clock" has been described as the first analog computer. The scribe/illustrator Faruq ibn Abd Al-Latif follows the Baghdad School's descriptive technique in depiction of figures, their attire, and actions. Similar to the illustrations of Hariri's Maqamat, Al-Jazari's main figures are haloed to signify their importance and status. The illustration is done in lineal style, showing the functionality of the device through a comprehensive diagram and realistic rendering. Al-Jazari's popular book

Fig. 8.10: Folio from Al-Jazari's illustration of the "Castle Clock," Ink, opaque watercolor and gold on paper, 39.37 x 27.62 cm (15 1/2 x 10 7/8 in.). Museum of Fine Arts, Boston.

ARAB ART DURING THE ISLAMIC PERIOD (800 - 1300)

Fig. 8.11: Illustrated detached manuscript folio from Al-Qazwini's book "The Wonders of Creation and the Oddities of Existence." H x W (verso angel): 9.9 × 9.4 cm (3 7/8 × 3 11/16 in). Freer Sackler Gallery of Art, Smithsonian Institution, Washington DC.

was copied continuously for centuries by different scribes and in different places.

The next example is an illustrated folio from Zakaria bin Muhammad bin Mahmud Abu Yahya Al-Qazwini (1203-1283), who was a physician, astronomer, geographer, writer and zoologist. The illustration comes from his encyclopedic book entitled "`Aja'ib Al-Makhluqat wa Ghara'ib Al-Mawjudat," or "The Wonders of Creation and the Oddities of Existence." Al-Qazwini's treatise covered an eclectic assortment of topics, from humans and their anatomy to mythical creatures, plants and animals, to constellations, stars and zodiacal signs. The book was extremely popular and was frequently translated and re-illustrated over the centuries into Persian and Turkish. The illustration is a visual depiction of Al-Qazwini's description of the four angels carrying the celestial throne of God (Fig. 8.11).

According to Muslim tradition, these four angels, called Karubiyyoun (singular Karoub), hold the throne of God. The word Karoub is an archaic South Arabian term used by the Sabaeans in 700 BCE, meaning "qareeb," meaning "close to the deity/divine entity." In the Qur`an and Islamic tradition they are the bearers of the throne. In this illustration they are depicted in the forms of human, lion, falcon, and bull. Interestingly, the iconography of the four angels matches that found in Christian visual descriptions of the Four Evangelists – Matthew, Mark, Luke, and John.

The Baghdad School, similar to many other cultural institutions of the time, suffered horribly when the Mongols swept through the Muslim regions, who pillaged and destroyed everything in their path. The Mongols invaded Baghdad and razed the city in 1258. Cultural and educational establishments like libraries and Bayt Al-Hikmah were burned and destroyed, with thousands of books thrown in the Tigris River. Cultural activities halted or moved out of Baghdad. Soon, the distinct style of the School of Baghdad began to fade in prominence, and a new Mongol style prevailed for the following two centuries.

Important example of manuscripts illustrated by the Baghdad School are: Maqamat Al-Hariri – discussed above; The Arabic translation of Dioscorides' medical treatise, De materia medica, dated 1224; the frontispiece to the book "The Epistles of the Sincere Brethren" (Arabic Ikhwan Al-Safa), which is a 10th-11th century collection of philosophical issues interpreted by Shi`i-Muslim scholars of Basrah; and "Kalila wa Dimna," which is an 8th century Arabic translation of a 4th century Sanskrit book "Panchatantra" that contains practical wisdom and intelligence presented in the pleasant form of animal fables. Other works executed in Mosul and Iran can be added to the list, such as "Kitab Al-Diryaq" and Al-Jazari automata, as discussed in this chapter.

THE ART OF THE FATIMIDS IN EGYPT

The Fatimid dynasty started first in Al-Mahdiyyah, Tunisia in 953, then expanded to Egypt, establishing Cairo as their capital in 969. The Fatimid Caliphs were patrons of the arts, culture, and knowledge, rivaling the Abbasids in Baghdad and the Umayyads in the Andalus, Spain. Under their patronage numerous architectural masterpieces were constructed, such as the Al-Azhar mosque and school, Al-Hakim mosque, Al-Aqmar mosque, and many splendid palaces. Muqarnas, geometric design and excellent compositions of Arabic calligraphy are found throughout the buildings. Pottery flourished under the Fatimids, as did Tiraz textile manufacturing, with a major factory in Cairo. Sources refer to a "Dar Al-Hikmah" and a major library connected with it in Cairo, along with the splendid decorated buildings.

The Fatimids maintained political and cultural contact with the rest of the Muslim empire, which facilitated the travel of artisans, ideas and artistic techniques from Iran, Iraq and Syria. Characteristics of the Baghdad School of visual art are noticeable in surviving Fatimid works, which spread through much of their domains including Sicily. Fatimid rule did not last long amid internal crises, economic decline, and the growing pressure of the Crusades. Their reign ended in 1171, when their palaces were pillaged, and libraries were looted. Following is a quick review of a few noteworthy examples of their art and architecture.

The Al-Aqmar Mosque, located in the heart of Cairo, is a small congregational mosque with a square courtyard. It was constructed in 1125 and is considered the first mosque in Cairo to have a decorated stone/brick facade. The facade of this mosque is an outstanding work of art, richly decorated with geometric, floral and Muqarnas elements. Perhaps the most astonishing aesthetic display is the elaborately decorated Arabic text, all executed in Kufic style. The inscription contains Qur`anic verses, names and

Fig. 8.12: Facade of Al-Aqmar Mosque, 1125, Cairo, Egypt.

titles of the Caliph and Wazir (minister), and dates of the foundation (Fig. 8.12).

The prominent inscriptions of the facade are found in a medallion above the central doorway of the mosque, inside the shelled pointed arch. The inner circle of the medallion contains the name of the Prophet Mohammed and `Ali, his cousin, son-in-law, the fourth Caliph, and the cornerstone figure in Shi`ism. These elements are encircled by a band containing part of Sura 33 of chapter 33 in the Qur`an, which addresses "Ahl Al-Bayt," or "the people of the house" of the Prophet: Mohammed, Fatimah, `Ali, Hasan, and Husain.

The entrance of the building therefore proudly pronounces the Shi`a doctrine, which was the sect of the Fatimids. Similar Shi`i references are found in other parts of the building. The splendor of the facade is marked by deep carvings that appear as three-dimensional compositions. Along with carefully selected text, Al-Aqsa Mosque is a prime example of Islamic "oratorical architecture," where the structure uses writing to interact and engage actively with visitors.

Fig. 8.13: Plaster wall painting fragment from a bath-house, 11th century, height 24.5 cm, width 60 cm. Fustat (Old Cairo), Egypt.

The next example is a fragment of a plaster wall painting (Fig. 8.13), and comes from Fustat in Old Cairo. The painting shows a youth holding a cup, dressed in fine decorated garments with a pleated head-dress. His posture and attributes allude to his courtly status. The style and details present a strong connection with depictions found in the Abbasid Palace at Samarra, primarily found on lusterware originating in Iran and Iraq, as well as with the pictorial program found on the Muqarnas ceiling of the Cappella Palatina in Palermo, Sicily.

The third example is composed of four ivory panels (Fig. 8.14) which denotes the exquisite mastery in carving that Fatimid artists were known for, as evidenced by many surviving examples found in wood. The organization of the carved narratives suggest that two were meant to be displayed horizontally while the other two vertically, likely to compose a frame. These panels may have originally been designed to decorate a secular court space such as a "Diwan," or "the audience hall;" furniture such as the ruler's seat, throne, or pedestal; or a door in a palace.

The narratives are carefully carved in a realistic, meticulous style. The iconography includes scenes of horse-riders, falcon-hunting, animal fighting, leisurely drinking, music playing, and dancing. The subject of this fine ivory carving is secular, displaying scenes of hunting, royal activities, and courtly pastime; themes that we have encountered in Arab art of the pre-Islamic and early Islamic Umayyad and Abbasid periods.

ARAB ART DURING THE ISLAMIC PERIOD (800 - 1300)

Fig. 8.14: Four ivory panels, Fatimids, 11th-12th century. Horizontal panels length 36.5 cm, width 5.8 cm. Vertical panels: height 30.3 cm, width 5.8 cm. Depth of panels 1–1.5 cm. Museum für islamische Kunst, Staatliche Museen, Berlin.

Selected Bibliography

In addition to the list in Chapter 6 and Chapter 7

Al-Jazari, Ibn Al-Razzaz. *The Book of Knowledge of Ingenious Mechanical Devices (Kitab fi ma'rifat Al-Hiyal Al-Handasiyya). Trans.* Donald Hill. Dordrecht: Dordrecht Publishing Company, 1974.

Allen, Roger M.A., *The Arabic Literary Heritage: The Development of Its Genres and Criticism,* United Kingdom: Cambridge University Press, 1998.

Annemarie Schimmel, *Islamic Calligraphy,* Leiden: Brill, 1970.

Atil Esin, *Renaissance of Islam: Art of the Mamluks,* Washington DC: Smithsonian Institution Press,1981.

Atiyeh George F. Ed., The Book in the Islamic World: The Written Word and Communication in the Middle East, State University of New York Press; (Washington DC): Library of Congress, 1995.

Bloom, Jonathan M. *Arts of the City Victorious: Islamic art and architecture in Fatimid North Africa and Egypt,* New Haven: Yale University Press, 2007.

_____, *Paper before Print: The History and Impact of Paper in the Islamic World,* New Haven: Yale University Press, 2001.

Carter Thomas F., *The Invention of Printing in China and its Spread Westward,* 2nd ed., rev. L. Carrington Goodrich, New York: The Ronald Press Company, 1955.

Josef W. Meri Ed., *Medieval Islamic Civilization: An Encyclopedia,* New York: Routledge, 2006.

CHAPTER 9

ARAB ART IN EUROPE DURING THE ISLAMIC PERIOD (800 - 1500) IBERIA (AL-ANDALUS)

The 7th century witnessed the expansion of Arab power in the fertile crescent – Syria, Palestine and the Sinai region, along with North Africa. They established major cities in North Africa, Egypt, Tunisia, and Iberia. It is particularly interesting to compare the earlier Arab expansion, with the Canaanites-Phoenicians, some 1000 years earlier, who followed a similar pattern: Phoenician Cartage and Arab Qayrawan in Tunisia; Sardinia and Sicily in the Mediterranean Sea; Cadiz and Malaga in Sothern Iberia––the Arab Al-Andalus.

The Arab-Muslim armies conquered southern Iberia in 711, and soon established the base of what would be Al-Andalus, which included most of present-day Spain and Portugal to the borders of France. The conquest of Iberia was consolidated after 756, when Abd Al-Rahman, a survivor of the ousted Umayyad dynasty in Syria, arrived in Cordoba, and was able to establish a strong independent state. The Arabs named it Al-Andalus, which according to Arab historians was a term derived from the word "Vandals." Al-Andalus became the most sophisticated and advanced state in Europe during the 10th-13th centuries. The increased pressure of the Iberian Christians in the north, coupled with the turbulent internal politics among the Arab rulers, soon impacted the state of Al-Andalus and an inevitable fragmentation took place. Al-Andalus turned into Tawa`if (singular Ta`ifah), semi-independent small Emirates unable to repel the charges of the northern Christian armies (Map 9).

Two major waves of military assistance came to the Arab-Muslims from North Africa. The first was with Al-Murabitun, the Almoravids (1086-1094). Al-Murabitun, plural of Murabit, refers to the Islamic tradition of frontier fighters, usually encamped in Rabats along frontier lines, and prepared to engage in military defense or attack. The other was Al-Muwahhidun, the Almohads, meaning "the proclaimers of the Oneness of God" (1146-1173). Both efforts of military assistance succeeded in delaying the eventual takeover by northern Christian kingdoms. The last Muslim Emirate of Granada surrendered to the armies of Castile and Aragon under Isabella and Ferdinand in 1492. The Arabs were expelled from Iberia after nearly 800 years, during which, they produced remarkable culture, arts, and architectural marvels. Al-Andalus was a vibrant crossroads, and key in the transmission of Arab-Muslim achievements in medicine, art, literature, philosophy and

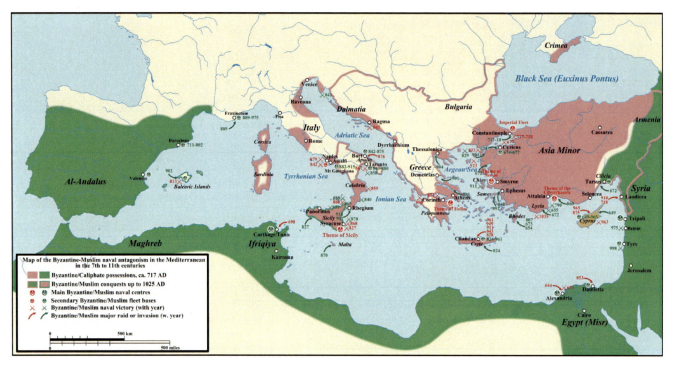

Map. 9 : Map of Iberia, Sicily and Malta in the Mediterranean region during Byzantine Muslim confrontation (7th -11th) centuries.

other fields to Europe. It became a conduit for knowledge, science, and advanced learning between the Muslim and Christian worlds, and contributed to the rise of the Renaissance.

In Al-Andalus, the Muslims applied the same political and social formula in dealing with the conquered population, offering protection and internal autonomy in religious practice to "Jizyah," or tax-paying non-Muslims. This tolerant atmosphere created cooperation and exchange amongst Muslims, Christians and Jews. Although the reign of the Arabs in Iberia ended politically at the end of the 15th century and physically at the beginning of the 17th century, nearly eight centuries of cultural history left a deep impact on Spain's present-day culture, language, and way of life; especially in the south.

The Great Mosque of Cordoba "Mezquita de Cordoba"

The Arabs created masterpieces of art and architecture in Iberia, as in the earliest example: the Great Mosque of Cordoba. The history of the Great Mosque is similar to its counterpart in Damascus. The Mosque of Cordoba was constructed in 784 on an ancient site formerly believed to have been used for rituals associated with different divinities, including a temple to the Roman god Janus. The temple was converted into a church by the invading Visigoths who seized the region in 572. After the Muslim conquest of Granada in 711, the church was divided into two parts, one for Muslims and one for Christians. This arrangement lasted until 784, when Abd Al-Rahman purchased the Christian part from the local Christian population of Granada and constructed the mosque on the site (784-86). The mosque was enlarged considerably later in the 9th and 10th centuries, ultimately reaching its present rectangular size of 190 meters by 140 meters (Fig. 9.1).

The Great Mosque of Cordoba has a courtyard that occupies about a third of the space, planted with orange trees. It is surrounded by a heavily fortified wall––about 1.14-meter thick, with 11 elaborately decorated doors (Fig. 9.5). There is

Fig. 9.1: The Great Mosque of Cordoba, 8th–10th centuries, Cordoba, Spain.

a strikingly ornamented Mihrab surrounded by a secluding space (the Maqsurah). The Mihrab is flanked by two structures harmonious in form: the first is the treasury––"Bayt Al-Mal," and the second is a private entrance that leads to the nearby palace of the ruler, through a roofed passage. Such an arrangement reflects the early Umayyad structures in Iraq and Syria. The Arabic inscription on the Mihrab (Fig. 9.6), which was done in mosaic, contains selected verses from the Qur`an and a line commemorating the Caliph Al-Hakam, who sponsored the renovation. In 951 a towering square Minaret was erected across the open courtyard on the north side, replacing the old minaret.

Cordoba was reconquered by the Christian armies in 1236, and the Spanish Catholic authorities consecrated the Great Mosque as the city's cathedral. For the next three centuries, only minor changes occurred in the mosque to accommodate Christian use. However, after the fall of Granada in 1492 and early in the 16th century, Catholic authorities proposed the construction of a new cathedral and the demolition of the mosque. The population of Granada objected, and an alternative action was endorsed by both the government and religious establishment: a large section of the prayer area of the Great Mosque was dismantled and a Gothic chapel was inserted in the heart of the structure.

The minaret was repurposed, with modifications done to the upper part to serve as a bell tower (Figures 9.1, 9.4). Further decoration and changes were added to the chapel area in the 17th and 18th centuries. The result is an unusual structure where a cathedral is inserted in the middle of a congregational mosque. Some scholars interpret the act as cultural destruction, while others see it as a display of multi-religious identity. At present, the overall concept

Fig. 9.2: Interior of the Great Mosque of Cordoba, Spain, 8th-10th centuries.

of the complex is still easily recognized as an Arab-Islamic architectural monument with an unrelated Gothic chapel at the center.

The original hypostyle plan and construction of the mosque resembled the Great Mosque of Damascus. Similar characteristics are the horseshoe arches, double-tier arches, the Ablaq method in alternating stone and brick with light and dark colors, and the mosaic decoration at the Mihrab-Maqsurah area (Fig. 9.6), along with the wide hypostyle prayer hall (Fig. 9.2). The features of the Great Mosque of Cordoba served as a basis for other mosques built in Al-Andalus.

Work on the building continued through the period of Arab rule, with subsequent additions and improvement. Significant architectural innovations found at the Great Mosque of Cordoba include the method of raising the height of the ceiling by employing double-tier arches; lower tiers are horseshoe-shaped while the upper are semi-circular. Furthermore, poly-lobed and interlocking arches are used for support and aesthetics; ribbed ceilings decorate interior domes; horseshoe arches highlight corridors; and the bold, rhythmic use of over 1300 arched columns support the 8.9 meter-high ceiling of the prayer hall. Most of the columns are spolia or recycled ancient Roman building elements. The captivating effect of the "Ablaq" technique runs throughout the mosque (Figures 9.2, 9.3).

Records indicate that Arab authorities requested Byzantine artisans to lay the mosaic decoration in the Mihrab during a 10th century renovation. The Great Mosque accommodated other functions besides congregational prayer in Cordoba. Major public announcements were made from the Minbar, and a pledge of allegiance to the Amir or Caliph also took place there. Moreover, it was a place for learning, where important classes, lectures and educational sessions would be conducted regularly.

Fig. 9.3: The dome in front of the Mihrab, the Great Mosque of Cordoba.

Fig. 9.4: Altar and Nave of the inserted Cathedral inside the Great Mosque of Cordoba, 16th century.

Fig. 9.5: "Puerta de San José," one of the 11 doors at the Great Mosque of Cordoba.

Fig. 9.6: Qur`anic verses and decoration, Mihrab of the Great Mosque of Cordoba.

ARAB ART IN EUROPE DURING THE ISLAMIC PERIOD

Fig. 9.7: Bab Al-Mardum Mosque, Toledo, Spain, 999.

Fig. 9.8 : Brickwork with Kufic inscription on the facade of the Bab Al-Mardum Mosque, Toledo, Spain.

Fig. 9.9 : The Cathedral of Seville on the site of the Great Mosque of Seville, Spain, 15th century.

Arab historians state that numerous mosques were built throughout Al-Andalus; especially in Granada, Seville, Toledo and other major cities. Most of the mosques did not survive the Reconquista except for a few that were repurposed or converted to churches. The Reconquista sentiments of Spaniards propagated the intentional destruction of Arab buildings throughout the land. Only a few structures survived because they were converted to churches or modified for practical use. The Great Mosque of Toledo was demolished in the 13th century, and a major church––the Catedral Primada Santa María de Toledo––was erected on its site. Such is the case with the Great Mosque of Valencia, which was demolished, and the Cathedral of Santissima Maria was constructed on its site in the 13th – 15th centuries. Similar acts of removing the vestiges of Arab-Muslim heritage was done countrywide.

Bab Al-Mardum Mosque "Ermita del Cristo de la Luz"

Among the list of surviving structures is a small mosque known as Bab Al-Mardum in Toledo (Fig. 9.7). The characteristics of this building follow closely those of the Great Mosque of Cordoba. It was built in 999-1000, according to an Arabic inscription in brickwork on the wall, which also gives the names of the architect and sponsor. The original mosque was a square building about 8 meters in dimension. After Toledo was claimed by the Reconquista in the 12th century, the mosque was converted to a church, and a semicircular apse was added, replacing the original Qiblah wall and Mihrab. The original brick decoration of interlacing arches and Kufic inscription bands are still visible on the facade (Fig. 9.8).

Fig. 9.10: The minaret of the Great Mosque of Seville--now the bell tower "La Giralda," Seville, Spain.

Fig. 9.11: Details of a bronze original door of the Great Mosque of Seville--now Puerta del Pardon.

Fig. 9.12 : Alcazar, courtyard, Seville, Spain, 9th - 13th centuries.

Fig. 9.13: Interior of the Reception Hall, Alcazar, Seville, Spain.

The Great Mosque of Seville, Cathedral of Santa Maria de la Sede and Geralda

The construction of this congregational mosque (1172-1198) took place during the Al-Muwahhidun – Almohads reign of Al-Andalus. It was constructed with bricks and plaster; rectangular in plan with an open courtyard filled with orange trees, similar to the Great Mosque of Cordoba. The prayer hall and the arcaded courtyard were enclosed by a crenelated wall, fortified by buttresses also constructed of brick and plaster. In 1184 the minaret was added, which was a lavishly decorated grand tower following the style of the Al-Kutubiyyin mosque minaret (1147-1154) in Marrakesh.

After the Christian conquest of Seville in 1248, the mosque was consecrated as the Cathedral of Santa Maria de la Sede, Saint Mary of the See (The Holy See). The structural conversion started in 1402 and was completed in 1506. Many original mosque elements were used in construction of the new cathedral, which followed the same rectangular plan of the mosque. In the 15th century, most of the structure of the mosque was destroyed and a Gothic cathedral was built on its site (Fig. 9.9).

The minaret of the mosque was appropriated to serve as the bell tower of the cathedral. Initially a bell compartment was added, but in 1568 a higher addition was constructed in the Renaissance style, surmounted by a colossal bronze statue representing "Faith" holding a weathervane called "El Giardiello;" hence the popular name "Giralda" (Fig. 9.10).

The former mosque was destroyed, except for the Minaret (Giralda), the court of oranges (Patio de los Naranjos), and one gate (now called Puerta del Perdon), with its exquisite bronze-plated door (Fig. 9.11). The spared parts were integrated, with modification, into the new 16th century construction of the cathedral.

Fig. 9.14: Example of the decorative program at Alcazar, Seville, Spain.

Fig. 9.15: Kufic calligraphy at Alcazar, Seville, Spain.

Alcazar Complex, Seville

The building name "Alcazar" is derived from the Arabic word Al-Qasr, meaning "the palace." Alcazar was originally built as a palace, probably in the 8th century. It was enlarged and renovated in the 12th century during the reign of the Almohads. After Seville was reconquered in 1248, the palace was used as a royal residence by Spanish kings. Extensive renovations and enlargements were done by Arabs who continued to live in Iberia after the Reconquista. They were known as Al-Mudajjanun, or Mudajers, the latter a corruption of the Arabic term Mudajjan, a designation given to Arab-Muslims who remained in Iberia after the Reconquista. Mudajer, meaning domesticated or tamed, was a term also used in art to identify the building and decoration style done in Iberia by Arab architects, artisans and craftsmen for Christian kings and officials (Fig. 9.12).

The 13th century work on Alcazar was done by artisans who applied classic Andalusian methods, plan, visual elements, and decoration program to the renovated palace. A second level was added, and the entire complex was dressed with exquisite tile work, carved stucco, Muqarnas ('honeycomb' vaults), and calligraphic composition. Work was done by local Toledo artisans, including Arabs. Furthermore, artisans were called in from Cordoba to aid in construction. The palace was planned to surround the rectangular garden-pool court on three sides. The facades of the three wings are decorated with geometric stucco patterns complemented by interlacing poly-lobed arches and Muqarnas. Behind the facade is the opulent reception hall. The interior of the reception hall is lavishly ornamented with colored glazed tiles, carved wooden doors, and calligraphic bands framing sections of the walls and arches (Fig. 9.13).

Fig. 9.16: Aerial view, Madinat Al-Zahra, Cordoba, 9th – 10th centuries.

Throughout the palace, we find Arabic text, executed beautifully in Kufic and modified cursive styles. The inscription bands display a variety of textual content and were used primarily for aesthetic effect. Nevertheless, there are references to King Pedro I as "Sultan," sponsor and builder of the palace, carved in stucco and wood. The famous phrase used by Nasirid rulers of Granada "Wala Ghaliba Illa Allah," or "there is no victor but Allah," found throughout the Alhambra Palace in Granada, is also found scattered at Alcazar. Other phrases include well wishes, glorification, exaltation and praises, such as "Continuous Glee;" "Pleasure and Delight;" "Glory to Our Master" (Sultan or king); "May Allah Support and Grant Him Victory;" "Thanks to Allah for His Bounty;" "Bestowal from Allah;" "Greatness is for Allah;" "Glory and Might for our Master Al-Sultan," and other related sentiments (Figures 9.14, 9.15). Arabic poetry is also present, as well as plenty of illegible words. Calligraphic decoration of structures using such phrases was common throughout Arab-Islamic regions in the 11th century and earlier. They were usually found in secular buildings, but were also used in religious structures, depending on the context of the selected text.

The visual beauty and captivating effects of the Arab architectural style and decorative epigraphic program at Alcazar was also applied to other buildings that were constructed for royal Spanish personalities after the Reconquista. The style was admired by the populations of Iberia, both Muslims and Christians, regardless of political views. Spanish kings and high-ranking officials sought Andalusian artistic tastes and employed them in their palaces during the 13th-15th centuries. The predilection for Andalusian visual culture began to diminish with the rise of official anti-Arab, anti-Muslim policies, especially during the 16th century. The Alcazar is merely one surviving example of Arab art and architecture in Iberia; other buildings with similar characteristics, built between the 13th and 16th centuries, are scattered across the region.

Fig. 9.17: Audience Hall, Diwan of the Caliph, Madinat Al-Zahra`, Cordoba, Spain.

Madinat Al-Zahra`

At Madinat Al-Zahra`, we have a fortified Arab royal city planned and sponsored by Abd Al-Rahman III (890-961). He started his career as Amir (Emir) of Cordoba and then proclaimed himself Caliph of all of Andalus in 929. He succeeded in resisting many rebellions, consolidating his control over divided Andalus. Abd Al-Rahman III acquired the title "Al-Nasir li-Din Allah," or "The Defender of God's Faith." In his Caliphal pursuit, he challenged the Caliphal tradition of the Abbasids and the Fatimids. He was a patron of the arts and architecture and contributed significantly to the restoration and expansion of the Great Mosque of Cordoba. After declaring himself the Caliph of Andalus, he began a massive and ambitious royal project, the Madinat Al-Zahra`, literally meaning "the shining, splendid city" which was built between 936-940 (Fig. 9.16).

The complex is located some 5 kilometers (3.10 miles) north of Cordoba and included royal ceremonial reception halls ("Diwan" or "Majlis"), mosques, administrative and governmental headquarters, a Mint, residential quarters, baths, gardens, military garrisons, and other facilities. The function of a royal complex of this nature extended a superior political image of the new Caliphal reign; it was an expression of power, wealth, and might. Madinat Al-Zahra` thrived for over half a century but was sacked and severely destroyed in the civil conflict of 1010. The Succeeding Ruler, Ibn Abi `Amir, abandoned Madinat Al-Zahra' and established a new royal Palace-City called Al-Madinah Al-Zahirah (The Glorious City). Built on a site east of Cordoba in 979, Al-Madinah Al-Zahirah was the new seat of power for Al-Andalus. By choosing a

Fig. 9.18: General view of the Alhambra complex. Granada, Spain, 9th – 15th centuries.

similar name and nearby location, the new ruler intended to outshine the memory of the splendor of Abd Al-Rahman III and Madinat Al-Zahra`. According to contemporary literary sources of the time, the complex of Ibn Abi `Amir was soon looted and destroyed, due to the growing internal political and civic turbulence. No traces have been identified of Al-Madinah Al-Zahirah.

The restored area at Madinat Al-Zahra` includes residential units with baths; the court complex with two impressive ceremonial audience halls, called "Diwan" or "Majlis;" gardens and pools; and the congregational mosque. The audience halls (Fig. 9.17) represent yet another lavish display of wealth and power. Contemporary Arab historians left detailed accounts of some of the ceremonial activities at Madinat Al-Zahra`, such as the Caliph receiving foreign delegations seeking to establish or renew treaties and alliances. The accounts recall ambassadors from the Christian kingdoms to the north, envoys from the Byzantine Empire and Ottonian courts, as well as dignitaries from North Africa. Along with the details of such events, the accounts provide vivid descriptions of the building, the royal atmosphere of the reception halls and the routine protocols that took place inside them.

The architectural vocabulary at Madinat Al-Zahra` echoes the established trends in Arab art found elsewhere in Al-Andalus: horseshoe and interlaced arches; geometric and floral designs; stucco work; the Ablaq technique of using light and dark colored stones and brick; and Kufic calligraphic inscriptions. In one audience hall called Salon Rico, a commemorative inscription was found exalting Abd Al-Rahman III for his patronage of the project. Names of builders, masons, and decorators are also found on the columns of many capitals.

The ensuing centuries witnessed further loss of Arab power in the Andalus, culminating in the total takeover by the "Reconquista" in 1492. Arab visual heritage was neglected or wasted, and in certain cases destroyed intentionally. At present, restoration efforts at Madinat Al-Zahra` are slowly advancing, but only a fraction of the site has been excavated. The remnants of the structures that have been found demonstrate innovative architectural planning and exquisite decoration programs that follow the broader trends found in the Andalusian artistic repertoire.

Al-Hamra` Complex, Alhambra

The Al-Hamra` or Alhambra royal palace complex in Granada was initially built by the Arabs in the 9th century as a small palace castle called "Qasabah." In the 13th century it was enlarged with additions and became the official royal palace of Granada. In 1333, more sections were added to the complex, including a defensive wall by the Nasirids "Banu Al-Ahmar," the last dynasty of Al-Andalus. It is commonly known as the Alhambra, which is a Spanish corruption of the

Fig. 9.19: Interior of upper level room, the "Lindraja Balcony" - "Ain Dar `Aisha," with glazed ceramic tiles and stucco, Alhambra, Granada.

original Arabic name Al-Hamra`, meaning "the red one," probably referring to the color of the building materials. The complex survives in relatively good condition, even though it suffered regular abuse and negligence beginning in the 15th century. Its architectural and decorative programs are considered the standard source for and prime example of Arab-Islamic royal architecture of the time. There are many palaces within the complex, constructed at different times, but follow the same general architectural plan (Fig. 9.18).

In 1492, the Spanish Christian armies took over Granada under the united leadership of King Ferdinand and Queen Isabella. Consequently, the complex was appropriated for their residential use. Later in the 16th century, King Charles V dismantled part of the complex, which included sections of the palace, gardens and burial sites, and built a palace in the Renaissance-Mannerist style. In the late 19th and early 20th centuries, attention was paid to the complex, which resulted in excavation and restoration efforts that are still under way today.

Fig. 9.20: Alhambra, Interior with stucco work, calligraphy and Muqarnas, Granada, Spain.

Fig. 9.21: Alhambra, "Hall of the Two Sisters" with Muqarnas work at the ceiling and base of the dome, Granada, Spain.

Most famed at Alhambra is the interior decoration program, which include typical Andalusian arches; colonnaded arcades; interlaced and intertwined arches; Muqarnas at the bases of domes, under arches and in ceiling corners; carved stucco; geometric and floral design work on marble, wood and plaster; glazed ceramic tiles on walls; elegant slender marble columns; and exceptional calligraphic decorations and inscriptions throughout the spaces of the complex (Fig. 9.19).

The skillful artists of Al-Andalus created a spectacular program of decoration that fills every inch of the complex. They managed to design intricate carvings of geometric, vegetal and floral patterns embraced by dynamic compositions of Arabic calligraphy, as well as seemingly impossible Muqarnas elements displayed in radiant and harmonious colors.

Researchers have recently uncovered a highly sophisticated pattern of mathematic formulas used in the creation of the architecture at Alhambra; both in small details and large structural elements alike. Muqarnas composition are derived from a calculated system of three-dimensional vaulting with repeated units in the shape of honeycomb that seemingly multiply infinitely in a given space. The purely aesthetic element is found in the corners of ceilings, under balconies, at the bases of domes, under arches,

Fig. 9.22: Details of calligraphic inscriptions inside Alhambra, Granada, Spain.

and around doors and gates. At the Alhambra, Muqarnas is used to create an awe-inspiring visual presence from within the walls of the complex (Figures 9.20, 9.21)

Calligraphic Decoration at the Alhambra

The distribution of the Arabic epigraphic program on the walls, spandrels, arches, crowns, and doorframes at Alhambra exemplify the unparalleled visual splendor found at the complex, this time through the use of decorative text. The text on the walls of the various spaces are executed in different calligraphic styles: old geometric Kufic, modified Naskh, and modified Thulth. In some instances, there is cross-over between the Naskh and Thulth. The text contains phrases of commemoration and praise of the builder––the Caliph––along with short statements of good wishes, such as the common axiom of the Nasirid dynasty: "There is no victor but Allah," "Wala Ghaliba illa Allah," repeated ubiquitously (Fig. 9.22). Some historians believe that this phrase was initiated by Zawi ben Ziri, who contested Al-Mansur in 1000 and succeeded in establishing the Zirid Emirate of Granada, proclaiming himself the first Amir (Emir) (1013- 1019). Other sources interpret the use of the motto as having political and psychological implications, likely related to the status of the declining Nasirid reign at the time.

Fig. 9.23: Wooden window framed with carved calligraphic stucco work. Example of the use of Arabic calligraphy in the decorative program at Alhambra, Granada, Spain.

The repetition of the saying "There is no Victor but Allah," which is derived from Sura 12, verse 21 of the Qur`an, along with the use of short declaratory statements such as "Glory to Allah," or "Eternity to Allah," creates a conceptual atmosphere with a message that reverberates throughout the space. The structure becomes a choir, chanting repeatedly to visitors with audio-visual resonance. The walls "speak" to the audience, addressing occupants as they enter the space. This communication between building and audience exalts the visitor to active participant, a required ingredient for the whole visual repertoire, making the Alhambra a chief example of Arab-Islamic art presented as "Oratorical Architecture." Perhaps the concept of audio-visual interaction culminates at the Alhambra where selections of poetry from Andalusian poets are found decorating walls of the complex and on the basin of the Lion Fountain.

These court poets were known for their prolific artistic abilities: Ibn Al-Jayyab (1274-1349), Ibn Al-Khatib (1313-1375), and Ibn Zamrak (1333-1393). Their poetry on the walls of the Alhambra is a combination of praise and glorification of the Caliph, along with eloquent descriptions of the beauty of the building. They rhapsodized about festivities and described the nobility of the official activities of the Diwan. It appears that the poets were commissioned to compose odes in praise of the interior decoration of specific parts of the complex. Amazingly and unexpectedly, such descriptions are sometimes recited on behalf of the building itself where "she," "the building" exults joyfully about

Fig. 9.24: Ibn Al-Khatib's poetry in the "Salón de Comares," Alhambra, Granada, Spain.

Fig. 9.25: Painting of the 10 figures on the central ceiling of the "Hall of Kings," Alhambra, Granada, Spain.

ARAB ART IN EUROPE DURING THE ISLAMIC PERIOD

"her" beauty, like a young attractive bride addressing the audience. An example of such self-proclaimed beauty is the poetic words on the arch and wall of the private apartment with a balcony known as the "Lindraja Balcony" from the Arabic "Ain Dar `Aisha," which means the "Eye of `Aisha's apartment," by Ibn Zamrak:

> "Every artist has conferred on me his splendid aesthetics. Granting me his opulence and perfection. He who sees me--will know the radiance of a newly-wedded bride. He who contemplates me--will be enveloped in my splendor.
>
> He will embrace the moon through my luminous reflection and crown of light."

At the Al-Hamra` complex, we are introduced to a new form of art that integrates pictorial rendering, textual narratives, colorful ingenuity, and skillful craftsmanship. We can imagine the sophisticated sensual aesthetic effects of the visual conceptuality created by these ingredients combined with natural light and atmosphere. The artists of Alhambra transformed artwork from separated object to an actively engaged, transcendent space, complete with innovative architectural design elements and the exquisite use of calligraphic compositions and poetic narratives, bringing every inch of the palace complex to life.

Fig. 9.26: Mertola, Arab castle and former mosque--now a church (Igreja Matriz de Mértola), Portugal.

Fig. 9.27: The Church of Nossa Senhora da Anunciação, former mosque, Mertola. Portugal.

The Paintings of the Alhambra, Sala de Los Reyes

The most exciting and perhaps most unexpected scene is that of the three painted ceilings in the Hall of the Kings––the Sala de Los Reyes. The name comes from a painting on the ceiling of the central arch in the magnificent official ceremonial space. It shows 10 dignified royal figures occupying a "Diwan – Majlis" setting and engaged in serious conversation. The hall is intricately decorated with calligraphic and floral decoration complemented by Muqarnas patterns and stucco work. Three painted oblong ceilings divided by arches cover the roof of the hall. The subject of the paintings on two of these ceilings depict what appear to be narratives from literary sources or folk tales. The main focus of the central painting seems to be the 10 persons of authority (Fig. 9. 25).

The identification of the near life size figures is still debated among scholars; the general consensus is that they represent important Nasirid rulers of the period, dating from the 14th or early 15th century. The painting is done on thin leather, stretched over a wooden base. Due to centuries of negligence, all three paintings are in poor condition; a campaign of conservation and restoration is presently under way. The iconography of the paintings are still being analyzed. The presence of such an Arab art form in the 14th century in Al-Andalus shouldn't be a surprise. It is a continuation of the old tradition

Fig. 9.28: Interior of the main church of Mertola—former mosque, Mertola, Portugal.

of presenting visual narratives in both painting and sculpture, that we find in the art of the Fatimids, Abbasids, Umayyads, and that of the pre-Islamic era.

The political power of the Arabs in the Iberian Peninsula ended in 1492, but the culture that developed over 700 years in Al-Andalus did not cease to exist. Although much of the cultural heritage of the Andalusian Arabs has since been neglected, a tremendous amount has survived, scattered in local museums, private collections, and other institutions. Interest in the Arab-Andalusian tradition has grown in recent times, though historically, scholarship has been generally reluctant to acknowledge the contributions of the heritage. Future objective research and archaeological work will certainly enrich our knowledge about Arab cultural history in Europe, especially with regard to the visual arts in Spain and Portugal.

PORTUGAL

The Arabs invaded and occupied Portugal, which they called "Gharb Al-Andalus," meaning the western part of Al-Andalus, for over five centuries (711-1249). The circumstances of Arab rule in Portugal were very similar to that of Al-Andalus, and marks of Arab culture are still evident, especially in visual art and architecture. The Arabs constructed mosques, castles, military defensive structures and palaces in major cities. In the 13th century, Christian armies from the north reconquered the region, and most of the Arab population departed to North Africa; the remaining Arabs were deported in the 16th century. Arab palaces, castles, fortresses and mosques were reused, converted or destroyed during the aftermath of the Reconquista. Two buildings are worth mentioning: the castle and mosque in the city of Mertola in the district of Beja (Fig. 9.26).

The city of Mertola was founded by the Phoenicians in the 4th century BCE and was utilized as an active trading center. The castle was originally a Roman fortress, destroyed in the 5th century and rebuilt by the Arabs, with space, details, and defensive elements added during the 12th century. More work was done by the Almohads in the same period, with walls, towers and palaces built within the settlement at Mertola.

Fig. 9.29: Remains of the upper section of the Mihrab of the former mosque, main church of Mertola, Portugal.

The Church-Mosque (Nossa Senhora da Anunciação)

This congregational mosque was built in the 12th century during Almohad rule. It was converted to a church after the Reconquista in the 13th century, initially with minor changes. Major alterations took place in the 16th century; modifications to the interior and exterior of the mosque were made to accommodate the function of the church (Fig. 9.27).

Many elements have survived unaltered, including the four horseshoe arched doors, the minaret, and the prayer area with its typical Andalusian architectural design (Fig. 9.28).

Remains of the original Mihrab are still present on the altar wall of the building, with three original poly-lobed blind arches carved in stucco decoration (Fig. 9.29).

The Reconquista did not stop at eliminating the Arab people from Iberia, but also aimed to remove and destroy any cultural materials associated with the ethnicity. The unfortunate dogmatic approach caused irreversible damage to or complete loss of Arab architecture throughout Al-Andalus. Nevertheless, there are still many sites in Portugal and Spain with Arab archaeological materials waiting to be systematically excavated and studied.

Selected Bibliography

Almond, Lan, *Two Faiths One Banner,* Cambridge, Mass: Harvard University Press, 2009.

Anderson, Glaire, D., and Mariam Rosser-Owen, eds. *Revisiting Al-Andalus: Perspectives on the Material Culture of Islamic Iberia and Beyond,* Leiden: B. J. Brill, 2007.

Barrucand, Marianne. *Moorish Architecture in Andalusia,* Cologne: Yaschen, 1992.

Bush, Olga, *Reframing the Alhambra: Architecture, Poetry, Textiles and Court Ceremonial,* Edinburgh: Edinburgh University Press, 2018.

Crespi, Gabriele, *The Arabs in Europe,* New York: Rizzoli International Publication Inc., 1986.

Dodds, Jerrilynn, D., *Architecture and Ideology in Early Medieval Spain,* Pennsylvania: Pennsylvania State University Press, 1994.

____, ed. *Al-Andalus: The Art of Islamic Spain,* New York: MET Publication, 1992.

Echevarria, Ana, *The Fortress of Faith: The Attitude Towards Muslims in Fifteenth Century Spain,* Leiden: B. J. Brill, 1999.

Ecker, Heather, *Caliphs and Kings: The Art and Influence of Islamic Spain,* Washington DC.: Arthur M Sackler & Freer Gallery, 2004.

Evans, Helen C., ed., with Brandie Ratliff, *Byzantium and Islam: Age of Transition,* New York: The Metropolitan Museum of Art, 2012.

Fairchild, Ruggles, D., *Gardens, Landscape, and Vision in the Palaces of Islamic Spain,* Pennsylvania: Pennsylvania State University Press, 2003.

Hill, Derek, and Golvin, Lucien. *Islamic Architecture in North Africa: A Photographic Survey.* London: Faber and Faber, 1976.

Kennedy, Hugh, *Muslim Spain and Portugal: A Political History of Al-Andalus,* London: Routledge, 1996.

Lane-Poole Stanley, *The Story of the Moors in Spain,* New York: G. P. Putman's Sons, 1903.

Montêquin, F. A. de. *Muslim Architecture of the Iberian Peninsula: Eastern and Western Sources for Hispano-Islamic Building Arts.* CT: West Cornwall, 1987.

Parker, Richard B., *A Practical Guide to Islamic Monuments in Morocco.* Charlottesville, N.C.: The Baraka Press, 1981.

Rosser-Owen Mariam, *Islamic Art from Spain,* London: Victoria & Albert Publishing, 2010.

Roth, Ann Mary, *Jews, Visigoths and Muslims in Medieval Spain: Cooperation and Conflict,* Leiden: B. J. Brill, 1994.

CHAPTER 10

ARAB ART IN EUROPE DURING THE ISLAMIC PERIOD (800- 1500)

SICILY (SIQILYAH)

The Arabs targeted Sicily as early as the 7th century through swift attacks, and in 827 they succeeded in a major conquest that was promptly consolidated with further land gains (Map 9). By 902 Sicily was under Arab control with Palermo as its capital, after Byzantine domination dating back to 535. Sicily continued to be under Arab rule until the Normans invaded and conquered in 1060, also taking southern Italy and Malta. The Arabs of Sicily were connected with Al-Andalus, the Aghlabids of North Africa, the Fatimids in Egypt, and the Abbasids in Baghdad. This strong network enabled independent Sicily to prosper under Arab rule; social and intellectual advancements were now available to them from the Arab world. The Normans ended the political power of the Arabs in Sicily and Malta, but the culture reverberated for centuries.

The Normans were skillful fighters and soldiers with superior military aptitude, but lacked administrative skills and ingenuity. They found Sicily a highly advanced, cohesive society that they could not easily govern. They prudently employed the Arabs, utilizing their knowledge in order to attend to state affairs. Hence, the Norman kings were closely connected to Arab culture, and even utilized Arabic as an official language along with Greek and Latin. The Normans adopted existing Arab administrative systems, hired Arab personnel amongst their official staff, consulted with the Arabs in military affairs, and employed Arab art, architecture, and even clothing into their official court aesthetic. Sicily was a multicultural society characterized by religious tolerance; especially under the reigns of King Roger II and his grandson William II. Eventually, the dogmatic sentiment that swept through western Europe during the 12th century reached Sicily around 1200.

By the 13th century, the Arab-Muslim populations of Sicily suffered pressure, religious bigotry and alienation, and were ultimately eliminated from the island. In 1240, the remaining Arabs of Sicily, especially in Palermo, were deported to and confined in Lucera and Apulia in lower mainland Italy. In the isolated city, authorities exploited the Arab population for military and agricultural work. By 1300, after some 250 years of rule in Sicily, the Arab population faced forced conversions and enslavement in Lucera. Still, what the Arabs left behind in Sicily attests to a remarkable level of achievement in art and architecture, although habitually presented by Western scholarship as being Norman or only vaguely influenced by the Arab-Muslims. It is important to mention that a parallel situation occurred in Malta.

ARAB ARCHITECTURE IN SICILY

The Great Mosque of Palermo– The Palermo Cathedral

As in the case of Al-Andalus, the Arab-Muslims constructed fortresses, mosques, castles, and palaces in many cities and towns throughout the island, with a focus on Palermo, which they made the capital; replacing the former Byzantine capital of Syracuse. Interestingly, the Phoenicians developed a thriving commercial trading settlement in Palermo in 734 BCE. In the 9th century, the Arabs erected a Great Mosque in Palermo at the site of an older Byzantine basilica, according to sources. In 1185 the Normans repurposed the mosque and constructed a church, with additions and enlargements built in the 14th and 15th centuries (Fig. 10.1).

Fig. 10.1: Palermo Cathedral, formerly the Great Mosque, Palermo, Sicily.

Fig. 10.2: Qur`anic text on the original mosque's pillar, now at the entrance of the Palermo Cathedral, Palermo, Sicily.

Historic evidence points to the mosque as still functional beyond Norman conquest of Palermo in 1072. It seems that conversion took place gradually over an extended period of time, paralleling the diminishing Muslim population in Palermo. Parts of the mosque were incorporated into the new church; notably the entrance, where a stone column still stands (Fig. 10.2), carved with Qur`anic text (Chapter 7:52).

> "For we have certainly sent into them (people of the book) a book based on knowledge, which we explained in detail a guide and a mercy to all who believe"

Remnants of the Mosque's Mihrab and prayer hall Muqarnas still stand behind the altar wall of the church near the tower (Fig. 10.3). Perhaps the most interesting aspect of the cathedral is the architectural style. Strong Andalusian features are clearly employed, such as the interlaced arches, pointed arches, square multi-section tower-minaret, and the use of decorative geometric designs. In fact, these trends were prevalent in both Arab and Norman structures. Who were the architects, builders, and decorators? The Arab architectural and stylistic repertoire was highly developed by the time the Normans had arrived; by contrast, the Normans did not possess any comparable sophistication in the realm of visual or architectural heritage, as was espoused by the Arabs.

Arab architects, artists, and craftsmen continued to live and work in Sicily, especially in Palermo. Some mosques were converted into churches, with modification, as was the case at the Palermo Cathedral and the Church of St. John the Hermit, "Chiesa di San Giovanni degli Eremiti" in Palermo. Similar converted mosques are found in Syracuse, Enna, Catania, Messina, Nicosia and other towns and cities. During the conversion process, some of the original structures were spared and incorporated into the new churches. The Normans utilized the expertise of Arab architects and craftsmen and employed them in their building programs, just as was done in Iberia with the Mudajjanun – Mudajers. The Normans were fond of the splendor found in Arab-Islamic building styles and decorative details; hence all Norman buildings, including their palaces and churches, reveal the incorporation of Arab-Islamic visual or architectural characteristics.

The Martorana,

(Concattedrale Santa Maria dell' Ammiraglio)

The Martorana is a church that was constructed in 1143, under the direct sponsorship of George of Antioch. George of Antioch, an Arab Syrian who served as minister to King Roger II, the Amir, also Emir (governor) of Palermo, served as the admiral of Roger's Navy fleet. Prior to his service at the Norman court, he worked for the Zirid Sultan in Tunisia, later defecting to Norman Sicily. The Martorana has many Arab elements, such as marble columns and a wooden door, likely taken from destroyed mosques or other Arab-Muslim structures in the city. The bell tower was designed in the square-minaret style, commonly found in mosques of North Africa and Al-Andalus (Fig. 10.4). Characteristics of this type of minaret, such as the multi-section composition, are distinctly North African, such as the minaret at the Great Mosque of Qayrawan (Also Kairauan) in Tunisia (670-675).

Inside the church and around the magnificent Byzantine style mosaic work, there are a few marble columns (spolia) reused from former mosques. Some columns have carved Arab-Muslim decorations present, such as vegetal and floral motifs along with Arabic writing. The example in Figure 10.5 shows a reused column with its original Arabic Qur`anic carved text. It reads:

> "For God is with those who restrain themselves and those who do good" (Qu`ran: 16:128).

At the Martorana, there is yet another curious feature. The wooden band at the base of the dome is inscribed with Arabic text in Kufic style. The content is the Greek Orthodox liturgical hymn "Anaphora" (Fig. 10.6). It reads:

Fig. 10.3: Remains of the original Mihrab of the Great Mosque of Palermo, now behind the altar of Palermo Cathedral, Palermo, Sicily.

Fig. 10.4: The bell tower of Santa Maria dell' Ammiraglio (the Martorana), Palermo, Sicily.

Fig. 10.5: Qur`anic text on a reused marble column at the Martorana church, Palermo, Sicily.

Fig. 10.6: Anaphora Hymn in Arabic at the base of the dome of the Martorana, Palermo, Sicily.

"In the Name of God, the Father, the Son, and the Holy Spirit Al-Quds (Jerusalem). Sacred, sacred, sacred, God of armies over heavens and earth. Who is coming in the name of Oshi'ana in the heights. We pray to you, glorify you, thank you O Allah, O Father, O Son, O Yasu' Masaya and Holy Spirit, Who is carrying the sins of the world Accept our prayers."

The architectural style known as Arab-Norman prevailed in Palermo under Norman rule. New cathedrals were constructed in this way at the Cefalu Cathedral (1131) and Monreale Cathedral (1174-1182). In both buildings, we find Arab-Islamic articulations: the minaret-tower, intertwined arches, and geometric mosaic decorations. At Cefalu Cathedral, there are beautifully painted secular scenes decorating the ceiling, depicting a banquet, musicians, hunting, animals fighting, and mythological scenes, presented in pure Arab style. The paintings may have been inspired by those on the ceiling of the Cappella Palatina in Palermo. The Arab-Sicilian artists who decorated the ceiling were following a familiar painting style found in Fatimid Egypt and North Africa (Fig. 10.7).

Historians agree that the Norman period (1060- 1230) was a time of relative tolerance, co-existence, and harmony among the populations of Sicily. This is reinforced by the marriage of different styles in the arts: Byzantine, Islamic, and Gothic. Examples of the application of multicultural elements are found in many buildings in Sicily; for example, the exterior decoration of the apse of the Cathedral of Monreale displays such diversity (Fig. 10.8). Intricate interlaced arches, pointed arches, and inlayed geometric patterns adorn the structure. The same Arab characteristics are found in other structures, such as the church of St. Cataldo and the Admiral Bridge in Palermo.

ARAB ART IN EUROPE DURING THE ISLAMIC PERIOD (800-1500)

Fig. 10.7: Painting on the ceiling of Cefalu Cathedral, 12th century, Palermo, Sicily.

The Arab Amirs had traditional court lifestyles in Sicily and built leisure palaces complete with Diwans and entertainment pavilions. Some of the palaces were later used by Norman authorities; a significant example is the Palazzo dei Normanni, formerly the palace of the Arab Amir in Palermo. Although many older palaces were reused, Norman leaders also employed Arab architects, builders, and artists to erect new palaces for their luxury. Examples in Palermo include the famous La Zisa, La Cuba, and Uscibene. These structures were commissioned by Norman rulers and erected by Arab engineers along the outskirts of Palermo, serving as countryside homes amid pleasing natural settings.

La Zisa Castle-Palace, Palermo

The construction of La Zisa castle started in 1165 during the reign of the Norman King William I and was completed later in 1180 by his son King William II (Fig. 10.9). The castle-palace was apparently part of a network of palaces designed to provide a summer residence for the King. The palace is located in a large hunting resort known as Genoardo, Arabic for Jannat Al-`Ardh, or "Earthly Paradise." Other important palaces connected to this project are La Cuba Sottana, La Cuba Soprano, and Uscibene Palace.

The design and architectural decoration was evidently done by Arab architects and craftsmen. The name of the palace, "Zisa," is derived from the Arabic word `Aziz, or "dear," hence Al-Qasr Al-`Aziz, meaning the "dear palace." Inside the entrance hall, there is an

Fig. 10.8: Exterior of Apse, Monreale Cathedral, 12th century, Monreale, Sicily.

impressive composition of Muqarnas cascading above a fountain (Fig. 10.10).

Above the entrance of La Zisa, passing the corridor, an Arabic poetry couplet carved in modified Naskh style announces the palace to visitors. The inscriptions decorate both sides of the entrance arch, welcoming and introducing the palace (Fig. 10.11). The Arabic poetry reads:

> ... You shall see the great king of the era in his beautiful dwelling-place, a house of joy and splendor which suits him well.... This is the earthly paradise "Genoardo" (Jannat Al-`Ardh), that reveal its beauty. And this is the King (William II) Al-Musta'iz *(the exalted one with support of Allah),* And this is the dear palace "La Zisa" (Al-`Aziz).

William II officially used the Arabic "Al-Musta`iz" as his honorific title, a formality learned from Fatimids and Abbasid Caliphs. His father, William I, was called "Al-Hadi bi Amr Allah," translating to "the one who leads to the right path with the guidance of Allah." His grandfather, Roger II, acquired the honorific title "Al-Mu`tazz bi Allah," meaning "the one who is proud and strengthened by Allah," which was originally the honorific title of the Abbasid Caliph in Baghdad (d. 869). These honorific titles are found written in Arabic: sealing official Norman documents and on gold and silver coins of the period.

Fig. 10.9: La Zisa Palace, 12th century, Palermo, Sicily.

Fig. 10.10: Muqarnas decoration and fountain at the hall of La Zisa Palace, 12th century, Palermo, Sicily.

Here, we encounter the unique trend of the transformation of space into oratorical interactive podium. According to historic accounts, the La Zisa Palace originally had a band of monumental Arabic inscription carved in high relief in the ashlar blocks along the upper edifice. In the 14th century, a merlon crenellation was added on the top of the roof, probably for the purpose of military defense, which caused the destruction of the inscription band. It seems that such an inscription would resonate with the content of the entrance inscription, functioning within the concept of praise rhetoric. Luckily, a similar "decorative" inscription has survived in another castle in the area—La Cuba.

La Cuba, Castello della Cuba

The palace of La Cuba's name was derived from the Arabic word "Kubbah" (also Qubbah), meaning dome. It was built in 1180 for King William II, in the park known as Genoardo, mentioned above. Genoardo contained other prominent structures for royal leisure: La Zisa, La Cuba Soprano, the Cubula, and Uscibene. These resort castles formed a network of retreats for the royal family, near to Palermo and surrounded by delightful natural scenery. Genoardo was lush with woods, orchards, vineyards, with birds and animals roaming freely in the open setting. Surrounding the palaces were man-made lakes, ponds and tranquil fountains. The Norman kings

Fig. 10.11: Arabic inscription at the entrance of the hall of La Zisa Palace, 12th century, Palermo, Sicily.

established these parks following the customs of the Arab Amirs, who had built such complexes in places like Syria and Al-Andalus. La Cuba is a majestic rectangular castle, soaring 25 meters high (Fig. 10.12).

The building is designed in Arab architectural style, but also incorporated Romanesque and Byzantine elements. Elegant Muqarnas formations adorn the interior space, and blind pointed arches cover the exterior of the over

Fig. 10.12: La Cuba Castle, 12th century, Palermo, Sicily.

Fig. 10.13: Monumental Arabic inscription on the upper part of La Cuba, 12th century, Palermo, Sicily.

31-meter-long and 17-meter-wide castle. Thick walls and minimal windows at the lower level of La Cuba derive from Arab architecture designs, meant to keep interiors cool in hot climates. The upper part of the roof is covered by a band of carved ashlars with Arabic monumental inscriptions in modified Naskh style (Fig. 10.13).

The monumental Arabic inscription was overlooked by scholars until the middle of the 19th century. Although much of it is in ruins, most has survived, thanks to the sturdy high relief carvings on the ashlar blocks. Today, the palace museum displays some of the fallen pieces, along with a replica of the longer section made by mold casting (Fig. 10.14). A few scholars have attempted to read and interpret the surviving inscription in the 19th and early 20th centuries, with only partial success. The Sicilian scholar Michael Amari, well acquainted with Arabic, was able to identify and translate phrases referring to King William II, hence pointing to the possible time of construction and carving of the inscription band. The significance of this monumental Arabic inscription is yet another example of the continuity of the Arab oratorical architecture trend; "the talking building."

Obviously, there is a need for further research in this realm; inscriptions like the one found at La Cuba, as well as the large body of materials scattered in museums throughout Sicily deserve significant consideration and analysis. The status of art and architecture of Sicily during the

12th century was unique. Muslim populations, architects, artisans and craftsmen were living and working under the rule of Christian Norman kings, in what can be described as an advanced, multicultural, and tolerant society in Palermo. Norman acquisition of Arab culture was not a temporary trendy approach; instead, the implementation of Arab cultural practices and aesthetics was a mark of high culture that the Normans sought to be identified with. Museums in Europe and especially in Sicily house numerous cultural materials of the era which attest to this point. Materials include the famous royal mantle of Roger II, designed and produced by Arabs at the Tiraz factory in Sicily in 1133-34; marble slabs adorned with Arabic poetry in colored inlay; inscriptions praising Roger II and his palace; many luxury ivory carved boxes; jewelry; Qur`anic manuscripts; and vast numbers of grave headstones with informative obituaries.

THE PAINTED CEILING OF THE ROYAL CHAPEL–THE CAPPELLA PALATINA, PALERMO, SICILY

The royal Norman chapel known as the Cappella Palatina in Palermo is the most fascinating space found at the palace of King Roger II. The inclusion of Arabic text and pictorial decorations on the ceiling of the church make it unprecedented in the history of Christian visual decoration. The chapel lies

Fig. 10.14: Fallen pieces and museum replicas of the monumental Arabic inscription on the upper part of La Cuba, La Cuba Museum, Palermo, Sicily.

Fig. 10.15: The Norman palace, formerly Arab Dar Al-Emarah, Palermo, Sicily.

Fig. 10.16: The Cappella Palatina, general view of the Muqarnas ceiling, Palermo, Sicily.

at the heart of the former Arab fortress-palace "Dar Al-Emarah," which existed for most of the period of Arab reign in Sicily, prior to Norman conquest of Palermo in 1072. The Arab travelers Ibn Hawqal (10th century), and Ibn Jubayr (12th century) described and identified the Amir's palace, confirming the same location as the later Norman royal palace. By the time Roger II had reached the age of 17, the palace of the Amir had been modified, and was incorporated into the new Norman seat of power, thus establishing continuity with its former Arab function and location (Fig. 10.15).

The interior of the chapel is decorated with typical Byzantine-style Biblical narratives. However, a wooden ceiling executed in Arabic-Islamic style and technique cascades above the nave and two flanking side aisles of the chapel. The entire ceiling is adorned with stunning decorations: figural compositions of humans, animals, and birds; geometric, floral and non-figurative motifs; as well as Arabic calligraphy, in various Kufic sub-styles and a Naskh-like cursive script (Figures 10.16, 10.17, 10.18).

The pictorial program on the ceiling of the Cappella Palatina displays a variety of subjects: seated dignitaries with attendants, figures in niches and in windows, characters drinking from goblets, and pairs of young men playing chess (or similar). There are scenes of male and female musicians seated under palm trees, playing instruments like the flute, `Ud, drums, tambourine, as well as others. Also included are depictions of dancers, singers, poets reciting, scenes of pleasure, romance and love, fun and pastimes, hunting, fighting, entertainment, fairy tales, travel narratives, and a variety of daily-life activities. There are mythological depictions, detailed interiors of royal tents, thrones, and a variety of other enigmatic scenes (Fig. 10.17).

Along with this rich display, there is an even richer program of geometric and floral designs that frame and connect the figurative representations found on the Muqarnas ceiling. Interestingly, Arabic calligraphic text is used to complement and unify the entire composition of the ceiling, producing a diverse but balanced work of art. The text contains short expressions

Fig. 10.17: Examples of paintings on the Muqarnas ceiling, the Cappella Palatina, Palermo, Sicily.

Fig. 10.18: Examples of Arabic text on the Muqarnas ceiling, the Cappella Palatina, Palermo, Sicily.

of blessing and support, but no certain name of king, ruler, or individual is found. The Arabic expresses sentiments of magnificence, grandeur, beauty, protection, might, safety, happiness, victory, triumph, good health, well being, beatitude, vivaciousness, permanence, as well as good omen and prosperity (Figures 10.18, 10.19, 10.21).

Scholars have exhaustively studied the architectural design of the Cappella Palatina, the iconography of its Biblical paintings, and the symbolism. The ceiling's iconography has been interpreted as a reflection of royal power and the luxury of the royal milieu associated with the court of Roger II. It has also been read as a reflection of the Islamic conception of paradise, and a symbolic representation of cosmological nature. Another topic that has been discussed is the identity of the artists who worked on the ceiling: it has been suggested that they may have been Faṭimid Egyptians, local Sicilians, Arab Christians influenced by Byzantine art, and Muslim artists working within the established tradition of pictorial narration, a style reflected in the art of Al-Andalus. The structure and decorative features have also been interpreted as a celebratory expression of diversity intended by King Roger II.

The Royal Palace of King Roger II and Qasr Al-Amir

Arabic sources refer to the palace of the Arab Amir (Dar Al-Emarah) in Palermo. These references are given primarily by: the 10th century geographer, historian and traveler Ibn Hawqal from Iraq; the 12th century geographer and cartographer Al-Idrisi from Al-Andalus, who spent considerable time at the palace in Palermo upon invitation and commission from Roger II, to compose a treatise on the geography of the world; the historian Ibn Al-Athir (1160-1233) from Al-Jazeerah; and the Andalusian geographer and traveler Ibn Jubayr (1145-1217). The accounts of these historians and others reveal important details about the location of Qasr Al-Amir. The palace, which later was repurposed as the Norman Palace, was constructed in the Maghribi tradition as a royal and military garrison fortress, similar to Qal'at Bani Hammad in Algeria or the fortified structures in Tunisia and Morocco. Qasr Al-Amir must have contained many facilities and pavilions. In the complex, there was likely a royal Diwan, along with smaller audience halls and courts: for the reception of dignitaries, ambassadors and foreign officials; signing of treaties and discussion of legal and strategic plans; and for public petition forums.

The royal Diwan would have accommodated other functions, including the entertainment of guests and the royal court of the Amir. Activities of the Diwan would include music, singing, dancing, and poetry recitation, along with display of fine exotic objects complemented by an abundant service of food and drink. Similar space are the Umayyad Qusayr `Amra (Chapter 7), as well as the palace of the Caliph in Samarra, known as Jawsaq Al-Khaqani (Chapter 8). The Diwan was an essential part of the palace of the Amir; there is a strong possibility that the Diwan of Qasr Al-Amir was located at or near the location of the later Cappella Palatina.

THE ARABIC TEXT ON THE CEILING OF THE CAPPELLA PALATINA

The bulk of the Arabic text on the ceiling of the Cappella Palatina is a composite of rhyming prose and short phrases of blessing, praise, and wishes for well-being, fortune, strength and power. As discussed above, there is no mention of a specific name or honorific title of a ruler found amongst the writing. Common to the studies on this subject are the misinterpretation of images and an incorrect reading of the text as referring to Roger II. The Arabic phrases on the ceiling are non-religious (non-Qur'anic, non-Biblical) in nature. Rather, they are secular, courtly and official, addressing the reader formally as opposed to individually or privately. There is no direct relationship between the phrases and the images adjacent to them. The Arabic text on the chapel ceiling is executed mainly in Kufic script, with variant sub-styles (Figures 10.18, 10.19, 10.21).

Although there is no other surviving example of a wooden Muqarnas ceiling similar to the one in the Cappella Palatina, the high quality of its workmanship suggests an established tradition of painted ceilings in Palermo and throughout Sicily. We already know of at least two slightly earlier but nearly contemporaneous Muqarnas ceilings in Morocco, those of the Mosque of Al-Qarawiyyin in Fez (815, rebuilt 1135) and the Great Mosque of Tinmel, north of Marrakesh (1153–54). As for the aisles, we can look at the wooden aisles of the Great Mosque of Qayrawan (670) for comparison.

The quality of the pictorial images and the Arabic text, along with the architectural Muqarnas design, show an accomplished artistic tradition in these crafts. We can reasonably assume that a tradition of constructing and

Fig. 10.19: Examples of Arabic text in variant Kufic styles on the Muqarnas ceiling, the Cappella Palatina, Palermo, Sicily.

decorating ceilings was already in place by the beginning of the 12th century, not only in Palermo but in the other parts of Sicily as well.

An excellent example attesting to the spread of the tradition is found with the painted ceiling of the Cathedral of Cefalu near Palermo, built shortly after the Cappella Palatina. Another example is the Cathedral of Nicosia in the province of Enna, which was built in the 14th century, over a pre-existing Norman edifice that may itself have been built over the former Great Mosque of that city. Nicosia Cathedral still contains a painted wooden ceiling similar to Cefalu, which is now covered by a newer ceiling. We should also consider the Palazzo Chiaramonte-Steri in Palermo, which is an early 14th century palace, whose grand hall (Sala) has a painted ceiling that echoes the same tradition.

The Tradition of the Arab Diwan

The secular and luxurious lifestyles rendered in the ceiling paintings mirrored the activities and events that took place underneath it: receptions and entertainment of guests and dignitaries, public performances, and poetic and literary readings. The spaces of Diwan and Majlis are well known in Arab culture, and have existed in various regions beginning in the pre-Islamic era and continuing to modern day. A few examples will serve to illustrate this point. In pre-Islamic times, we have records of Diwans in palaces mentioned before, such as Al-Khuwarnaq, Ghatfan, Al-Ablaq, Qasr Bariq and Dhu Al-Shurufat. As we have seen, the Umayyad Caliphs continued the tradition, and their Diwans are still standing in Syria,

Fig. 10.20: Painted panels on the north aisle of the Muqarnas ceiling, the Cappella Palatina, Palermo, Sicily.

Jordan and Palestine in royal palaces such as Khirbat Al-Mafjar, Quṣayr 'Amra, and many others discussed earlier (Chapter 7). There are references to the Diwans of the Abbasids, Fatimids and later periods, with descriptions of similar secular settings and activities (Chapter 8).

This tradition was strong in Al-Andalus, with surviving Diwans, though in ruins, in the Alhambra complex: inside the Palace of the Lions and the Hall of the Kings. It was also employed in Madinat Al-Zahra` near Cordoba, in the Diwan of the Caliph 'Abd Al-Rahman III. The Arabic text on the Muqarnas and side aisle ceiling, along with their designs, were rendered by professional calligraphers and scribes who were fluent in Arabic; in other words, they were executed by native Arab-Sicilian artists (Figures 10.18, 10.21). Planned, designed and executed by learned people fluent in Arabic, the epigraphic program would have been intended to be consumed by a public similarly fluent in Arabic. That is to say, the artists, calligraphers and master designers of the ceiling would have conceived the Arabic text on the ceiling with the understanding that their patrons were highly learned Arab officials, be they Amirs, honored guests, or members of the aristocracy.

The Muqarnas Ceiling and the Chapel

The characteristics of the visual imagery on

Fig. 10.21: Detail of one of the 20 large eight-pointed stars along the central axis of the Muqarnas ceiling, the Cappella Palatina, Palermo, Sicily.

the ceiling and its text do not directly relate to the Norman king or his governmental officers. Arab Sicilian panegyrists like 'Abd Al-Rahman Al-Buthayri, composed poetry praising Roger II by name, and Arabic poetry inscribed on marble slabs meant for Roger's palaces in Messina and Palermo also contain messages of glorification, addressing the King by name directly. Why, then, would the Cappella Palatina's ceiling be missing names and titles? Was the ceiling constructed during the transformation of the old space to the new church? If so, where did the ceiling originate? Was it reused from another structure or another part of the palace? Or could it belong to the former Diwan of the palace of the Amir?

It is possible that the ceiling was part of the previous palace before the construction of the chapel in 1130. Another interesting question raised is about whether or not this ceiling is the only example of such construction, Could there have been other similar ceilings that have not survived? The answer to these questions depends further literary research and archaeological evidence. Several Arab royal palaces existed in Palermo, according to historical accounts, and some of their ruins are extant – as in the case of the already mentioned palace of the Arab Kelbite Amir in the Favara (Arabic Fawwarah, meaning fountainous) complex in Sicily, the Palace of Uscibene, and

Fig. 10.22: The Cappella Palatina, general view of the throne side, Palermo, Sicily.

Fig. 10.23: View of the Muqarnas ceiling, the Cappella Palatina, Palermo, Sicily.

others.

According to Arab historian Ibn Al-Athir (1160-1233), Roger II imitated Muslim leaders in many ways, including the establishment of a new Diwan called "Diwan Al-Madhalim," or Office of Grievances. Ibn Al-Athir described Roger II in this way:

> "... He (Roger II) copied and followed the royal etiquette of Muslim kings and established "Diwan Al-Madhalim," The court of grievances, where he listened to complaints and justly judged them even if he had to punish his own son..."

It is possible that he adopted the original Arab Diwan and used it for that purpose. The Diwan mentioned above was later modified and consecrated as a chapel in 1140, and probably used as a church and Diwan at the same time by Roger II, until his death in 1154. Such dual usage was practiced by the 8th century Emperor Charlemagne in the royal chapel at Aachen in Germany. The layout of the Cappella Palatina reveals that functionality, where the raised platform of the throne is positioned across the Altar (Fig. 10.22).

Roger II utilized the ceiling as part of his new royal chapel–the Cappella Palatina–probably for its visual splendor, but also because of his knowledge and taste for Arab traditions, thereby associating his official personage with the culture of the Arabs. Arab heritage was prevalent in the region; associated with education, sophistication, and intricacy. Before the Diwan at the complex was converted to church, the space may have functioned as the Diwan of Grievances for the Norman King; in which citizens of Sicily, including Arab and Muslim clients, would have attended the space. King Roger II maintained cultural continuity for his Arab populace; he acquired an Arab-Muslim honorific title, used Arabic as the official language in his Diwans and on buildings and currencies, and most importantly, he preserved the traditions of Arab Sicily, clearly visible with the Muqarnas ceiling at the Diwan of Grievances. The Muqarnas ceiling at the Cappella Palatina is a key monument of Arab art; it is a visual treasure that represents the richness and diversity of the cultural era of the Arabs in Sicily (Fig. 10.23).

Selected Bibliography

In addition to the list in Chapter 9

Abbas Ihsan, *Al-Arab fi Siqilliyya, The Arabs in Sicily* (Arabic), Beirut, Lebanon: Dar Al-Thaqafah, 1975.

Ahmed Aziz, *History of Islamic Sicily*, Edinburgh: Edinburgh University Press, 1975.

Agius Dionisius A., *Siculo Arabic,* London & New York: Kegan Paul International, 1996.

Al-Baladhuri, *Futuh Al-Buldan, History of Islamic Conquest* (Arabic). Ed. Abdallah A. Al-Tabba, Beirut, 1987.

Al-Baladhuri, *Futuh Al-Buldan* (English). Trans., Philip Khuri Hitti, under *The Origin of the Islamic State*, Beirut, 1965.

Al-Idrisi, *Nuzhat Al-Mushtaq fi Ikhtiraq Al-Afaq, The Pleasant Journey of the Seeker to Explore the Faraway Lands,* (Arabic), Cairo: Al-Thaqafah Al-Diniyyah Bookstore, ND.

Al-Imad Al-Asfahani Al-Katib, *Kharidat Al-Qasr wa Jaridat Al-`Asr,* (Arabic), Tunisia 1986.

Al-Musarrif, Naji Zain Al-Din, *Musawwar Al-Khatt Al-'Arabi,* (Arabic), Baghdad, 1974.

Al-Siqili, Ibn Al-Qata', *Al-Durrah Al-Khatirah fi Shu'ara' Al-Jazirah (Siqilyah),* (Arabic), being an anthology of Arab Sicilian poets, edited by Bashir Al-Bakkush, Beirut: Dar Al-Gharb Al-Islami, 1995.

Al-Tawil, Hashim, "The Arabic Calligraphy on the Ceiling of the 12th century Cappella Palatina in Palermo, Sicily: Function and Identity", in *Calligraphy and Architecture in the Muslim World,* Eds. M. Gharipour and Irvin Schick, Edinburgh: Edinburgh University Press, 2014.

Amari Michele, *Le Epigrafi Arabiche di Sicilia: Transcritte,* Tradotte e Illustrate, 3 parts, Palermo, 1875, reprint Palermo: S. F. Flaccovio, 1971

___, (ed.), *Biblioteca arabo-sicula,* Torino and Roma: Ermanno Loescher, 1880-1889.

Atil Asin, *Renaissance of Islam: Art of the Mamluks*, Washington DC: Smithsonian Institution, 1981.

Costa P. M. "Early Islamic Painting: from Samara to Northern Sicily", *New Arabian Studies 3*, Ed. Rex Smith and others, Exeter, UK: University of Exeter Press, 1996, 14-32.

Curtis Edmund, *Roger of Sicily and the Normans in Lower Italy 1016-1154,* New York: G. P. Putnam's Sons, 1912.

Dennis, George, and Murray, John, *A Handbook for Travellers in Sicily,* London 1864, reprinted by University Publication of America.

Ettinghausen, Richard, *Arab Painting*, New York: Rizzoli International Publication, 1977.

Gabrieli, Francesco and Scerrato Umberto (ed.): *Gli Arabi in Ltalia:* cultura, contatti e tradizioni. Saggi di P. Balog, A. Bausani, E. Guidoni, A.M. piemontese, A. Ragona. (Antica Madre, a cura di G. Pugliesi Carratelli.) Milan: Libri Scheiwiller for the Credito Italiano, 1979.

Gelfer-Jorgensen, Miriam, *Medieval Islamic Symbolism and the Painting of the Cefalu Cathedral*, Leiden: B. J. Brill, 1986.

Grube, Ernst J., & Johns Jeremy, *The Painted Ceilings of the Cappella Palatina,* New York: The Bruschettini Foundation for Islamic and Asian Art, The East-West Foundation, Italy, 2005.

Houben, Hubert, *Roger II of Sicily: Ruler between East and West:* (translated by Graham A. Loud and Diane Milburn), Cambridge, UK: Cambridge University Press, 2002.

Ibn Al-Athir, *Al-Kamil fi Al-Tarikh* (Arabic), Beirut: Dar Al-Kutub Al-`Ilmiyyah, 1987.

Ibn Al-Athir, *The Chronicle of Ibn Al-Athir for the Crusading Period from Al-Kamil fi Al-Tarikh,* Part 1. Translated by

D.S. Richards, Crusade Texts in Translation, London: Aldershot, Ashgate, Farnham, 2006.

Ibn Hawqal, *Surat Al-Ardh* (Arabic), Beirut: Dar Maktabat Al-Hayat, 1992.

Ibn Jubayr, *Rihlah Ibn Jubayr, The Travel of Ibn Jubayr* (Arabic), Beirut: Dar Sadir, ND.

Jansen Katherine L., Drell Joanna, and Andrews Frances, Ed., *Medieval Italy: Text in Translation,* Philadelphia: University of Pennsylvania Press, 2009.

Johns, Jeremy, *Arabic Administration in Norman Sicily: The Royal Diwan,* Cambridge Studies in Islamic Civilization, Cambridge: Cambridge University Press, 2002.

____, The Bible, the Quran, and the Royal Eunuchs in the Cappella Palatina, Thomas Dittelbach (ed.) *Die Cappella Palatina in Palermo* - Geschichte, Kunst, Funktionen. Forschungsergebnisse der Restaurierung Hg. im Auftrag der Stiftung Würth, Künzelsau: Swiridoff Verlag, 2010.

Kitzinger, Ernst, & Ćurčić Slobodan, *The mosaics of St. Mary's of the Admiral in Palermo,* Washington DC: Dumbarton Oaks Studies, Harvard University, 1990.

Kreutz, Barbara, M., *Before the Normans: Southern Italy in the Ninth & Tenth Centuries,* Philadelphia: University of Pennsylvania Press, 1991.

Mallette, Karla, *The Kingdom of Sicily, 1100-1250*, Philadelphia: University of Pennsylvania Press, 2005.

Metcalfe, Alex, *Muslim of Medieval Italy,* Edinburgh: Edinburgh University Press, 2009.

Monneret de Villard, Ugo, *Le pitture musulmane al soffitto della Cappella Palatina in Palermo,* Roma: La Libreria dello Stato, 1950.

Nercessian, Nora Nouritza, *The Cappella Palatina of Roger II: The Relationship of its Imagery to its Political Function,* Unpublished Ph.D. Dissertation, University of California, Los Angeles, 1981.

Norwich, John Julius, *Sicily: An Island at the Crossroads of History,* New York: Random House, 2015.

____, *The Kingdom in the Sun, 1130 -1194,* New York: Penguin, 2004.

Petrus de Ebulo, *Liber ad honorem Augusti sive de rebus Siculis* translated to German and annotated by Gereon-Becht-Jördens, Jan Thorbecke Bonne: Verlag, 1994.

Simon-Cahn, Annabelle, *Some Cosmological Imagery in the Decoration of the Ceiling of the Palatina Chapel in Palermo,* Unpublished Ph.D. Dissertation, Columbia University, 1978.

Starke, Mariana, *Travels in Europe*, 9th edition, Paris: A. and W. Galignani and Co., 1836.

Taylor, Julie Ann, *Muslims in Medieval Italy: The Colony at Lucera,* London: Lexington Books, 2003.

Tronzo, William, *The Cultures of His Kingdom, Roger II and the Cappella Palatina in Palermo,* Princeton, NJ: Princeton University Press, 1997.

____, "The Medieval Object-Enigma, and the Problem of the Cappella Palatina in Palermo", *Late Antiquity and Medieval Art of the Mediterranean World,* Ed. Eva R. Hoffman, New York: Blackwell Publishing, 2007, 367-388.

Waern, Cecilia, *Medaeival Sicily: Aspects of Life and Art in the Middle Ages,* London: Duckworth & Co., 1910.

CHAPTER 11

ARAB CULTURAL IMPACT AND EXCHANGE

Arab culture, including the realm of visual arts and architecture, developed through a long process of assimilation, integration and adaptation other cultures. Contact with other cultures has occurred consistently throughout the history of the Arab populations. In turn, cultural exchange has had multiple impacts on the culture: it has manifest influence, spread influence, or functioned to influence both populations, inspiring cultures reciprocally. The most sensitive characteristics of any culture, when under the impact of another culture, would reflect on the language, the art, the architecture, and other social features such as religious or ritual practices. In this chapter, we will take a brief look at Arab cultural exchange throughout its historic phases and explore some highlights, especially from the period of its peak (900-1600).

Cultural Exchange Through Trade and Commerce

Early indications of such occurrences come from the Phoenician-Canaanite expansion in the Mediterranean Sea during their height (1500 BCE – 400 BCE). The Arabs were in direct contact with the Assyrians, Egyptians and Greeks. Their trade and commercial activities with powerful empires resulted in the absorption of outside influences as well as the extension of their own influence abroad. The Phoenicians impacted the early Greeks in the formation of their language and in artistic compositions of the Archaic period, sometimes referred in art history as the "Orientalizing" style of Greek Art. Furthermore, trade and commercial activity with the Assyrians and the Egyptians disseminated the established imperial artistic styles of both empires to the Phoenicians, as we have seen in Chapter 1.

The Nabataeans in Petra and Palmyra developed their art and architecture, rooted in the culture of the ancient South Arabian kingdoms. They were also impacted by Hellenistic culture, especially the Roman visual vocabulary, as evidenced in Petra and Palmyra when the Romans dominated their territories (see Chapter 3). Similar situations are found in the art and architecture of the Arabs of Hatra under the Parthians; Hirah under the Sassanids; and the Ghassanids under the Byzantines (see Chapters 4 and 5). The Arab activity in the commercial operations of the Silk Road contributed to the cultural exchange, and hence to assimilation and inspiration. Arab confederates and semi-kingdoms demonstrated active roles in monitoring, servicing, and controlling much of the transactions of trade highways that passed through the regions of Arabia and adjacent territories in Syria and Iraq. Those commercial activities necessitated frequent travel to foreign lands along with the receiving and hosting of unfamiliar populations. Arabs were exposed to foreign languages, beliefs, rituals, and ways of life. This multi-level exchange also impacted the development of visual art traditions.

With the rise of Arab power in the 7th century, a new artistic trend was born: Islamic art. The essence of Islamic art depended heavily on the indigenous Arab traditions that had existed for centuries in the area. Islamic art became the official cultural forum of the new rising empire during the period of the Rashidun Caliphs, and more clearly with the Umayyads. Two major cultural stimuli contributed to the formation of Islamic art: Byzantine and Sassanian. However, the crucial, dynamic apparatus was the tradition of Arab art, with its roots in South Arabia, Syria and Iraq. A major element in the Islamic visual tradition became the use of the Arabic language. On one hand, the power of the Arabic language made it an apt vehicle in teaching Islamic theology and performance of rituals. On the other hand, the monumental artistic use of Arabic calligraphic compositions substituted figurative narratives, as they were deemed inappropriate for use in religious spaces. This new visual concept of non-figurative narratives spread throughout the Arab-Muslim world, including to newly conquered lands and Isles in the Mediterranean.

Arab-Islamic Art Abroad

As we have seen in Chapter 10, Arab art was firmly established in Al-Andalus–in Southern Iberia for over 700 years, and in Sicily for over 250 years. Both Sicily and Al-Andalus were frequently visited by European seekers of knowledge, who attended learning institutions in Toledo, Seville, and Salerno in southern Italy. Traditionally, such learning institutions were housed in major Mosques in key cities next to schools, in Arabic "Madrasa" (also Medrasa; plural Madaris). Scholars occupied a corner of the mosque as their own classroom to teach students. European knowledge seekers joined their Arab colleagues in this educational process, translating into Latin the Arabic corpus of science that was compiled, annotated, critiqued, and added to in Baghdad from ancient Greece between the 8th and 10th centuries. Arab scholars of the 11th and 12th centuries in Iberia and Sicily were instrumental in advancing and transmitting the legacy of Greco-Roman intellectual heritage back to Europe after centuries of neglect. The Arab contribution played a critical role in the European awakening that eventually led to the Renaissance. Concurrently, aspects of Arab visual art reached many European locations outside Al-Andalus and Sicily, through trade, travel, diplomacy and war.

War and Diplomatic Relationships

The crusades opened direct access to the Arabs starting in the 11th century: the Reconquista in Spain and Portugal; the Norman invasion in Sicily; and the collective repeated systematic military campaigns along the eastern shores of the Mediterranean—Palestine, Syria, Egypt and North Africa. Extended contact provided exposure and awareness of the Muslim architectural methods and building techniques, which was later utilized in the construction of Romanesque churches and culminating with Gothic cathedrals. Most noticeable are the use of pointed arches and ribbed ceilings, which both reduced structural thrust, a practical solution in achieving the desired height of Gothic churches. Moreover, the structure of the square bell tower, again found in Gothic cathedrals, emulated the distinct Muslim minarets of Toledo, Seville and Granada. Furthermore, geometric and vegetal designs, a signifying factor of Islamic art, are commonly found decorating the Rose Windows of Gothic churches.

The Abbasid Caliph Harun Al-Rashid's Gifts to Charlemagne

The Arab-Muslim states in the east and the west of the Arab-Islamic empire maintained diplomatic channels with their adversaries; whether it was the "Rum"—the Byzantines in the east, or the "Frenj"—the Franks, Frankish, the different kings and emperors of the Holy Roman Empire, and the papal office in the west. Historic records indicate the nature of diplomatic exchanges, which included gifts of extravagant textiles, jewelry, or other luxurious objects. The Abbasid authorities established diplomatic alliance with the Carolingians in the 8th and 9th centuries, possibly to face the growing power of the Umayyads in Al-Andalus. In 798 Charlemagne, the emperor of the Holy Roman Empire, dispatched an embassy to Baghdad, seeking an alliance with the Caliph Harun Al-Rashid. The envoy spent months in Baghdad, which was the most advanced city of the time, likely taking note of the customs, advanced ways of life, and visual splendor of architecture and art. They returned to Aachen with gifts from the Caliph in Baghdad, and similar embassies were repeated years later.

Historical records describe the gifts that the Abbasid Caliph Harun Al-Rashid sent to Charlemagne in 807, which included an intricately carved ivory horn, a decorated golden tray and pitcher, a water jug, perfumes, a set of chessmen, fine cloth, a large tent-pavilion, and a richly woven mantle of honor embroidered with the Arabic phrase "La Ilaha Illa Allah" (There is but one God). The list of gifts to Charlemagne also included an albino elephant, two tall elegant engraved brass candlesticks, and a fancy complicated water clock. The clock had 12 brass balls that struck the hour by falling on a cymbal, and 12 carved horsemen, who came out of small windows to parade. Sadly, the clock has been lost, but was detailed in the 807 CE in "Annales regain Francium," a journal that chronicled daily life in Charlemagne's court. Many gifts are housed in various treasuries of European cathedrals, abbeys, and monasteries. One such object, believed to have been one of the gifts provided by Harun Al-Rashid, is a golden rose-water jug elaborately decorated with precious stones. It is now in the treasury of the Abbey of Saint-Maurice, Valais in Switzerland (Fig. 11.1). We know that similar relations with the Byzantine emperors were also established, as evidenced in exchange of embassies and trade. Notable is the embassy sent by the Abbasid Caliph Al-Muqtadir to the King of the Volga Bulgars in 921. Among the members of the delegation was Ibn Fadhlan, the secretary of the Ambassador. Ibn Fadhlan wrote a detailed account of the trip, known as "Risalat Ibn Fadhlan", also "Rihlat Ibn Fadhlan", or the Journey of Ibn Fadhlan.

Arab Decorative Visual Vocabularies in European Art

The so called pseudo-Kufic decoration, also Kufisque/Cufisque and pseudo-Arabic, appeared in the architecture, painting, sculpture, stained glass, furniture and other art objects in Christian Europe as early as the 11th century, if not earlier. The use of pseudo-Kufic decoration in European art was a prominent phenomenon that scholars and historians are often puzzled by. These pseudo–Kufic stylizations continued to appear on the walls and floors of many churches; in works of religious paintings; sculptural monuments; and metal works through the 17th century. What were the reasons or intentions of such artistic decisions? What are the iconographies of the compositions, and how do they serve the religious spaces they occupy? The majority of scholars who have studied this subject argue that it was the result of imperfect copying of Kufic script that would have been seen on imported luxury textiles, pottery, jewelry, furniture, illuminated manuscripts, metalwork and other goods. Other scholars see it as an attempt to introduce an element of exotic or foreign attraction to a work. It seems that European civil and religious authorities, intellectuals, and artists agreed that there was merit in the visual

Fig. 11.1: Rose-water jug, believed to be a gift from Harun Al-Rashid to Charlemagne, 766-809, gold, precious stones and enamel. The Treasury of the Abbey of Saint-Maurice, Valais, Switzerland.

art of Arab-Islamic culture. But why were Arab-Islamic visual elements used mostly in the art of Christian subject matter?

To understand the reason for such appreciation, we have to fully comprehend the cultural impact created by Arab culture in Europe during the period of the 8th–17th centuries. The Arabs conquered European lands during the height of their advancement in civilization, during the so-called "Golden Age" of Islam (800-1400). They brought with them great advancements and invested them in the newly conquered territories of Iberia, Sicily and elsewhere. Among their advancements and technologies were elaborate agricultural structures; extensive irrigation systems; dams and water reservoirs; new crops, fruits and plants; as well as the transformation of the dilapidating feudal serfdom and slave labor into a system of till-sharing farming. They introduced paper-making, public education, better healthcare technologies and services, and many other advanced ways of life to Europe, which was crumbling under the burden of the "Dark Ages."

Cities under the control of the Arabs in Al-Andalus and Sicily in turn became bridges that transmitted Arab art to Europe. Additionally, major Italian ports like Venice, Bari, Naples, Salerno, Florence and others were busy receiving goods from Muslim ports on the Mediterranean. Among these materials were portable objects of exquisite quality and craftmanship. The list includes carpets, textile, ceramics, metal works, jewelry, woodcarvings, glasswork, and illustrated manuscripts. These items contained a variety of visual decorations and narratives along with remarkable calligraphic compositions. Illustrated Arabic manuscripts of philosophical, geographical, medicinal and mathematical treatises reached Europe in both Arabic and Latin editions and were used in major institutions. This funneling in of Arab-Islamic intellectual, social, technological and artistic innovation provided a promising landscape against the backdrop of the European "Dark Age."

KNOWLEDGE EXCHANGE AND DISSEMINATION

During the 12th–14th centuries, Arab science and knowledge were valued by European educational circles. Such a repertoire was sought after, especially among the religious and civil authorities. A few noteworthy examples illustrate this point. The first example is the 12th century Andalusian Ibn Rushd—Averroes—; a polymath who excelled in logic, philosophy, theology, jurisprudence, psychology, political theory, geography, math, astronomy, physics, medicine and other fields of knowledge. One of his books, Al-Kullyat fi Al-Tibb, *Principles of Medicine*, was translated into Latin under the title Colliget. It became a major textbook in Europe beginning in the 12th century and for centuries beyond (Fig. 11.2). The High Renaissance Italian artist Raphael included Ibn Rushd among major philosophers and thinkers from different civilizations, though mostly Western, in the famous Vatican fresco mural known as "The School of Athens." Why did he include Ibn Rushd? Raphael's chosen subject matter reflects the general mentality of the Renaissance, which held in high regard great thinkers relevant to Europe, a list which included Ibn Rushd.

Ibn Rushd was known in Europe as "The Commentator," because of his extensive commentary regarding the philosophy of Aristotle; Ibn Rushd even criticized dogmatic Islamic views that existed among fundamentalist Muslim theologians. He reconciled Islamic traditions with ancient Greek thought, propagating the importance of independent critical thinking. His publications reached Europe through translations in Greek and Latin, which were not well received by rigid Christian authorities, but welcomed by those who adopted a knowledge-seeking humanistic attitude. It was Averroes who introduced "Humanism" to Europe through his book "The Commentaries" (Fig. 11.3). As his philosophies spread, a new school of thought developed in Europe, called Averroism. The movement swept through Europe, opposed by the church and theological dogma at first, but later his philosophies flourished among wide circles of Christians and Jews. His teachings were so popular that his texts were translated and used at major universities in Paris, Padua, London and others.

Ibn Rushd, known to the West as Averroes, reintroduced the ancient Greek concept of "Humanism," in a more critical, practical and realistic structure to the Arab-Muslim and European worlds. "Humanism" was the philosophical foundation for what would later become the 16th century Renaissance. Raphael's inclusion of Ibn Rushd represents the impact

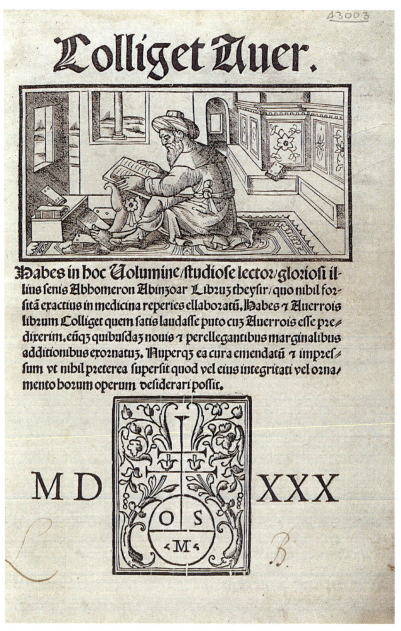

Fig. 11.2: A Latin copy of Averroes Colliget, *Principle of Medicine,* dated 1530. Yale University, Cushing/Whitney Medical Library.

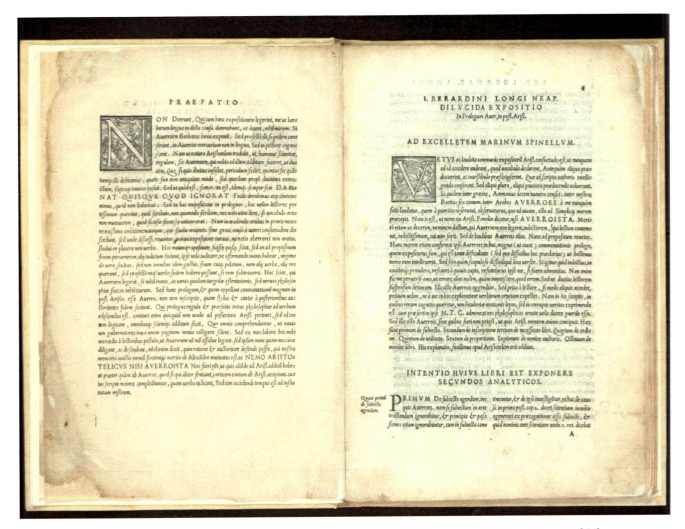

Fig. 11.3: Latin translation of Averroes's Commentaries, printed in Napoli 1551, Qatar National Library.

of an important thinker on European culture. Ibn Rushd's philosophies caused an intellectual tremor in late Medieval Europe, paving the way for the intellectual rebirth experienced during Raphael's lifetime. Arab-Islamic culture gained high esteem among intellectual circles, civil authorities, and religious powers in Europe; which helps explain the preference of the use of pseudo-Kufic decoration in European artistic spaces, as we will see later in this chapter.

The second example is the Arabic book Al-Qanoon fi Al-Tibb, or *Canon of Medicine*, which is an encyclopedic work by Ibn Sina (Latin: Avicenna)(980-1037). A Muslim from the Eastern Islamic lands, Ibn Sina was known for his prolific intellectual work and innovative mind. His medical encyclopedia was translated from Arabic to Latin in Al-Andalus. It soon reached Europe and was used as a textbook in major medical schools beginning in the 11th century to as late as the 18th century. Many prestigious universities in Europe carry his name on their buildings. The Canon was translated to Latin by Gerard of Cremona in the 13th century under the title *"Canon Medicinae"* and was adopted in the curricula of many universities in Europe from the 14th century on (Fig. 11.4).

The third example comes from Mohammed Al-Idrisi (1100-1165) in Al-Andalus. Al-Idrisi was a brilliant geographer, cartographer and traveler-explorer. The Norman King Roger II was interested in the field of geography and sought a scientific scheme of the geography of his kingdom, as well as the known world at the time. He was aware of the inept production of cartographic maps made by Europeans, which mostly depicted the locations of the "Garden of Eden" and "Paradise," usually at the top of the map with "Jerusalem" at the center. Maps of this kind were filled with depictions of mythological monsters, dragons, and ominous fantastic creatures occupying the unexplored regions. Hence, King Roger II turned to Arab scholars, and invited and commissioned Al-Idrisi to create a geographical account of the known world. Roger II in effect established and supervised a "Geographical Academy" with Al-Idrisi as its director in Palermo in the 12th century.

Al-Idrisi spent 18 years in Palermo living and working at the Norman Royal Palace, under direction of the king and alongside tens of assisting geographers and astronomers, mostly Arabs. He finished his project in 1154, producing a book of maps and a model of the earth. It was a great silver disk––80 inches in diameter, and weighing over 300 pounds, inscribed and marked with information derived from his book. The Arabic title of the book, Nuzhat Al-Mushtaq fi Ikhtiraq Al-Afaq, translates to *"The Pleasant Journey of the Seeker to Explore the Faraway Lands."* It is also known as "The Book of Roger," or Tabula Rogeriana. This remarkable treatise was the first serious geographical account of the known world produced in the Middle Ages and based on factual information (Fig. 11.5).

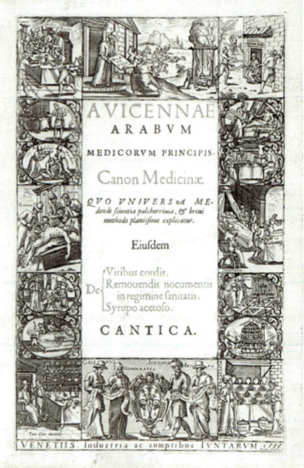

Fig. 11.4: Arabic Page from Ibn Sina, Avicenna's Canon (Qanoon) (left), and the frontispiece of the Latin version printed in Venice 1559 (right).

Roger II died in 1154, and Al-Idrisi continued working for his son, King William I on a similar and more comprehensive project. In 1160, a rebellion led by the barons of Sicily erupted: the royal palace was looted, the academy was destroyed, records, accounts and maps were burned, and the silver disc disappeared, probably cut to pieces and melted down for silver. The barons also attacked the Arab-Muslim populations of Sicily, and Al-Idrisi promptly fled to North Africa. His book became an essential source in Europe and the Muslim world. "The Book of Roger" was published in Rome by the Medici press in 1592. The Latin version became available in Europe by the 17th century.

The legacy and impact of Idrisi's work was significant in the Mediterranean and Muslim worlds. Arab-Muslim geographers of the 13th to 16th centuries produced maps with geographical details based heavily on Idrisi's work. The Arab Moroccan explorer Ibn Battuta's (1304-1369) book Tuhfat Al-Nudhdhar fi Ghara'ib Al-Amsar wa 'Aja'ib Al-Asfar," A Gift to Those Who Contemplate the Wonders of Cities and the Marvels of Traveling, also known under the title "The Travels of Ibn Battutah" was greatly influenced by Idrisi. Scholars speculate that explorers Marco Polo (1224-1324) and Christopher Columbus (1451-1506) were well aware of and perhaps benefited from the "Tabula Rogeriana" during their respective careers.

The Arabic number system reached Europe in the 10th century through the Arabs of North Africa, Al-Andalus and Sicily. It was a practical and convenient system, streamlining everything from daily transactions at the bazaar to complicated banking. It was soon adopted in Europe, and replaced the complicated Roman number system. In 1202 the Italian mathematician Fibonacci (born in 1175) transmitted the system to Italy, after learning it from his travels in North Africa. His book was called the *Liber Abaci* (Book of Calculations). During the 8th century, the Arabs developed and used the Hindu-Arabic numeral system. Mohammed ibn Musa Al-Khawarizmi (780-850), was a scholar, astronomer, mathematician, and geographer, appointed by Caliph Al-Ma`mun as chief astronomer and director of the library of the House of Wisdom in Baghdad around

Fig. 11.5: Al-Idrisi map of the world, from the Book of Roger, 1154. Bibliotheque Nationale de France, Paris.

820. He and other Arab and Muslim scholars contributed to the development of "Al-Jabr"- Algebra, Logarithms, and the invention of the digit zero. Cultural exchange continued to pave the way for further developments throughout the late Medieval times in Europe.

THE TOLEDO SCHOOL OF TRANSLATORS

The Italian Gerard of Cremona was one of many European scholars, who translated Arabic scholarly books found in libraries in Toledo to Latin, after the takeover of the city by the Spaniards in 1085. Realizing the significance of the Arab heritage in the field of knowledge, the Catholic authorities promptly began a project to translate texts from Arabic to Latin. In fact, they followed the Arab–Muslim tradition and established the famous "Toledo School of Translators" at the Toledo Cathedral–the former Great Mosque of Toledo. The project, which was fully supported by the religious authorities, was designed to translate Arabic manuscripts to Latin. Some were later translated to the Castilian language.

The works of major Arab and Muslim scholars from different parts of the Islamic empire were available in Toledo and the rest of Al-Andalus and Sicily. They were translated to Latin and other European languages, and used as textbooks in major universities in Paris, Rome, London and other places for centuries. The campaign of translation in Toledo, Seville, Salerno and other cities was a collaborative effort led by Arab, Muslim, Christian and Jewish scholars from Europe and the Islamic world. Other important European translators in the 12th century were John of Seville, who teamed up with Dominicus Gundissalinus--the director of the School of Translators--to translate Arabic text to Castilian. Other prominent Arabic-to-Latin translators were the 12th century Flemish scholar Rudolf of Bruges and the 13th century Scottish scholar Michael Scot.

The Arabic works that were translated to Latin were comprised of the work of scholars of the 9th-13th centuries and include Al-Battani's Math and Astronomy; Al-Khawarismi's Algebra; Al-Kindi's Optics; Al-Farghani's Astronomy; Al-Farabi's work on philosophy, political science, and ethics; Al-Razi's work in Chemistry and Medicine; the works of the physician and astronomer Thabit Ibn Qurra; the 10th century works of Al-Zahrawi's in medicine and surgery; and the works of the physician and scientist Hunayn Ibn Ishaq. The illustration in Figure 11.6 shows a folio from the translated work of the Cordoban–Andalusian scholar Abu Al-Qasim Al-Zahrawi, known in the West as Albucasis (d. 1010). The work is called Kitab Al-Tasrif, a 30-volume medical encyclopedia dealing with a broad coverage of medical topics.

Hunayn Ibn Ishaq Al-Ibadi, known as Iohannitius (809-873), was a prolific Arab Christian scholar, physician and scientist. He studied and learned Greek, and along with his fluency in Syriac–Aramaic and Arabic, he became a prominent and productive translator. The Caliph Al-Ma`mun appointed him in charge of Bayt Al-Hikmah (House of Wisdom) in Baghdad, where he supervised and directed other learned scholars. He contributed tremendously to the project of translating original Greek medical treatises into Arabic. He also wrote many treatises on ophthalmology, philosophy and medicine. One of his major works was a medical encyclopedia called "Al-Masa`il fi Al-Tibb Lil Muta`allimin (Introduction to Medicine for Beginners). The work, which echoes ancient Greek medical practices—especially that of Galen—was translated into Latin by Constantine with the title Isagoge (Fig. 11.7). Many Arab scholars translated Greek medical and scientific works to Arabic with splendid illustrations (see Chapter 8 and Figures 8.6, 8.7).

The wealth of scientific and philosophical works from Arab scholars appearing in Europe occurred at a time when Christian theological dogma was losing power. The growing appeal of philosophies which propagated critical thinking, along with increased trade and therefore cultural exchange, accelerated the process of social and intellectual change in Christian Europe.

PSEUDO-KUFIC DECORATION

As mentioned before, so-called pseudo-Kufic decoration appeared in Christian Europe; both in the eastern Byzantine territories and in western Europe. European architecture, painting, sculpture, textile, metalwork, coins, ceramic work, and illustrations make use of Arab-Islamic inspired decorative elements as early as the 8th century. Artists, mostly Italian, were intrigued by the aesthetics of the Arabic calligraphy, and repeatedly included stylizations of Arabic text in their paintings beginning in the early Renaissance until the 16th century. Recent research has shown that Italian art was influenced by Arab-Islamic art practiced by Muslim artists in Sicily and southern Italy, especially in Apulia and Calabria, from the 11th century on. Bands of Arabic Kufic inscriptions and modified cursive--similar to those found on the ceiling of the Cappella Palatina and elsewhere in Sicily--are also found painted in fresco on walls or executed in mosaics on the floors of churches and cathedrals constructed during that period.

Pseudo-Arabic in Byzantium

Byzantine cultural exchange with the Arab-Islamic world was prominent in territories in

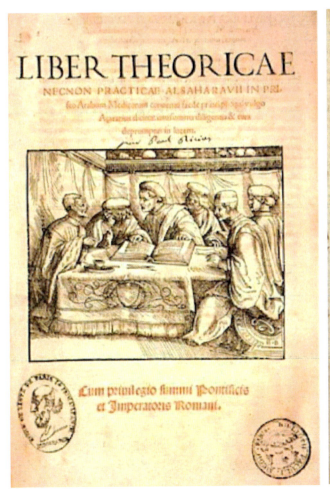 

Fig. 11.6: Frontispiece and a page of the Latin Translation of Al-Zahrawi Kitab Al-Tasrif, printed in Basil in 1541 by the printshop Henricus Petrus. US National Library of Medicine.

Fig. 11.7: Latin folio from Hunayn Ibn Ishaq, Isagoge "Introduction to Medicine for Beginners" and detail. US National Library of Medicine.

southern Italy, Malta, Sicily and other islands of the Mediterranean. In the 8th century, Arab forces from Al-Andalus invaded and conquered the Byzantine-controlled island of Crete. The Arabs established a prosperous Emirate principality, which lasted about a century and a half (820-961), until the Byzantine Empire managed to recapture it. Scholars speculate that the Byzantine recapturing led to the displacement of Arabs, including craftsmen, to other parts of the Mediterranean including the Greek mainland. Besides archaeological evidence of Muslim structures in Greece, such as the mosque in Athens, there is also strong evidence of the use of pseudo-Arabic decoration in many places; Arab inspired decoration was appreciated among the Greek Christian populations.

The monastery of Hosios Loukas in Boeotia, Greece is an excellent example which points to evident popularity of Arab inspired or pseudo-Arabic decorative programs. The monastery contains two churches: the smaller and older is Panagia (Theotokos) and the larger is Katholikon, built in the 10th - 11th centuries. Bands of monumental pseudo-Arabic decorative text adorn the exterior of the church (Figures 11.8, 11.9).

The inscription carved in Kufic style is dominating, with visual power equal to that found in the figurative narratives on the tympana of Romanesque churches. Similar carved pseudo-Kufic inscription is found inside the church. In the crypt of the church, pseudo-

Kufic script is painted on the wall, and decorates the marble slab of a tomb (Fig. 11.10). Other remains of Arab inspired decorative programs adorn surviving fragments of carved marble, and on part of the iconostasis, which is the screen that separates the sanctuary from the nave (Fig. 11.11).

Another striking example of the use of Arab-Islamic visual elements are found in the fresco painting at the church of Hosios Loukas. Part of the surviving fresco shows a portrait of the Biblical figure Joshua, also called "Jesus of Navi" (Fig. 11.12).

The rim of the helmet is decorated with pseudo-Arabic decorative design; so is the border of the garment covering his head under the helmet (Fig. 11.13). The text is illegible, which is typical of pseudo-Kufic designs found all over the region among Christian objects, paintings, sculpture and buildings. Researchers have posed the question of why 10th century Byzantine artists used a writing style associated with the Arabs to decorate the helmet of the Biblical figure Joshua? In the Islamic tradition, Biblical Joshua is known as the Prophet Youshi` Ibn Noon. Arab sources state that his tomb was in Baghdad; there is a shrine, or "Maqam," dedicated to Yashu` in Jordan, the Christian name for Youshi`.

Fig. 11.8: East facade of the Theotokos, Hosios Loukas Monastery, Greece, 10th century.

Fig. 11.9: Details of the pseudo-Arabic inscription on the east facade of the Theotokos, Hosios Loukas Monastery, Greece, 10th century.

Fig. 11.10: Details of the pseudo-Arabic inscription on the wall of the crypt, Hosios Loukas Monastery, Greece, 10th century.

Fig. 11.11: Details of the pseudo-Arabic inscription on a fragment of the iconostasis, Hosios Loukas Monastery, Greece, 10th century.

The presence of Arabic visual art and pseudo-Kufic inscription in the monastery of Hosios Loukas in Greece since the 10th century indicates the impact of Arab culture in the region. The pseudo-Arabic decorative text, whether legible or illegible, was used by Byzantine artists as a signifier of sacred icons and was applied to religious sacred figures and buildings. This trend continued and appeared in later Byzantine churches of Attica, Boeotia, and the Aegean Islands. It is plausible that a theological understanding for the affinity between the Christian dogma and the Islamic tradition existed and was appreciated reciprocally.

Pseudo-Arabic in Southern Italy

Scholars have identified many churches containing Arab-Islamic inspired decorations with bands of epigraphic pseudo-Kufic, pseudo-cursive Arabic, and geometric patterns. These churches were constructed in the late 12th to early 13th century in Apulia and nearby regions. They are St. Pietro at Otranto, St. Nicholas in Bari, St. Maria di Cerrate at Squinzano, St. Marco at Massafra, St. Maria d'Anglona in Tursi, and St. Giovanni in Monterrone (Fig. 11.14). Perhaps there were many more churches with similar visual elements in south Italy.

Art historians struggle with the question of why the use of Arab-Islamic elements was adopted in Christian buildings. Arab-Muslim artists and craftsmen from Sicily and those living in southern Italy were an important source of such visual expressions. The attraction of Arab architecture and decoration was appreciated by the Christian Europeans in Italy, the Normans in Sicily, and the Spaniards, who were fighting Al-

Fig. 11.12: Fresco painting of Joshua, Hosios Loukas Monastery, Greece, 10th -11th centuries.

Andalus "Tawa`if" mini-states, as we have seen in Chapters 9 and 10. Arab artistic impact on Romanesque architectural style is well known and documented in southern France, Spain and Italy. To sum up, Arab art was sought after, alas mixed with religious hostility reciprocated by both sides.

Arabs in Southern Italy

The 7th - 9th centuries comprised the period that followed standards set forth of imperial invasion and conquest, as seen with the Greeks and the Romans in the Mediterranean. The Byzantine Empire continued the norm of imperial colonization. With this in mind, it is an error to apply the negative connotation of "colonialization" to events that happened in the

Fig. 11.13: Detail of the fresco painting of Joshua, Hosios Loukas Monastery, Greece, 10th-11th centuries.

Medieval era. The Arab power thrust should be seen through that historical perspective. The 9th century represented the peak of that thrust when the Arabs targeted the Mediterranean region, Iberia, and Italy. They wrestled with the Byzantines in southern Italy and succeeded in acquiring territories in Apulia, especially Bari. By the middle of the 9th century, the Arabs managed to control Sicily, Malta, and a portion of southern Italy, while continuing their expansion northward.

In 846 they attacked and besieged Rome unsuccessfully. Years later, they tried again, but were repelled. Pressure by the Arabs continued over the next period, and the Pope was forced to pay an annual tribute to stop their military campaign against Rome. Eventually, the Franks and Byzantine forces drove the Arabs out of central Italy, but Bari remained under Arab control for over 25 years (847-871). The sources indicate that fortresses, palaces and a mosque were erected in Bari, but were apparently demolished after Franco-Lombard armies headed by Luis II took Bari in 871. The presence of Arab-Muslims in Bari and Apulia is still traceable in surviving remains of their forts and other spaces. This cultural presence may help to explain the presence of pseudo-Kufic and other Arab decorative motifs in Christian churches of the 11th-13th centuries in southern Italy, Greece and Macedonia.

The mere fact that the area was home to Arabs for extended periods of time explains the strong presence of Arab-Islamic art in that region. Additionally, in 1240, the Emperor Frederick II of the Hohenstaufen dynasty deported

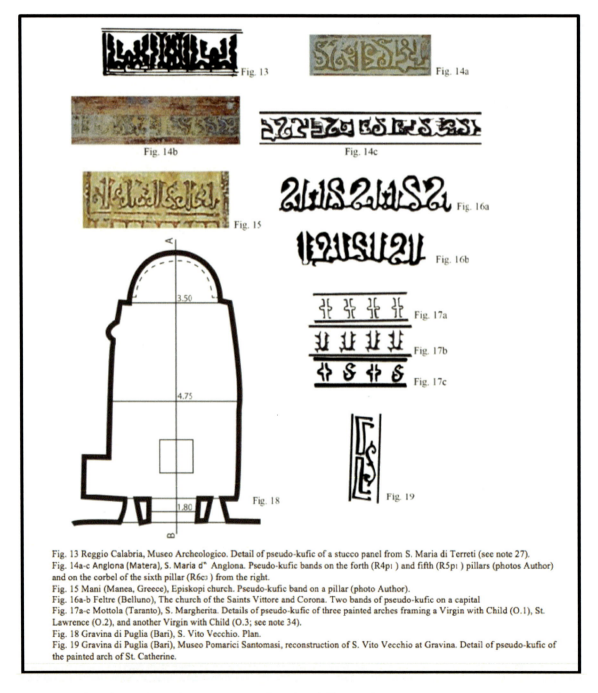

Fig. 13 Reggio Calabria, Museo Archeologico. Detail of pseudo-kufic of a stucco panel from S. Maria di Terreti (see note 27).
Fig. 14a-c Anglona (Matera), S. Maria d" Anglona. Pseudo-kufic bands on the forth (R4p1) and fifth (R5p1) pillars (photos Author) and on the corbel of the sixth pillar (R6c3) from the right.
Fig. 15 Mani (Manea, Greece), Episkopi church. Pseudo-kufic band on a pillar (photo Author).
Fig. 16a-b Feltre (Belluno), The church of the Saints Vittore and Corona. Two bands of pseudo-kufic on a capital
Fig. 17a-c Mottola (Taranto), S. Margherita. Details of pseudo-kufic of three painted arches framing a Virgin with Child (O.1), St. Lawrence (O.2), and another Virgin with Child (O.3; see note 34).
Fig. 18 Gravina di Puglia (Bari), S. Vito Vecchio. Plan.
Fig. 19 Gravina di Puglia (Bari), Museo Pomarici Santomasi, reconstruction of S. Vito Vecchio at Gravina. Detail of pseudo-kufic of the painted arch of St. Catherine.

Fig. 11.14: Examples of pseudo-Arabic inscriptions found in different churches in southern Italy, 12th-13th centuries.

remaining Arab-Muslims from Palermo, a number estimated at 20,000, and confined them in Lucera-Apulia (see Chapter 10). We can presume that among them were highly skilled architects, artisans, and craftsmen. Local Italian artisans inspired by Arab art produced works with pseudo-Kufic decoration and geometric designs. We can also consider the possibility that church authorities employed Arab artisans of Lucera in the actual decoration process of their churches. The Emperor Frederick II depended greatly on the military skills of Arab archers from Sicily who were then living in Lucera; their knowledge in other fields such as agriculture were also utilized, so the implementation of their artistic practices was also likely.

Pseudo-Arabic as a "Humanistic Mark"

The term pseudo-Kufic can more accurately be described as pseudo-Arabic; styles other than Kufic calligraphy were used, including modified Thulth and Naskh which were both popular. The use continued through the 14th, 15th, and 16th centuries in western Europe, especially Italy. Major artists of the early Renaissance applied a variety of such compositions in their paintings, especially works of religious narratives pertaining to the Virgin Mary, Jesus, and other holy figures. The Madonna of Humility (Figures 11.15, 11.16, 11.17) is a tempera painting on wood panel, measuring 56 cm × 41 cm (22 in × 16 in), painted by the late Medieval-Gothic Italian artist Gentile da Fabriano. It is dated to 1420-1423 and is now on display at the National Museum of San Mattero, Pisa, Italy. The subject of the painting is a typical presentation of the Virgin Mary holding the newly born baby Jesus on her lap. Intriguing is the inclusion of the "decorative" Arabic script: inside the halo, on the border of her dress, and most importantly, on the border of the blanket upon which Jesus lies. Italian scholars have tediously tried to explain the iconography of the work in relation to the Arabic text, but most conclude that the pseudo-Arabic used in the work is merely decorative. However, upon careful analysis of the inscription, a semi-legible reading appears and closely resembles an important Islamic creed.

The pseudo-Arabic inscription on the border of the garment-blanket (Fig. 11.17) resembles the Islamic "Shahadah," the declaration of faith: "I affirm that there is no god except Allah, and I affirm that Muhammad is the Messenger of Allah." *La Ilaha Illa Allah, Muhammad Rasul Allah"*. Some scholars contest such a reading, arguing it is simply decorative design. Fabriano produced many other icons on the subject of the Madonna, with similar presentations embellished with pseudo-Kufic decorations. Many contemporary Gothic artists used pseudo-Kufic and pseudo-Arabic randomly in their composition, but in the case of the Fabriano painting "The Madonna of Humility," we are looking at a very specific text. The dominant iconographic interpretation for such use of pseudo-Kufic is that it is an incidental decorative agent meant to beautify the visual impact of the painting. But with the selection of certain text being represented, we have to look deeper.

Such a phenomenon raises many questions: was Fabriano aware of the religious Arabic text? Was he knowledgeable of the Arabic language? What was his understanding of Arab-Islamic culture, considering he lived in a region historically rich with Arab traditions and populations, whether living there or visiting while on trade missions in Venice, Napoli, Florence and other ports? Was his choice of this Arabic phrase intentional? If so, was he informed about Islamic theology and the celestial merit of Mary and Jesus in the Qur`an? These inquiries would require investigation of Fabriano's background, his early years, and his exposure to Arab culture, Islamic religion, and art. These critical and contextual approaches are necessary when examining similar works from other artists who utilized pseudo-Arabic inscriptions in their works.

Fig. 11.15: Gentile da Fabriano, The Madonna of Humility, Tempera on wood, 56 cm × 41 cm (22 in × 16 in), 1420-1423, National Museum of San Mattero, Pisa, Italy.

Fig. 11.16: Gentile da Fabriano, The Madonna of Humility, details of the pseudo-Arabic inscription inside the halo.

An example of pseudo-Arabic as a signifier of humanistic concepts is found in the painting of the 15th century artist Giovanni Bellini, "The Blessing Christ" (Fig. 11.18). It is a small intricate portrait of the resurrected Jesus, executed in tempera on wood. There is an elaborate pseudo-Kufic inscription on the hem of the collar and arm bands of Jesus' dress. The decorative inscription here works like an exclamation of the "holy," and an announcement of the "sacred" (Fig. 11.19).

Among the widely circulated interpretations for the use of pseudo-Arabic text in religious figures of the period states that the artists were copying the motifs they saw on imported objects of metalwork, fabrics, woodworks, and a variety of other items. Such arguments are based on the fact that during the 14th -15th centuries, there was a steady growth in trade with the Muslim world, especially with Venice and Florence. However, this argument does not consider that the artists were not isolated from the rest of the world, and the source for their use of Arab-Islamic visual elements cannot totally depend on their knowledge of imported objects. Travel was available, as many artists were known to have done, and Arab structures in southern Italy, Sicily and Al-Andalus were easy to reach and experience first-hand. Furthermore, translated Arab manuscripts on many subjects were abundant.

Fig. 11.17: Gentile da Fabriano, The Madonna of Humility, details showing the pseudo-Arabic inscription on the edge of the garment where Jesus is lying.

The use of pseudo-Arabic inscriptions discussed points to the consideration that Arabic was used to reinforce religious iconography and the images of the "holy": Jesus, Mary, Saints, and so on. According to this argument, the image of the holy was associated with the "Oriental" in order to signify Jerusalem, Heaven, and the Holy Land. Italian artists, familiar with sacred religious Islamic texts and Islamic narratives related to Jesus and Mary, found pseudo-Arabic to be a fitting visual vocabulary, one which would represent the "Oriental" holy atmosphere. However, recent research proposes that pseudo-Arabic in European art signifies the Islamic philosophy of humanism, which as discussed, later represented the foundation of Renaissance thought in Europe. Before the Renaissance, Arab-Islamic culture cultivated a humanistic civilization that propagated scholarly innovation, rational thought, and individual achievement through education. Within such a humanistic framework, Islamic intellectual culture nurtured a philosophic and scientific repertoire inspired by diverse traditions, later translated and elaborated upon in the Arabic language, as we have mentioned. This research argues that the inclusion of pseudo-Arabic script in a European context came to act as recognition for Arab-Islamic humanism; therefore aligning the Italian Renaissance with the social and educational ideals that flourished in the Arab-Muslim world.

Pseudo-Arabic text represented sacred writing and humanist lettering, and soon became a visual trend that was used through the 14th, 15th, and 16th centuries. Many other artists followed the trend, including: Ugolino di Nerio, Masaccio, Duccio di Buoninsegna, Giotto di Bondone, Antonio Filarete, Andrea del Verrochio, Bicci di Lorenzo, Masaccio, Jacopo Bellini, Giovanni di Paolo, Francesco Squarcione, Andrea Mantegna, Antonio Vivarini, Filippo Lippi, Fra Angelica, Henri Bellechose, Paolo Veneziano, Michelozzo, Donatello, Fernando Yañez de la Almedina, and Raphael, along with countless others.

Pseudo-Arabic as a Signifier of "High Status"

At the "Basilica of the Most Holy Annunciation," the Capella della Madonna at Santissima Annunziata in Florence, there is a tondo––a circular painting of stained glass with the Medici coat of arms design, surrounded by pseudo-Arabic calligraphy in a style that is a cross of modified Thulth and Naskh (Figures 11.20, 11.21).

Fig. 11.18: Giovanni Bellini, Blessing Christ, tempera on wood, 58 × 46 cm (22.8 × 18.1 in), 1465-70, Louvre Museum, Paris, France.

Fig. 11.19: Giovanni Bellini, Blessing Christ, details of the pseudo-Arabic inscription on the collar and arm bands.

The stained-glass work has been attributed to Alessio Baldovinetti and dated 1465. The influential Medici dynasty rose to power in Florence in the 15th century as a major banking family, and later extended their political power to the government and the church in Florence and across Tuscany. The basilica itself was an important religious site that goes back to the 13th century, dedicated to the miraculous image of the Annunciation that attracted pilgrims for centuries. The Medici family acquired religious significance by associating themselves with the Basilica. Moreover, it was Lorenzo di Piero de Medici who took things further and extended political power to the family. Piero was aware of the significance of Arab-Islamic culture; he corresponded with Muslim authorities including the Mamluk Sultan of Egypt Qait Bay, who bestowed him with honorific epithets and titles. Piero must have experienced the feeling of utmost clout through such correspondence.

His admiration of the official epithets bestowed on the Sultan were influential; Piero intentionally emulated the use of the dignifying titles in the grand decoration of Santissima Annunziata. Most of the Arabic words surrounding the Medici coat of Arms are legible and are typical of the honorific epithets usually addressed to the Caliph, Sultan, Emir (Amir) and similar high authorities. These honorific titles are found in many royal objects spaces, adorned with phrases like: *Al-Mu`adhdham*, meaning the greatest or the aggrandized; *Al-Mansur*, or the Victorious; or *Al-Kamil*, the perfect one. The Sultan's name, Qait, is a Turkic word derived from the Arabic "Qa`id," meaning leader, or commander in a military affair. His full name carries such epithets: *Sayf Al-Din*, the sword of the religion; and *Al-Ashraf*, the most noble. Piero wished to emulate the honorific and lofty image he observed; by including Arabic text in the coat of arms, he was able to self-project or identify with the noble status.

The Arabic calligraphy here resembles a typical band of text found on horizontal registrars of the interior of an Arab mosque or palace. It can also be compared to calligraphic decoration found on Tiraz–medieval Arab textiles embroidered with calligraphic decoration and ornamentation. Similar decorations can also be found on pottery and metal objects, especially from the Mamluk period. The question remains: Why did the association of Arabic script with churches and religious icons intentionally materialize? Could it have been a signal of diplomatic collegial appreciation of the increasing commercial trade, especially with the Ottomans of that period, as some scholars suggest? Or was it the conscious emulation of Arab-Islamic culture, held in high regard? What was the connection between sacred Christian icons, such as images of Jesus or Mary, and pseudo-Arabic script?

It seems probable that artists and intellectuals of the Gothic and Renaissance periods looked at Arab-Islamic culture with high esteem, especially when we consider the level of multifaceted accomplishments made by the Muslims in science, philosophy, medicine, math, astronomy, geography, art and architecture. The impressive list of artists across time who participated in the use of pseudo-Arabic elements in their works indicates that such decisions were not random or a result of temporary fashion. European authorities, intellectuals, and artists not only celebrated education and the potential of the individual through an education, but recognized the Arab-Islamic culture as responsible for developing and transmitting knowledge to them; the Arab-Muslims were regarded in high reverence to Europeans of the time. In turn, they viewed the visual culture of the Arabs—in this case, Arabic writing—as a signifying mark of excellence; hence it became an artistic vehicle to represent that concept in their works. Nonetheless, more in-depth analysis about this artistic trend will shed greater light on the intriguing subject.

THE DECLINE OF ARAB ART (1700-1900)

By the 17th century, with the assertive growing power of the Ottomans in the Mediterranean region and Europe, approbation declined rapidly and as cultural hostilities grew. Disparaging terms such as "Saracens" and "Moors" occupied European literature and political discourse, which continued throughout the 18th and 19th centuries to the present time.

By the 16th century, the Arab state received two major blows: in the east, the Mongols devastated the Abbasid empire, and by 1258 Baghdad was captured and destroyed. In the west, Al-Andalus and Sicily were retaken and the Arabs in both locations were displaced to North Africa and other regions. The Arab retreat continued through the 17th century and well into the 18th. Europe was fully mobilized to conquer the world with advanced armies and more sophisticated military means. Major empires raced in this conquest, especially Spain, France, Britain, and Portugal. By the 19th century, the Arabs were marginalized while governed by the declining Ottoman Empire, which eventually succumbed to the might of the new powerful and determined imperial Europe.

In 1507, Portuguese forces invaded and occupied the Strait of Hurmuz in Oman, and colonized Muscat and Bahrain. The colonization was ended by the Safavid coalition with the Arabs and the support of British forces in 1622, and the Hurmuz port of entry to the Gulf was promptly taken by the British. The 19th century witnessed French colonization of Algeria in 1834 and Tunisia in 1881. France also invaded Egypt and Syria (1798-1801), Italy colonized Libya (1911-34), and in 1882 the British occupied Egypt. After World War I (1914-1917), the British invaded and colonized Iraq and Palestine, and much of the region was divided between France and Britain, with new forced entities and borders drawn by the European invaders. Most of the Arab lands fell under the sway of British-French colonialism. The effects of that colonialism continues to reverberate to the present time.

The period from the end of the 19th century

Fig. 11.20: Stained glass window, Santissima Annunziata, Florence, 1465.

to the mid 20th century was a time of intense Arab struggle with European colonialism. As a result, Arab culture retreated and suffered loss to its unifying characteristics. Colonialism promoted European culture, language and art against the indigenous Arab culture, under the guise of "modernization," which in turn produced Arab intellectuals and politicians who supported the mentality and essentially aided imperial propaganda. European artists of the 19th century, active in the Neo-Classical, Romantic and especially Oriental movements, created works that facilitated the imperialist worldview. Depictions of the Arab people were often represented as violent villains or backwards barbarians living in lawless places. At

Fig. 11.21: Stained glass window details, Santissima Annunziata, Florence, 1465.

the same time, these works presented Western European culture as the enlightened antithesis to the Arab way of life. Artists like Antoine Jean Gros, Jacques Louis David, Eugene Delacroix, Jean-Leon Gerome and Henri Regnault popularized the image of diabolical men and passive, sexualized women in the occupied Arab society. The compositions of these works were often embellished with inaccurate but visually attractive exotic scenery.

Regardless of the adverse socio-political impact of colonialism, the legacy of Arab art did not perish completely in Europe. The aesthetics of Arab-Islamic architectural and decorative vocabularies appeared in European structures of the 19th and early 20th century in many forms. An example of such an appearance is the Royal Pavilion in Brighton, United Kingdom (Fig. 11.22). The architect John Nash was inspired by diverse sources, including Greek, Egyptian, Gothic and Indian. The crowning influence was that of Arab-Islamic, derived from Arab-Andalusian stucco screens, Islamic Minarets and the domes of Mughal architecture.

Other examples include the home of the artist Fredric Leighton in London––also known as "London's Arab Hall," which was constructed in the second half of the 19th century; the palace "Iranistan" designed by Austrian-American architect Leopold Eidlitz in Bridgeport, Connecticut (destroyed by fire in 1867); the Vorontsov Palace in Crimea, Ukraine (1828-1848); and the Tivoli Gardens in Copenhagen in 1843. Artists of the early Modern style movement also reflected inspiration from Arab-Islamic aesthetics in their paintings. Prominent among them were Auguste Renoir, Henri Mattise, Paul Klee and Wassily Kandinsky after their visit to Tunisia in 1914.

The 19th century rising European empires conquered major regions in the Arab world militarily and ideologically. European literary and visual art works depicting Arab-Muslim society through the lens of Orientalism essentially conveyed the discriminatory assertion that Western culture was superior to that of the Arabs. This concept swept throughout Europe and was ingrained into standard education. The effect of this profound Eurocentrism was ultimately transmitted to the colonized Arab people, mobilizing many individuals to facilitate European political agendas. During the first half of the 20th century, many educated Arab professionals, misguided by such systematic and misleading information, inadvertently promoted and perpetuated the concept.

Meanwhile, an awakened spirit grew among educated Arabs wishing to reconcile this cultural disconnect felt in the aftermath of imperialism. The unifying movement of *Pan-Arabism*, also referred to as *Arab Nationalism* became popular in major Arab countries, especially after World War II. Arab Nationalism, a secular movement, attracted people from diverse backgrounds across the Arab world. After World War II and the United Nations creation of Israel, the "Middle East" became a hot spot for the ensuing Cold War era, and a desired economic target for the newly emerging wealth of oil. The strategic location of the Arab world and the abundance of natural resources made it a prized target pursued by Western powers throughout the 20th -21st centuries, through direct or indirect interventions. Many secular Arab countries opposed the restructuring of the Middle East at the hands of Europe, such as Syria, Egypt, Iraq, Libya, Yemen and others. These countries constituted an obstacle to the political ideology of the West, which is still being applied in region, as as was seen with the invasion of Iraq in 2003, the military intervention in Libya, the division of Sudan in 2011, and the ongoing war in Yemen.

MODERN ARAB ART

With this historic context in mind, modern Arab art during the second half of the 20th century gravitated towards the influence of Western artistic trends, leaving behind indigenous traditions and expressions. The fields of the Fine Arts, Visual Arts, and Art History drew curricula, teaching methods, and studio training from European practices, focusing on styles such as Neo-Classicism, Romanticism, Realism, Impressionism, German Expressionism and Abstraction. Furthermore, "Islamic Art" came to be understood as the Eastern antithesis of Western realism: purely non-figurative, aniconic, and decorative.

The cultural scene in the Arab world between 1960 and 1980 witnessed the importation of other modern European and American trends including Abstraction, Surrealism, Social Realism, and Minimalism, among others. Later, movements such as Pop Art, Op Art, Super Realism, and modified versions of other styles reached the Arab world. Conversely, trends such as Performance, Conceptual, and Feminist Art did not gain as much traction, probably due to themes and visual elements that conflicted with growing conservative Islamic cultural sentiments. This attitude continued through Post Modernism, where Arab artists found it easier to engage in such trends while living abroad.

The development of Modern Arab art can thus be viewed as an introduction of the prevalent Western styles to the Arab world, though modified in expression and variety. It was a faithful transmission and diffusion of the sweeping Western visual experience to the Arab world. Western technological advancement greatly impacted the development of modern Arab art in providing needed tools, art supplies, and equipment in various fields of artistic production. In the process, however, the spirit of foundational Arab art was subdued and almost completely overshadowed by the appeal of Western Modernism and Post-Modern trends, which at the time acquired the meaning of being "progressive" and "contemporary."

Missing in this transformational process was the Arab visual art tradition both in subject

Fig. 11.22: John Nash, the Royal Pavilion, Brighton, United Kingdom, 1815-1818.

matter and presentation. Pioneers of Arab Modern art were students of Western European art schools, and their works reflected the approach in the choices of medium, technique, style, subject and composition of their works. Artists were likely aware of the compelling quality of the aesthetics of Arab artistic traditions, but were not interested in engaging them in their expressions. This early period that comprised the formation of Modern Arab art also witnessed a lack of associated studies in aesthetics, art history, and art criticism related to Arab history. As a result, pioneering Arab artists did not have the opportunity to chronologically study in-depth the development of visual arts, especially Arab-Islamic art. The long history of the development of Arab art was overlooked and marginalized; compartmentalized as topics such as Arabic Calligraphy or Islamic Ornamentation in curricula.

The preceding chapters have shown the development of Arab art and architecture since the earliest stages against the backdrop of major civilizations: Mesopotamian, Egyptian, and Hellenistic, beginning around 2000 BCE. Arab-Muslim artists later developed and employed the aesthetic power of Arabic letters and textual compositions. The visual presence of the Arabic word was applied to different artistic forms, such as in manuscript illumination, pottery, glassworks, metalworks, and most importantly, architecture. However, the dominance of Western socio-political influence in the Arab world in the 20th century was shaped by an Orientalist perspective that deemed the culture of the Arab-Muslim "Ottomans" as inferior to the civilized and superior culture of the West. In turn, this perspective greatly impacted the visual arts produced by Arabs and Europeans alike.

Arab-Islamic visual traditions came to be considered as cherished antiquities, though an outdated culture of the past. This perception was reiterated and transmitted through literature that contributed to the making of "Modern Arab art." However, most early Modern Arab artists—who studied art in Europe—were aware of this issue in cultural identity, and found ways to express the long tradition of Arab visual culture while assimilating Western styles. Many were able to develop distinct styles that visually combined the language of Arab-Islamic heritage with Modern European artistic trends. Such expressions that consciously applied Arab cultural heritage commenced among Arab artists in Egypt, Iraq, Syria, Morocco, Tunisia and other parts of the Arab world, culminating throughout the second half of the 20th century. In Iraq, artists pioneered the movement of indigenous awareness in Arab art, which was especially practiced at the Baghdad School of Painting. In the last quarter of the 20th century, Baghdad became a hub for Arab artists of this sentiment and methodology to showcase their works and participate in academic discourse.

This renewed sense of cultural awareness culminated in the initiation of annual and biannual artistic events such as the Arab International Biennial Art Festival and Al-Wasiti International Festival, both launched in Baghdad. Al-Wasiti Festival was inaugurated in 1972 and focused on the works of the 13th century Iraqi artist Al-Wasiti (see Chapter 8).

Similar endeavors that exalted the aesthetics of traditional Arabic calligraphy commenced in Arab capitals beyond Baghdad. Today, new generations of young and educated Arab artists are beginning to consciously reexamine the visual value of Arabic text within the context of modern art. These artists come from different parts of the Arab world, especially Tunisia, Morocco, Sudan, Yemen, Egypt, Syria, Lebanon, Qatar, Saudi Arabia and Iraq.

At the present time, Modern Arab visual artists continue to experiment on an international scale, with various trends, using a variety of techniques and styles. Meanwhile, there is a rapidly growing renewed interest in revisiting the heritage of Arab art, elements of which continue to be incorporated into the visual aesthetics of contemporary Arab artists. The establishment of major museums and centers for the study and preservation of Arab art in Arab capitals such as Baghdad, Cairo, and Damascus have served as an essential foundation in the promotion of the art and culture of the Arabs. The latest in this effort is the founding of museums, galleries, and research centers, especially in Qatar and the United Arab Emirates. Such endeavors, backed by adequate support, show promise in energizing further advancement of the study and preservation of this important field of creativity.

Selected Bibliography

In addition to the list in Chapter 9 and 10

Al-Tawil, Hashim, "The Formation of Identity in Modern Iraqi Visual Art: A New Perspective" Bulletin of the Royal Institute for Inter-Faith Studies 8, nos. 1 & 2, 2006, 95-118.

_____, "The Visual Absence of the Dot and its Conceptual Presence in the Arabic Inscriptions of the Ceiling of the 12th Century Cappella Palatina in Palermo Sicily", *Nuqtah, a Discourse,* 7th Sharjah Biennale on Arabic Calligraphy, Sharjah, UAE, 2016, pp. 93-126, 156-163.

Al-Tawil, Wihad. *Arabic Pseudo-Script and the Italian Renaissance.*, Unpublished master's thesis, Wayne State University, 2015. http://digitalcommons.wayne.edu/oa_theses/430

Auld, Sylvia, "Kuficising Inscriptions in the work of Gentile da Fabriano", *Oriental Art,* 32, No. 3, 1986, 213-328.

Bradley J. Cavallo, Of Medici and Mamluk Power: Islamic Forms in a Renaissance Florentine Stained Glass Window, *Viator*, 45, no. 1 (Spring, 2014), 311-330.

Burnett, Charles and Contadini, Anna, eds., *Islam and The Italian Renaissance,* London: Warburg Institute Colloquia, 1999.

Cardini, Franco. *Europe and Islam.* New Jersey: Blackwell Publishing, 2001.

Fontana Maria Vittoria, "Byzantine Mediation of Epigraphic Characters of Islamic Derivation in the Wall Paintings of Some Churches in Southern Italy", in Burnett, Ch., Contadini, A. (eds), *Islam and the Italian Renaissance,* London, 1999, 61-75.

_____, Kufic Ornamental Motifs in the Wall Paintings of Six Churches in Southern Italy, *IOSR Journal Of Humanities And Social Science (IOSR-JHSS)*, Volume 21, Issue 12, Ver. 2 (December. 2016), 56-73.

Mack, Rosamond E., *Bazaar to Piazza: Islamic Trade and Italian Art, 1300–1600*, Oakland, CA: University of California Press, 2001.

Metcalfe, Alex, *Muslims of Medieval Italy*, Edinburgh: Edinburgh University Press, 2009.

Miles, G. C., "Byzantium and the Arabs: Relations in Crete and the Aegean Area", *Dumbarton Oaks Papers,* 18, 1964, 1–32.

Morgan, Susan Martin, "The Ontology of the Venetian Halo in its Italian Context", Ph.D. Thesis, UK: University of Plymouth, 2012.

Richard Ettinghausen, "Kufesque in Byzantine Greece, the Latin West and the Muslim World," A Colloquium in Memory of George Carpenter Miles (1904–1975) *The American Numismatic Society,* 1976, 28–47.

Said, Edward W., *Orientalism*, New York: Random House Inc., 1979.

Safran, L. (ed.) *Heaven on Earth: Art and the Church in Byzantium*, The Pennsylvania State University Park, PA: University Press, 1998.

Strickland, Debra Higgs. *Saracens, Demons & Jews: Making Monsters in Medieval Art*, Princeton, N.J.: Princeton University Press, 2003.

Images & Maps Credits

Fig. 1.1: Sarcophagus of Ahiram, King of Byblos, 1000 BCE, Carved, Limestone; Beirut National Museum, Lebanon. Credit: G. Eric and Edith Matson Photograph Collection, Prints and Photographs Division, Library of Congress (1936).
https://www.loc.gov/search/?in=&q=Sarcophagus+of+Ahiram&new=true&st=. Accessed 10 January 2018.

Fig. 1.2: Silver-gilt bowl, Mid 8th century BCE, H. 1 1/4 in. (3.1 cm) diameter 6 5/8 in. (16.8 cm), MET Museum, NY. Credit: The Cesnola Collection.
https://www.metmuseum.org/art/collection/search/243823. Accessed 10 January, 2018.

Fig. 1.3: Tayma` Stele, sandstone, 111cm H, 43 cm W and 12 cm D, 6th century BCE, found in Tayma`, Louvre Museum, Paris, France. Credit: Unknown - Jastrow (2007), Public Domain, https://commons.wikimedia.org/w/index.php?curid=1527793. Accessed 12 January 2018.

Fig. 1.4: Stone panel from the North Palace of Ashurbanipal (Room L, nos. 9-13), Nineveh, northern Iraq, Neo-Assyrian, around 645 BCE, Limestone, Length: 134.62 cm., Width: 226.06 cm., Credit: Trustees of the British Museum.
https://www.google.com/culturalinstitute/beta/asset/stone-panel-from-the-north-palace-of-ashurbanipal-room-l-nos-9-13/bgFeReNGcLGPvA. Accessed 12 January 2018.

Fig. 1.5: Fragment of Assyrian relief panel, North Palace of Ashurbanipal, 680-636 BCE, Limestone, Height 39 cm., Credit: Vatican museum.
http://www.museivaticani.va/content/museivaticani/en/collezioni/musei/museo-gregoriano-egizio/sala-ix--rilievi-e-iscrizioni-dei-palazzi-assiri/rilievo-con-tende-degli-arabi-date-alle-fiamme.html Accessed 12 January 2018.

Fig. 1.6: Assyrians engaged in warfare with Arabs, Limestone relief panel, 650 BCE, Credit: Trustees of the British Museum.
www.bmimages.com Accessed 10 January 2018.

Fig. 2.1: The ruins of the ancient city of Baraqish, Yemen. Credit:
https://commons.wikimedia.org/wiki/File:Barakisk_flickr01.jpg Accessed 13 January 2018.

Fig. 2.2: Wall with Minaean inscriptions, Baraqish, Al Jawf province, Yemen, 5th-1st century BCE. Photo Sabina Antonini de Maigret.
https://whitelevy.fas.harvard.edu/people/sabina-antonini-de-maigret. Accessed 15 January 2018.

Fig. 2.3: Votive alabaster stele carved in relief sculpture with Minaean inscription, 6th to 4th centuries BCE. Private Collection. Credit:
https://www.christies.com/lotfinder/Lot/a-south-arabian-alabaster-revetment-plaque-circa-3924019-details.aspx. Accessed 22 June 2018.

Fig. 2.4: The remains of ancient Ma'rib, Yemen. Credit: Bernard Gagnon. https://commons.wikimedia.org/wiki/File%3AAncient_Ma'rib_01.jpg Accessed 7 February 2018.

Fig. 2.5: Barran Temple, Ma`rib, Yemen, Credit:
http://www.aljazeera.net. Accessed 7 February 2018.

Fig. 2.6: Calcite incense burner showing a camel rider, Sabaean, 3rd century BCE, From Shabwa, Yemen, Credit: Trustees of the British Museum, www.bmimages.com. Accessed 7 February 2018.

Fig. 2.7: Painted limestone incense burner, 5th-4th century BCE, Height: 9.50 cm. Width: 9.50 cm Thickness: 9.50 cm. Trustees of the British Museum, www.bmimages.com. Accessed 7 February 2018.

Fig. 2.8: Calcite statue of Standing female figure, 3rd - 2nd centuries BCE, Height: 74.5 cm, Width: 33 cm (at shoulder), Thickness: 24 cm, Sabaean from Ma`rib or Qataban, Yemen, Credit: Trustees of the British Museum,
www.bmimages.com. Accessed 7 February 2018.

Fig. 2.9: Dedication calcite Stele: Ghalilat, daughter of Mafaddat, 1st c. BCE- 1st c. CE Width: 27.50 cm, Credit: Trustees of the British Museum,
www.bmimages.com. Accessed 7 February 2018.

Fig. 2.10: Aylward Stela- Funerary Qatabanian calcite Stele, Wadi Bayhan (Qataban), Hayd ibn Aqil (Timna)Yemen, 1st c. BCE- 1st c. CE. Height: 29 cm, Width: 27 cm, Thickness: 6.3 cm, Credit: Trustees of the British Museum,
www.bmimages.com. Accessed 7 February 2018.

Fig. 2.11. `Awam Temple "Mahram Balqis", Sabaean, near Ma`rib. Credit:
http://mapio.net/pic/p-36591639/ . Accessed 10 February 2018.

Fig. 2.12: Mahram Balqis, interior. Credit:
http://www.archaeophysics.com/bilqis/index.html. Accessed 10 February 2018.

Fig. 2.13: Sabaean hunting scene, Alabaster carving, Yemen, 500 BCE, Height. 88 Cm, Width 32.5 Cm, Thickness 6 Cm., Credit: Società Geografica Italiana
http://societageografica.net/wp/en/. Accessed 10 February 2018.

Fig. 2.14: Funerary commemorative slab of `Aban of the tribe of Mahdhar, Calcite-alabaster stele, Height: 30 cm, Width: 19.01 cm, Thickness: 7 cm (at nose) 1st c. BCE – 2nd c. CE. Trustees of the British Museum,
www.bmimages.com. Accessed 7 February 2018.

Fig. 2.15: Life size stone relief of alleged Himyarite king, Dhafar, Yemen, 450- 525 CE., 1.70 meters height, Credit: Paul A. Yule, Heidelberg University,
http://heidicon.ub.uni-heidelberg.de/pool/zafar. Accessed 8 February 2018.

Fig. 2.16: Funerary dedication of a man head, calcite-alabaster Stele, Timna`, Yemen, 1st c. BCE – 2nd c. CE, Credit: Trustees of the British Museum,
www.bmimages.com. Accessed 7 February 2018.

Fig. 3.1: Al-Khaznah- The Treasury, Petra, Jordan. Credit: Berthold Werner
https://commons.wikimedia.org/w/index.php?curid=8566120. Accessed 7 April 2018.

Fig. 3.2: Al-Dayr, The Monastery, Petra, Jordan. Credit: Diego Delso, Accessed 17 February 2018.
https://creativecommons.org/licenses/by-sa/4.0/legalcode

Fig. 3.3: The tomb of Uneishu, Petra, Jordan. Credit: Bernard Gagnon,
https://commons.wikimedia.org/wiki/User:Bgag#/media/File:Silk_Tomb,_Petra.jpg. Accessed 5 February 2018.

Fig. 3.4: Axonometric drawing of the altar, Khirbat Al-Tannur, north of Petra, 1st Century CE. Credit:
http://tannur.omeka.net/items/show/76. Accessed 8 March 2018.

Fig. 3.5: Sandstone Relief sculpture of Nabataean deity Qaws (Qos, Koz), h. 115 cm., 2nd Century BCE- 1st Century CE, Khirbat Al-Tannur, Petra, Jordan. Credit: Cincinnati Art Museum.
https://www.surveymonkey.com/r/CAMNearEast. Accessed 8 March 2018.

Fig. 3.6: Limestone relief sculpture of the bust of the "Grain Goddess", h. 27 cm., 2nd Century BCE- 1st Century CE, Khirbat Al-Tannur, Petra, Jordan. Credit: Cincinnati Art Museum.
https://www.surveymonkey.com/r/CAMNearEast. Accessed 8 March 2018.

Fig. 3.7: Limestone relief sculpture of the winged goddess (Nike) carrying the Goddess (Tyche)- Arab Allat surrounded by a presentation of the Zodiac, Khirbat Al-Tannur, Petra, Jordan, 2nd Century BCE- 1st Century CE, Credit: Cincinnati Art Museum.
https://www.surveymonkey.com/r/CAMNearEast. Accessed 8 March 2018.

Fig. 3.8: Limestone relief sculpture of the Sun deity (Helios), h. 55 cm., Khirbat Al-Tannur, Petra, Jordan, 2nd Century BCE- 1st Century CE, Credit: Cincinnati Art Museum.
https://www.surveymonkey.com/r/CAMNearEast. Accessed 8 March 2018.

Fig. 3.9: Limestone Sculptural presentation of eagle wrestling with a serpent, h.46.1 cm., Khirbat

Al-Tannur, Petra, Jordan, 2nd Century BCE- 1st Century CE, Credit: Cincinnati Art Museum. https://www.surveymonkey.com/r/CAMNearEast. Accessed 8 March 2018.

Fig. 3.10: Remains of the temple of Allat, Palmyra, Syria. Credit: Marco Prins. http://www.livius.org/pictures/syria/tadmor-palmyra/palmyra-temple-of-allat/temple-of-allat/. Accessed 12 March 2018.

Fig. 3.11: "The lion of Allat" after conservation, Limestone ashlars, h. 3.5 m., 1st century CE., Palmyra, Syria. Credit: Photo Mappo - Own work, Public Domain, https://en.wikipedia.org/wiki/Lion_of_Al-lāt#/media/File:Lion_in_the_garden_of_Palmyra_Archeological_Museum,_2010-04-21.jpg. Accessed 15 March 2018.

Fig. 3.12: Relief sculpture of the deity Allat, Palmyra, Syria. Credit: Owen Cook. https://upload.wikimedia.org/wikipedia/commons/4/42/Allat_Palmyra_RGZM_3369.jpg. Accessed 20 March 2018.

Fig. 3.13: Limestone funerary portraits of female figures, Allat Temple, Palmyra, Syria, 2nd century CE., Courtesy of Palmyra Archaeological Museum, inv. 3/77 & B 23198520 (Bartosz Markiewicz). https://www.researchgate.net/publication/305728647_Palmyrene_portraits_from_the_temple_of_Allat_New_evidence_on_artists_and_workshops. Accessed 20 March 2018.

Fig. 3.14: Temple of Ba`l from the south, Palmyra, Credit: Bernard Gagnon https://commons.wikimedia.org/wiki/File%3ATemple_of_Bel%2C_Palmyra_02.jpg. Accessed 20 March 2018.

Fig. 3.15: Baal Shamin flanked by Aghlibel and Malakbel, Palmyra, 1st century CE, Louvre Museum, Paris, France. Reproduced under a Creative Commons License. http://philipharland.com/greco-roman-associations/honors-for-soadu-part-2-132-ce/ . Accessed 20 March 2018.

Fig. 3.16: Tower Tomb "Ilahbel", 103 CE, Palmyra, Syria (destroyed 2015). Credit: Photo B. Gagnon, 2010. https://commons.wikimedia.org/wiki/File:Tower_of_Elahbel,_Palmyra.jpg. Accessed 20 March 2018.

Fig. 3.17: Interior of Tower tomb, Palmyra, Istanbul Archaeological Museum, Turkey, Credit: Photo Hashim Al-Tawil.

Fig. 3.18: Funerary Relief of a Woman and Two Children, Palmyra, 150 CE., Carved limestone, 71.5 cm h x 56.5 cm w x 27 cm d (28 1/8 x 22 1/4 x 10 5/8 in.) Credit: Harvard Art Museums/Arthur M. Sackler Museum, Gift of Alden Sampson, Richard Norton, and Edward W. Forbes, 1908.3.

Fig. 3.19: Funerary bust of a priest, Limestone, 25" x 21", 50-150 CE, Palmyra, British Museum. http://www.britishmuseum.org/research/collection_online/collection_object_details/collection_image_gallery.aspx?assetId=30791001&objectId=282719&partId=1. Accessed 12 March

IMAGES & MAPS CREDITS 281

2018.

Fig. 3.20: Bust of woman, relief limestone, 20" x 16.5", (51 x 42 cm.), British Museum.
http://www.britishmuseum.org/research/collection_online/collection_object_details/collection_image_gallery.aspx?assetId=413534001&objectId=282713&partId=1. Accessed 12 March 2018.

Fig. 3.21: Hatra, aerial view (from Henry Stierlin, "Cités du désert: Pétra, Palmyre, Hatra", found in "Hatra, Citta' del Sole" catalogue of an exhibition organized by the Italian Archaeological Mission to Hatra).
http://www.esicomos.org/Nueva_carpeta/info_IRAKUNESCO.htm. Accessed 3 April 2018.

Fig. 3.22: Plan of the circular city of Hatra showing the location of the Grand Temple. Credit: Andrea Walker, Hatra. Nach Aufnahmen von Mitgliedern der Assur-Expedition der Deutschen Orient Gesellschaft. I. Allgemeine Beschreibung der R. Leipzig (J. C. Hinrichs) 1908. Wissenschaftliche Veroffentlichung der Deutschen Orient-Gesellschaft, 9).

Fig. 3.23: General view of Hatra with Temple of Shamsh in the back. Credit: Photo Wendy Butts. Public Domain.
https://www.dvidshub.net/image/71339/city-sun-god. Accessed 22 February 2018.

Fig. 3.24: Bronze coin from Hatra shows Radiate head of Sun God "Shamash" with Aramaic text, and an eagle on the observe side., 2nd century CE., Credit: Public Domain, Classical Numismatic Group, Inc. Credit: Johny Sysel
https://en.wikipedia.org/wiki/Hatra#/media/File:Coin_of_Hatra.jpg. Accessed 3 March 2018.

Fig. 3.25: Façade of the temple of Allat, Hatra, Credit: Public Domain,
http://whc.unesco.org. Accessed 11 March 2018.

Fig 3.26: Female head adorned the façade of the temple of Shamsh in Hatra, Credit: Photo Véronique Dauge. Public Domain,
http://whc.unesco.org/en/documents/109734. Accessed 13 March 2018.

Fig. 3.27: Details of figural representations on the façade of the temple of Shamsh, Hatra, Credit: Public Domain, Photo Véronique Dauge,
http://whc.unesco.org/en/documents/109732

Fig. 3.28: Relief sculpture of male head with Aramaic inscription, The grand temple, façade of Iwan, Hatra. Credit: Photo Erick Bonnier
https://www.erickbonnier-pictures.com/reports-travels/iraq-hatra/. Accessed 20 April 2018.

Fig. 3.29: King Sanatruq and his son `Abadsamia on the façade of the temple of Allat, Hatra. Credit: Public Domain,
http://whc.unesco.org. Accessed 19 March 2018.

Fig. 3.30: Head portrait of Arab king wearing a crown adorned with eagle, Limestone, 35 cm h., 2nd century BCE, Credit: Hatra, The Iraqi Museum.
http://tempxyp2440ym0wn.blogspot.com/2011/11/baghdad-museum-project.html. Accessed 19 March 2018.

Fig. 3.31: Monumental statue of royal female "Bubint Damyoun", Limestone, 210 cm. h., located within the grand temple, Hatra. Courtesy:
www.Baghdadmuseum.org. Accessed 11 May 2018.

Fig. 4.1: Temple of Ba`l, outside the wall. Dura, Syria. Credit:
https://commons.wikimedia.org/wiki/File:DuraEuropos-TempleOfBel.jpg. Accessed 2 March 2018.

Fig. 4.2: Conon Sacrifice: Details of the wall painting in the temple of Ba`l, 1st century CE., Dura, Credit: National Museum, Damascus, Syria. Public Domain
https://commons.wikimedia.org/wiki/File:Dura_Europos_fresco_Sacrifice_of_Conon.jpg. Accessed 2 March 2018.

Fig. 4.3: Julius Terentius Performing a Sacrifice, wall painting, Temple of Ba`l, Dura. Credit: Photography © 2011 Yale University Art Gallery
http://popular-archaeology.com/issue/june-2011/article/treasures-of-ancient-dura-europos-released-for-all-to-see. Accessed 11 March 2018.

Fig.4.4: Interior of the Jewish Synagogue, Dura, Syria with wall paintings of Old Testament narratives, 245-256 CE. Tempera on plaster wall. National Museum Damascus, Syria.
http://cyarthistory.wikispaces.com/synagogue+at+dura+europos. Accessed 3 March 2018.

Fig. 4.5: The Christian house-church (Baptistery), Dura, Syria, 250 CE. Reconstructed at Yale University Art Gallery. Credit: Public Domain.
https://en.wikipedia.org/wiki/Dura-Europos. Accessed 14 March 2018.

Fig. 4.6: Depiction of Jesus as the Good Shepherd, wall painting, House-Church, Dura, Reconstructed at Yale University Art Gallery. Credit:
https://commons.wikimedia.org/wiki/File:Dura_Europos_Baptistry_Good_Shepherd.jpg. Accessed 2 April 2018.

Fig. 4.7: Aerial view of the remains of Qaryat Al-Faw, Arabian Peninsula.
Credit: Al-Ansari, Qaryat Al-Faw: A Portrait of Pre-Islamic Civilization in Saudi Arabia, 1982.
https://archive.org/details/QaryatAl-fawAPortraitOfPreislamicCivilisationInSaudiArabia1982. Accessed 3 April 2018.

Figure 4.8: Aerial view of the remains of Qaryat Al-Faw, Arabian Peninsula – details. Credit: Al-Ansari, Qaryat Al-Faw: A Portrait of Pre-Islamic Civilization in Saudi Arabia, 1982.
https://archive.org/details/QaryatAl-fawAPortraitOfPreislamicCivilisationInSaudiArabia1982. Accessed 5 January 2018.

Fig. 4.9: Foundation of a temple. Qaryat Al-Faw, Credit: Al-Ansari, Qaryat al-Faw: A Portrait of Pre-Islamic Civilization in Saudi Arabia, 1982
https://archive.org/details/QaryatAl-fawAPortraitOfPreislamicCivilisationInSaudiArabia1982. Accessed 5 January 2018.

Fig. 4.10: Carving depicting the deity Kahl (Wadd), Qaryat Al-Faw, Credit: Al-Ansari, Qaryat al-Faw: A Portrait of Pre-Islamic Civilization in Saudi Arabia,1982
https://archive.org/details/QaryatAl-fawAPortraitOfPreislamicCivilisationInSaudiArabia1982 Accessed 5 January 2018..

Fig. 4.11: Upper part of a male figure may represent king Mu`awiyah Bin Rabi`ah, Limestone, Qaryat Al-Faw, Department of Archaeology, King Saud University, Riyadh. Credit: Al-Ansari, Qaryat Al-Faw: A Portrait of Pre-Islamic Civilization in Saudi Arabia, 1982
https://archive.org/details/QaryatAl-fawAPortraitOfPreislamicCivilisationInSaudiArabia1982. Accessed 5 January 2018.

Fig. 4.12: Clay figure painted and incised with south Arabian Musnad., Qaryat Al-Faw, Department of Archaeology, King Saud University, Riyadh. Credit: Al-Ansari, Qaryat Al-Faw: A Portrait of Pre-Islamic Civilization in Saudi Arabia (1982)
https://archive.org/details/QaryatAl-fawAPortraitOfPreislamicCivilisationInSaudiArabia1982. Accessed 5 January 2018.

Fig. 4.13: Fragment of a wall painting with a banquet scene, 2nd century CE, black and red paint on white plaster, 58x32 cm, from Qaryat Al-Faw, residential district. Department of Archaeology, King Saud University, Riyadh. Credit: Al-Ansari, Qaryat Al-Faw: A Portrait of Pre-Islamic Civilization in Saudi Arabia (1982)
https://archive.org/details/QaryatAl-fawAPortraitOfPreislamicCivilisationInSaudiArabia1982. Accessed 5 January 2018.

Fig. 4.14: Fragment of a wall painting with a head of man "ZKY", 2nd century CE, black, yellow and red paint on white plaster, Qaryat Al-Faw, residential district. Department of Archaeology, King Saud University, Riyadh. Credit: Al-Ansari, Qaryat Al-Faw: A Portrait of Pre-Islamic Civilization in Saudi Arabia (1982)
https://archive.org/details/QaryatAl-fawAPortraitOfPreislamicCivilisationInSaudiArabia1982. Accessed 5 January 2018.

Fig. 4.15: Fragment of a wall painting depicts a tower house with inhabitants (3rd century BCE – 3rd century CE), black, red and yellow paint on white plaster, 59 x 64 cm, from Qaryat al-Faw, Saudi Arabia. Credit: Department of Archaeology Museum, King Saud University, Riyadh.
http://www.wikiwand.com/en/Qaryat_al-Faw. Accessed 5 January 2018.

Fig. 5.1: Statue of a man, broken at knee height, 4th–3rd centuries BC, Red sandstone, 230 x 83 cm, Al-`Ula, Credit: Department of Archaeology Museum, King Saud, University, Riyadh, 137D4 and 136D4.

http://www.wikiwand.com/en/Qaryat_al-Faw. Accessed 5 January 2018.

Fig. 4.2: Colossal sandstone statues, Al-`Ula, 4th-2nd century B.C.E. Courtesy of the Department of Archaeology Museum, King Saud University, Riyadh, Saudi Arabia.
http://www.wikiwand.com/en/Qaryat_al-Faw.

Fig. 5.3: Colossal statue of male figure, Northwest Arabia, 3rd-1st century BCE, Istanbul Archaeology Museum, Turkey. Credit: Photo Hashim Al-Tawil.

Fig. 5.4: Colossal head of male figure, North west Arabia, 3rd-1st century BCE, Istanbul Archaeology Museum, Turkey. Credit: Photo Hashim Al-Tawil.

Fig. 5.5: Relief sculpture of Allat flanked by two female attendants above a lion, Hatra, 2nd century CE., Limestone, 115 cm. h., 75 cm. w., Credit: The Iraqi Museum, Baghdad, Iraq.
https://www.pinterest.com/pin/540150549039327507/. Accessed 15 May 2018.

Fig. 5.6: General scene of façades of a tomb in Mada`in Salih. Credit: Photo Marjory Woodfield.

Fig. 5.7: Recesses carved in the walls of Mada`in Salih tombs.
Credit:
https://jeddahblogdotcom.files.wordpress.com/2013/05/madain-8.jpg. Accessed 15 January 2018.

Fig. 5.8: Qasr Al-Bint, Mada`in Salih. Credit:
https://scth.gov.sa. Accessed 10 January 2018.

Fig. 5.9: Qasr Al-Farid, Mada`in Salih, Credit:
https://commons.wikimedia.org/wiki/File%3AQasr_al_Farid.JPG. Accessed 10 January 2018.

Fig. 5.10: Eusebius of Cesarea and Ammonius of Alexandria, Folio 2r, the Rabbula Gospels, Zaghba, Syria, 586, Tempera on Parchment 13" x 10.5", Biblioteca Medicea Laurenzina, Florence, Italy.
https://commons.wikimedia.org/wiki/File:RabulaGospelsFolio14vPentecost.jpg. Accessed 12 January 2018.

Fig. 5.11: Crucifixion and Resurrection, folio 13r, the Rabbula Gospels, Zaghba, Syria, 586, Tempera on Parchment 13" x 10.5", Biblioteca Medicea Laurenzina, Florence, Italy.
https://commons.wikimedia.org/wiki/File:RabulaGospelsFolio14vPentecost.jpg. Accessed 12 January 2018.

Fig. 5.12: Folio 4v, Canon Table with the Prophets Samuel and Joshua and the Annunciation to the Virgin, the Rabbula Gospels, Zaghba, Syria, 586, Tempera on Parchment 13" x 10.5", Biblioteca Medicea Laurenzina, Florence, Italy.
https://commons.wikimedia.org/wiki/File:RabulaGospelsFolio14vPentecost.jpg. Accessed 12 January 2018.

Fig. 5.13: Arabic epitaph of "Imri`ul-Qays" inscribed in Nabataean script. H. 45 cm (17 ½ in.), W. 1.73 m (5 ft. 8 in.), D. 15 cm (5 ¾ in.), Basalt, dated 328 CE. Found at Namara in the Hawran (Southern Syria), Louvre Museum. Credit: Jastrow (2007), Public Domain.
https://commons.wikimedia.org/w/index.php?curid=1527958. Accessed 5 March 2018.

Fig. 5.14: Tracing of the original Nabataean text of "the Namara Inscription" and its Arabic interpretation by Dussad. Credit: Sabulhab.
https://commons.wikimedia.org/w/index.php?curid=21798437. Accessed 5 March 2018.

Fig. 5.15: Remains of possible Nestorian monastery, Hirah, Iraq. Credit: Associated Press. https://www.sfgate.com/world/article/Ruins-in-Iraq-could-be-Hira-3782003.php. Accessed 5 March 2018.

Fig. 5.16: Details of stucco beams at the ruins of a Nestorian monastery, Hirah, Iraq. Credit: Associated Press.
https://www.sfgate.com/world/article/Ruins-in-Iraq-could-be-Hira-3782003.php. Accessed 5 March 2018.

Fig. 5.17: Stucco work at the ruins of a Nestorian monastery, Hirah, Iraq, Credit: Photo Alaa Al-Marjani, Associated Press.
https://www.sfgate.com/world/article/Ruins-in-Iraq-could-be-Hira-3782003.php. Accessed 5 March 2018.

Fig. 5.18: Example of plaster stucco of wall decoration in the monastery, Hirah, Iraq. Credit: Associated Press.
https://www.sfgate.com/world/article/Ruins-in-Iraq-could-be-Hira-3782003.php. Accessed 5 March 2018.

Fig. 5.19: Sample of Nestorian crosses found in Hirah, Iraq. Credit: Al-Kufah Journal, 3rd year, Issue 1, 2014, P. 129.

Fig. 5.20: Marble plaque for Abd Al-Maseeh, 6th century, Hirah. Credit: Al-Kufah Journal, 3rd year, Issue 1, 2014, P. 128.

Fig. 5.21: Jesus and St. Mina, paint on wood, Deir Baweet, Egypt, late 6th – early 7th century, 75 cm x 75 cm x 2 cm, Louvre museum, Paris, France.
https://www.louvre.fr/en/departments/egyptian-antiquities/highlights?page=20. Accessed 15 May 2018.

Fig. 5.22: Wall painting of Coptic ascetics, from the monastery of Saint Jeremiahs, Saqqara, Egypt, late 6th- early 7th century. Credit: the Coptic Museum, Cairo, Egypt.
https://www.pinterest.com/pin/300826450086339790/. Accessed 24 June 2018.

Fig. 6.1: General view of the Ka`ba inside the sacred Mosque in Mecca. Saudi Arabia. Credit: http://www.nourallah.com. Accessed 15 March 2018.

Fig. 6.2: Diagram of the interior of the Ka`ba of Mecca. Credit: IslamicLandmarks.com. https://www.islamiclandmarks.com/category/makkah-haram-sharief. Accessed 18 February 2018.

Fig. 6.3: Placing a new Kiswa on the Ka`ba, 2015. Credit: Majid Waris
https://www.youtube.com/watch?v=Y1r5wKQGeIg. Accessed 18 February 2018.

Fig. 6.4: Details of the calligraphic decoration on the door of the Ka`ba. Credit:
http://www.quransurat.com. Accessed 18 February 2018.

Fig. 6.5: 14th century Illustration in Jami` Al-Tawarikh of Rashid Al-Din of the event of placing the black stone during 605 CE rebuilding of the Ka`ba. After David Talbot Rice, Illustrations to the "World History" of Rashid Al-Din, Edinburgh University Press 1976, pp. 100-01. Edinburgh University Library, MS. Or. 20.

Fig. 6.6: The destruction of the statues of the idols of the Ka`ba, Safavid manuscript entitled Mir Khawand's Universal History, (Rawdhat Al-Safa) and dates to 1585-1595. After Markus Hattstein and Peter Delius, Islam, Art and Architecture, Konemann, Verlagsgesellschaft mbH, 2000, p. 29.
http://miniaturasmilitaresalfonscanovas.blogspot.it/2012/06/el-islam-mahoma-3-los-grandes.html. Accessed 10 February 2018.

Fig. 6.7: The destruction of the idols of the Ka`ba, page of a book relates the life stories of religious people. Colors and gold on paper, 24 x 14 cm, 18th century, Kashmir, India. Credit: The Museum of Ethnography, Rotterdam (Wereldmuseum Rotterdam) Netherlands. Published in "Dreaming of Paradise: Islamic Art from the Collection of the Museum of Ethnography", Rotterdam, (Rotterdam 1994), PP. 82-83, inventory number 68236 in the Islamic Collection. Photo courtesy Wereldmuseum Rotterdam by Erik Hesmerg, Sneek.

Fig. 6.8: Mohammed approaching the Ka`ba and the destruction of the sculptural representations of the idols, color and gold on paper, 32 x 20 cm., India 1808. Credit: Bibliotheque nationale de France, Paris, BNF, Manuscrits, suppl. persan 1030 f. 305v-306.

Fig. 6.9: Aerial view of Khayber Fort, Tabuk area, Saudi Arabia. Photo 2017. Credit:
www.EarthTeam.com. Accessed 10 February 2018.

Fig. 6.10: Hypothetical floor plan and perspective drawing of the Prophet Mohammed's house in Medinah Credit: (after Creswell), Nasser Rabbat / Aga Khan Program for Islamic Architecture, MIT.

Fig. 6.11: Mihrab and Minbar at the mosque of `Amr ibn Al-`As, (Fustat), Cairo, Egypt. Credit: Zishan Sheikh,
https://www.flickr.com/photos/zishansheikh/. Accessed 10 February 2018.

Fig. 7.1: The Great Mosque of Al-Kufah and the adjacent Dar Al-Imarah, Kufa, Iraq. Photo taken in 1915. Credit: Courtesy of The National Archives, London. Royal Air Force.
https://www.rafmuseum.org.uk/research/default/archive-collection.aspx. Accessed 10

IMAGES & MAPS CREDITS

February 2018.

Fig. 7.2: Floor plan of the Great Mosque of Al-Kufah, Credit: Saeed Arida, Archnet.org. https://archnet.org. Accessed 10 February 2018.

Fig. 7.3: Dar Al-Imarah, plan, Kufah. Creswell, K. A. C.. A Short Account of Early Muslim Architecture. Rev. ed. Allan, James W., 1989, Aldershot, Scolar Press, P. 13.

Fig. 7.4: The sacred Precinct, Jerusalem: Locations of the Aqsa Mosque, the Dome of the Rock, and the Umayyad Royal Residential - Palatial Complex. Credit: Andrew Shiva / Wikipedia. https://www.google.com/

Fig.. 7.5: Dome of the Rock, General view, Jerusalem, Palestine, completed 691. Credit: Andrew Shiva / Wikipedia.
https://en.wikipedia.org/wiki/Dome_of_the_Rock#/media/File:Israel-2013(2)-Jerusalem-Temple_Mount-Dome_of_the_Rock_(SE_exposure).jpg. Accessed 18 March 2018.

Fig. 7.6: Sectional axonometric view through the Dome of the Rock. Credit: Sawyer Fischer.
http://www.sawyer.cgsociety.org/art/architecture-3ds-max-rendering-vray-illustration-3d-dome-rock-410396. Accessed 18 March 2018.

Fig. 7.7: Qur`anic inscription in the inner face of the arcade, the Dome of the Rock, Jerusalem. Credit:
https://squarekufic.com/2016/01/26/the-dome-of-the-rock-its-inscriptions-and-the-religions-in-early-islamic-jerusalem/. Accessed 23 June 2018.

Fig. 7.8: Mosaic work, interior of the Dome of the Rock, Jerusalem.
https://mustseeplaces.eu/dome-of-the-rock-jerusalem. Accessed 18 March 2018.

Fig. 7.9: Aerial view of the Great Mosque of Damascus, Syria, (705-715). Credit:
https://www.skynewsarabia.com/ . Accessed 18 March 2018.

Fig. 7.10: Interior view of the Great Mosque of Damascus, Syria, Credit: Agha Khan Visual Archive. Photo: Nasser Rabbat.
https://dome.mit.edu/handle/1721.3/28419. Accessed 18 March 2018.

Fig. 7.11: Mosaics at the western side of the courtyard. Great Mosque of Damascus, Syria.
Credit: Photo by Heretiq.
http://creativecommons.org/licenses/by-sa/3.0/, via Wikimedia Commons. https://commons.wikimedia.org/wiki/File:Umayyad_Mosque-Mosaics_west.jpg. Accessed 18 March 2018.

Fig. 7.12: Aerial view of Qusayr `Amra, 8th century, Jordan. Credit: AtlasTour.Net.
https://atlastours.net/jordan/desert-castles/. Accessed 18 March 2018.

Fig. 7.13: Astronomical chart of the constellations, painting on the ceiling of the bath, Qusayr

`Amra, Jordan. Credit:

http://pennycaravan.com/royal-retreats-of-east-jordans-desert-castle-loop/ Accessed 18 March 2018.

Fig. 7.14: Painting of female dancer, server on the spandrel, Qusayr `Amra, Jordon. Credit: http://slsongtravel.blogspot.com/2012/07/. Accessed 18 March 2018.

Fig. 7.15: Reproduced painting of the "Six Kings", Qusayr `Amra, Jordan
Credit:
http://www.metmuseum.org/exhibitions/listings/2012/byzantium-and-islam/blog/where-in-the-world/posts/qusayr-amra, Public Domain, https://commons.wikimedia.org/w/index.php?curid=29024344. Accessed 18 March 2018.

Fig. 7.16: Aerial view of Mshatta complex, Jordan. Credit: http://www.apaame.org. Accessed 18 March 2018.

Fig. 7.17: Part of the outer wall of the Mshatta complex at the Pergamon museum in Berlin. Credit: Photo Hashim Al-Tawil.

Fig. 7.18: Aerial view of Khirbat Al-Mafjar, Jericho, Palestine. Credit:
http://www.soniahalliday.com/category-view3.php?pri=IS573-1-36.jpg. Accessed 18 March 2018.

Fig. 7.19: Mosaic work at the bath-house area, Khirbat Al-Mafjar, mid 8th century, Jericho, Palestine. Credit: Sara Toth Stub, the Rockefeller Archaeological Museum.
https://www.archaeology.org/issues/232-1611/features/4939-khirbet-desert-castle#art_page4 Accessed 18 March 2018.

Fig. 7.20: Examples of stucco statues from Khirbat Al-Mafjar, Jericho, Palestine. Credit: Palestinian Department of Antiquities and Cultural Heritage.
https://en.wikipedia.org/wiki/Department_of_Antiquities_(Mandatory_Palestine) Accessed 18 March 2018.

Fig. 7.21: Stucco of the dome cap of the Diwan. Khirbat Al-Mafjar, Palestine. Credit:
https://www.alfajertv.com. Accessed 18 March 2018.

Fig. 8.1: Illustration of Baghdad, the round city. Credit: Illustration: Jean Soutif/Science Photo Library
http://www.amusingplanet.com/2016/07/the-round-city-of-baghdad.html. Accessed 2 April 2018.

Fig. 8.2: Al-Jazari's illustration of the automaton horse rider atop the Green Dome, the Caliph's palace, Baghdad. Credit:
http://historiautomatas.blogspot.com/2010/06/s-xii-al-jazari.html. Accessed 2 April 2018.

Fig. 8.3: Al-Mustansiriyyah school, Baghdad, 13th century. Credit: Photo Mustafa Waad Saeed https://creativecommons.org/licenses/by-sa/4.0)], via Wikimedia Commons. https://commons.wikimedia.org/wiki/File:المدرسة المستنصرية في بغداد.jpg. Accessed 2 April 2018.

Fig. 8.4: Main entrance, Al-Mustansiriyyah school, Baghdad, 13th century. Credit: Zzztriple2000 https://commons.wikimedia.org/wiki/File%3AMustansiriya_school_main_entrance.jpg. Accessed 2 April 2018.

Fig. 8.5: Façade of the entrance, Ince Minareli Medrasa, Kpnya, Turkey, 13th century. Credit: Photo Donnyhoca.
https://commons.wikimedia.org/wiki/File%3AInce_minare_entrance.jpg. Accessed 2 April 2018.

Fig. 8.6: Folio from "Kitab Al-Diryaq" Book of Antidotes of Pseudo-Galen,12th century, Mosul, Iraq. Credit: Bibliothèque nationale de France.
http://gallica.bnf.fr/ark:/12148/btv1b8422960m/f40.item. Accessed 8 April 2018.

Fig. 8.7: Folio from "Kitab Al-Diryaq" Book of Antidotes of Pseudo-Galen,12th century, Mosul, Iraq. Credit: Bibliothèque nationale de France.
http://gallica.bnf.fr/ark:/12148/btv1b8422960m/f34.item. Accessed 8 April 2018.

Fig. 8.8: Folio 19 Recto: Illustration of Maqamah # 7, celebration the end of Ramadan. Bibliothèque nationale de France. Credit:
http://gallica.bnf.fr/ark:/12148/btv1b8422965p/f47.item.r=Hariri. Accessed 8 April 2018.

Fig. 8.9: Folio 29 Verso: Illustration of Maqamah # 11, The burial at Sawa Cemetery. Credit: Bibliothèque nationale de France
http://gallica.bnf.fr/ark:/12148/btv1b8422965p/f68.highres. Accessed 8 April 2018.

Fig. 8.10: Folio from Al-Jazari's illustration of the "Castle Clock", Ink, opaque watercolor and gold on paper, 39.37 x 27.62 cm (15 1/2 x 10 7/8 in.), Credit: Museum of Fine Arts, Boston.

Fig. 8.11: Illustrated detached manuscript folio from Al-Qazwini's book "The Wonders of Creation and the Oddities of Existence". H x W (verso angel): 9.9 × 9.4 cm (3 7/8 × 3 11/16 in). Credit: Freer Sackler Gallery of Art, Smithsonian Institution, Washington DC.

Fig. 8.12: Façade of Al-Aqmar mosque, Cairo, 1125. Credit:
https://commons.wikimedia.org/wiki/File%3AAl_aqmar_facade.jpg. Accessed 28 May 2018.

Fig. 8.13: Plaster wall painting fragment from a bath-house, Fustat (old Cairo), 11th century, Height 24.5 cm, width 60 cm. Credit: Museum of Islamic Arts, Cairo, Egypt.
http://www.museumwnf.org. Accessed 3 January 2018.

Fig. 8.14: Four ivory panels, Fatimids, 11-12th century. Horizontal panels length 36.5 cm, width 5.8 cm. Vertical panels: height 30.3 cm, width 5.8 cm. Depth of panels 1–1.5 cm. Credit: Museum für islamische Kunst, Staatliche Museen, Berlin. http://www.smb.museum/en/home.html. Accessed 3 April 2018.

Fig. 9.1: The Great Mosque of Cordoba, 8th – 10th centuries, Cordoba, Spain. Credit: Toni Castillo Quero.
https://commons.wikimedia.org/wiki/File:Mezquita_de_Córdoba_desde_el_aire_(Córdoba,_España).jpg. Accessed 3 April 2018.

Fig. 9.2: Interior of the Great Mosque of Cordoba, Spain, 8th-10th centuries. Credit: Berthold Werner.
http://cryptojudaism.com/2016/05/24/the-concept-of-taqiyya-and-its-impact-on-iberian-jewry/. Accessed 3 April 2018.

Fig. 9.3: The dome in front of the Mihrab, the Great Mosque of Cordoba. Credit:
https://pufflesandhoneyadventures.wordpress.com. Accessed 3 April 2018.

Fig. 9.4: Altar and Nave of the inserted Cathedral inside the Great Mosque of Cordoba, 16th century. Credit:
http://keywordsuggest.org/gallery/352728.html. Accessed 3 April 2018.

Fig. 9.5: "Puerta de San José", One of the 11 doors of the Great Mosque of Cordoba, Credit: Américo Toledano.
https://commons.wikimedia.org/wiki/File:Puerta_de_San_José_-_Mezquita_de_Córdoba.jpg. Accessed 3 April 2018.

Fig. 9.6: Qur`anic verses and decoration, Mihrab of the Great Mosque of Cordoba. Credit:
https://dome.mit.edu. Accessed 3 April 2018.

Fig. 9.7: Bab Al-Mardum Mosque, Toledo Spain, 999. Credit: photo PMR Maeyaert.
http://www.pmrmaeyaert.com. Accessed 3 April 2018.

Fig. 9.8: Brickworks with Kufic inscription on the façade of the Bab Al-Mardum Mosque, Toledo, Spain. Credit: Solbaken. Credit:
http://www.gnu.org/copyleft/fdl.html. Accessed 3 April 2018.

Fig. 9.9: Cathedral of Seville on the site of the Great Mosque of Seville, Spain, 15th century, Credit:
http://www.ihistory.co/tales-of-alhambra/. Accessed 3 April 2018.

Fig. 9.10: The minaret of the Great Mosque of Seville -now the bell tower "La Giralda", Seville, Spain. Credit: Jebulon.
https://commons.wikimedia.org/wiki/File:La_Giralda_August_2012_Seville_Spain.jpg. Accessed 3 April 2018.

Fig. 9.11: Details of a bronze original door of the great mosque of Seville – now the Puerta del Pardon. Credit: Jebulon via Wikimedia Commons.

IMAGES & MAPS CREDITS

https://commons.wikimedia.org/wiki/File:Door_knocker_Puerta_del_Perdon_Seville_Spain.jpg. Accessed 3 April 2018.

Fig. 9.12: Alcazar, courtyard, Seville, Spain, 9th - 13th centuries. Credit: By Kiko León (Own work) [CC BY-SA 4.0 (https://creativecommons.org/licenses/by-sa/4.0)], via Wikimedia Commons.
https://upload.wikimedia.org/wikipedia/commons/0/0f/Reales_Alcázares_de_Sevilla_-_Patio_de_las_Doncellas.jpg. Accessed 10 April 2018.

Fig. 9.13: Interior of the Reception Hall, Alcazar, Seville. Credit: Dos de Arte Ediciones SL
https://www.dosde.com/discover/en/the-royal-alcazar-of-seville/. Accessed 10 April 2018.

Fig. 9.14: Example of the decorative program at Alcazar. Credit: https://ramblingsofanarabicstudent.wordpress.com/tag/arabic-spanish-overlap/. Accessed 10 April 2018.

Fig. 9.15: Kufic calligraphy at Alcazar. Credit John M Philips.
http://skepticphoto.blogspot.com/2014/10/seville-alcazar.html. Accessed 10 April 2018.

Fig. 9.16: Aerial view, Madinat Al-Zahra, Cordoba, 9th – 10th centuries. Credit:
http://www.discoverislamicart.org/database_item.php?id=monument;isl;es;mon01;2;en. Accessed 10 April 2018.

Fig. 9.17: Audience Hall, Diwan of the Caliph, Madinat Al-Zahra`, Cordoba. Credit:
https://www.artehistoria.com. Accessed 10 April 2018.

Fig. 9.18: General view of the Alhambra complex. Granada, Spain, 9th – 15th centuries.
Credit: Photo by Slaunger.
https://commons.wikimedia.org/w/index.php?curid=35203662. Accessed 10 April 2018.

Fig. 9.19: Interior of upper level room, the "Lindraja Balcony" - "Ain Dar `Aisha", with glazed ceramic tiles and stucco, Alhambra, Granada. Credit:
http://travelbetterwiththefunfactor.com/409-2/. Accessed 10 April 2018.

Fig. 9.20: Alhambra Interior with stucco work, calligraphy and Muqarnas, Granada, Spain
Credit: Photo Jaritah Lu.
https://creativecommons.org/licenses/by-sa/4.0), via Wikimedia Commons. http://buffaloah.com/a/virtual/spain/gran/alham/comext/tc.html. Accessed 10 April 2018.

Fig. 9.21: Alhambra, "Hall of the Two Sisters" with Muqarnas work at the ceiling and base of the dome, Granada, Spain.. Credit: jvwpc - Flickr,
https://commons.wikimedia.org/w/index.php?curid=1615140. Accessed 10 April 2018.

Fig. 9.22: Details of calligraphic inscriptions inside Alhambra. Credit:
http://entertablement.com/about-us/. Accessed 10 April 2018.

Fig. 9.23: Wooden window framed with carved calligraphic stucco work. Example of the use of Arabic calligraphy in the decorative program at Alhambra. Credit: http://entertablement.com/about-us/. Accessed 10 April 2018.

Fig 9.24: Ibn Al-Khatib's poetry in the so called "Salón de Comares", Alhambra. Credit:
http://viajes.kinestravel.com.ar/wp-content/uploads/2017/04/arco-de-entrada-al-Salón-de-Comares.jpg. Accessed 10 April 2018.

Fig. 9.25: Painting of the 10 figures on the central ceiling of the "Hall of Kings." Credit: https://histoireislamique.wordpress.com. Accessed 10 April 2018.

Fig. 9.26: Mertola, Arab castle and former mosque- now a church (Igreja Matriz de Mértola), Portugal. Credit: By Femidio.
https://commons.wikimedia.org/wiki/File:Castelo_de_Mértola_ao_entardecer.jpg. Accessed 10 April 2018.

Fig. 9.27: The Church of Nossa Senhora da Anunciação, former mosque, Mertola. Credit: https://commons.wikimedia.org/wiki/File:Igreja_Matriz_de_Mértola.jpg.
Accessed 15 April 2018.

Fig. 9.28: Interior of the main church of Mertola – former mosque. Credit: Courtesy of IPPAR. https://commons.wikimedia.org/wiki/File:Mertola-MatrizChurch.jpg. Accessed 10 April 2018.

Fig. 9.29: Remains of the upper section of the Mihrab of the former mosque, main church of Mertola. Credit:
http://www.islamichistoryandtravel.com/igreja_matriz_church_old_mosque_mertola_photos.html. Accessed 10 April 2018.

Fig. 10.1: Palermo Cathedral, formerly the Great Mosque. Credit: Hashim Al-Tawil 2007.

Fig. 10.2: Qu`anic text on the original mosque's pillar now at the entrance of the Palermo Cathedral, Palermo, Sicily. Credit: Hashim Al-Tawil 2007.

Fig. 10.3: Remains of the original Mihrb of the Great Mosque of Palermo, now behind the altar of Palermo Cathedral. Credit:
http://palermodintorni.blogspot.com/2016/02/cattedrale-di-palermo-la-cripta.html. Accessed 6 February 2018.

Fig. 10.4: The bell tower of Santa Maria dell'Ammiraglio (the Martorana), Palermo, Sicily. Credit: Hashim Al-Tawil 2007.

Fig. 10.5: Qur`anic text on a reused marble column at the Martorana church, Sicily. Credit: Hashim Al-Tawil 2007.

Fig. 10.6: Anaphora Hymn in Arabic at the base of the dome of the Martorana, Palermo, Sicily.

IMAGES & MAPS CREDITS

Credit: http://thewanderingscot.com/. Accessed 6 February 2018

Fig. 10.7: Painting on the ceiling of Cefalu Cathedral, Sicily, 12th century. Credit: http://www.discoverislamicart.org/. Accessed 6 February 2018.

Fig. 10.8: Exterior of Apse, Monreale Cathedral, Monreale, Sicily, 12th century. Credit: Hashim al-Tawil 2007.

Fig. 10.9: La Zisa palace, Palermo, Sicily 12th century. Credit: Hashim Al-Tawil 2007.

Fig. 10.10: Muqarnas decoration and fountain at the hall of La Zisa palace, Palermo, Sicily 12th century. Credit: Sandro Scalia.
http://www.discoverislamicart.org/. Accessed 6 February 2018.

Fig. 10.11: Arabic inscription at the entrance of the hall of La Zisa palace, 12th century, Palermo, Sicily. Credit: Hashim Al-Tawil 2007.

Fig. 10.12: La Cuba castle, Palermo, Sicily, 12th century. Credit: Hashim Al-Tawil 2007.

Fig. 10.13: Monumental Arabic inscription on the upper part of La Cuba, Palermo, Sicily, 12th century. Credit: Hashim Al-Tawil 2007.

Fig. 10.14: Fallen pieces and museum replica of the monumental Arabic inscription on the upper part of La Cuba, La Cuba museum, Palermo, Sicily. Credit: Hashim Al-Tawil 2007.

Fig. 10.15: The Norman palace, former Arab Dar Al-Emarah, Palermo, Sicily. Credit: Hashim Al-Tawil 2007.

Fig. 10.16: The Cappella Palatina, general view of the Muqarnas ceiling, Palermo, Sicily. Credit: James B. Kiracofe.

Fig. 10.17: Cappella Palatina, examples of paintings on the Muqarnas ceiling, Palermo, Sicily. Credit: Hashim Al-Tawil 2007.

Fig. 10.18: Cappella Palatina, examples of Arabic text on the Muqarnas ceiling, Palermo, Sicily. Credit: Hashim Al-Tawil 2007.

Fig. 10.19: Cappella Palatina, examples of Arabic text in variant Kufic styles on the Muqarnas ceiling, Palermo, Sicily. Credit: Hashim Al-Tawil 2007.

Fig. 10.20: Painted panels on the north aisle of the Muqarnas ceiling, Cappella Palatina, Palermo, Sicily. Credit: Hashim Al-Tawil 2007.

Fig. 10.21: Detail of one of the 20 large eight-pointed stars along the central axis of the Muqarnas ceiling, Cappella Palatina, Palermo, Sicily. Credit: Hashim Al-Tawil 2007.

Fig. 10.22: The Cappella Palatina, general view of the throne side, Palermo, Sicily. Credit: http://www.salentoacolory.it/larte-litica-nella-cappella-palatina-palermo/. Accessed 6 February 2018.

Fig. 10.23: View of the Muqarnas ceiling, Cappella Palatina, Palermo, Sicily. Credit: Hashim Al-Tawil 2007.

Fig. 11.1: Rose water jug, believed to be a gift from Harun Al-Rashid to Charlemagne, 766-809, Gold, precious stones and enamel. The Treasury of the Abbey of Saint-Maurice, Valais, Switzerland.
https://commons.wikimedia.org/wiki/File:Kanne_Karls_des_Gro%C3%9Fen.jpg
Credit: Whgler GFDL (http://www.gnu.org/copyleft/fdl.html) or CC BY-SA 4.0. Accessed 6 February 2018.

Fig. 11.2: A Latin copy of Averroes Colliget, Principle of Medicine, dated 1530. Yale University, Cushing/Whitney Medical Library.
https://wellcomecollection.org/works/ex3u83dz. Accessed 6 February 2018.

Fig. 11.3: Latin translation of Averroes's Commentaries, printed in Napoli 1551, Qatar National Library.
https://www.qdl.qa/العربية/archive/qnlhc/10684.5. Accessed 6 February 2018

Fig. 11.4: Arabic Page from Ibn Sina, Avicenna Canoon, and the frontispiece of the Latin version printed in Venice 1559.
http://www.muslimheritage.com/article/ibn-sinas-canon-medicine. Accessed 6 February 2018.

Fig. 11.5: Al-Idrisi map of the world, from the Book of Roger, 1154. Bibliotheque Nationale de France. Credit: TabulaRogeriana.jpg: Al-Idrisi derivative work: PHGCOM (TabulaRogeriana.jpg) [Public domain], via Wikimedia Commons.
https://commons.wikimedia.org/wiki/File:TabulaRogeriana_upside-down.jpg. Accessed 6 February 2018.

Fig. 11.6: Frontispiece and a page of the Latin Translation of Al-Zahrawi Kitab Al-Tasrif, printed in Basil in 1541 by the printshop Henricus Petrus. Credit: Public Domain. Courtesy of the US National Library of Medicine,
https://www.nlm.nih.gov/exhibition/odysseyofknowledge
https://www.wdl.org/en/item/9552/. Accessed 19 February 2018.

Fig. 11.7: Latin folio from Hunayn Ibn Ishaq, Isagoge "Introduction to Medicine for Beginners" and detail. Credit: Public Domain. Courtesy of the US National Library of Medicine,
https://www.nlm.nih.gov/exhibition/odysseyofknowledge. Accessed 19 February 2018.

Fig. 11.8: East Façade of the Theotokos, Hosios Loukas Monastery, Greece, 10th century. Credit: http://projects.beyondtext.ac.uk/project_gallery.php?i=16. Accessed 19 May 2018.

Fig. 11.9: Details of the pseudo-Arabic inscription on the East Façade of the Theotokos, Hosios Loukas Monastery, Greece, 10th century. Credit:
http://projects.beyondtext.ac.uk/project_gallery.php?i=16. Accessed 19 May 2018.

Fig. 11.10: Details of the pseudo-Arabic inscription on the wall of the crypt, Hosios Loukas Monastery, Greece, 10th century. Credit:
http://projects.beyondtext.ac.uk/project_gallery.php?i=16. Accessed 19 May 2018.

Fig. 11.11: Details of the pseudo-Arabic inscription on a fragment of the iconostasis, Hosios Loukas Monastery, Greece, 10th century. Credit:
http://projects.beyondtext.ac.uk/project_gallery.php?i=16. Accessed 19 May 2018.

Fig. 11.12: Fresco painting of Joshua, Hosios Loukas Monastery, Greece, 10th -11th centuries. Credit:
http://projects.beyondtext.ac.uk/project_gallery.php?i=16. Accessed 19 May 2018.

Fig. 11.13: Detail of the fresco painting of Joshua, Hosios Loukas Monastery, Greece, 10th -11th centuries. Credit:
http://projects.beyondtext.ac.uk/project_gallery.php?i=16. Accessed 19 May 2018.

Fig. 11.14: Examples of Pseudo-Kufic inscriptions found in different churches in Southern Italy, 12th – 13th centuries. Credit: Fontana Maria Vittoria, Kufic Ornamental Motifs in the Wall Paintings of Six Churches in Southern Italy, IOSR Journal Of Humanities And Social Science (IOSR-JHSS), Volume 21, Issue 12, Ver. 2 (December. 2016) PP 56-73.

Fig. 11.15: Gentile da Fabriano, The Madonna of Humility, Tempera on wood, 56 cm × 41 cm (22 in × 16 in), 1420-1423, National Museum of San Mattero, Pisa, Italy. Credit: Public Domain.
https://commons.wikimedia.org/wiki/File:Gentile_da_fabriano,_madonna_col_bambino,_pisa.jpg. Accessed 19 May 2018.

Fig. 11.16: Gentile da Fabriano, The Madonna of Humility, details of the pseudo-Arabic inscription inside the halo. Credit: Public Domain.
https://commons.wikimedia.org/wiki/File:Gentile_da_fabriano,_madonna_col_bambino,_pisa.jpg. Accessed 19 May 2018.

Fig. 11.17: Gentile da Fabriano, The Madonna of Humility, details showing the pseudo-Arabic inscription on the edge of the garment where Jesus is lying.

Fig. 11.18: Giovanni Bellini, Blessing Christ, tempera on wood, 58 × 46 cm (22.8 × 18.1 in), 1465-70, Louvre Museum, Paris, France. Credit: [GFDL (http://www.gnu.org/copyleft/fdl.html) or CC BY 3.0
https://creativecommons.org/licenses/by/3.0)], from Wikimedia Commons. https://en.wikipedia.org/wiki/Christ_Blessing_(Bellini)#/media/File:Giovanni_Bellini_Le_Christ_Benissant_1465_1470.jpg. Accessed 19 May 2018.

Fig. 11. 19: Giovanni Bellini, Blessing Christ, details of the pseudo-Arabic inscription on the collar and arm bands.

Fig. 11.20: Stained glass window, Santissima Annunziate, Florence, 1465. Credit photo: Francesco Guazzelli.

Fig. 11.21: Stained glass window details, Santissima Annunziate, Florence, 1465. Credit photo: Francesco Guazzelli.

Fig. 11.22: John Nash, the Royal Pavilion, Brighton, UK, 1815-1818. Credit: By Qmin [CC BY-SA 3.0 (https://creativecommons.org/licenses/by-sa/3.0)], from Wikimedia Commons
https://commons.wikimedia.org/wiki/File:Brighton_royal_pavilion_Qmin.jpg. Accessed 23 May 2018.

Map Credits

Map 1: The Arabian Peninsula and the trade routes around 1000 BCE.
Credit:
https://gazetawarszawska.net/historia/1313-isil2#!/ccomment. Accessed 2 January 2018.

Map 2: Phoenician Expansion in the Mediterranean Region around 800 BCE. Credit:
http://doi.org/10.137/journal.pone.0190.g001. Accessed 3 February 2018.

Map 3: Routes of the Silk Road through the Arabian Peninsula (1000 BCE-700 CE). Credit: www.Unisco.org. Accessed 23 May 2018.

Map 4: Nabatean cities and trade routes. Credit: Rababeh, S. 2005. How Petra was built, Figure 1.13, British Archaeological Reports, 1460, Oxford:
www.archaeopress.com. Accessed 23 April 2018.

Map 5: Nabataean expansion around 270 CE. Credit: Sémhurderivative: Attar-Aram Syria -
https://commons.wikimedia.org/wiki/File:Middle_East_topographic_map-blank.svg, Accessed 23 May 2018.

Map 6: Major trade cities on the Silk Road in the Jazeerah region including Hatra.
http://judithweingarten.blogspot.com/2015/03/elegy-for-hatra.html. Accessed 23 May 2018.

Map 7: The location of Qaryat Al-Faw, the Arabian Peninsula. Credit: Helene David, Louvre Museum,
https://en.wikipedia.org/wiki/Ancient_towns_in_Saudi_Arabia. Accessed 11 May 2018.

Map 8: Map of the territories of the Ghassanids and the Lakhmids (Munthirids), 6th-7th centuries. Credit: Thomas Lessman.

https://creativecommons.org/licenses/by-sa/3.0)], from Wikimedia Commons. https://en.wikipedia.org/wiki/Ghassanids#/media/File:NE_565ad.jpg. Accessed 31 May 2018.

Map 9: Map of the location of Iberia, Sicily and Malta in the Mediterranean region during the Byzantine Muslim confrontation (7-11) centuries. Credit: Cplakidas.

https://commons.wikimedia.org/wiki/User:Cplakidas#/media/File:Byzantine-Arab_naval_struggle.png. Accessed 31 May 2018.

search?q=Aqsa+Mosque,+the+Dome+of+the+Rock,+and+the+Umayyad+Royal+Residential&source=lnms&tbm=isch&sa=X&ved=0ahUKEwiOntKC6bLbAhVNslMKHda_BwcQ_AUICygC&biw=984&bih=734#imgrc=ThjBz5AS7czzCM: Accessed 17 March 2018.

Fig. 7.5: Dome of the Rock, General view, Jerusalem, Palestine, completed 691. Credit: Andrew Shiva / Wikipedia. https://en.wikipedia.org/wiki/Dome_of_the_Rock#/media/File:Israel-2013(2)-Jerusalem-Temple_Mount-Dome_of_the_Rock_(SE_exposure).jpg. Accessed 18 March 2018.

Fig. 7.6: Sectional axonometric view through the Dome of the Rock. Credit: Sawyer Fischer.

http://www.sawyer.cgsociety.org/art/architecture-3ds-max-rendering-vray-illustration-3d-dome-rock-410396. Accessed 18 March 2018.

Fig. 7.7: Qur`anic inscription in the inner face of the arcade, the Dome of the Rock, Jerusalem. Credit: https://squarekufic.com/2016/01/26/the-dome-of-the-rock-its-inscriptions-and-the-religions-in-early-islamic-jerusalem/. Accessed 23 June 2018.

Fig. 7.8: Mosaic work, interior of the Dome of the Rock, Jerusalem. https://mustseeplaces.eu/dome-of-the-rock-jerusalem. Accessed 18 March 2018.

Fig. 7.9: Aerial view of the Great Mosque of Damascus, Syria, (705-715). Credit: https://www.skynewsarabia.com/ . Accessed 18 March 2018.

Fig. 7.10: Interior view of the Great Mosque of Damascus, Syria, Credit: Agha Khan Visual Archive. Photo: Nasser Rabbat. https://dome.mit.edu/handle/1721.3/28419. Accessed 18 March 2018.

Fig. 7.11: Mosaics at the western side of the courtyard. Great Mosque of Damascus, Syria.
Credit: Photo by Heretiq. http://creativecommons.org/licenses/by-sa/3.0/, via Wikimedia Commons. https://commons.wikimedia.org/wiki/File:Umayyad_Mosque-Mosaics_west.jpg. Accessed 18 March 2018.

Fig. 7.12: Aerial view of Qusayr `Amra, 8th century, Jordan. Credit: AtlasTour.Net. https://atlastours.net/jordan/desert-castles/. Accessed 18 March 2018.

Fig. 7.13: Astronomical chart of the constellations, painting on the ceiling of the bath, Qusayr `Amra, Jordan. Credit: http://pennycaravan.com/royal-retreats-of-east-jordans-desert-castle-loop/ Accessed 18 March 2018.

Fig. 7.14: Painting of female dancer, server on the spandrel, Qusayr `Amra, Jordon. Credit: http://slsongtravel.blogspot.com/2012/07/. Accessed 18 March 2018.

Fig. 7.15: Reproduced painting of the "Six Kings", Qusayr `Amra, Jordan

Glossary

'Amru Ibn Luhayy: A native Arab from the Meccan region in pre-Islamic time. According to Islamic tradition, he introduced visual representations (statues) of polytheistic deities to Mecca that he brought from the Syrian region or Iraq in the pre-Islamic era.

'Ud also **Oud:** Arabic stringed musical instrument, a short-neck lute type.

Ablaq: Arabic for particolored or piebald. An ancient Syrian architectural decorative technique alternating rows of light and dark color stone or masonry on the façade of a building.

Abyssinia: Arabic Al-Habashah, the old Ethiopian kingdom in Africa.

Acanthus: Greek for broad leave plant commonly used as a decorative pattern in architecture.

Ahl Al-Bayt, also **`Al Al-Bayt:** Arabic for "people of the house", referring to the family of the Prophet Mohammed which includes: The prophet Mohammed, his cousin and son in law `Ali, his daughter Fatimah, and his grandsons Hasan and Husain.

Ahnaf also **Hunafa`**, singular **Hanif:** In Arab-Islamic tradition, Ahnaf are the Arab people who maintained their monotheistic––Abrahamic belief and did not participate in polytheism during the pre-Islamic era. Islamic traditions consider Abraham as the first Hanif.

Aksumites also **Axumites:** The inhabitants of the Kingdom of Aksum, also Axum (100 CE-940 CE). An ancient African Kingdom in present northern Ethiopia and Eritrea. Aksum was the center-capital of the Kingdom, and an important city on the trade route connecting the Roman Empire with India.

Al-'Uzza: Arabic for the "dear", the "dearest", the "strong", and the "mighty". A Major pre-Islamic female deity along with others, was worshiped in different regions of the Arabian Peninsula, Syria, and Iraq. Her worship signified power and protection.

Al-Isra` wa Al-Mi`raj: Isra` is Arabic for "travel during the night", **Mi`raj** is "ascension". The term refers to the two parts of the Night Journey that, according to Islamic tradition, the prophet Mohammed commenced around the year 621 from Mecca to Jerusalem to Heaven.

Al-Khuwarnaq and **Al-Sadir:** The names of the two legendary luxurious palaces that the Lakhmid king of Hira constructed in the 5th century CE in the suburb of Hirah, Iraq.

Al-Musawwir: Arabic for the shaper, the maker of image, painter, sculpture, and creator.

Al-Musnad Al-Janubi: South Arabic script, and **Al-Musnad Al-Shamali:** North Arabic script: Ancient Arabic writing system that was developed in the south and the north of the Arabian Peninsula concurrently around 1000 BCE. Both the north and south scripts contributed to the development of many dialects culminated in the Aramaic which eventually produced the traditional Arabic language.

Al-Wasiti: Yahya ibn Mahmud Al-Wasiti, was a 13th century Arab painter, illustrator, and calligrapher from Wasit, Iraq. He was famous for his elaborate illustrations of the literary work known as Maqamat Al-Hariri (the Assemblies of Al-Hariri).

Alhambra: Spanish for the Arabic Al-Hamra`, the red fortress: It is a palace complex built by the Arabs of the Andalus - southern Iberia initially in the 9th century but more intricately with expansions and additions in the 14th century. Located in the suburb of Granada and was the governmental-residential complex to the end of the Arab reign in Iberia in 1492.

Allat also **Al-Lat:** A chief pre-Islamic female deity signifying power, domestic guardianship, protection and fertility. She was worshiped in different regions of the Arabian Peninsula, Syria, and Iraq. Allat identity was fused with similar deities such as Ishtar, Atargatis and Athena from neighboring cultures.

Almohads: The word is the English inaccurate transliteration of the Arabic word Al-Muwahhidun, those who promote a strict puritanical understanding to the oneness of Allah. Almohads dynasty developed in North Africa and centered in Morocco. They ruled most of that region along with the Andalus in southern Iberia during the 12th century.

Almoravids: The word is the English inaccurate transliteration of the Arabic word Al-Murabitun, which means standby trained combatants in a fortified convent Rabat. The Almoravids dynasty was established in the 11th century (1040-1147) and controlled vast area of western north Africa and Al-Andalus. They were overpowered by Almohads.

Andalus, also **Al-Andalus:** The territories occupied by Arabs in the Iberian Peninsula starting at 711. It included southern present Spain and Portugal to the boarder of France. The geographical span of Al-Andalus continued to shrink, and by 1492 was merely the city of Granada and its surroundings. The Arabs called it Andalus, which may have been derived from the Germanic Vandals or Gothic term.

Ansab: plural of Arabic **Nasub, Nusb,** meaning **Sanam,** which is a visual representation of a pagan deity.

Aramaic: A Semitic language that prevailed in the North and Northwest regions of the Arabian Peninsula since about 1000 BCE. Aramaic dialects were used among Canaanite-Phoenicians, Nabataeans in the Syrian region, and at Hatra and Hirah in Iraq. It is ancestral to Hebrew, Syriac and Arabic Alphabets.

Ashlar: Finely cut and hewn stone masonry used to dress walls in building to achieve unified surfaces. Ashlar masonry was used by many ancient civilizations.

Asnam: An Arabic plural of Sanam. In the Arab-Islamic tradition, it means a statue of a glorified and worshiped deity as in the case of the statue of Hubal, Allat and Manat in pre-Islamic time.

Assurbanipal: King of the Neo-Assyrian Empire in Mesopotamia (ruled 668-627 BCE).

Averroism: is a Medieval intellectual philosophical movement spread in Europe among young intellectual Europeans in the late 13th century. The movement was based on the philosophical interpretation and discourse of the 12th century Arab philosopher Averroes (Arabic Ibn Rushd). He reinterpreted the then forgotten Greek concept of "Humanism", in a more critical, practical and realistic new Arabic structure. He contended Aristotle's discourse, and established a reconciliation of Aristotelianism with the teaching of the Islamic faith. The movement continued to be strong even though the Catholic church condemned it and was banned by other official offices in Europe.

Awthan: Arabic plural of Wathan which is a term for a statue of idol of pagan deity.

Ba`l also **Baal:** Major ancient male deity, lord of heaven, the storm god, and head of the pantheon. Baal was worshiped by many Semite groups in different regions. His cult prevailed among the Canaanite-Phoenicians, the Nabataeans, the Mesopotamians at Hatra, Egypt, Syria, Palestine and other places.

Bayt: Arabic for house.

Bayt 'ilhy: Aramaic and Arabic for "House of the Gods"

Bayt Al-Hikmah, also "Dar Al-Hikmah": Arabic for "the **House of Wisdom**" which was a major Abbasid educational and scientific center in Baghdad, established in the 8th century. Bayt Al-Hikmah was the nucleus of what evolved to a full academic and scientific center for researching, studying and translating the known knowledge body that was collected from various cultures. The Abbasid authorities fully supported and funded its operation in recruiting multi-religious multilingual scholars from all over the Muslim Empire. It was in Bayt Al-Hikmah that scholars critically studied, annotated and translated to Arabic major Greek philosophical and scientific works. The project was replicated in other Muslim centers in Egypt, Syria and Al-Andalus. The original Bayt Al-Hikmah of Baghdad along with its observatory and library were destroyed by the Mongols in 1258. All its valuable manuscripts were burned and wasted.

BCE: Abbreviation for Before the Common or Current Era, referring to the time span from the pre-historic to the year 1.

Black Stone is a corner stone set into the eastern corner of the building of the Ka`ba in Mecca.

Canaanites: Ancient Semitic ethnic group, Aramaic speaking, occupied vast erea in the regions of Syria, Palestine and the Sinai since around 2000 BCE. The Greek identified them as Finiki and Punic, hence known as Phoenicians. They were active traders in the Mediterranean region and conducted trade activities with the Ancient Egyptians, Mesopotamians and Greeks. At their highest power (8th–4th centuries BCE), they expanded their territories to North Africa, Cyprus, Sicily, Malta, and Spain while centered their administration in the Levant at Sidon, Sur Haifa, and other coastal cities in the Mediterranean region.

CE: Abbreviation for the Common or Current Era, which refers to the time span from the year 1 to the present time.

Copt: The word copt or Gobt is the name the ancient Greek used- Gobt- to identify the people of Ancient Egypt. The Arabic Qibt and or Aqbat are used in Arabic to identify the Christian Egyptians followers of the Eastern Church of St Mark.

Dahis and Ghabra': An incessant pre-Islamic war between Arab tribes in the central Najd region of the Arabian Peninsula. It lasted approximately 40 years¬¬ (from around the end of the 5th century and the beginning of the 6th century CE.)

Dar Al-Emarah, also **Dar Al-Imarah:** The place that represents Government House in the Arab-Islamic tradition. It contains the legislative and consultative bodies and the decision-making power.

Dhullah also Zulla: Arabic for any roofed structure that provides shelter from sun heat, cold or rain.

Diwan also Majlis: Audience hall were high authority bodies meet, receive guests of honors, delegations, and conduct official matters.

Diwan Al-Madhalim: The Court of Grievances that the Norman King Roger II established in the 12th century in Palermo, Sicily emulating the Arab-Islamic model.

Dumya: Arabic word refers to a doll, statue, or any figurative visual representation.

Ewan, also **Iwan:** Persian word for the rectangular architectural space that is vaulted and walled on three sides, with one end open to a courtyard. It was developed in Islamic Iran around the 11th century and based on the Persian pre-Islamic prototype.

Favara: A city in Sicily with the Arabic name Fawwarah, which means "Gurgling water pool".

Frenj: Arab historians used this word to identify the Franks, Frankish, or the different kings and emperors of the Holy Roman Empire in the medieval time.

Genoardo: is the Italian rendering of the original Arabic Jannat Al-`Ardh, which means Paradise on Earth. The term was used by the Arabs of Sicily to describe the beauty of the vast park area in Palermo that contains the luxurious palaces La Zisa, La Cuba and others.

Gharb Al-Andalus: Arabic for the Western part of Al-Andalus, in reference to Portugal.

Ghassanids, also **Al-Ghasasinah** and **Banu Ghassan.** An Arab tribal confederacy occupied territories in Syria and became a mini-state agent to the Byzantine Empire after converting to Christianity during the 5th-7th centuries.

Giralda: Spanish La Giralda, is the bell tower of the Seville Cathedral. Originally built in 1198 as the Minaret for the Great Mosque of Seville in Al-Andalus during the reign of the Almohads dynasty. The mosque was converted to Cathedral after 1248, and the Minaret was used as the bell tower with later architectural addition at the top in the Renaissance style.

Hatra: From the Arabic Al-Hadhar, was an ancient Arab kingdom in the Ninewa, also Nineveh region in north Iraq. Its strategic location controlled the trade route and operation in that region. Its history spans from around 300 BCE to 200 CE.

Haykal: Arabic for structure, temple, body, sanctuary, and altar.

Hirah, also **Hira:** From Arabic **Al-Hirah,** was the capital of a Christian Arab kingdom of Lakhamids-Munthirites confederacy, located on the lower Euphrates in Iraq. Hirah controlled and managed the thriving trade activity passing through the city. The kingdom was a vessel of the Sassanian Empire. It flourished during the 4th–7th centuries.

Hypostyle: A basic structural form in Islamic architecture, consists of roofed space, supported by columns and arches. It was used to create the prayer hall in early Islamic mosques.

Iwan: See Ewan

Jahiliyyah: Arabic word from the Jahala, to be unaware and ignorant, in reference to the pre-Islamic time.

Jizyah also **Jizya:** it was a regulated tax that non-Muslim, living in Muslim land, had to pay annually.

Ka'ba: also, **Kaaba** is the cubic building located at the center of the most sacred site, that is the Meccan Great Mosque in the city of Mecca in present Saudi Arabia. The Ka`ba is associated with the daily prayers, where Muslims face the Ka`ba, and it is the site of the pilgrimage. The Ka`ba signifies the permanent presence of God-Allah.

Karubiyyoun (singular **Karoub**): According to Islamic tradition, there will be four angels called Al-Karubiyyoun, carrying the throne of God- Allah, on the day of Judgement. The word Karoub is an archaic south Arabian term used by the Sabaeans -700 BCE and means qareeb – close to the deity/divine entity. The four carriers of the throne are described in the forms of human, lion, falcon, and bull, hence reflecting the Christian definition of the four evangelists Mathew, Mark, Luke, and John.

Kiswa, also **Kiswah:** Arabic word means the cloth that covers the Ka`ba (Kaaba) in Mecca. It is annually made of fine silk dyed in black color and embroidered with silver and gold threads and decorated with Qur`anic verses along with commemorative epigraph. The Kiswa is changed annually during the Hajj – Pilgrimage rituals.

Kitab: Arabic for book.

Kubbah also **Qubbah:** Arabic for tomb, shrine, and dome.

Kufah also **Kufa:** Was a city located on the lower Euphrates river near Hirah, south of Baghdad. It was established in 638 as a military Garrison during the reign of the second Caliph `Umar Ibn Al-Khattab. In 657 the fourth Caliph `Ali Ibn Abi Talib transferred the seat of Khilafah from Medinah to Kufah.

Kufic script also **Cufic script** is the oldest Arabic calligraphic style that was developed in the city of Kufah in Iraq during the second half of the 7th century. Early Kufic script evolved from the angular Aramaic script, hence the similarities in the formation and shapes of the letters.

Kufisque also **Cufisque, Pseudo-Kufic, Pseudo-Arabic:** A decorative trend appeared in the architecture, painting, sculpture, stained glass, furniture and other art objects in Christian Europe as early as the 11th century. Pseudo-Arabic patterns were usually imitation of Arabic Kufic calligraphic bands, mostly illegible and continued to appear on the walls and floors of many churches in Italy; in works of religious paintings; sculptural monuments; and metal works through the 17th century. The use of Pseudo-Arabic signified the impact of Arab-Islamic culture on European intellectuals and artists. It was also used to indicate high culture, sacred identity and prestigious status.

Madinah also **Madina** and **Medinah:** Arabic for city, but specifically the name of the former Yethrib city in the Hijaz region of the Arabian Peninsula. Located north of Mecca and contained the tomb and mosque of the prophet Mohammed and considered the second holiest city in Islam after Mecca. It is also called Al-Madinah Al-Munawwarah, the radiant city, and Madinat Al-Nabi, the city of the prophet in reference to the prophet Mohammed's migration and settling in it in the year 622 CE, which is the first Hijri year in the Islamic calendar.

Madrasah also **Madrasa,** plural Madaris, is Arabic for general educational school and college for Islamic studies.

Manarah also **Manara:** Arabic for lighthouse tower. In early Islam the need for a high place to perform the "Athan", the call for prayer, triggered the development of a tower like structure-higher than the building of the mosque "Mi`thanah" to call for the prayer. The top part of the Mi`thanah was equipped with lanterns and lamps to indicate the location of the mosque, hence the tower was called Manarah.

Manat also **Manah:** Major pre-Islamic female deity, worshipped in many parts of the Arabian Peninsula including the region of Mecca.

Maqamah plural **Maqamat:** Arabic for Assemblies. Maqamah is any prosimetric literary work that contains rhymed prose and verses of poetry in classical Arabic literature.

Maqsurah: Arabic word for the enclosed space near the Mihrab area in Islamic mosque. It was designed for the protection of the Caliph, Amir, or the ruler of the Muslim community leading the course of prayer. The tradition was initiated by the Umayyads in Syria.

Medici, the House of Medici: A prominent Italian banking and financiering family thrived during the the reign of Cosimo de Medici in Florence, Italy in the 15th century.

Medinah see Madinah

Mi`thanah Arabic for the tower from which the call for the prayer "Adhan" is performed. See Minaret.

Mihrab: A blind niche in the Qiblah wall of the mosque, indicating the direction of prayer toward the Ka`ba in Mecca.

Minbar, also **Minber:** An elevated seat, similar to a pulpit, used by the Imam, leader of the community to give the sermon to the congregation in a mosque.

Monophysites: Early Orthodox Christians in Egypt and Syria, who held that Jesus Christ has only one nature, the divine and possibly a mix divine-human nature.

Monophysitism: Early Arab Orthodox Christians who rejected the theological discourse of the Byzantine Council of Chalcedon in the 5th century.

Moors: A coarse term used by the Europeans during the Medieval time, refereeing to the dark-skinned Arabs, North Africans, and Muslims in Spain, Sicily, and Malta and other Mediterranean locations. Perhaps originally the word was derived from Mauri in reference to the people of Mauretania. It is a derogatory term implying uncivilized and infidels.

Mu`athin also **Muazzin:** Arabic name of the person who performs the call for prayer Athan.

Mudajer, Mudajers: European term from the original Arabic Mudajjan, Mudajjanun meaning tamed or domesticated. It was the name given to Muslims of Al-Andalus who remained in Iberia after the Reconquista and did not convert to Christianity. Mudajer is also used to identify the artistic, especially architectural trend that combines both Arabic-Islamic and Christian medieval, mostly Gothic style.

Muqarnas: A unique Islamic architectural decorative elements, resembling honeycomb formation. It is an elaborate form of geometrically calculated squinches, vaults, and mini copula or corbel. Muqarnas decoration developed in the 10th century in the eastern Islamic land, and promptly spread to other regions in Iraq, Syria, North Africa, Sicily and Al-Andalus.

Nabataeans: Arabic Anbat, they were Arab population, Aramaic speaking, inhibited the Syrian region in Petra, Palmyra, Busra and other places (4th century BCE-300 CE). They controlled the trade operation and activity along the trade route passing through their territory into the Mediterranean through Palestine, Syria and the Arabian Peninsula.

Naskh: Arabic calligraphic style, was developed and derived from another calligraphic style called Thulth in the 10th century. The Iraqi scholar and calligrapher ibn Muqlah is credited for the development of Naskh style.

Nasirids also **Nasrids:** The Nasrid dynasty, also known as Banu Al-Ahmar, was the last Arab-Muslim Dynasty in Iberia (1230-1492).

Oratorical Architecture: Arab-Islamic architecture employs text to decorate the exterior and interior of buildings. The choice of text and its contextual relation to the functionality of the building transforms the structure to a talking architecture or speaking building.

Palmyra: The Greek name of the capital of the Nabataean territory in Syria. The Arabic name is Tadmur. Palmyra developed to a major state in the 2nd century CE but was swiftly conquered by the Romans.

Parthians: A major Persian power revolted against the Seleucid Empire and established their dominion in the 2nd century BCE. The Parthians expanded their power to include all of Persia and Mesopotamia followed by continuous struggle with the Romans. Their power ended by the 3rd century CE.

Poly-Loped Arch: An Islamic arch that has many decorated lopes, used in the interior and exterior of spaces in buildings. Most noticeable of that type of arches are to be found in Al-Andalus.

Qal`at** also **Qal`ah is Arabic word for castle, fortress and fort.

Qasabah: Arabic word for city, or the old part of a city.

Qiblah: From the Arabic to face toward. It is commonly used to indicate the direction of prayer toward Mecca.

Rabbula Gospels: A 6th century illustrated Bible-New testament, written in Aramaic and illustrated with colors on parchment by certain Rabbula. Not much is known about the person, or monk Rabbula. The name however may be derived from the Aramaic to mean "rab alaha" (God-Allah is the Lord), or "rab `elaya" a cognate of the Arabic expression "rab Al-`ula" (God of Heaven). The illustrated Rabbula Gospels was produced in a monastery in Syria.

Rashidun: The Arabic word for the guided ones. A term applied to the four Caliphs who succeeded the Prophet Mohammed: Abu Bakr, `Umar Ibn Al-Khattab `Uthman Ibn `Affan, and `Ali Ibn Abi Talib. They are called Al-Khulafa` Al-Rashidun, the Guided Khulafa`, Caliphs.

Rassam: Arabic for painter or artist who creates figurative images.

Reconquista: Spanish word for "Reconquest" of Iberia from the Arab-Muslims during a period of continuous military struggle from the 8th century and ended in removing the Arabs from the Iberian Peninsula in 1492.

Register, also **Registrar:** A horizontal, vertical or combination of bands on the exterior or interior of a façade contains decorative elements, calligraphic text or both.

Sabaeans: A prominent old south Arabian kingdom ruled in the region of Yemen (700 BCE-575 CE).

Sanam: Singular of Asnam. See Asnam.

Sassanian, also **Sassanid:** The Sasanian Empire was the last phase of the Persian Empire. They ruled Persia, Mesopotamia, Syria, Egypt, Eastern and Southern parts of the Arabian Peninsula, Anatolia and much of Central Asia (224-651). The Sassanian empire was defeated by the new rising Arab-Muslim power in 651.

Sayf Ibn Dhi Yazan: (516-578), A Himyarite King of Yemen. With Sassanian support, he was able to end the Eksumite, also Exumite control in southern Arabia.

School of Baghdad: A stylistic art movement that developed gradually in Baghdad within the field of manuscript illumination and reached its highpoint in the 12th-13th centuries. Major artist of the movement was Mahmoud ibn Yahya Al-Wasiti's whose style epitomized that artistic trend. The movement ended with the Mongol destruction of Baghdad in 1258.

Seleucids: The Seleucid Empire (312-63 BCE) was a hellenistic state founded after the division of the Greek Empire. The Seleucids controlled Persia, Mesopotamia, Central Anatolia, Syria, and territories in Central Asia.

Semite, Semitic, Semitism: An Old Testament term identifying the culture and ethnicity of the population in the Arabian Peninsula and adjacent regions in Mesopotamia, Syria, Palestine, Egypt and East Africa in ancient time. The use of the terms Semite, Semitic, and Semitism alludes to certain racial and ethnic identities, and convey veiled nepotism.

Shamash: The Sun God in ancient Mesopotamian cultures.

Siqilyah also **Siqilliyya:** Arabic for the Island of Sicily.

Spandrel: The triangular space between arches, a wall and the ceiling of framework in traditional buildings.

Tahreek: The use of diacritical marks in Arabic punctuation.

Taifa also **Ta`ifah,** Plural **Tawa`if:** Arabic for sects or Semi- Independent principalities, that developed among the Arabs of Al-Andalus in Iberia after the beginning of the decline of the central leadership in the 11th century.

Theotokos: Greek term for Mother of God used in the Eastern Orthodox church.

Thulth: Arabic calligraphic style.

Timthal: Arabic for statue.

Tiraz: Arabic for embroidered fancy garments associated with the royal office of the Caliph, Emir, or the ruler in Medieval Islam. It is usually made of fine silk and textile, gold and silver threads, and decorated with text and other decorative patterns. Tiraz may also refer to the place of manufacturing such materials: Dar Al-Tiraz.

Umayyads: An Arab dynasty assumed power over the Islamic Empire 661-750 from Damascus in Syria, and in Al-Andalus, Iberia 756-1031.

Wathan: Arabic for an idol, a statue representing a deity. Arabic plural is Awthan.

Yethrib: The name of a city north of Mecca, which was renamed "Madinah", the city, meaning "the city of the Prophet Mohammed" upon his arrival in the first Hijri year 622 CE.

Zukhruf: Arabic for ornament.

Index

A

Aachen, 241, 247
Abadsamia, 58, 62, 281
Aban, 22–23, 279
Abbas, 100, 124
Abbasid authorities, 167, 170, 247, 300
    Caliph Al-Mansur, 100
    Caliph Al-Muqtadir, 247
    Caliph Al-Mustansir Billah, 173
    Caliph Harun Al-Rashid, 247
    CAPITAL, 170
    cities, 176
    Empire, 170, 176, 269
    Palace, 169, 186
Abbasids, 128, 169, 184, 203, 213, 217, 239, 300
Abdah Ibn Al-Tabib, 121
Abd Al-Fulan Al-Najjar, 131
    Al-Malik, 137
    Al-Maseeh, 109, 114, 285
    Al-Rahman, 85, 189–90
    Al-Buthayri, 240
Abd Al-Rahman III, 203-04, 239
Abd Shams, 121
Abdullah Ibn Al-`Ajlan, 124
    Al-Zubayr, 136, 137, 151
Ablaq, 149, 155, 192, 204, 238, 298
Abraham, 69, 88, 125, 128, 133, 298
Abrahamic measurements, 137
Abraham's Sacrifice, 69
Abu Al-Fadhl Ibrahim, 143
    Bakr, 305
    Rafi, 131
    Tammam, 123
    Tujarah, Tujrat 131
Abyssinia, 9, 22, 88, 116, 126, 129, 161, 298

Abyssinian, 88, 116–17, 131
    builder, 129
    incursion in Yemen, 24
    ruler Ibraha, 99
    style, 100
    viceroy in Yemen, 88
Achaemenids, 9
Adam, 97, 126, 128, 149
Aden region, 25
Adhan, 304
Adhlal, 18
Admiral Bridge in Palermo, 224
Adna, 149
Adomites, 27
Adonis, 68
Aegean, 1, 275, 259
Affan, 305
Africa, 11, 22, 298
African companion, 140
Aghlabids, 217
Aghlibel, 46–47, 280
Agius Dionisius, 243
Agra, 154
Ahiram, 3, 277
Ahl Al-Bayt, 185, 298
Aḥmad Ibn Al-Rashid, 143
    Ibn Abi Ya'qub, 143
Ahnaf, 126, 298
Aishah, 123, 205, 211, 291,
Aja'ib Al-Asfar, 253
    Al-Makhluqat, 183
Ajlan, 121, 124
Akhbar Mecca, 136
Al-Akhtal, 124
Akkadians, 1, 58
Aksum, 9, 298
Albucasis, 254

Alcazar, 198–202, 291
Alexander, 27
Alexandria, 103, 115, 284
Algebra, 254
Algeria, 236, 269
Alhambra, 170, 204–12, 216, 239, 291–92, 299
Allah, 97, 104, 126, 128, 209, 224, 227, 263
  al-Mu'tazz bi, 227
  oneness of, 127, 152, 299
  there is no victor but, 202, 208
Allat, 30, 34, 42–43, 45–46, 58, 60, 62, 76, 93–95, 101, 124, 280–81, 284, 299–300
Almaqah-Allumqah, 20
Almohads, 189, 199, 201, 214, 299, 302
Almoravids, 189, 299
Alqamah Al-Fahal, 121
Al-'Uzza, 99, 124
Ambo, 140
Amir, 192, 203–4, 220, 235, 237, 239–40, 268, 304
Al-'Amkinah wa Al-Biqa`, 143
Amman, 65, 85, 118, 125, 158, 162
Amm-'Anas, 93
Amm-dhara, 14
Ammiraglio, 220, 222, 292
Ammonius, 103, 284
Amr, 107
Amra, 157–60, 166–67, 237, 239, 287–88
Amr Ibn Al, 141, 286
Amru, 125–26
Amru Ibn Qam'ah Ibn Luhayy Al-Kindi Al-Jurhami, 88, 125–26, 298
Ana, 216
Anaphora Hymn, 224, 292
Anatolia, 27, 42, 54, 145, 161, 170, 306
Ancient Arab Diwan, 82
    Arabic, 299
    Arab kingdom, 302
    Arab tradition, 155
    Egypt, 115, 301
    Greek concept, 249–250, 301
    Iraq, 1
    Ma'rib, 16, 278
    Mesopotamian, 60, 306
  Semitic, 10, 300
  SOUTH ARABIA, 11
Al-Andalus, 169, 184, 189–90, 192, 196, 201–4, 207, 209, 212–13, 215–18, 216, 220, 236, 246–47, 249, 251, 253–54, 256, 299–302, 304–7

Andalusian scholar Abu Al-Qasim Al-Zahrawi, 254
Andalus in southern Iberia, 299
Andromachus, 176
angular Aramaic script, 303
Anna, 275
Annunciation, 106, 268, 284
Ansab idols, 122
Antarah, 124
anti-Arab, 202
Antidotes, 170, 176–78, 289
Antigonnus, 27
Antioch, 220
Antoine Jean Gros, 271
Anunciação, 212, 214, 292
Aphlad, 68
Apulia, 217, 255, 259, 261–62
Aqaba, 95
Aqbat, 301
Al-Aqmar Mosque, 184–85, 289
Aqmat daughter, 50
Aqsa, 149-51, 156, 166, 185, 287
Arab Allat, 38, 279
Arab architects, 201, 215, 218, 220, 225, 231, 259
Arab art, 119, 145, 154, 164, 166, 169, 186, 189, 242, 246, 260, 263, 269, 271, 274
  development of, 169, 273
  development of modern, 272
  employed, 217
  foundational, 272
  transmitted, 249
    and architecture in Iberia, 202
    form, 212
    artists, 272, 274
  contemporary, 274
    buffer states, 28
    castle, 211, 292
    characteristics, 73, 116, 224
    -Christian, 28, 102, 105, 109, 236
    cities, 5, 67–68, 179
    confederates and semi-kingdoms, 245
    Contribution, 167, 246
Arab culture, 27, 116, 213, 217, 232, 238, 245, 259, 263, 270
  in Europe, 249
  Dar Al-Emarah, 233
  Decorative Visual Vocabularies in European Art, 247
  deities, 34, 42, 69, 76, 97

Diwan, 238, 241
expansion, 189
geographer-historian Al-Hamdani, 101
heritage, 241, 254
historian Al-Azraqi, 100
    Ibn Al-Athir, 241
    Ibn Al-Kalbi, 88
Arab historians, 88, 90, 99, 102, 121, 124-25, 130, 137, 139, 189, 196, 273, 301
Arabia, 9-10, 13, 26, 30, 42, 75-76, 88-90, 95, 97-98, 138, 102, 246, 296
Arabian deities, 95, 125
    Gulf, 95
    mythological entities, 32
    Peninsula, 1, 4-5, 9, 11-12, 14, 27, 29-30, 45, 87-89, 119-20, 124, 126, 282, 296, 298-99, 303, 305-6
    Al-Habashah, 298
    Al-Hadhr, 302
    Al-Hamra, 299
    Al-Hijr, 95
    Alphabets, 299
    Anbat, 304
    Al-Qanoon, 251
Arabic calligraphy, 152, 176, 184, 207, 209, 235, 243, 246, 255, 268, 273-4, 292, 303, 305, 307
    corpus of science, 246
    Dhullah, 138
    epigraphic program, 208
    epitaph, 285
    expression, 104, 305
    Fawwarah, 240
    Grammar, 126
Arabic historical tradition record, 28, 109
Arabic, 108, 191, 196 229, 231-32, 275, 285
Arabic-Islamic style and technique, 235
Kufic inscriptions, 255, 303
    language, 1, 28, 107, 170, 173, 246, 263, 266, 299
    letters, 273
    lexicographer, early, 126
    Literary Heritage, 188
    Literature, 143
    major Greek philosophical and scientific works, 300
    manuscripts, 181, 254
        Mi'thanah, 139
Arabic monumental inscriptions in modified Naskh style, 231

Mudajjan, 304
name, 162, 304-5
    Fawwarah, 301
    number system, 253
    poetry, 102, 202, 227, 232, 240
Pseudo-Script, 275
punctuation, 306
Qibt, 301
rhymed prose, 179
script, 176, 263, 269
term Mudajjan, 201
text, 152, 184, 202, 220, 232, 236-37, 239, 252, 254-55, 263, 268, 274, 293
translation, 184
    visual art and pseudo-Kufic inscription, 259
word, 225, 229, 268, 273, 301-2, 304-5
    Al-Murabitun, 299
    Al-Muwahidun, 299
    Al-Qasr, 201
    for castle, 305
    for city, 305
    KHAZZAF, 120
    RASSAM, 120
Arab-Islamic aesthetics, 271
    architectural monument, 154, 192, 305
    art, 209, 246, 255, 262, 273
    culture, 249, 251, 263, 266, 268-69, 303
    elements, 259
    empire, 247
    heritage, 274
    humanism, 266
    inspired decorations, 255, 259
Arab-Islamic tradition, 298, 300-301
    visual elements, 249, 257, 265, 273
Jews, 102
Kelbite Amir, 240
King, 5, 32, 63, 105, 282
kingdoms, 27, 75, 88, 119
lexicographers, 99
    literal memory, 119
    Modern art, 273
    monks and priests, 104
    Moroccan, 253
Arab-Muslim artists, 259, 273
    dynasty in Iberia, 305
    geographers, 253
    heritage, 196
    honorific title, 242

populations of Sicily, 217, 253
Arab-Muslims, 189, 201, 218, 250, 262–63, 269, 273, 305
    in Bari and Apulia, 262
Arab-Nabataean deities, 34, 46
    design, 34
Nabataeans, 60, 69, 87
    Nationalism, 272
    nomadic groups in Samaria, 5
    -Norman, 224
Arab oratorical architecture trend, 154, 173, 185, 209, 229, 231, 305
    Painting, 243
    palaces, 214
    palaces in Hirah, 147
    pictorial trends, 105
    poet Jarir, 121
    populations, 4, 27, 34, 214, 217, 245, 304
    Qayrawan, 189
    region, 27, 235, 299
    royal palaces, 240
    rule, 192, 213, 217
Arabs, 1, 4–5, 8–10, 100–102, 119–20, 166, 189–90, 213–18, 241–43, 245–46, 252–54, 256–57, 260–62, 269–75, 298–99
  ancient, 154
  pre-Islamic, 34, 122
Arabs and Arab culture, 116
Arab scholars, 246, 252, 254
    science and knowledge, 181, 249
    semi-kingdoms, 78
Arab-Sicilian, 224, 240, 242
Arabs in Al-Andalus and Sicily, 249
    in military affairs, 217
    in sanctuary cities of major deities, 45
    in Sicily and Malta, 217, 217, 301
    in Southern Italy, 260
    in Yemen and Nabataea, 117
    of Al-Andalus in Iberia, 306
    of Hatra, 245
    of Hirah, 87
    of Kindah, 82
    of North Africa, 253
Arab-Syrian goddess Atargatis, 95
Arab traditions, 42, 117, 165–66, 241, 263
    traveler Ibn Hawqal, 235
Arab tribes, 5, 9, 89, 102, 109, 301
Aramaic, 1–2, 4, 28, 30, 42–43, 45, 48, 50, 57–58, 60–62, 67–69, 73, 104, 107, 119, 169–70, 254, 281, 299–300, 304–5

arco-de-entrada-al-Salón-de, 292
Ardh, 41, 225, 227, 301
Arethas, 100
Aribi, 5
Ariha, 164
Aristotelianism, 300
Aristotle, 249
armed Athena, 95
art
  early Muslim, 166
  influenced Hatran, 54
  pre-Islamic, 109
  south Arabian, 25
Art and Architecture of Islam, 167
Artemis, 68
Artuqid dynasty, 181
Arus, 48, 143
Asad, 107
Al-A'sha, 100, 122-123
Ashlar, 300
Al-Ashraf, 268
Ashurbanipal, 5–8, 10, 277
Al-Asma'i, 126
Assemblies, 170, 180-81, 299, 303
Assurbanipal, 4, 8, 300
Assyria, 10
Assyrians 1, 3-5, 8–9, 11, 67, 245, 277
astronomer Thabit Ibn Qurra, 254
Astronomical chart, 158, 287
Atargatis, 34, 45, 60, 68, 95, 299
Ate'aqab, 50
Athan, 303
Athena, 60, 95, 299
Athens, 249, 256
Athtar, 14, 19–20
Athtar-de-Qabdu, 14
Atiqatayn Al-Ma'i'atayn, 143
Averroes, 249–51, 294-300
    Colliget, 250, 294
Averroism, 250, 300
Avicenna, 251-52
    Canoon, 294
Awwam Temple, 20, 99, 278
Awdh, 93
Awm, 22
Axonometric, 35, 279
Axumite, 78, 126, 298
Aylward Stela, 19, 278
Azd, 101
Al-Azhar Mosque, 169, 184

Al-Azraqi, 90, 100, 125, 132, 136, 138

B

Baal, 300
Baalbek, 9, 54
Ba'alsamin, 95
Ba'alshamin, 95
Baal Shamin, 280
Ba'altega, 50
Bab Al-Mardum Mosque, 195–96, 290
Babylon, 27, 124
Babylonian King Nebonidus, 4
Babylonian pantheon, 69
Babylonians, 1, 3-4, 69, 125
Badi, 181
Badr, 124
Baghdad, 169–74, 176, 179, 181, 184, 243, 246–47, 253–54, 257, 274, 284, 288–89, 300, 303, 306
Baghdad School, 181–82, 184, 306
    School of Painting, 274
    School of visual art, 184
Bahrain, 269
Baird, 65, 85, 118
Ba'l, 42, 45–46, 68–71, 280, 282, 300
    temple of, 69
Al-Baladhuri, 90, 145, 243
Balqa, 125
Balqis' castle, 99
Ba'l Shamin, 46–47
Banu Al-Ahmar, 204–05
    Al-Harith, 100
    Ghassan, 136, 302
    Ghatafan, 99
    Salim, 121
Baptist, 154
Baptistery, 73, 282
Baraqish, 13–14, 26, 277
Bari, 249, 259, 261–62
Barran Temple, 16, 18, 278
Bashshar Ibn Burd, 124
Basrah, 145–47, 149–50, 170–71, 176, 179, 184
    mosque, 145
    school of Arabic Grammar, 126
    war, 88
Al-Battani's Math, 254
Bay'at Najran, 100
Al-Baydha, 138, 143
  Bayhan valley, 25

Al-Bayt, 298, 300
Bayt Al-Hikmah, 169-170, 184, 254, 300
    Al-Mal, 147, 191
    zukhruf, 138
Beirut, 3,143, 243–44, 277
Beja, 214
Bellini, 295
  Giovanni, 267–68, 295–96
Bet Mar Yohannan, 104
Bible, 72, 244
Biblical, 69, 71, 73, 104–05, 116, 125, 133, 236
  Joshua, 257
    prophets, 149
    scenes, 69
    themes, 71
    theology, 73
Bilal, 139–40
Biqa, 27
Bishr Ibn Abi Khazim, 124
Blessing Christ, 267–68, 295–96, 265
Book of Antidotes of Pseudo-Galen, 170, 176–78, 289
    of Calculations, 253
    of Gifts and RaritiesS, 143
    of Idols, 131, 143
    of Knowledge of Ingenious Mechanical Devices, 170, 181, 188
        Tuhfat Al-Nudhdhar fi Ghara'ib Al-Amsar, 253
Borgia, 65, 85, 118
Bosra, 27–28, 30, 43
Bostra, 30, 102
British-French colonialism, 269
Bubint Damyoun, 63–64, 282
Al-Bujayrawan, 100
Al-Bukhari, 90, 124–25
Busra, 95, 102, 304
Byblos, 3, 9, 277
Byzantine-Arab, 297
  art, 236
  artisans, 192
  artists, 259
  churches of Attica, 259
  client state of Aksumites, 9
  island of Crete, 256
  Council of Chalcedon, 304
  Emperor Justinian, 102
    Nikephoros, 102
  emperors, 99, 161, 247
  Empire, 9, 22, 78, 88, 115, 119, 204, 256,

INDEX

260, 302
Greece, 275
influence, 104, 152
mosaic tradition, 152
Muslim confrontation, 190, 297
Byzantines, 27-28, 88-89, 102, 104-5, 109-10, 115, 119, 125, 145, 149, 154, 156, 166, 170, 245-47
in southern Italy, 261
style, 100
world, 9, 73
Byzantium, 88, 216, 255, 275

C

Cadiz, 189
Cairo, 116, 141, 143, 167, 169-70, 184-85, 243, 274, 285-86, 289
Calabria, 255
Calcite-alabaster stele, 22, 24, 279
incense burner, 17, 278
statue, 18, 278
Caliph Abu Bakr, 138
Al-Hakam, 191
Al-Ma'mun, 253-54
Al-Walid, 155
Harun Al-Rashid, 247
Hisham, 164
of Andalus, 203
Caliph's Palace, 169, 172, 288
calligrapher ibn Muqlah, 305
calligraphy, pseudo-Arabic, 267
Canaanite-Phoenicians, 1, 3, 32, 189, 299-300
artists and craftsmen, 2
city-states, 9
Canon, 106, 251, 284
Medicinae, 251
Canonical Tables, 104
capital Shabwa, 25
Tamna, 25
Cappella Palatina, 154, 165, 186, 224, 232, 234-44, 255, 293-94
Muqarnas, 170
Caravan Kingdoms, 26
Carolingians, 247
Carthage, 1
Castello, 229, 292
Castile, 189
Castilian, 254
Castle Clock, 182, 289

Catania, 220
Catedral Primada Santa María, 196
cathedral Al-Qullays, 100
of Seville, 196, 290, 302
Cecilia, 244
Cefalu, 238
Cefalu Cathedral, 224-25, 238, 243, 293
Central Anatolia, 306
Arabia, 4, 75, 88-89, 166
Asia, 28, 145, 169, 306
Iraq, 147
Cerrate, 259
Cesarea, 103, 284
Cesnola Collection, 277
Chalcedon, 304
Chaldean, 119
Charlemagne, 241, 247-48, 294
Chiesa, 220
China, 11-12, 28, 34, 41, 130, 161, 169-70, 181, 188

Christ, 72, 116, 152, 295, 304
Christian Arabs, 11, 88, 117, 302
scholars, 170
Christian Building, 85, 118, 259
churches, 33, 97, 100, 120, 151
conquest of Seville, 199
dogma, 259
Egyptians, 301
Europe, 247, 255, 259, 303
Christian house-church, 68, 71, 73, 282
Christianity, 22, 71, 73, 88, 100, 102, 116, 302, 304
doctrinal, 88, 102
eastern Orthodox Jacobite Arab, 102
Christianity and early Christians, 102
Christian kingdoms, 126, 204
kings, 201
martyrs of Najran, 100
motifs, 99
name for Youshi, 257
Norman, 232
population of Jerusalem, 152
Christians, 71-72, 85, 102, 104, 109-10, 118, 126, 132, 149, 154, 184, 190-91, 250, 254, 262
of Najran, 22, 101
subject matter, 249
Church-Mosque, 214
Church of Abyssinia, 116

of Jerusalem, 116
of Nossa Senhora, 212, 292
The city of Basrah, 145
the city of the Prophet Mohammed, 307
Classical Arabic language, 1, 11, 88, 109
    literature, 303
    Numismatic Group, 281
Cologne, 216
colonized Muscat, 269
Columbus, Christopher, 253
the Commentaries, 250
the Commentator, 249
Concattedrale Santa Maria, 220
Conon Sacrifice, 70, 282
Constantine, 254
Constantinople, 88, 102, 155
Contemporary Arab, 204
    Gothic artists, 263
Copt ascetics, 117
Coptic, 24, 116–17
    art imbeds, 117
    ascetics, 116, 285
    church, 116
    community, 116
    roots, 24
    tradition, 116
Copts, 115–16, 301
Cordoba, 155, 169, 189–94, 196, 199, 201–3, 239, 290–91
Corinthian columns, 46
    portico, 43
    style capitals, 33
Corsica, 1
Cosimo, 304
Cosmological Imagery, 244
Costa, 243
Crimea, 271
Crucifix, 122
Crusaders, 149
Crusade Texts, 244
Crusading Period, 243
Cuba, 225, 229–32, 293, 301
    Castle, 230, 293
Cuba Soprano, 225, 229
Cuba Sottana, 225
Cubula, 229
Cufisque, 247, 303
Cyprus, 301

D

Dahis, 88, 301
Damascus, 70–71, 138–39, 147, 149, 154–56, 166, 170–71, 190, 192, 274, 282, 287, 307
Dar Al-Emarah, 145–48, 150, 235–36, 301
    Al-Gharb Al-Islami, 243
    Al-Hikmah, 169, 184, 300
    Al-Imarah, 145, 286–87, 301
    Al-Tiraz, 307
Dark Ages, 249
decorations
  carved Arab-Muslim, 220
  pseudo-Arabic, 256–57
  pseudo-Kufic, 247, 251, 255, 263
Dedan, 5, 13, 27–8, 90, 95
Deir Baweet, 115, 285
deities, pre-Islamic female, 299
    Manat, 95
    Allat, 44–45, 99, 280
    Al'uzza, 99
    Attar, 19
    Dhu Al-Khalasa, 101
    Haddad, 154
    Hubal, 97, 132
    Kahl, 79, 283
    Nergal, 60
    Thul-Sharah, 98
Delacroix, Eugene, 271
Delius, Peter, 286
design
  architectural Muqarnas, 237
  contemporary Palestinian textile, 164
Dhafar, 23–24, 279
Dhahran, 89
Dhat Al-Rusum, 137
Dhat-Himyam, 20
Dhu Al-Ka'bat, 109
Dhu al-Ka'batayn, 110
Dhu Al-Khalasa, 93, 101
Dhu Al-Shara, 34, 93, 95
Dhu Al-Shurufat, 109, 238
Dhu La'wah, 98
Dhullah, 301
Dhushara, 30
Dibon, 125
Dioscorides, 184
Diwan, 157, 161, 164–65, 186, 203–4, 209, 237–41, 241–42, 288, 291, 301
    Al-Madhalim, 241, 301

of grievances, 242
Donatello, 267
Doughty, 89
Duccio, 267
Duma, 123–24
Dumya, 123, 301
Dura-Europos, 28, 43, 62, 65, 67, 69, 85, 95, 118, 166, 282
    House-Church, 71
    House-Synagogue, 69, 85, 118
    Synagogue Paintings, 85, 118
Al-Durrah Al-Khatirah, 243
Dusares, 34, 93, 98

E

Early Arab Icons, 65, 85, 118
    Orthodox Christians, 304
    Sculpture, 85, 118
Early Islamic Art in Jerusalem, 143
    Painting, 243
    poet Al-Hasan Ibn Hani, 121
Early Muslim Architecture, 143, 287
    Orthodox Christians in Egypt, 304
    Roman Empire, 65, 118
East Africa, 129, 306
eastern Byzantine territories, 255
    Church of St Mark, 301
    Islamic lands, 251
    Jazirah, 65, 85, 118
Ebulo, 244
Edessa, 27
Egypt, 1–3, 9, 11, 25, 27, 29–30, 115–17, 141–42, 145, 169, 184–86, 188–89, 246, 269, 274, 285–86, 300, 306,
Egyptian Hieroglyphic-Demotic, 2, 116
Egyptians, 1, 3, 34, 37, 80, 90, 117, 130, 245, 271, 273
Egypt Qait Bay, 268
Eksumite, 306
Elahbel, 280
Emessa, 27
Emir, 203, 208, 220, 268, 307
Emirates, 189
Emperor Frederick II, 262–63
empires
  declining Ottoman, 269
  early Byzantine, 87
Enna, 220, 238
Eremiti, 220

Eritrea, 298
Eternity to Allah, 209
Ethiopia, 24, 116-117, 126, 298
Euphrates, 1, 28, 54, 67, 146, 109, 181, 302

Eurasian continent, 41
Eurocentrism, 272
Europe, 2, 181, 189–90, 213, 216–17, 232, 244, 246, 249–51, 217, 253–55, 263 266, 269, 271–72, 274–75, 300
  European Art, 247, 266
    artistic spaces, 251
    artists, 270
    authorities, 269
    awakening, 246
    cathedrals, 247
    colonialism, 270
    context, 266
    culture, 251
European empires, 271
  invaders, 269
  knowledge seekers, 246
  languages, 254
  political agendas, 272
  Europeans, 170, 249, 252, 269, 273, 300, 304
  scholars, 254
Eusebius, 103, 284
Evangelists, 184, 302
Exodus, 116
explorers Marco Polo, 253
Exumite control, 306

F

Fabriano, 263–66, 275, 295
Al-Farabi's work on philosophy, 254
Al-Farazdaq, 123, 143
Al-Farghani's Astronomy, 254
Fatimah, 185
Fatimids, 128, 184–85, 187-88, 203, 213, 217, 224, 227, 236, 239, 289
Favara, 240, 301
Feminist Art, 272
Ferdinand, 189, 206
Fertile Crescent, 1, 65, 189
Filippo Lippi, 267
Finiki, 300
Florence, 103, 105–6, 249, 263, 265, 267–68, 270–71, 284, 296, 304

fortified convent Rabat, 299
France, 5, 47, 107, 115, 169, 177–80, 189, 260, 267, 269, 277, 280, 285–86, 289, 294–95, 299
Frankincense Trade, 26
Frankish, 247, 301
Franks, 247, 261, 301
Frenj, 247, 301
fundamentalist Muslim theologians, 249
Fustat, 141, 186, 286, 289
Futuh Al-Buldan, 243

G

Galen, 176, 254
Gaza, 27
Genoardo, 225, 227, 229, 301
Gentile, 263–66, 275, 295
Geographical Academy, 252
geometric Kufic, 208
Geralda, 199
German Expressionism, 272
Germanic Vandals, 299
Germany, 162, 241
Ghabra, 88, 301
Ghalilat, 18–19, 278
Ghamdan, 102
Ghara'ib Al-Mawjudat, 183
Gharb Al-Andalus, 213, 301
Ghassanids, 28, 87–88, 102, 104, 109–10, 119, 136, 138, 156, 166, 245, 296–97, 302
Ghatfan, 238
Gindibu, 5
Giotto, 267
Giovanni, 220, 267, 295
Giralda, 199, 290, 302
Gobt, 301
God, 14, 62, 69-7, 104, 120, 122, 124, 126–27, 152, 183–84, 189, 203, 220, 224, 305, 307
    God-Allah, 302, 305
Goddess Athena, 95
Golan, 102
Good Shepherd, 72, 74, 282
Gothic, 191-2, 199, 224, 246, 269, 271, 299, 304
Governor's House, 146–47
Grain Goddess, 37, 279
Granada, 154, 189–91, 196, 202, 204–10, 246, 291, 299
Great Mosque in Palermo, 170, 218, 221, 292
    of Al-Kufah, 146–47, 286–87
    of Basrah, 145–46
    of Cordoba, 155, 169, 190–94, 196, 199, 203, 290
        of Damascus, 139, 149, 154–56, 166, 192, 287
    of Kufah, 146-47
    of Qayrawan, 169, 220, 237
    of Samarra, 169
    of Seville in Al-Andalus, 302
    of Tinmel, 237
    of Toledo, 196
    of Valencia, 196
    of Wasit and Dar Al-Emarah, 147
Greco-Roman, 27, 42, 46, 68, 95, 115, 169, 246
Greece, 2, 245–46, 256–62, 294–95
Greek Christian populations, 256
    cities, 2
    city-states, 9
    concept, 300
    deities Nemesis, 60
    Empire, 306
    Helios, 34, 39
    Heracles, 60
    imperial power, 27
    inscription, 99
    knowledge, 181
    language, 42, 116
    Nike, 38
    Orthodox, 220
Greeks, 1–2, 27–28, 30, 60, 67–69, 73, 102, 104, 115, 139, 169–70, 245, 249, 298, 300–301
Greeks-Seleucids, 67
Greek Tyche, 38
    word Ekklesia, 99
Green Dome, 171–72, 288
Grievances, 241–42, 301
Guided Khulafa, 305
Gundi-Shapur, 170

H

Al-Hadhar, 54, 65
Hadhramawt, 1, 12, 15, 22, 25, 82
Al-Hadi bi Amr Allah, 227
Hadith, 90, 100, 124–25
Hagagu, 50
Hagam, 4
Haifa, 301
HA'IL, 98

Hairan, 50
Hajj, 126–27, 303
Al-Hakim mosque, 184
Hamdan, 101
Al-Hamdani, 90, 100–101, 122
Hamedan, 181
Al-Hamra, 154, 170, 204, 211, 209
Hamza, 122
Handasiyya, 188
Hanif, 298
Hani ibn Tafsy, 96
Al-Haram Al-Makki, 128
Al-Hariri, 100, 121, 170, 180–82, 179, 289-99
Al-Harithah, 100
Al-Harith Al-Rabi, 32
Hashim Al-Tawil, 65, 85, 243, 275, 292–94
Hatem Al-Ta'i, 124
Hatra, 27–28, 30, 34, 43, 45, 54–56, 57–65, 67–	68, 73, 94–95, 125, 281–82, 284, 296, 299–300, 302
    Hatran and Mesopotamian characteristics, 68
        coins, 60
            dialects, 67
            iconography, 95
            sculptures, 62
            Shamash, 58
Hawran, 95, 102, 107, 285
Haydari Campaign, 133
Hayderabad, 143
Hayd ibn Aqil, 19, 278
Hebrew, 67, 119, 169, 299
Hit, 125, 132
Hegra, 95
Helios, 34, 279
Hellenistic, 9, 11, 28, 30, 32, 34, 37, 42, 69, 71, 73, 80, 104, 116–17, 169, 273
    culture, 67, 245
    elements, 30, 34
    influence, 28
    pantheon, 34
    style, 32, 104
    world, 169–70
Hermes, 60
Hermits, 121, 123, 220
High Renaissance Italian, 249
Higrah, 126
Hijaz, 89, 95, 145, 303
Al-Hijr, 27, 95–96
Hijrah, 121, 124, 126, 138
Hijri year, 303, 307

Hims, 27
Himyarite King, 23-4, 88, 101, 117, 279, 306
  Kingdom, 22, 88, 101
       palace, 98
Himyarites, 12, 22–25, 126
      sanctuary, 101
      scripts, 1
      Territories, 22
Hindu-Arabic numeral system, 253
Hirah, 11, 28, 30, 34, 73, 87–89, 95, 102, 109–14, 120–21, 125, 146–47, 156, 166, 285, 298-99, 302–3
  client Arab mini-state, 9
Hisham, 143
Hispano-Islamic Building, 216
Holy Land, 266
      Roman Empire, 247, 301
      See, 199
      Sepulcher, 149, 151
         Spirit Al-Quds, 224
Hoor ibn Ahi, 96
Hosios Loukas, 256–61, 259, 294-95
House of Wisdom in Baghdad, 253
Houses of Dura-Europos, 65, 85, 118
Hubal, 90, 93, 95, 132
  statue of, 132–33, 300
Huber, 89
Humanistic Mark, 263
Humanities, 275, 295
Humility, 263–66, 295
Hunafa, 298
Hunayn Ibn Ishaq, 254, 256, 294
Hur, 123
Huris, 124
Hurmuz, 269
Husain, 185, 298
Hyderabad, 143
Hypostyle, 302

I

Iarhibol, 69
Iberia, 189–90, 201–2, 215, 220, 246, 249, 261, 297, 299, 304–7
Iberian Christians, 189
    Peninsula, 169, 213, 216, 299, 306
Ibn, Malik, 121
    Abi Talib, 203-04,146, 303, 305
    Al-Athir, 90, 143, 241, 243, 236
  Al-Bawwab, 176

Al-Jayyab, 209
Al-Kalbi, 90, 100, 110, 122, 125, 130–31, 143
Al-Khatib, 209–10, 292
Al-Qata, 243
Al-Razzaz, 188
Al-Zubayr, 143
Battutah, 253
Fadhlan, 247
Hawqal, 244, 236
Hisham, 90, 125
Ishaq, 90, 133, 136, 143
Jubayr, 235-36, 244
Muqlah, 176
Noon, 257
Rushd, 249–51, 300
Sa'd, 90, 137, 143
Sina, 251–52
Tulun Mosque, 169
Zamrak, 209, 211
Ibraha, 88, 99
Ibrahim, 125, 133, 137
Al-Idrisi, 236, 243, 251–53, 294
Igreja Matriz, 211, 292
Ikhwan Al-Safa, 184
Ikhtiraq Al-Afaq, 243, 252
Al-Iklil, 143
Ilahbel, 48, 280
Al-Imad Al-Asfahani Al-Katib, 243
Imam, 304
Impressionism, 272
Imri'ul-Qays, 105, 107, 285
Ince Minareli Madrasah, 174–76, 289
India, 11, 28, 34, 41, 130, 133, 136, 154, 169–70, 181, 286, 298
Indian, 170, 271
leaders, 161
sciences, 170
indigenous Arab traditions, 246
indigenous South Arabian characters, 25
inscriptions praising Roger II, 232
Iohannitius, 254
Iran, 133, 142, 145, 147, 170, 181, 184, 186
Iranian Pahlavi, 67
Iranistan, 271
Iraq, 9, 11, 27–28, 30, 55–65, 109–14, 145–48, 177–79, 246, 269, 272, 274, 284–86, 289, 298–99, 302-4
Iraqi scholar and calligrapher ibn Muqlah, 305
Isa, 136

Isagoge, 256, 294
Al-Isbahani, 110
Ishmael, 133
Ishtar, 69, 299
ISIS (Islamic State of Iraq and Syria), 46, 48, 63, 67
Islam, 9–11, 26, 28, 89, 97, 100, 102, 119, 121–22, 126, 128, 131, 138, 167, 243, 249, 275, 303
Islamic arch, 305
Architecture, 58, 143, 216, 286, 302
Art, 166–67, 216, 246, 272, 286, 289
art and architecture in Fatimid North Africa, 188
calendar, 303
Calligraphy, 188
city, 147
Civilization, 244
conception of paradise, 236
Conquest, 243
Culture, 89, 167
Empire, 176, 254, 307
era, 154
faith, 89, 126, 300
Forms, 275
history, 133
Iberia, 216
intellectual culture, 266
Iran, 301
lands, 147, 154, 304
Minarets, 271
Monuments, 216
mosque, 302, 304
narratives, 266
PERIOD, 45, 104, 109, 119, 123, 145, 169, 189, 217
philosophy of humanism, 266
religion, 263
rule, 104, 137
schools of Jurisprudence, 173
Sicily, 243
sources, 99
Spain, 216
State, 145, 169, 243
Islamic State of Iraq and Syria (ISIS), 46, 48, 63, 67
territories, 142
theology, 246, 263
time, early, 119, 137

Trade and Italian Art, 275
tradition, 95, 97, 126, 128, 149, 151, 184, 249, 257, 259, 298, 302
tradition of frontier fighters, 189
visual tradition, 246
World, 143, 170, 188, 254
Isma'il, 125–26
Isra, 298
Israel, 272, 287
Italian Art, 255, 275
    artists, 266
    banking, prominent, 304
    Context, 275
    mathematician Fibonacci, 253
    Renaissance, 266, 275
    scholars, 263
Italy, 103, 105–6, 217, 261, 243, 253, 259–61, 263–64, 269, 284, 295, 303–4
Ithra, 98
Ittila, 143
Iturea, 27
Iylia, 100

J

Al-Jabr, 254
Jacopo Bellini, 267
Jacques Louis David, 271
Jahala, 302
Al-Jahidh, 101
Jahiliyyah, 119, 302
Jami`, 129, 131, 286
Jannat, 225, 227, 301
Jaridat, 243
Jarir, 143
Jawahir Al-Qamus, 143
Jawf, 14, 277
Jawsaq Al-Khaqani, 169, 237
Al-Jazari, 171–72, 182, 184, 188, 288–89
Al-Jazari automata, 184
Jazeerah, 54, 181, 136, 243, 296
Jean-Leon Gerome, 271
Jebel Druze, 95
    Ghunaym, 98
    Tannur, 34
Jebulon, 290
Jeddah, 125, 129
Jerash, 65, 85, 118
Jericho, 163–65, 288
Jerusalem, 100–101, 116, 138, 143, 149–53, 157, 169–70, 173, 224, 252, 266, 287, 298
Jerusalem-Temple, 287
Jesus, 72, 74, 104–5, 115, 136, 257, 263, 265–66, 269, 282, 285, 295
Jewish, 11, 37, 85, 118, 120–21, 138, 254
    house-synagogue, 68–69, 71
    King Dhu Nuwas, 78, 100
    Synagogue, 72, 97, 282
Jews, 71, 121, 126, 149, 169, 190, 216, 250
Jizyah, 190, 302
Joshua, 106, 260–61, 284, 295
Judaic, 67
Judaism, 22, 71, 73, 76, 88, 101
Judeo-Christian tradition, 116
Jundi-Shapur, 170
Jundub, 5
Jupiter, 68, 154
Justinian, 88
Juynboll, 143

K

Kaaba, 126, 302
Ka'ba, 60, 90, 97–101, 109–10, 121, 125–37, 140–41, 149, 285–86, 300, 302, 304
Al-Ka'bah Al-Shamiyyah, 101
    Al-Yamaniyyah, 101
Ka'ba idols, 133
Ka'bat Al-Yamamah, 101
    Ghatafan, 99
    Najran, 100–101
    Sindad, 102, 109
Kaf, 98
Kalilah wa Dimnah, 170, 184
Al-Kamil, 268
Al-Kamil fi Al-Tarikh, 143, 243
Karoub, 184, 302
  Al-Karubiyyoun, 184, 302
Kashmir, 133, 286
Kaslul, 107
Katholikon, 256
Al-Khali, 82
Al-Khamis, 167
Kharidat Al-Qasr, 243
Kharrana, 157
Al-Khawarismi's Algebra, 254
Khayber, 138–39, 286
Al-Khaznah, 31–32, 279
Khilafah, 147, 303
Khirbat, 279

Khirbat Al-Mafjar, 132, 163–66, 239, 288
Khirbat Al-Tannur, 34–40, 65, 279
Al-Khulafa, 305
Khurasan, 132, 171
Khusraw Anushiruwan, 88, 121
Al-Khuwarnaq, 102, 238, 298
Khuza'ah, 88, 125, 137
Kindah, 67, 75, 82, 85, 88–89, 95, 118–19
  Al-Kindi's Optics, 254
Kindites, 75–76, 78
King Charles V, 206
Kingdom of Aksum, 298
        of Sicily, 244
king Mu'awiyah, 283
        Mu'awiyah Bin Rabi'ah, 80
        Obodas I, 33
        of Saudi Arabia, 128
        Pedro I, 202
        Roger II, 217, 220, 232, 236, 242, 252
        Shalmaneser III, 5
        William I, 253
        William II, 229, 231
Kiswah, 127-29, 286, 302
Kitab, 303
        Al-Asnam, 130, 143
        Al-Buldan, 143
        Al-Diryaq, 170, 176-78, 184, 289
        Al-Jawharatayn Al, 143
        Al-Maghazi, 143
            Al-Tabaqat Al-Kabir, 137, 143
        Al-Tasrif, 254
        Al-Thakha'ir, 143
        Al-Tijan, 143
Kitab fi Ma'rifat Al-Hiyal Al-Handasiyyah, 170, 181, 188
        Sirat Rasul Allah, 143
Konya, 174–75, 289
Koz, 36, 279
Ku'ayb, 100
Kubbah, 229, 303
Kufah, 109, 146–50, 146-47, 170–71, 176, 285-87, 303
Kufesque in Byzantine Greece, 275
Kufic, 109, 152, 195-96, 201-02, 204, 237, 255, 263, 275, 291, 295, 303
Kuficising Inscriptions, 275
      style, 152, 176, 184, 220, 256, 247
      sub-styles, 235
Kufisque, 247, 303
Al-Kullyat fi Al-Tibb, 249

Kut in central Iraq, 147
Al-Kutubiyyin mosques, 169, 199
Kuwait, 145

L

La Giralda, 197, 290
La Ilaha Illa Allah, 247
Lakhamids-Munthirites, 28, 87–88, 102, 109–10, 119, 146, 156, 166, 296, 298, 302
Al-Lat, 280, 299
La Zisa, 227–29, 293
Lebanon, 3, 27, 54, 102, 104, 157, 243, 274, 277
Lectern, 140
Libya, 269, 272
Lihyanites, 1, 27–28, 95
Lindraja Balcony, 205, 211, 291
los Naranjos, 199
Los Reyes, 212
Lucera, 217, 244, 263
Luis II, 262
Luke, 184, 302
Luz, 196

M

Ma'ab, 125, 132
Ma'an, 50
Macedonia, 9, 27, 262
Mada'in Salih, 89-90, 93, 95–99, 125, 284
Madhij, 107
Al-Madina Al-Zahira, 169
Madinah, 89, 120, 155, 303, 307
Al-Madinah Al-Munawwarah, 303
      Al-Zahirah, 203–4
      region of Hijaz, 95
Madinat Al-Nabi, 303
      Al-Salam, 170
      al-Shams, 65
      Al-Zahra, 202–4, 239, 291
Madonna of Humility, 263–66, 295
Madrasah, 173, 246, 303
Mafaddat, 18–19, 278
Maghribi tradition, 236
Mahdhar, 22–23, 279
Al-Mahdiyyah, 184
Mahmoud ibn Yahya Al-Wasiti, 181, 306
Mahram Balqis, 20–21, 278
Ma'in, 12–14

Majlis, 203, 212, 238, 301
Malaga, 189
Malakbel, 46–47, 280
male deities Kahl, 76
Malik, 121, 137
Malta, 190, 217–18, 255, 261, 297, 301, 304
Mamluk, 132, 188, 243, 269, 275
Mamluk Sultan of Egypt Qait Bay, 268
Manaf, 93
Manara, 303
Manarah, 139, 303
Manat, 69, 76, 93, 95, 300, 303
Al-Mansur, 208, 268
Mantegna, Andrea, 267
manuscript, translated Arab, 265
Map Credits, 296
Map of Iberia, 190
Al-Maqah, 20
Maqam, 257
Maqamah, 180–81, 303
Al-Maqamah al-Barqa'idiyyah, 180
Maqamah, 179–80, 289
Maqamat Al-Hariri, 170, 176, 179, 184, 299
Maqsurah, 146, 155, 191, 304
Marasid, 143
Ma'rib, 12, 14–16, 18, 20, 25, 99, 102, 278,
Marrakesh, 199, 237
Al-Marrar Ibn Munqidh, 124
Martorana, 220, 222, 224, 292
Maryam, 136
Masaccio, 267
Masaya, 224
Masjid, 138
Massafra, 259
Al-Mas'udi, 90, 124, 137
Mattero, San, 263–64, 295
Matthew, 184
Mattise, Henri, 271
Mauretania, 304
Mauri, 304
Mecca, 88–90, 97, 99–101, 119, 121–23, 125–28, 28–33, 88, 128, 132–33, 136–38, 140–41, 149, 151, 285, 298, 300, 302–5, 307
Meccan Great Mosque, 302
　　　　sanctuary, 99
Medici, 267–68, 253, 275, 304
Medieval, 243, 300
　　Art, 244, 275
　　era, 261
　　Islam, 188, 307
　　Italy, 244, 275
　　Spain, 216
Medinah, 89–90, 100, 126, 131, 137–42, 145–47, 149, 286, 303–4
Al-Medinah Al-Munawwarah, 126
Mediterranean, 1–3, 11–2, 14, 27–28, 30, 34, 166, 189–90, 244–46, 249, 253, 256, 260–61, 269–97, 301, 304
Medmarm, 22
Melkite and Syriac churches, 102
Mertola, 211–14, 292
Mesopotamia, 1–4, 9, 11, 25, 28, 30, 34, 37, 41–42, 46, 54, 60, 80, 125–26, 130, 273, 300-01, 305–6
Mesopotamian characteristics, 68
　　deity Ba'l, 46
　　Empire, 5
　　kings, 5
　　Marduk, 69
　　prototypes, 90
　　sites, 125
　　sources, 34
　　temples, 69
Messina, 220, 240
Mezquita, 190, 290
Mihrab-Maqsurah area, 192
Mihrb, 292
Milan, 243
Minaean inscriptions, 14–15, 277–78
　Kingdom, 12–13
Minaeans, 13, 25, 26, 28
Minarah, 139, 246
Minbar, 140–42, 146, 192, 286, 304
Minimalism, 272
mini-states, independent Arab, 27
Mi'raj, 298
Mir Khawand, 133–34, 286
Misan, 27
Mi'thanah, 139, 303
Mithraeum, 67, 68
Moab, 125
Modern Arab art, 272–74
　　Iraqi Visual Art, 275
modified Naskh style, 227, 231
Mohammed, 126, 129, 131–33, 138, 143, 185, 286
Mohammed ibn Musa Al-Khawarizmi, 253
Mohammed's cousin, 133
　　uncle, 122
monastery of Saint Jeremiahs, 116, 285

Mongol destruction of Baghdad, 306
Mongols, 170, 184, 269, 300
Monophysites, 102, 116, 304
Monreale, 224, 226, 293
Monterrone, 259
Monumental Arabic inscription, 231, 293
    Statues in Mecca, 125
monument Sahar, 14
moon deity Almuqqah, 18
Moors, 216, 269, 304
Moqimu, 50
Morocco, 169, 216, 236–37, 274, 299
Mosaic, 100, 152–53, 155, 163–64, 220, 287–88
Moscati, 10
Moses, 69, 116
Mosque of Al-Qarawiyyin, 237
    of Cordoba, 190
Most Holy Annunciation, 267
Mosul, 54, 170, 176–78, 180–81, 184, 289
Mount-Dome, 287
Mount Moriah, 149
    Tannur, 34
MRW, 125
Mshatta, 161–62, 288
Al-Mu'adhdham, 268
Mu'athin, 304
Mu'aththin, 139-140, 304
Mu'awiyah, 80, 138, 146
Muazzin, 139, 304
Mudajers, 201, 220, 304
Mudajjanun, 201, 220, 304
Mudhhij, 80
Mughal, 271
Muhammad, 183, 263
Muhammad ibn Abi Al-Fath, 176
    Rasul Allah, 263
Mu'jam Al-Buldan, 102
Muluk Himyar, 143
Mundhirids, 28, 102, 109, 119, 296
Muqarnas, 154, 165, 184, 186, 201, 206–8,
    227, 234–39, 241–42, 291, 293–94, 304
    composition, 207
    decoration, 228, 293, 304
    elements, 184, 207
    formations, 230
    patterns, 212
    work, 207, 291
Murabit, 189
Al-Murabitun, 189
Mushatta, 157

Muslim and Christian worlds, 190
    Architecture, 216
    army, 145
    Art, 167
    artists, 236
    artists in Sicily and southern Italy, 255
    authorities, 268
    centers in Egypt, 300
    clients, 242
    community, 126, 138, 304
  conquest of Granada, 190
    Emirate of Granada, 189
    empire, 169–70, 181, 184, 300
    Historiography, 143
    kings, 241
    lands, 166, 170, 181, 302
    leaders, 127
    mosque, 155
    newcomers, 121
    period, 128
    population in Palermo, 220
    populations, 125, 232
    ports, 249
    prayer, 149
    regions, 184
Muslims, 104, 119, 126, 149, 154, 169, 190,
    244, 246, 251, 254, 269, 275, 302, 304
    scholars, 254
    scientists, 181
    in Fifteenth Century Spain, 216
    in Medieval Spain, 216
    of Al-Andalus, 304
    sources record, 140
    Spain and Portugal, 216
    retook Jerusalem, 149
    state, 128
    structures, 104, 256
    territory, 138, 169
    tradition, 184, 254
    tribe, 121
    World, 133, 143, 243, 253, 265, 275
Musnad, 81, 126
Al-Musnad Al-Janubi, 1, 299
Al-Musnad Al-Shamali, 1, 299
Al-Musta'iz, 227
Al-Mustansiriyyah School, 173–74, 289
Al-Muwahhidun, 189. 199, 299
Muzahim Al, 121

N

Nabataea, 28, 117
Nabataean, 1, 28–30, 34, 41–42, 65, 67, 71, 95, 120, 122, 125, 130, 154, 245, 299–300, 304
    art, 37
    cities, 29
    deity Qaws, 36, 279
    era, 125
    expansion, 41, 296
    inscription, 125
    King Aretas IV, 32
    sanctuary, 98
    script, 1, 107, 285
    Sculpture, 65
    states, 28
    structures, 125
    style, 34
    territory, 305
    text, 108, 285
    tradition, 34
    Aramaic text, 107
    cities, 296
Nabonidus, King, 8
Najd, 89, 119, 301
Najran, 22, 34, 90, 100–102, 107, 120, 131–32
Nakrah, 14, 26
Namara Inscription, 105, 108, 285
Naples, 249
Napoli, 251, 263, 294
Naqa'idh, 143
Nash, John, 273, 296
Nasirid, 202, 204, 208, 305
Al-Nasir li-Din Allah, 203
Naskh, 176, 208, 263, 267, 305
Nasr, 93
Nasub, 299
Negus, 161
Namara, 107, 285
Neo-Assyrian, 6, 277, 300
Neo-Babylonian, 5, 138
Neo-Classicism, 272
Nercessian, 244
Nestorian Christian Arabs, 88, 109
    crosses, 113, 285
        Nestorian monastery, 109-11, 285
Netherlands, 133, 135, 286
New Testament, 72, 104
Nicator, 27

Nicosia, 220, 238
Nike, 34, 279
Nile, 117
Nineveh, 6, 8, 10, 277, 302
Noah flood, 125-26
Norman, 217-18, 220, 225, 232, 235, 243-44, 259
    invasion, 246
    King Roger II, 251, 301
    kings, 217, 229, 240, 242
    King William I, 225
    leaders, 225
    period, 224
    Royal Palace, 235, 252
    rule, 224
    rulers, 225
North Africa, 9, 147, 166, 169, 189, 204, 214, 216–17, 220, 224, 246, 253, 299, 301, 304
  North Africans, 3, 220, 304
North Arabia, 1, 27, 120, 125
North Arabian Peninsula, 28
    sites, 120
North Arabic, 1, 28, 299
Northeastern Arabia, 143
northern Arabia, 1, 5, 30, 80, 90, 122
  northern Christian armies, 189
    kingdoms, 189
northern Ethiopia, 298
Northern Iraq, 6, 54, 99, 181, 277, 302
    Sicily, 243
North Palace of Ashurbanipal, 6, 8, 10, 277
Northwest Arabia, 88–90, 93, 95, 284
Nossa Senhora, 212, 214, 292
Al-Nuhayradan, 100
Nuhm, 93
Nuqtah, 275
Nuzhat Al-Mushtaq, 243, 252

O

Old Cairo, 186
    City of Jerusalem, 149
      Mosque of Basrah, 145
    Testament, 69, 72, 282
Oman, 269
Ontology, 275
Oratorical Architecture, 154, 173, 185, 209, 305
Oriental, 266, 275
Orientalism, 271, 275
Orientalist, 166, 273

Orientalizing style, 245
Oriental movements, 270
Orthodox Arab Christian church, 104
Oshi'ana, 224
Otranto, 259
Ottomans, 128, 152, 269, 273
Ottonian courts, 204
Oud, 298

P

Padua, 250
Pahlavi, 28, 169
Palace, Norman, 233, 236, 293
    Raydan, 102
Palatial Complex, 149–50, 157, 287
Palatina Chapel in Palermo, 244
Palazzo Chiaramonte-Steri in Palermo, 238
Palermo, 154, 170, 186, 217–25, 227–41, 243–44, 252, 263, 292–94, 301
  Palermo Cathedral, 218–20, 292
    Sicily, 275
Palestine, 5, 27, 29–30, 42, 73, 102, 117, 122, 145, 151–53, 157, 163–64, 287–88, 300, 305–6
Palestinian architects, 150
Palmyra, 9, 11, 23, 27–28, 41–54, 62, 65, 67–69, 73, 95, 102, 165, 245, 280, 304–5
Palmyra, 28, 280
Palmyran Allat, 95
    and Hatran dialects, 67
    architects, 42
    art and architecture, 42
    artists, 50
    funerary limestone relief, 50
    Gods, 69
Palmyrans, 41–42, 46, 48, 68–69, 122
    territories, 42
    woman, 50
Palmyre, 281
Panagia, 256
Pan-Arabism, 272
Panchatantra, 184
pantheon, pre-Islamic Arabian, 90
Paolo, 267
Parthia, 65
Parthian art, 85, 95, 118
    attacks, 54
    authorities, 28
    Empire, 54

Parthians, 28, 34, 41–42, 46, 54, 67–69, 71–73, 245, 305
Parthian-Sassanians, 28, 54
Persia, 9, 27, 41, 129, 166, 169, 181, 305-06
Persian artists, 121
    characteristics, 104
    colonists, 67
    control, 9, 54
    elements, 42
    Empire, 306
    influence, 11
    King, 121
    manuscript, 133
    mythological themes, 42
    occupation, 73
Persian-Parthian, 60
Persians, 9, 12, 27–28, 37, 67–68, 88, 115, 166, 170, 183, 301
    Sassanians, 102
Petra, 9, 11, 27–28, 30–42, 45, 54, 62, 65, 68, 73, 95, 98, 245, 279–80, 296
Petran styles and techniques, 96
Petra's architecture, 30, 33
Pharaoh, 69
Pharaonic, 117
Phoenicia, 9, 42
Phoenician Aramaic, 2
    art, 3
    artifacts, 2
Phoenician-Canaanite expansion, 245
    cities, 1, 9, 189
Phoenician-early Aramaic, 3
    Expansion, 2, 296
    language, 2
Phoenicians, 2, 3, 9, 119, 154, 214, 218, 245, 301
Pioneers of Arab Modern art, 273
poet Hassan Ibn Thabit, 122
poetry, pre-Islamic, 1, 123, 125
poets
  early Islamic, 121, 124
  pre-Islamic, 121, 123–24
Poly-Loped Arch, 305
Pop Art, 272
Portugal, 189, 211–16, 246, 269, 292, 299, 301
Post Modernism, 272
Pre-Islamic Arabia, 65, 85, 90, 93, 98, 118, 131, 138, 155
    Arabian Names, 143
    Civilization, 85, 118, 282–83

era, 45, 82, 119, 130, 142, 166, 213, 238, 298
KA'BAS, 97
literary sources, 110
literature, 98, 119–22
Mecca, 65, 85, 118, 130
period, 1, 87–89, 120, 125, 128, 131, 138
poet Al-A'sha, 101
poet Al-Aswad ibn Ya'fur, 110
poet Juma'ah Al-Bariqi, 137
poetry collections, 1
population, 90, 120-21, 123, 126, 132
time, 109, 298, 300, 302
priest Sahr, 14
Prophet, 69, 100, 129, 131–33, 136, 138–42, 145, 152, 185, 303
Abraham, 126
Mohammed, 89–90, 100, 119, 125, 131–33, 136, 138, 140, 142-43, 145–47, 151, 185, 298, 303, 305
Salih, 95
Prophet's house-mosque, 139–40, 142, 149, 155
Samuel, 106, 284
Youshi, 257
pseudo-Arabic inscription, 258–59, 262–63, 265–66, 268, 295–96
patterns, 303
script, 266, 269
text, 265–66
Pseudo-Galen, 170, 176–78, 289
pseudo-Kufic, 259, 262–63, 303
designs, 257
inscription, 259, 265, 295
Ptolemaic dynasty, 115
Ptolemies, 9, 27
Puerta, 198-199, 290–91
de San José, 194, 290
Punic, 300

Q

Qabdu, 14
Qahtan, 80
Qa'id, 268
Qait, 268
Qal'ah, 305
Qal'at Bani Hammad, 236
Al-Qalis, 99
Qanoon, 252

Al-Qarawiyyin and Al-Kutubiyyin mosques in Morocco, 237, 169
Qaryat Al-Faw, 24, 75–85, 117–118, 137, 166, 282–83, 296
and Al-Rabadhah, 90
Qasabah, 204, 305
Qasr Al-Amir, 236–37
Al-Bint, 96, 98, 284
Al-Brays and churches, 104
Al-Farid, 96, 99, 284
Al-Hayr Al-Gharbi, 157, 165
Al-Hayr Al-Sharqi, 157
Al-Mashta, 157
Al-Minya, 157
Bariq and Dhu Al-Shurufat, 238
Burqu, 157
Harrana, 157
Wardan, 104
Qataban, 18–19, 25–26, 278
Qatabanian Kingdom, 1, 12, 14, 25
Qatar, 251, 274, 294
Qatif, 89
Qaws, 34
Al-Qawwaynin, 121
Qayrawan, 169, 220, 237
Al-Qays, 95, 107
Al-Qazwini, 183, 289,
Qedar, 5
Qiblah, 139–41, 146–47, 149, 155, 164, 196, 304-05
Qubba, 100–01, 229, 303
Queen Shaqillath II, 34
Al-Qullays, 99–100
Qur'an, 90, 95, 120, 122, 125-26, 131, 151-52, 156, 184–85, 191, 209, 220, 224, 263
Qur'anic calligraphic inscription, 140
exegete, 132
inscription, 153, 287
manuscripts, 232
text, 127, 152, 219–20, 223, 292
verses, 127, 174, 184, 194, 290, 302
Quraysh, 88
Qurayshites, 132, 137
Qurayyah, 98
Qusayr, 157–60, 166–67, 239, 287–88
Qusayy Ibn Kallab, 137
Qutabanians, 22

R

Rababeh, 296
Al-Rabadhah, 90
Rabats, 189
Al-Rabbah, 93
Rabbis, 101, 121
Rabbula, 104, 104, 305
Rabbula Gospels, 103-04, 105-6, 117, 284, 305
Al-Rabi, 100
Rabi'ah, 80, 109, 283
Raha, 27
Rahim, 42
Ramadan, 179, 181, 289
Raphael, 249-51, 267
Raqqa, 102, 104
Rasafa, 102, 104
Al-Rashid, Harun, 247-48, 294
Rashid Al-Din, 129, 131, 286
Rashidi Caliph, 149
Rashidun Caliphs, 145-46, 246, 305
Rassam, 305
Rawdhat Al-Safa, 133-34, 286
Ray, 181
Rayda, 121
Al-Razi, 254
Reconquista, 196, 201-2, 204, 214-15, 246, 304-5
Red Sea, 9, 11, 89, 95, 129, 138
Regnault, Henri, 271
Renaissance, 190, 199, 246, 249, 266, 255, 263, 266, 269, 302
    Florentine Stained-Glass Window, 275
    Mannerist style, 206
  of Islam, 188, 243
Renoir, Auguste, 271
Resurrection, 105, 284
Rihlah Ibn Jubayr, 244
    Ibn Fadhlan, 247
Riyadh, 75, 80-83, 85, 89, 91-92, 118, 283-84
Riyadh Saudi Arabia, 84
Roger II, 227, 232, 236-37, 241, 243-44, 252-53
Roger's palaces in Messina and Palermo, 240
Roma, 243-44
Roman, 9, 30, 32-4, 37, 42-3, 46, 54, 69, 71, 154
Roman emperor Marcus Julius Philippus, 102
    Empire, 9, 12, 29, 41, 67, 102, 298
Romanesque, 230, 260
Romanesque churches, 246, 256
Roman fortress, 214
    influence, 30, 32
Roman mythology, 32, 42
    occupation of Palmyra, 42
    Palmyra, 65
    province of Arabia, 30
    rule in Dura, 71
Romans, 9, 12, 27-28, 30, 41, 54, 60, 67-69, 72-73, 87-8, 95, 102, 107, 245, 305,
    styles, 30
    Syria, 65, 85, 118
    territories, 11, 22, 42
Romanticism, 272
Rome, 65, 253-54, 261
  besieged, 261
Royal Diwan, 236-37, 244
Royal Eunuchs, 244
Royal Pavilion, 271, 273, 296
Ruhayma, 100
ruined Mundhirids palaces, 147
Rum, 247

S

Saawah, 181
Al-Saawiyyah, 181
Saba, kingdom of, 14
Sabaean alabaster stele, 20
    alphabet, 18
    hunting scene, 21, 278
    inscription, 19
    Kingdom, 14
    moon, 20
Sabaeans, 1, 12, 14-5, 17-18, 20, 22, 25, 120, 184, 278, 302, 306
Sabaeans kings, 15
sacred Precinct, 149-50, 287
sacrifice of Conon, 69
Sa'd, 22, 93
Al-Sadir, 102, 298
Safaitic, 1, 67
Safavid 133-34, 269, 286
Al-Safra, 143
Safran, 275
Sahool, 121
Saint Jeremiahs, 116, 285
    Mary, 199
    Maurice, 247-48, 294
Sala, 212, 238

INDEX

Salerno, 249, 254
Salm, 4
Salón de Comares, 210, 292
    Rico, 204
Samaria, 5
Samarra, 169, 186, 237, 243
Sam'ay, 101
Samuel, 69
San'a, 22, 99–101, 137
Sanatruq, King, 58, 62, 281
Santa Maria, 199, 222, 292
Santissima Annunziata, 266–68, 270–71
    Maria, 196
Saqqara, 116–17, 285
Saracens, 269, 275
Sarah, 121
Sardinia, 1, 189
Sasanian Empire, 9, 306
    building techniques, 147
Sassanians, 9, 24, 27, 67, 69, 72, 78. 87–89, 102, 109-10, 115, 119, 145, 156, 161, 166, 245–46, 302, 306
Saud, King, 91–92, 283
Saudi Arabia, 76–78, 80–83, 85, 89, 91–92, 95–99, 118, 127–28, 139, 274, 282–86, 296, 302
Sawa Cemetery, 180, 289
Sayf Ibn Dhi Yazan, 88, 306
Seleucid Empire, 305–6
Seleucids, 143, 306
Semite groups, 300
Semites, 28, 306
Semitic, 119, 306
    family, 1–2
    language, 67, 299
    origins, 11
Semitism, 306
Seville, 169, 196–201, 246, 254, 290–91, 302
Shabwa, 25, 278
Shahba, 102
Shakespeare, 89
Shalmaneser III, 5
Shamash, 42, 57–60, 281, 306
Shammar, 107
Sheba, 20, 26, 69
Shi'a doctrine, 185
Shi'i-Muslim scholars, 184
    references, 185
Sicilian poets, 243
    scholar Michael Amari, 231
Sicily, 1, 3, 165–66, 170, 184, 186, 189–90, 217–44, 246, 249, 253–55, 259, 292–94, 301, 304
Sidon, 9, 301
Silk Road, 11–12, 14, 54, 245, 296
Sinai, 27, 30, 42, 73, 117, 122, 189, 300
Sindad, 109–10
Al-Siqili, 243
Siqilyah, 217, 243, 306
Social Realism, 272
Souq Al-Warraqin, 170
South Arabia, 1, 9, 11-3, 19, 25, 30, 78, 82, 88–89, 95, 117, 120, 125–26, 165–66
South Arabian, 1, 12, 20, 75–76, 81, 88–89, 101, 104, 130, 138
    inscriptions, 101, 120
    Musnad, 76, 78, 80, 283
South Arabic, 1, 9, 24, 26, 88, 90, 109, 122, 299, 306
Southeast Asia, 11–12, 28
Southern Iberia, 189, 246, 299
    Iraq, 9, 87, 109, 145
    Italy, 166, 217, 244, 246, 255, 259–62, 265, 275, 295
    Spain, 1, 3, 147
    Syria, 102, 107, 285
Spaniards, 196, 254, 259
Spanish Catholic, 191, 209
Sphinx, 3
Stained glass window, 270–71, 296
St. Cataldo, 224
    Jeremiads, 117
    John, 104, 154, 220
    Marco, 259
    Maria, 259
    Mark, 116, 301
    Mary, 244
    Mina, 115, 117, 285
    Nicholas, 259
    Onophrious, 117
    Pietro, 259
    Simon Basilica, Qal'at Sam'an-, 65, 104
styles
    blended Arab art, 166
    local Arab-Nabataean, 73
    modified Thulth-Naskh, 173
    new Mongol, 184
    variant Kufic, 237, 293
Sudan, 272, 274
Sultan, 202, 268

Sumerian, 58, 60
Sun God, 57–58, 281, 306
Super Realism, 272
Surrealism, 272
Synagogue of Dura-Europos, 118
Syracuse, 218, 220
Syria, 27–30, 41–46, 67–68, 70–75, 87–88, 102–6, 145–47, 154–57, 246, 280, 282, 284, 287, 298–300, 304–7
Syriac, 116, 119, 254, 299
    churches, 102
        building technique, 149
        Ghassanid origin, 102
        Ka'ba, 101
        Najran, 102
Syrian region, 9, 25, 99, 102, 105, 122, 149, 298–99, 304

T

Tabala, 101
Al-Tabari, 90, 132, 139, 143
Tabula Rogeriana, 252–53, 294
Tadmur, 41, 305
Al-Taghiyah, 93
Al-Ta'if, 93, 89–90, 101, 125, 131
Ta'ifah, 189, 306
Taj Mahal Mausoleum, 154
Ta'lab, 101
Tamathil, 120, 123–24, 138
Al-Tannur, 34, 280
Tarafah Ibn Al-'Abd, 121–22
Tawa'if, 189, 260, 306
Tayma, 4–5, 89, 98, 120, 277
Tayy, 124
Teban, 101
Tedmor, 65
Templar Knights, 149
Temple Mount, 149
    of Allat, 42–43, 45, 58, 62, 280–81
    of Nakrah, 26
    of Shamash, 57, 59, 60
    of DURA-EUROPOS, 69
    WADI AL-SIRHAN, 98
Thaj, 89
Theodora, 102
Theotokos, 256–58, 294–95, 307
Thulth, 208, 263, 267, 305, 307
Thulth calligraphy, 127, 174
Al-Tibb, 251

Tiglath Pileser III, 5
Tigris River, 1, 54, 147, 173, 181, 184
Tigris rivers in ancient Iraq, 1
Tihama, 138
Timna, 19, 24, 278–79
Timthal, 120, 123–24, 307
Tinmel, 237
Tiraz, 184, 268, 307
    factory in Sicily, 232
Toledo, 195–96, 246, 254, 290
    SCHOOL, 254
Torah niche, 69
Tower tomb, 34, 42, 48–49, 280
Trajan, 30
tribe of Banu Al-Harith, 100
    Mahdhar, 22–23, 279
Tubba, 101
Tunisia, 142, 169, 184, 189, 220, 236, 243, 269, 271, 274
Turkey, 49, 93, 174–75, 280, 284, 289
Tyche, 34, 279
Tyre, 9

U

UAE, 275
Ubaydah, 33, 124
Ubaydullah Al-Harithi, 100
Uday Ibn Zayd, 123
Udhayb, 110
Udhra, 124
Ukhaydir, 169
Ukraine, 271
Al-'Ula, 89, 283
Ulrike, 167
Uman, 88
Umar, 123, 125, 132, 143, 146, 149
    Ibn Al-Khattab, 303, 305
Umayyad, 145–47, 149, 151, 160, 162, 166–67
    Caliph Abd Al-Malik, 150
    Caliph Al-Walid, 124, 132, 138, 140
    Mosque in Damascus, 154
    palaces, 132, 138
    Period, 143, 147, 164, 166
    poet, 124
    Qusayr, 237
    reign, 132, 141
    royal family, 149
    royal palace complexes, 157
Royal Residence, 149–50, 287

INDEX

royal retreat, 158
Umayyads, 24, 25, 102, 104, 137-38, 145-47, 149, 151, 156, 160, 162, 164, 166-67, 184, 186, 191, 213, 246–47, 287, 304, 307
   Umrah, 126
Umru Ibn Luhayy, 125
Uneishu, 33-4, 279
Uscibene, 225, 229, 240
Al-'Uzza, 30, 76, 93, 95, 298

V

Valencia, 196
Vandals, 189
Vatican fresco mural, 249
Venice, 249, 252, 263, 265, 294
Virgin Mary, 133, 263
Visigothic Spain, 161, 216

W

Wadd, 14, 76, 78–79, 93, 283
Wadi Al-Sirhan, 98
   Bayhan, 19, 278
Wahab'il, 18
Wahb Ibn Munabbih, 125, 143
Al-Walid, 132, 139, 141
Al-Walid II, 161–62, 164
   Waqah, 14
Al-Waqidi Mohammed, 143
Wasit, 147, 179, 299
Wassily Kandinsky, 271
Wazir, 185
WDDM, 78
Western visual experience, 272
Wihad, 275
Wijdan, 167
William I, 227
   II, 227
World War I, 269
   II, 272

Y

Yaghuth, 93
Yahya ibn Mahmoud Al-Wasiti, 179, 180-81, 188, 274, 299
Yamamah region, 4, 101
Al-Ya'qubi, 143
Yaqut Al-Hamawi, 101, 143
Yashu, 257
Yasu, 224
Yathil-Baraqish, 13
Ya'uq, 93
Ya'wsi, 14
Yehbeshi, 62
Yemen, 5, 9, 11, 13–27, 30, 78, 88–89, 98, 101–2, 128–29, 166, 272, 274, 277–79, 306
Yemen, 1, 11, 13, 100, 306
Yemenite, 9, 121, 125, 137
   Ka'ba, 100–101
Yethrib, 34, 89, 120–21, 125–26, 131, 137, 307
Youshi, 257
Yusuf ibn 'Umar, 132

Z

Zabiba, 4
Al-Zabidi, 143
Ẓafār, 24
Zaghba, 103-6, 284
Al-Zahrawi, 254-55, 294
Zakaria, 183
Zamzam, 131
Zawi, 208
Zebida, 50
Zebido, 62
Zengid rulers of Mosul, 181
Zenobia, 41, 65
Zeus, 68
Zirid Emirate of Granada, 208
   Sultan, 220
Zisa, 225, 227–29, 293, 301
Zodiac, 38, 279
Zoroastrianism, 88
Zukhruf, 122, 307
Zulla, 138, 301
Zuqaq Al-Naqqashin, 137